The Victorian Debate

Literature and Society

General Editor: Herbert Tint

The Victorian Debate

English Literature and Society
1832 - 1901

Raymond Chapman

BASIC BOOKS, Inc., Publishers

New York

To my wife

Library of Congress Catalog Card Number: 68–8984
Printed in the United States of America

Contents

So complete was my father's reliance on the influence
of reason over the minds of mankind, whenever it is
allowed to reach them, that he felt as if all would be
gained if the whole population were taught to read,
if all sorts of opinions were allowed to be addressed to
them by word and in writing, and if by means of the
suffrage they could nominate a legislature to give
effect to the opinions they adopted.

JOHN STUART MILL: *Autobiography*

The ordinary man would not have put his case as it
was put by Wordsworth, or Maurice, or Carlyle, but
the error in the ruling philosophy of the time that
provoked those writers was the injustice in life that
provoked those rebels.

J. L. AND BARBARA HAMMOND: *The Bleak Age*

The Victorian Age

We are still near to the Victorians; our approach to them is one of shared experience as well as of historical imagination. There are plenty of them still alive, alert inhabitants of the later twentieth century. Most of us have known people born before the middle of Queen Victoria's reign, and the photographs of the period seem disturbingly familiar. These were people alternately excited and dismayed, as we are, by the rapid progress of science, the technological revolution, the speed at which men and ideas could move around the world. From the faded prints they gaze at us, confident yet bewildered.

For our part, we gaze back at them no longer as their children who must assert our new adult status and reject all that they accepted. There is no need for a Lytton Strachey to make us laugh at the great ones whose achievements had seemed to stunt the growth of another generation until they could be buried in amused condescension. Totally refusing the values of Thomas Arnold and General Gordon once seemed to be the only alternative to being constricted by them. More recently the tendency has been rather to idealize, to envy the Victorians for their stability; instead of dismissing them as prigs. We find a paradise of calm in those suburban parlours, and those great country houses with their established social ritual. We see a golden age, suffering no doubts about rights and duties in society, an age with clear loyalties upheld by established religion.

Perhaps we can now find a way between the extremes, encouraged to hope that the closeness which makes us a little uneasy in the company of the Victorians can also help us to see through their eyes and understand with their minds. 'The period of reaction against the nineteenth century is over; the era of dispassionate historical valuation of it has begun', wrote a modern historian who was, as he himself pointed out, a product of the Victorian age.[1] We have a view of consequences which the Victorians inevitably lacked, though many of them looked to the future with a clarity that makes nonsense of regarding them as complacent. Many of their problems have grown into our own; it is better neither to worship nor to condemn, but to pay the ultimate human tribute of trying to understand.

The fact that Victoria did not become Queen until 1837 need not set us running to find a new label for extending the period back to the First Reform Act of 1832, but it may remind us not to see a false unity in the longest British reign. In the outward signs of life, in fashion and furniture and ways of spending money, there were three Victorian ages. In the realm of ideas, attitudes and beliefs, there were two, overlapping and sometimes conflicting. The decade of the sixties saw the main transition, the decade when the urban worker gained the vote and when the relationship between the individual and the state was subjected to most rigorous scrutiny. The first generation struggled with the problems which it had inherited: thrust headlong into the modern world, it succeeded in holding together the society which was threatening to disintegrate.

The second generation found new uncertainties and suffered the realization that society had avoided revolution but was still far from perfect balance and stability. Many of its members became strongly critical of their age and of those people who were satisfied with what had been achieved. Without losing a cheerful zest for exploration of new possibilities, they became more serious. A certain flamboyance running on from the Regency years was dimmed in the later decades. The outward show of feeling disappeared into a general sober restraint. By the end of the century the masculine tear, shed copiously by Englishmen of earlier ages, was taboo.

As doubt became deeper and controversy keener, it was no longer possible to address oneself only to a few sympathetic hearers. The common stock of accepted belief had diminished: new ideas had to be promulgated or never known. Communications were improving; printed matter was becoming cheaper and more readily accessible; above all, more and more

[1] G. M. Trevelyan in *Ideas and Beliefs of the Victorians* (London, 1949), p. 15.

people were learning to read. Writing for publication was no longer the outlet of the talented creative artist alone, but also the most effective means of influencing a changing society. Literature itself became more polemical, more aware of contention.

It is unwise to look for a perfect and integrated expression of any society in its arts. The expectation is a denial of the artist's protest and rejection – activities no less important to society and to himself than his acceptance and interpretation. Yet the artist is part of his own society and his own generation: if we are to understand the literature of an age, we need to understand the main preoccupations and assumptions of that age.

Any system, be it theological, political, social or economic, tends to inhibit the creative imagination. Despite all systems, however, the imagination will find its subjects and its modes of expression in the reality surrounding it, and may open the way for a supersession of what seems to be fixed for ever. It was often through the most depressing facts and the most abstruse theories that the imaginations of Victorian writers found their fullest expression.

Our search for the Victorians may begin where they were most often to be found: at home. The basic unit of the family seemed as much a part of the natural order as the monarchy; and the Royal Family itself followed the pattern of many children and strong parental authority. For millions indeed there was little real family life, after long hours in field or factory followed by a return to housing so wretched that it could barely be endured except as a shelter from the worst weather. Yet the more fortunate – and the number of them grew with each year of the reign – were proud of their homes and spent a great deal of time in them. Going out in the evening was rare except for the richest and the poorest. For the increasing middle class it was a time for reading, often for reading aloud by one member of the family as an accompaniment to sewing and embroidery; a time for conversation; a time for making music which was becoming a more popular domestic recreation.

Even in the middle and upper classes, however, domestic life was full of discomfort and inconvenience. Although in some ways we can feel that the Victorians were sharing our present problems, other aspects of their lives seem to separate them from us more radically. One did not have to be very rich to employ at least one servant – there were over a million persons in domestic service in 1851 – but servants could not change the coldness of the house in winter if one moved a few yards from the fire. The drawing room might be the family's centre of evening security, but it was poorly lit and stuffy with heavy curtains and thick carpets that collected every particle of dust. In the kitchen there was no refrigeration; cooking and hot water usually depended on one of the large ranges that devoured coal (cheap, but carried laboriously up from the cellar) and poured out still more smoke into the polluted air. A low cloud of fog hung above the rooftops of the large towns for a great part of the year.

Housing was a major social problem, and one which the Victorians never fully solved. The slums of London and the new industrial centres were appalling throughout the century. At the other end of society, the nobility spent their time between the country manors which were a feature of rural England and the fine eighteenth-century London houses. Those who were as rich but of less ancient lineage built for themselves vast edifices in a mixture of styles and with a maximum of exterior ornamentation. At the beginning of the period there was virtually no planning at either the private or the public level of urban development. The few restrictions which were imposed were mostly fire precautions, concerned with the thickness of walls and depth of windows and not with appearance, sanitation or living conditions. Even in areas that were far from being slums, speculators would crowd in as many houses as possible within a plot of land, neither they nor their customers caring a great deal about light and fresh air. The tax on every window over eight in a house, levied until 1851, did not give much incentive for improvement.

In the year when window-tax was abolished, Prince Albert played a large part in planning and achieving against opposition the Great Exhibition in Hyde Park. His own exhibit was a block of 'model houses' for working-class families – humble enough homes with their 'two up and two down' but including the rare luxuries of a scullery, cupboards, a water-closet and a proper supply of fresh water.[1] It was the lack of these things more even than the actual overcrowding that made so many poor Victorian houses intolerable. After the Exhibition a small block of this type was opened at Kennington Park, an augury of a better planned future that still lay far ahead.

Although the old towns seemed to be in a hopeless muddle, the new phenomenon of the suburb was growing. In the ten years from 1881, the London suburbs had the highest rate of population-growth in the whole country.[2] Here the clerk or the shop assistant could separate himself from the really poor, could feel that he was at last a member of the middle class. The possession of an individual house, however tiny and inconvenient, was a symbol of superiority over those who occupied part of a large tenement or even of a terraced row. The relatively low cost of land a few miles from the central area allowed for a garden back and front. The suburb became a world of lilliputian fantasy, where a new society established a code based on living in a house with a name, instead of a number. The railway both followed and helped to develop the trend, as suburban lines proliferated all around London and offered quick transport to the City. The Cheap Trains Act of 1883 gave the Board of Trade power to enforce the issue of cheap workmen's fares on certain trains.

Furniture kept pace with the increasing fussiness and elaboration of houses. The fine, strong lines of good Regency furniture went out of fashion early in the period and no steady tradition was preserved. The 1851 Exhibition revealed an extraordinary jumble of styles, some faintly derivative from earlier fashions and some from classical or oriental cultures, but all notable for their excessive ornamentation. The forties saw a love for every conceivable object made of *papier mâché,* japanned black and often gilded or inlaid with patterns. This distressing style was almost frivolous in comparison with the general tendency towards solidity, full stuffing and thick upholstery. Early Victorian furniture seemed to become elaborate as a demonstration less of wealth than of security. There could be no threat of violence, from domestic passion or ravaging mob, in those

[1] Marjorie and C. H. B. Quennell, *A History of Everyday Things in England* (London, 1933), Vol. 3, p. 173.
[2] H. J. Dyos, *Victorian Suburb* (Leicester, 1961), p. 20.

parlours crammed full with heavy but vulnerable pieces of furniture and ornaments. This is by no means the only Victorian example of exaggeration to counter unresolved fears.

There was little enthusiasm in the early period for antique furniture: the old was merely the old-fashioned. It was not until the eighties that Norman Shaw began to guide the revival of interest which led to a flood of imitation Chippendale, Hepplewhite and Sheraton. William Morris started a medieval revival, producing massive furniture with exposed joints to prove the honesty of the workmanship. Unfortunately, things meant for the ample baronial hall were cumbersome in the nineteenth-century villa, and they were also uncomfortable. Yet what Morris did was a valuable corrective, as was the more practical design of plain oak furniture by Ambrose Heal in the last years of the century, of a failing not confined to one aspect of manufacture. The new productive skills were tending to develop into an excess of the cheap and nasty, encouraging the fall in sensitive awareness which moved Ruskin and Arnold as well as Morris to literary denunciation. Labour at home was cheap and, though the best timber had to be imported, Britain was largely self-sufficient for finished products. Seen apart from the stifling surroundings which they once occupied, many pieces of early Victorian furniture now have considerable charm.

Clothing, like furniture, was heavy and elaborate. Since it was improper for a woman to show so much as an ankle, dresses with long skirts were worn in the factory and workshop as well as in the home. Fashions became simpler for a time after the Queen's accession, as if the young girl on the throne had set a style of pure simplicity, with a call to expunge all traces of the gay, worldly Regency. Skirts gradually became fuller until the arrival of the hooped crinoline from Paris about 1854. The crinoline remained in vogue for over twenty years, the epitome of the mid-Victorian, middle-aged, middle-class woman. Its wearer seemed firmly planted on the earth, a matriarch, majestic in repose and awe-inspiring in progress.

The crinoline was followed by the bustle skirt, straight up in front and drawn up with padding at the back. Then came a short period of more extravagant and frivolous styles, derived from those of the Second Empire and coinciding with a feeling of reaction against stuffiness and Germanophilia, in the seventies when Pater produced *Studies in the History of the Renaissance* and Butler started *The Way of All Flesh*. The next decade saw women more earnest in appearance, the dresses bunchy and concealing the figure: it was the decade for serious minds, for the founding of the Fabian Society and the challenging social surveys of Booth and Sims. The century ended with a hint of freer and lighter clothing, a hint that tennis and cycling had arrived and that the new woman like Wells's Ann Veronica was near at hand.

For most of the period, the men dressed severely and sombrely. Tight trousers confirmed the general air of constraint. The starched white collar and cuffs, or their detachable celluloid substitutes, made the line of demarcation between the manual and the non-manual worker. The aristocracy no longer distinguished themselves by a quantity of lace and bright colours, but tended increasingly to dress like better-tailored imitations of their own upper servants. The moustache was not fashionable until the middle fifties, when the Crimean War brought its extension from purely military wear. The full beard came into vogue about the same time and held its own for the rest of the period, though side-whiskers were more fashionable towards the end of the century. Although Victorian males adorned their faces with these symbols of virility, it need hardly be said that cosmetics were out of the question for respectable women.

The eating and drinking of the English had been a pride to themselves and a wonder to other nations for many centuries. The economic reality at the beginning of the period was that a considerable part of the population was inadequately fed and that some people starved to death. Those who were better off, however, often ate very well indeed. The consumption of food was heavy by modern standards. Yet while we gasp at the description of Archdeacon Grantley's breakfast,[1] we do well to remember that it was not always the right sort of food for health.

The adulteration of food, which had been increasing with the retail demands of townspeople who could not produce for themselves, was very bad when Victoria became Queen. A number of articles on the subject in *The Lancet* helped towards the formation of a Select Parliamentary Commission in 1855

[1] Trollope, *The Warden* (1855), Ch. 8.

and eventually to the Food and Drugs Act of 1860. This was an important step in legislation, but had little practical effect until the first appointment of Government inspectors and analysts in 1872. Some national prejudices encouraged adulteration: for instance, the quality of bread was judged by its whiteness so the poor preferred bread blanched with alum to the products of barley and rye. Fresh milk was so much valued in the towns that nobody worried about the unsavoury keeping of cows in urban cellars. Butter was often rancid, its badness masked by a skilful process of washing and flavouring; margarine came into use in the last twenty years of the century after a good deal of initial prejudice and opposition.

The average British diet was high in protein, compared with contemporary Continental eating. There was enough pasture to produce plenty of meat and enough seas around the shores to yield quantities of fish. The condition of these commodities by the time they were sold was another matter: many of the open markets could show little if any advance on those of the Middle Ages in point of cleanliness. It was not until the second half of the century that there was any serious understanding of the diseases caused by tainted meat. Even bad meat was beyond the reach of the very poor, who endured a monotonously starchy diet principally of bread, potatoes and milk. One interesting social change in eating dates from about the fifties, when oysters became expensive and made old history of Sam Weller's contention that 'poverty and oysters always seem to go together'.[1]

Eating was, like other aspects of nineteenth-century life, greatly affected by technical progress. New methods in the preservation of food improved the health of the national stomach but jolted the national economy. The first frozen meat from Australia arrived in 1880, to be followed by frozen mutton from New Zealand in 1882 and a shipment from the Argentine in the next year. The United States had been sending both live and canned meat across the Atlantic during the preceding decade.

The Englishman's cup of tea was already proverbial. From the forties it became increasingly an afternoon ritual although more old-fashioned households continued to use it as a late

[1] Dickens, *The Pickwick Papers* (1837), Ch. 22.

8

evening drink after an early dinner. In spite of the curious arithmetic by which William Cobbett had once worked out that a labourer could spend one-third of his total income on tea,[1] consumption of tea had been growing steadily, and, by the seventies it reached nearly four pounds annually per head of the population. Although tea-drinking still had its opponents, it was favoured by the growing temperance movement which found its strongest adherents among the nonconformists but was representative of all Christian denominations. A good deal of time and energy was spent throughout the reign in proving that certain social changes would lead to drink among the working classes – or alternatively would save them from it.

The public house was the 'poor man's club' as Shaw's dustman describes it,[2] used not only for drinking but for all kinds of meetings, auctions, friendly societies, for such debased sports as rat-catching, as the home of the 'free-and-easy' which gave birth to the music hall. For many it was a refuge from the squalor of their homes; it offered warmth, light, company and a means of escape from the realities of the long working day. There was indeed strength and virtue in the aims of the temperance movement, but its leaders tended to concentrate on the abolition of alcoholic drink without considering the social conditions which drove men to it. The word 'temperance' came to mean total abstinence, and its exponents were a powerful pressure-group in politics by the seventies. They worked mainly through the Liberals, while the brewing interests looked to the Conservatives. The problem began to solve itself as the conditions of life improved and new interests for leisure developed, but well into the next century there were still terrible scenes on pay-nights, and the admonitory lantern-lectures of the reformers were still being given.

Public houses were common enough, but public eating was comparatively rare. Few people ate anywhere except in their own or other people's homes, though the situation changed as travel became more frequent. There were indeed eating-houses and refreshment-rooms of different social levels but they were used in necessity rather than in pursuit of social or gustatory pleasure. Dickens cannot be dismissed as simply *laudator*

[1] Cobbett, *Cottage Economy* (1822), Introduction, paras. 23ff.
[2] Shaw, *Pygmalion* (1912), Act 2.

temporis acti for his gloomy assessment of the situation.[1] In the early eighties one of the ABC bread shops started serving cups of tea and heralded something new in British life. The first Lyons teashop opened in Piccadilly on 20 September 1894, a date which in its own way is as important as many more famous ones. It is evidence of more money and leisure, of the freer movement of women about their own business, of the growth outwards of the suburbs which made it impossible for people to rush home for a meal at any time of the day.

Smoking was not respectable in mixed company until the end of the century. Men were entitled to smoke, with due precautions of special clothes and a separate room so that the female nose would not be polluted. Bret Harte shocked a dinner party in 1879 with his unconventional American habit of smoking when ladies were present.[2] The pipe was solid and respectable; cigarettes came in about the time of the Crimean War but were considered 'fast' then and for many years afterwards. The cigar was popular, and by no means the luxury which it later became. Good cigars were smoked even by the Prince of Wales, when his mother was not around; but an unsavoury reputation went with many of the cheap 'cigar divans' like the one into which Trollope's Mr Harding innocently wandered when he came to London.[3]

It was essentially a man's world, although there was no lack of henpecked husbands as many of the comic writers testified. In the matter of official rights, women were an under-privileged class fighting for status. In spite of the eighteenth-century tradition of the learned woman who could converse with men on equal terms – a tradition carried on by such originals as Mrs Grote of the Benthamite circle – women were not expected to know more than the routine of domestic management. Such education as they received was to give them 'accomplishments' rather than knowledge. The upper and middle classes, taught at private schools or by governesses, were less favoured in this way than the poor who, if they got any teaching at all, usually got the same as the boys.

After being trained to run a home, the woman who did not

---

[1] 'Refreshments for Travellers', in *All the Year Round,* 24 March 1860.

[2] Marion Lochhead, *The Victorian Household* (London, 1964), p. 74.

[3] Trollope, *The Warden* (1855), Ch. 16.

marry was a problem. Many households were over-staffed with unmarried aunts and sisters. The increasing production of ready-made goods reduced the scope of household occupations and idleness became a fashionable cult. While poor women worked alongside men in factories and workshops, the more favoured classes sat at home, immobilized in their heavy clothes, sewing for missions and charities. Were they indeed the more favoured? It was little wonder that many of them became permanent invalids or fell into mysterious 'declines', showing their insecurity by the only kind of exhibitionism that was socially acceptable, and giving added interest and employment to their bored sisters. Robert Browning's hearty irruption into the Wimpole Street sickroom was symbolic of a breakthrough that was needed everywhere.

There were enough surplus women to create a problem, one which was talked about but not taken very seriously. Working women were gradually given legislative protection but a woman's domestic rights were strictly limited. As for the vote, even the Chartists did not demand more than manhood suffrage and only a few eccentric Liberals like John Stuart Mill came to realize the logical justice of giving the vote to women. Though the vote was still a dream for the future, a measure of equality was won in other ways. Acts of Parliament during the period gave women the right to keep their children after being deserted, the right to divorce, the right to keep their property after marriage. Women's trade unions had existed for many years and became an effective force in the seventies. Female clerks were employed when the new electric telegraph started as a Government concern in 1870, and during the next thirty years women became essential in office work. Two female factory inspectors were appointed in 1892.

Those unmarried women who neither stayed at home nor worked with their hands often became governesses, a depressed and disregarded class but one which provided a key to emancipation. When F. D. Maurice helped to start Queen's College in Harley Street in 1848 it was mainly with the idea of providing a better education for governesses. Its intake soon spread to other young women, and it proved to be a pioneer of schools and colleges where a segregated but adequate education could be obtained.

Emancipation was gained not only by the few who campaigned directly for it. It came largely from the achievements of women who showed that they could outdo men in every field, who overcame the supposed inferiority of women simply by ignoring it. Emancipation was the gift to their sex of women as diverse in accomplishment as Florence Nightingale, Harriet Martineau, Mary Kingsley and Mrs Humphry Ward. It also owed something to the growing popularity of the Queen, who had no patience with it at all.

Female emancipation was part of a wider human emancipation. The cheap bicycle at the end of the century came as a climax to the widening of opportunities for ordinary men and women. At the beginning of Victoria's reign, many people would not travel farther in a lifetime than their feet could carry them, but wider explorations gradually became possible. Townspeople began to rediscover the countryside out of which their grandparents had been forced by industrialization; excursions to the seaside became popular; there was more interest in sport and personal exercise. The bicycle stood for increased leisure, greater purchasing power, the rights and responsibilities of the individual. In offering more personal choice of travel, it gave an extension to something which the railways had begun.

We shall see that the railway took a prominent and often symbolic place in the imaginative world. The greatest railway boom came in the forties: there were some five hundred miles of rail in 1838, ten times that distance a decade later. The railways became a mania, an outlet for wild speculation, a challenge to traditional interests, a monstrous terror to the timid. At the height of the fever a York linen-draper, George Hudson, headed a 'railway party' in the House of Commons. Bill after Bill for the establishment of new lines went through; Gladstone's attempt in 1844 to secure some Government control of the development was mutilated before being passed. There was fierce competition, with rival lines sometimes running parallel to each other between the same towns. By the end of the forties the great boom was over, though expansion continued. Investigations into Hudson's activities revealed how he had gambled and speculated with shares until he was deeply in debt.

The railways of Britain were given neither systematic planning nor national ownership during the nineteenth century. There were royal commissions and select committees; an Act of 1871 gave the Board of Trade the right to certain information from the companies, but there was scarcely any economic control. Legislation for the benefit of passengers was more effective, gradually establishing better conditions in the cheaper classes of travel.

Railway travel was an important factor in the development of a more precise sense of time, associated with the general speeding up of communications through the penny post, the telegraph and eventually the telephone. At the end of the eighteenth century the services in a country parish depended on the parson's clock. The villagers came when the church bell rang, but the few who possessed clocks of their own were likely to arrive late if the clerical time was fast.[1] By 1860 a visiting clergyman whose worldly affairs detained him would arrive late and find to his disgrace that the service had already begun.[2] Between the old and the new is the railway expert like the mill-owner, Mr Head, whom Disraeli's Coningsby meets in Manchester – 'Train tomorrow at 7.25, get a fly at the station and you will be at Millbank by 8.40.'[3]

The progress of the railways was both a cause and a result of the general industrial expansion. The turnpike roads and canals had carried the traffic of the first stage of the Industrial Revolution: it was the railways that bore it through its later development. It is important to remember that the Victorians did not create the industrialization of Britain. They inherited it and spent a great deal of time and energy trying to improve the situation which it had given them. The first phase, competitive and individualistic, was over by 1832. The next twenty years saw fewer new inventions than had appeared in the previous generation, but an increasingly wider application of existing methods and a steady increase in production.

The growth of production between 1830 and 1850 was startling. Exports nearly doubled in value, as the power of steam was applied to more and more processes especially in the

---

[1] James Woodforde's *Diary*, entry for Sunday, 20 November 1791.
[2] Trollope, *Framley Parsonage* (1860), Ch. 7.
[3] *Coningsby* (1844), Bk. 4, Ch. 2.

textile industries. Weaving was overtaken by the same revolution that had made spinning a factory job. In 1830 there were some sixty thousand power looms in the whole country and nearly a quarter of a million handlooms; twenty years later it was the power looms which had reached the quarter-million mark. This was the development in cotton, and the same was happening only a little more slowly with wool, silk and linen. The processes of finishing, as well as those of primary production, were being mechanized and improved. Iron production was nearly trebled between 1830 and 1850; coal was more than doubled between 1836 and 1856.

The bald figures seem triumphant, but the cost in social upheaval and human suffering was high. The machines made long hours of working both possible and desirable for their owners. The minding of them did not call for great skill or physical strength, so the more exacting work of the men could be supported by the employment of women and children. As the industrial towns encroached on the countryside, the male labourer was turned into a factory worker and all his family became part of the insatiable demand for production. It is true that child labour was nothing new, that long hours and insanitary conditions had been common in the old cottage industries. Yet what is insanitary in one family is intolerable when multiplied a hundred times. Weariness in the familiar home with bed only a few steps away is not the same as the traumatic daily exile to a distant building, where work is not part of a discernable totality but a meaningless vigil disciplined by alien authority.

It was the children who stirred the national conscience. Their protection seems to us to have come slowly and hesitantly whereas the whole evil system should have been swept away in one Act of Parliament. We have to remember, however, that legislative interference with the conditions of labour was a revolution of thought as great as the revolutions in methods of production. A man's labour, and that of his family, was seen as his birthright to dispose of as he thought fit, while the employer was equally entitled to make the best possible terms for himself. The laws of political economy would ensure that it all worked out for the best interests of society.

The truth forced itself upon the nation in the hesitant but

compelling tones of those who gave evidence before the Select Committee on Factory Children's Labour in 1831–2. The initiative of Peel and Owen had already in 1819 produced an Act prohibiting the use of children under nine in cotton mills. The scope was limited, but the principle was established that the state might regulate contracts between employer and worker. In 1832 young children in other industries were still working as much as nineteen hours a day in appalling conditions. The father of one such family appeared before the Committee;[1] the dry dialogue-form of the record does not conceal the personal tragedy:

Question 5065: Were the children excessively fatigued by this labour?

Answer: Many times; we have cried often when we have given them the little victualling we had to give them, and they have fallen to sleep with their victuals in their mouths many a time.

The story was the same wherever the factories had come to dominate employment. The mess was gradually cleared up by legislation, though the prevailing refusal to interfere directly in what a man did with his own labour restricted the reforms to women and children. Although the Liberals have won most of the credit for legislation, it was a period when party ties were not so strong as they afterwards became. Private members had more freedom in voting and in the introduction of measures; controversial issues could bring a conflict of loyalties. One man at least was single-minded on this issue. It was Henry Cooper Ashley, afterwards Lord Shaftesbury, who made it certain that the principle of State regulation would be confirmed and increased.

Following the report of the Committee, the Factory Act of 1833 limited the hours of workers under eighteen years of age and took the important steps of spreading control to all textile industries and of appointing inspectors to see that the law was obeyed. It seemed to many employers like the portent of anarchy, but the adult workers still endured long hours, unhealthy conditions and positive danger. Gradually, however, Shaftesbury and others dug away at the seemingly impregnable

[1] *Report of the Select Committee on Factory Children's Labour* (1831–2), XV, pp. 192 ff.

defences of individualism and the free market, to increase the inspection of factories, enforce safety measures and eventually, in 1847, to secure the ten-hour day for women and young persons.

The struggle continued all through the reign. Commissions on the employment of children met again in 1843 and 1863, each time to reveal horrors which no legislation had touched. Shaftesbury's Mines Act of 1842 forbade the employment below ground of women and of children under ten. The scope of the Factory Acts was continued by legislation and extended first to jobs linked with the production of textiles, then to other industries. The plea that such intervention was contrary to individual freedom was heard less often, and by 1860 the voice of resistance had sunk to a whimper.

Yet if there was less opposition in the latter part of the century to the reform of working conditions, there was apathy in plenty. There were still the small workshops and home labour which all legislation had passed by: the garment-workers driven to exhaustion on piece-rates, the pullers of rabbit fur choking in the one room where they lived and worked, the makers of matches whose faces glowed in the dark from phosphorus poisoning. These things were less often the subjects of polemical fiction: their exposure passed into the hands of those who could observe and correlate, could use scientific and statistical methods to show the social results of poverty and exploitation. The reforming novelist gave way to men like Charles Booth with his four-volume survey *Life and Labour of the People of London* (1891–1903), in which he was assisted by the zealous young Fabian Beatrice Potter who later married Sidney Webb. Here was a generation that could start from the observed facts and not from prevailing economic theories.

The problem of working conditions was only one of the unwelcome legacies which fell to the Victorians. The population as a whole had grown during the years of the early industrialization, and although the birthrate fell sharply after 1840, the deathrate fell also. The population of Great Britain rose from about sixteen million in 1831 to nearly twenty-one million in 1851, twenty-six million in 1871 and thirty-seven million by the end of the century. The increase brought its troubles, but it was a witness to the gradual improvement on conditions which had caused high mortality in earlier years. Only in Ireland did famine, disease and emigration lead to a fall in population.

Thomas Robert Malthus in his *Essay on Population* (1798) had said that population tended to increase more quickly than the means of subsistence unless it was kept in check by such human misfortunes as war and sickness. It was a theory that fitted well enough into the economic doctrine of the Utilitarians and their successors. The fear of over-population and the consequent struggle for survival troubled even those minds who cared little for the minutiae of economics. Dickens might laugh at it in the creation of the prolific Micawber family but Tennyson felt it more sombrely:

Slowly comes a hungry people, as a lion, creeping nigher,
Glares at one that nods and winks behind a slow-dying fire.[1]

The growth of population was not evenly distributed. The greatest weight of population shifted from the south to the north of England and from the country to the towns. New urban concentrations grew up in north-west England, in South Wales and between the Forth and the Clyde. The industrial centre was a magnet to the surrounding countryside and the result was overcrowding, squalor and disease. There was no tradition in planning large towns, no pattern to guide even had the will to plan existed. The workers poured into cellars, into back-to-back houses around ill-ventilated and undrained courts. The rich and the middle class fled into the new suburbs which constantly spread outwards before the advancing tide of slums.

The problem of housing remained a prick to the public conscience throughout the period. As late as 1884–5 a Royal Commission on Housing, with the Prince of Wales among its members, revealed conditions which can still arouse nausea in the mere reading. Yet some of the attendant problems were tackled, the initial drive coming largely from one man. Edwin Chadwick did for public health what Shaftesbury did for women and children in industry.

It would not be a great exaggeration to say that scarcely any measures to safeguard public health had been passed since the withdrawal of the Roman occupation. Such laws as had been made were usually directed towards one particular nuisance,

[1] *Locksley Hall* (1842), lines 112ff.

limited in scope and in area of application. The sudden growth
of the towns had raised questions of water-supply, the disposal
of sewage, the prevention and control of infection. London was
not given main drainage until the sixties, and such sewers as
existed earlier discharged into the river so that Members of
Parliament could not bear to use their Terrace in the summer.

Chadwick's work in public health grew out of his duties as a
member of the Royal Commission which met in 1832 to
consider the question of Poor Relief. Its report, for which he
was largely responsible, showed up the degradation and
inefficiency which then existed. The 'Speenhamland system'
by which inadequate wages were made up from the rates had
resulted in a shift of responsibility from the employer to the
parish. The overseers appointed each year to administer parish
relief were overwhelmed by the problem; many of them shirked
their duty and allowed things to get worse, while some found
personal profit in the exploitation of pauper labour. The
workhouses were corrupt and corrupting, casting the sick, the
senile, the insane and the able-bodied unemployed into a
ghastly community of semi-starvation.[1]

The tone of the new report was not favourable to the pauper.
It recommended that relief should be given in such a way as to
deter the thriftless, and make it a last, desperate resort:

Rendering the person who administers the relief the hardest
taskmaster and the worst paymaster that the idle and dissolute can
apply to.[2]

This efficient but harsh document was received with approval
by those who believed that poverty called for natural checks
and private benevolence rather than public relief, a view which
outlived the century in which it was conceived. The Poor Law
Amendment Act of 1834 adopted the principles of the report,
setting up a central Poor Law Department to guide the local
amateur officials. The parishes were grouped in 'unions' with
boards of guardians to control the workhouses for each group.
Outdoor relief was curtailed, though not abolished.

The new Poor Law was hated by those who suffered under it

[1] For a poet's account of the workhouse before the Act of 1834 see Book 1 of
The Village (1783), by George Crabbe.
[2] *Report of the Royal Commission for inquiring into the Administration and Practical
Operation of the Poor Laws* (1834), XXIX, iii, 29.

and this resentment contributed to the growing feeling of unrest, especially in the north. 'These hell-hounds of commissioners have set up the command of their master the devil, against our God', declared the Chartist leader Richard Stephens.[1] In some respects his words were not too strong, but the establishment of the new law had two more creditable results. It innovated something which was to be important in the development of social legislation: an administrative body carrying out the will of Parliament but not directly controlled by a Minister. Secondly, it had Edwin Chadwick as its first secretary.

Chadwick had already recognized the link between extreme poverty and disease. Such epidemics as the cholera outbreaks of 1832 and 1837 were becoming more terrible as overcrowding increased. It was with the backing of the Poor Law Commission that Chadwick produced his *Report on an Inquiry into the Sanitary Condition of the Labouring Population of Great Britain.* Factual and unemotional, backing its assertions with evidence and statistics, this report revealed what many had partly known and chosen to ignore, what others learned with incredulous horror. It revealed the high death-rate among the poorest townspeople, the appalling housing, the lack of sanitation and fresh water, the doomed children, the failure even to make fit provision for the burial of the dead.

The public was to be disturbed more than once before the century was over by sudden acquaintance with unpleasant facts. Chadwick's achievement was to make these things a national concern and to point out that they were remediable and not a part of the natural order. He stated his findings and recommendations in a manner typical of the time, inspired more by utility than by compassion. Better drainage would be cheaper in the long run than loss of work from sickness; bad living conditions tended to breed bad moral habits.

A Public Health Board was set up in 1848, to give direction to local authorities. The establishment of local boards of health was permitted, not compelled: the response varied from one place to another, and the new burden on the rates did not endear the central board to the residents of towns where its direction was followed. The board was dissolved in 1854, and a

[1] Quoted in Max Hovell, *The Chartist Movement* (Manchester, 1918), p. 97.

new one without Chadwick to lead it lasted until 1858, when its functions were divided between the Privy Council and the Home Office. The slow reform was carried on by successive pieces of limited legislation until the Public Health Act of 1875 rationalized and consolidated the law, as it affected areas outside London. The problems of public health and poor relief continued into the twentieth century but the publication of Chadwick's report saw the beginning of their solution.

The work for public health gave impetus to the devolution of power to local authorities. The Municipal Corporations Act of 1835 gave councils elected by householders the right to make byelaws and impose rates. In the same year it became compulsory for municipal boroughs to set up police forces, on the lines of the London force started by Robert Peel six years before. The development of local government was slow and often painful, with disputes about overlapping authorities, the liability of councils for illegal acts and omissions, the ultimate sanction of the central government. The counties gained little of this new power at first but remained dependent for many administrative matters on their Justices of the Peace in petty and quarter sessions. County Councils were set up in 1888, when the establishment of the County of London with its own council began a new phase of reform and innovation under local jurisdiction.

In local government, as in parliamentary representation and the reform of working conditions, the towns first gained new privileges and the counties followed more slowly. Yet in the 1851 census, out of a total population of 15,771,000 over ten years of age, there were 1,790,000 employed in agriculture: a number greater than the combined strength of those working in cotton, wool, coal-mining, iron and building. The rise of industry was tending to the decline of agriculture but the movement away from the land was notable for its concentration in certain areas rather than for its overall numbers. Our image of the Victorian period tends to be one of industrial work and urban life, perhaps because these were the conditions which first produced reforming legislation and which received the main attention of writers who depicted social conditions.

We shall not understand the period fully unless we realize the continuing importance of the land. The enclosures which had been going on for centuries, with increasing momentum since the middle of the previous century, continued well into the reign of Victoria. The ending of the open-field system often meant the ruin of smallholders through the cost of fencing and the loss of common rights. They drifted into the new towns and became part of the urban problem, or emigrated. The labourers who held no land were faced with falling wages, rising prices and often the loss of 'living-in' benefits. If the problems of early Victorian towns were new, at least in magnitude, those of the countryside were the primeval ones of food and shelter.

The decisive trial of strength between agricultural and urban interests came over the Corn Laws. Since 1818 the importation of foreign wheat had been forbidden, until the price of home-grown wheat had reached a certain level. This meant protection for the farmers and expensive bread for those who had to buy their flour retail. The Anti-Corn-Law League, founded in 1839 to campaign for repeal, was typical of the time: a movement largely middle class in leadership and support, using every new technique to make its voice heard. Pamphlets were distributed everywhere, aided by the new penny post of 1840; candidates for Parliament were sponsored; electors were canvassed. When Peel refused to act in 1842 a band of some five hundred highly respectable people marched to London to press their demand. The struggle sharpened as landlords, farmers, parsons with agricultural glebeland, mounted opposition and sometimes intimidated tenants who supported the League. At last, convinced by a ruinous English harvest and the failure of the potatoes in Ireland, Peel introduced the Bill which resulted in the repeal of the Corn Laws in 1846.

This did not lead to the extinction of British agriculture which the landed interests had prophesied. On the contrary, conditions began to improve as farmers learned to apply new scientific methods of cultivation and to use machinery to offset the shortage of labour. Agriculture shared in the general boom and rising prices from about 1853, and for the next twenty years the nation continued to depend mainly on home-grown food. The acquisition of land was something socially desirable for those who had grown rich in trade or manufacture, and although some of them bought it mainly for the snob-value of hunting and shooting, many of them used their technical skill to improve their property. The middle third of the century was the time of 'high farming', with larger holdings, better breeding and rearing of stock, more permanent pasture, developed in place of wheat.

The poorest class of agricultural worker did not profit much from the general prosperity. A Royal Commission on Women and Children in Agriculture which sat from 1867 to 1870 found that the reforms won for industry had not touched the land. There was the familiar story of long hours, bad conditions, inadequate food. Conditions were worst in the south, where there was scarcely any industry competing for labour. Then, from the middle seventies, agricultural prosperity declined. A succession of bad harvests led to bigger importation of wheat and falling prices; the improvements in method were halted or abandoned, and less land came under cultivation. Another Royal Commission in 1882 blamed the weather, and one meeting in 1893 blamed foreign competition. The latter conclusion was the more pertinent, for Britain was now indeed dependent on the export of manufactures and the import of food. Between 1871 and 1901 the acreage under corn fell by twenty-five per cent, and the increasing quantity of imported meat and dairy produce frustrated attempts to balance the loss by putting more land to pasture.

It was a result of the belief that free trade was ultimately beneficial to both buyers and sellers. The doctrines of Adam Smith had become axiomatic; apart from the clash over the Corn Laws, almost all voices were united in praise of free trade. As the home market expanded, there seemed no more need for protection. The annual budgets had reduced the muddle of tariffs and taxes which had grown in the earlier part of the century. For over twenty years from 1850 there was a steady expansion of British trade. Then came a period of slumps and unemployment, as the nation felt the impact of over-production and unwise investment, coupled with growing foreign competition, especially from Germany and the United States. Was free trade really the panacea that had been supposed? Britain was setting up few trade barriers, but her exports met restrictions when they reached other countries. A Royal Commission in 1886 advised home industries to bestir themselves, to cheapen the costs of production and adopt new methods; the country as a whole was urged to provide better technical and commercial education. It all has a strangely modern sound. By the end of the century the British economy was stronger, but still vulnerable.

A new pattern of reform has appeared in this account of national events: private initiative leading to public pressure, followed by a Royal Commission or Select Committee, and resulting eventually in legislation. The law-making machinery was put into motion over questions which would not formerly have engaged the interest of Parliament. The story of Victorian Britain is a story of growing political responsibility for the individual, coupled with extension of the power of the state. While citizenship had always been understood to incur certain duties, it was now increasingly held to confer certain privileges. The struggle for representation, both individual and collective, became a major issue.

For most people in the early nineteenth century, the monarch seemed to be part of the ordained scheme of things, the titular head of a system which was the best possible for mankind. Yet the loyalty was to an ideal rather than to a person. When Victoria came to the throne in 1837 the monarchy was low in public estimation. Her predecessor and uncle, William IV, was an amiable and harmless enough man but without the character to dispel the bad image which the Georges had left behind them: 'a weak, ignorant, commonplace sort of person' commented *The Spectator* when he died.[1] The nineteenth-century myth of progress might well have drawn support from the advancing status of the monarchy. The new strength came not in direct political power – though the Queen made several attempts to control such turbulent ministers as Palmerston and Gladstone – but in prestige and security.

The eighteen-year-old girl who was suddenly called to be Queen began with the advantage of sentimental approval inspired by her youth and her sex. Her German cousin, Albert of Saxe-Coburg Gotha, did little at first to save her popularity, which was beginning to wane by the time he became her husband. His attempts to assert more control over political

[1] Quoted in David Thomson, *England in the Nineteenth Century* (Harmondsworth, 1950), p. 170.

affairs did not endear him to the politicians, and his austere, narrow character was no passport to the hearts of the people. Gradually his real devotion to the affairs of his adopted country won him respect if not affection, and there was a wave of true sympathy for Victoria when he died in 1861.

As the Queen continued her years of mourning and seclusion, refusing even to perform such traditional duties as opening Parliament, sympathy passed through impatience to exaspera-tion. There were murmurs for her abdication and even talk of a republic. She gave way at last, and began the climb to a regard that was almost reverential. Her Golden Jubilee in 1887 was a fulsome expression of national loyalty; her Diamond Jubilee ten years later was the apotheosis of Britain as an imperial power. The country and the Queen had survived together through the problems of the century, overcoming one difficulty after another and now basking in fitful sunshine as the shadows lengthened.

Less for what she did than for what she was, and because so much of good and bad lay both in her and in the time, Victoria deserved to have that long period remembered by her name. The small woman had expressed in herself so many of the ideals of her people, so much of their pride and their insecurity, their sense of duty and their personal tensions. The extravagant grief which had once made her unpopular came at last to sanctify the idea of the family. She was the perfect image for an age which worshipped the ideal of womanhood and was upset by many of its realities.

The monarchy had fallen low in estimation when Victoria acceded but the prestige of Parliament was high. The years of reaction and penal legislation following Waterloo had seen a growing demand for political reform, a demand not new in itself as the many 'reform clubs' of the previous century had shown, but one for which support had never been so widespread or so vociferous.

The reform movement, like much else within the succeeding years, was largely a movement of the growing middle class. The new industrial towns often had no direct representatives in Parliament, while hamlets that were the ruins of medieval boroughs still returned their two members at the will of the local magnate. The struggle for reform was part of the trial of

ffective support from the trade unions. Like Chartism,
ers' attempts to combine for their betterment had
from diffusion of aims in the bitter years after 1815.
d been clubs and friendly societies of journeymen in
crafts since the beginning of the eighteenth century.
quent rise of associations of textile workers in the
s had come to be regarded as potentially seditious,
overnment became alarmed when miners and un-
urers started collective bargaining on wages and
The Combination Acts of 1799 and 1800 made such
illegal and continued in force until 1824, when their
ght the rapid growth of new unions.
ncy now was for small local societies to give way to
al unions of workers in the same trade or industry.
attempt to present a united labour front was made
t Owen created the Grand National Consolidated
n. The Scots visionary, undeterred by the recent
utopian experiment in America, had previously
rmation of national unions which could assume
ustry. Now the large and the small unions, the
the agricultural workers, flocked enthusiastically
d National.
ers, often sympathetic to the smaller unions which
with open and identifiable negotiators, were
es brought retaliatory lock-outs and the im-
'document' – a compelled promise not to take
ctivities. The Combination Acts had gone but
be prosecutions for molestation, obstruction
e law of master and servant. At Tolpuddle in
of labourers sought advice from the Grand
ow to combine to prevent a further fall in their
ceremony at which they pledged their unity
ution for taking an unlawful oath: an offence
at the time of the Nore Mutiny in 1797 and
. They were sentenced to transportation for

cks as this the Grand National collapsed, and
of little consequence for a decade. Although
ists tried to win the help of the unions, their
ntical. There was talk of the 'National

strength between land and money, between agriculture and industry. On the level of overt propaganda it enlisted such improbable associates as William Cobbett and Jeremy Bentham. More diffusely, it reached out and caught the imagination of the unenfranchized workers, who were coming to see that political reform was the gateway to a higher standard of living and that injustices would not be remedied without representation. For the majority of them, reform was a weapon in a desperate situation, a successor to machine-wrecking, rick-burning and unsuccessful attempts at trade unionism.

William IV had his moment of political power, not indeed through any wish or initiative of his own, in the passage of the First Reform Act of 1832. The Prime Minister, Lord Grey, persuaded him to agree to the creation of enough Whig peers to pass the measure through the House of Lords if the Tory opposition there continued to block it. The threat was enough, and the reformers won the first round of the fight for popular representation which remained a major issue for most of the century.

Despite the threatened and actual civil disturbances before its passage and the national jubilation which greeted it, the Reform Act of 1832 proved a disappointment. Some of the worst abuses of rotten boroughs had been removed and the size of the electorate increased; but those who could vote for the new House of Commons numbered only some fifty per cent more than those who had voted for the old one. The new system of registering voters gave more importance to party organization and made it easy enough for unscrupulous agents to manipulate things in favour of their own supporters.

It was a disappointment, but not a complete failure. The industrial interests were better represented and even the slight increase in the electorate proved that the right to vote was capable of extension. It had been shown that economic and popular pressure could influence the course of government. Above all, the appetite for reform had been whetted and was to make more demands.

The franchise was still based on property and did not satisfy the old Radical demand for 'one man, one vote'. The new movement which came to be called Chartism was less spontaneous than the old workers' associations. Bearing a deeper sense of wrong, its leaders were also inspired with a more positive hope and made more specific requests. Chartism grew, as material conditions began to show the slight improvement that political means could make still larger. It canalized and made coherent several different grievances and united for a time several different groups. Its heterogeneity was its strength, and eventually its undoing. Yet, though none of its demands was met during the years of the active movement, nearly all of them are now part of the British Constitution.

The idea of the Charter began with the London Working Men's Association, founded in 1836 by William Lovett with the aims of political equality, social justice, a cheap press and a national system of education. It was small in membership but its aims were spread through a number of sympathetic or affiliated associations in other parts of the country. It was Fabian rather than revolutionary, working for reform through public opinion: violence was seen as the ultimate ally of defence rather than as an essential part of political attack. The Charter itself was intended as a Bill to be presented to Parliament. It was a long document, but the famous 'six points' which won wide support were:

1. Universal adult manhood suffrage.
2. Annual Parliaments.
3. Electoral voting to be by secret ballot.
4. Equal electoral districts.
5. Abolition of the property qualification for Members of Parliament.
6. Members of Parliament to be paid a salary.

Lovett and his followers hoped that the workers would concentrate on the Charter and not disperse their strength in piecemeal attempts to remedy more specific and local grievances. In fact, the Charter became the watchword of two other groups. Attwood's Political Union, centred on Birmingham, represented the middle-class aims of those who looked to reform of the monetary system as the cure for economic depression. Both Lovett and Attwood were essentially peaceful in their methods, but a more militant group developed in the north, where industrial conditions were worst, and was supported principally by factory workers and miners.

The northern leadership pass
O'Connor, a brilliant orator wit
that toppled over into madness
spread into other regions, the n
the 'moral force' and the 'physi
ing hope of reconciliation to
Chartist Convention met resp
the north saw huge open-a
played bearing skulls and t
sent to command the nort
with Chartist ideals but
efficiency against the thre

The petition for the Ch
1839 and again in 1842,
each occasion. As dissen
were riots in South Wa
petition was planned in
an assembly on Kenni
steps for the defence c
veteran Duke of Well
houses barricaded. T
procession would b
ment, O'Connor su
was taken quietly
signatures proved
was again rejecte
never another m

The contrast b
of the Anti-Cor
into the grasp
firmly behind
calico-printer
issue, and Joh
powerful but
precise in its
The Charti
reaction in
changes in
them.

A furth

Holiday' – a general strike which would force the Government to capitulate – but there was neither the strength nor the organization to make it effective. Yet the activities of particular unions showed that the strike weapon was an important one. Although the dream of a large general union of all workers was never fulfilled, the years after 1850 saw the growth of bigger unions and new aims. The new trade union leader was not the desperate rebel of the repressive days, but a man who knew how to use every loophole in the existing law. He did not see himself as the sworn enemy of the existing order, but rather as one who could make terms within it and obtain its recognition of workers' rights. He built up the funds of his union, spent some of them on libraries and reading-rooms, put his faith in the results of education rather than violence.

Meanwhile the struggle for the franchise continued in a minor key. The years after the collapse of Chartism were calmer and more prosperous; a feeling of comparative contentment settled over the country and the attempt to extend the vote was weak and half-hearted. Parliament went on in its traditional way, the small Cabinet still containing more peers than commoners. Yet the precedent of the Public Health Board was being followed and private lives were receiving more interference from the Government. At the same time, the ancient and often anomalous system was becoming more complex and harder to understand. Its procedures were slow; the picture which Dickens gave in *Little Dorrit* of the 'Circumlocution Office' was not a wild exaggeration.

The belief that those who were to be affected by legislation had a right to choose the legislators gradually strengthened. The zeal which was overthrowing dynasties on the Continent found an outlet in Britain through new campaigns to widen the franchise. The power of the Commons was growing, and despite frequent bickering between the Houses it was coming to be recognized that it was not the Lords who held the national mandate. The demand for manhood suffrage became strong again in the early sixties – it was men, not property, that Parliament should represent. The trade unions lent their new strength to the cause; John Stuart Mill accepted the principle of general suffrage, with certain provisos.[1] Nevertheless, the

[1] J. S. Mill, *Representative Government* (1861), Ch. 8.

proposals of Russell and Gladstone to extend the franchise in 1866 brought the defeat of the Liberal government.

Disraeli was more successful and steered the Second Reform Act through Parliament in 1867, adding some million voters to the register and giving the franchise to the town workers. It was a gift worth less than its face value, since elections were still open and the pressures of employer or landlord could prevail. Gladstone's Secret Ballot Act of 1872 was the real liberator of working-class power. His Reform Acts of 1884 and 1885 gave the vote to all adult males and secured fairer representation for the new towns.

The working man had become a full political shareholder in the state, but his economic stake was still unequal. The property qualification for Members of Parliament had been abolished in 1858, and with this Chartist dream come true there was no constitutional barrier to the election of working men. The London Working Men's Association (not to be confused with Lovett's earlier organization) was founded in 1866 and made little impression on national politics, but the Labour Representation League of 1870 launched a more determined and successful effort. Thirteen Labour candidates stood in the 1874 election and two of them – both miners – were returned.

At the same time the trade union movement lost sympathy through the 'Sheffield outrages' of 1866, outbreaks of violence during a strike which led to the setting up of a commission to inquire into trade unionism as a whole. The unions had suffered adverse legal judgements in their attempts to justify their function as friendly societies, and their activities had been held to be illegal as in restraint of trade. The new inquiry seemed to be a threat, but it ended as a triumph. A succession of union witnesses impressed the commission with their integrity and responsibility. The Sheffield outrages occupied only a small part of the final report, which was largely favourable to the unions. A consequent Act in 1871 made it certain that a trade union could be registered as a friendly society and was not illegal merely by being in restraint of trade.

The struggle was not yet over. While the industrial unions were gaining recognition, the shadow of Tolpuddle stretched over the agricultural worker. It was not until 1872 that the Warwickshire labourer Joseph Arch stood up on a pig-stool and strength between land and money, between agriculture and industry. On the level of overt propaganda it enlisted such improbable associates as William Cobbett and Jeremy Bentham. More diffusely, it reached out and caught the imagination of the unenfranchized workers, who were coming to see that political reform was the gateway to a higher standard of living and that injustices would not be remedied without representation. For the majority of them, reform was a weapon in a desperate situation, a successor to machine-wrecking, rick-burning and unsuccessful attempts at trade unionism.

William IV had his moment of political power, not indeed through any wish or initiative of his own, in the passage of the First Reform Act of 1832. The Prime Minister, Lord Grey, persuaded him to agree to the creation of enough Whig peers to pass the measure through the House of Lords if the Tory opposition there continued to block it. The threat was enough, and the reformers won the first round of the fight for popular representation which remained a major issue for most of the century.

Despite the threatened and actual civil disturbances before its passage and the national jubilation which greeted it, the Reform Act of 1832 proved a disappointment. Some of the worst abuses of rotten boroughs had been removed and the size of the electorate increased; but those who could vote for the new House of Commons numbered only some fifty per cent more than those who had voted for the old one. The new system of registering voters gave more importance to party organization and made it easy enough for unscrupulous agents to manipulate things in favour of their own supporters.

It was a disappointment, but not a complete failure. The industrial interests were better represented and even the slight increase in the electorate proved that the right to vote was capable of extension. It had been shown that economic and popular pressure could influence the course of government. Above all, the appetite for reform had been whetted and was to make more demands.

The franchise was still based on property and did not satisfy the old Radical demand for 'one man, one vote'. The new movement which came to be called Chartism was less spontaneous than the old workers' associations. Bearing a deeper sense of wrong, its leaders were also inspired with a more positive hope and made more specific requests. Chartism grew, as material conditions began to show the slight improvement that political means could make still larger. It canalized and made coherent several different grievances and united for a time several different groups. Its heterogeneity was its strength, and eventually its undoing. Yet, though none of its demands was met during the years of the active movement, nearly all of them are now part of the British Constitution.

The idea of the Charter began with the London Working Men's Association, founded in 1836 by William Lovett with the aims of political equality, social justice, a cheap press and a national system of education. It was small in membership but its aims were spread through a number of sympathetic or affiliated associations in other parts of the country. It was Fabian rather than revolutionary, working for reform through public opinion: violence was seen as the ultimate ally of defence rather than as an essential part of political attack. The Charter itself was intended as a Bill to be presented to Parliament. It was a long document, but the famous 'six points' which won wide support were:

1. Universal adult manhood suffrage.
2. Annual Parliaments.
3. Electoral voting to be by secret ballot.
4. Equal electoral districts.
5. Abolition of the property qualification for Members of Parliament.
6. Members of Parliament to be paid a salary.

Lovett and his followers hoped that the workers would concentrate on the Charter and not disperse their strength in piecemeal attempts to remedy more specific and local grievances. In fact, the Charter became the watchword of two other groups. Attwood's Political Union, centred on Birmingham, represented the middle-class aims of those who looked to reform of the monetary system as the cure for economic depression. Both Lovett and Attwood were essentially peaceful in their methods, but a more militant group developed in the north, where industrial conditions were worst, and was supported principally by factory workers and miners.

The northern leadership passed into the hands of Feargus O'Connor, a brilliant orator with an unbalanced temperament that toppled over into madness before his death. As his influence spread into other regions, the movement began to split between the 'moral force' and the 'physical force' sections, with diminishing hope of reconciliation to present a single front. While the Chartist Convention met respectably at a London coffee-house, the north saw huge open-air rallies where banners were displayed bearing skulls and tokens of violence. General Napier, sent to command the northern garrison, had some sympathy with Chartist ideals but organized his troops with ruthless efficiency against the threat of rebellion.

The petition for the Charter was presented to Parliament in 1839 and again in 1842, and was overwhelmingly rejected on each occasion. As dissension grew within the movement, there were riots in South Wales and other places. A new and bigger petition was planned in 1848, to be carried to Parliament from an assembly on Kennington Common. The Government took steps for the defence of London, entrusting its command to the veteran Duke of Wellington: bridges were guarded, shops and houses barricaded. The end was an anticlimax; warned that the procession would be an illegal attempt to intimidate Parliament, O'Connor suddenly gave up the idea and the petition was taken quietly in three cabs. The boasted five million signatures proved to be less than two million and the petition was again rejected. The Convention dissolved and there was never another meeting in the name of Chartism.

The contrast between the failure of Chartism and the success of the Anti-Corn-Law League is instructive. Instead of falling into the grasp of unreliable demagogues, the League remained firmly behind its two responsible leaders: Richard Cobden, a calico-printer with a genius for mastering the details of the issue, and John Bright, a Quaker cotton-spinner with the gift of powerful but restrained oratory. The League was limited and precise in its aims, whereas Chartism became vague and diffuse. The Chartists were split between progress in politics and reaction in opposing industrialism: the League recognized the changes in the national situation and acted logically within them.

A further reason for the failure of Chartism was its inability to win effective support from the trade unions. Like Chartism, the workers' attempts to combine for their betterment had suffered from diffusion of aims in the bitter years after 1815. There had been clubs and friendly societies of journeymen in the urban crafts since the beginning of the eighteenth century. The subsequent rise of associations of textile workers in the small towns had come to be regarded as potentially seditious, and the Government became alarmed when miners and unskilled labourers started collective bargaining on wages and conditions. The Combination Acts of 1799 and 1800 made such associations illegal and continued in force until 1824, when their repeal brought the rapid growth of new unions.

The tendency now was for small local societies to give way to large national unions of workers in the same trade or industry. In 1834 the attempt to present a united labour front was made when Robert Owen created the Grand National Consolidated Trades Union. The Scots visionary, undeterred by the recent failure of his utopian experiment in America, had previously urged the formation of national unions which could assume control of industry. Now the large and the small unions, the industrial and the agricultural workers, flocked enthusiastically into the Grand National.

The employers, often sympathetic to the smaller unions which presented them with open and identifiable negotiators, were alarmed. Strikes brought retaliatory lock-outs and the imposition of the 'document' – a compelled promise not to take part in union activities. The Combination Acts had gone but there could still be prosecutions for molestation, obstruction and breach of the law of master and servant. At Tolpuddle in Dorset a group of labourers sought advice from the Grand National about how to combine to prevent a further fall in their wages. The pitiful ceremony at which they pledged their unity led to their prosecution for taking an unlawful oath: an offence in an Act passed at the time of the Nore Mutiny in 1797 and re-enacted in 1819. They were sentenced to transportation for seven years.

Under such attacks as this the Grand National collapsed, and trade unionism was of little consequence for a decade. Although the northern Chartists tried to win the help of the unions, their aims were not identical. There was talk of the 'National

Holiday' – a general strike which would force the Government to capitulate – but there was neither the strength nor the organization to make it effective. Yet the activities of particular unions showed that the strike weapon was an important one. Although the dream of a large general union of all workers was never fulfilled, the years after 1850 saw the growth of bigger unions and new aims. The new trade union leader was not the desperate rebel of the repressive days, but a man who knew how to use every loophole in the existing law. He did not see himself as the sworn enemy of the existing order, but rather as one who could make terms within it and obtain its recognition of workers' rights. He built up the funds of his union, spent some of them on libraries and reading-rooms, put his faith in the results of education rather than violence.

Meanwhile the struggle for the franchise continued in a minor key. The years after the collapse of Chartism were calmer and more prosperous; a feeling of comparative contentment settled over the country and the attempt to extend the vote was weak and half-hearted. Parliament went on in its traditional way, the small Cabinet still containing more peers than commoners. Yet the precedent of the Public Health Board was being followed and private lives were receiving more interference from the Government. At the same time, the ancient and often anomalous system was becoming more complex and harder to understand. Its procedures were slow; the picture which Dickens gave in *Little Dorrit* of the 'Circumlocution Office' was not a wild exaggeration.

The belief that those who were to be affected by legislation had a right to choose the legislators gradually strengthened. The zeal which was overthrowing dynasties on the Continent found an outlet in Britain through new campaigns to widen the franchise. The power of the Commons was growing, and despite frequent bickering between the Houses it was coming to be recognized that it was not the Lords who held the national mandate. The demand for manhood suffrage became strong again in the early sixties – it was men, not property, that Parliament should represent. The trade unions lent their new strength to the cause; John Stuart Mill accepted the principle of general suffrage, with certain provisos.[1] Nevertheless, the

[1] J. S. Mill, *Representative Government* (1861), Ch. 8.

proposals of Russell and Gladstone to extend the franchise in 1866 brought the defeat of the Liberal government.

Disraeli was more successful and steered the Second Reform Act through Parliament in 1867, adding some million voters to the register and giving the franchise to the town workers. It was a gift worth less than its face value, since elections were still open and the pressures of employer or landlord could prevail. Gladstone's Secret Ballot Act of 1872 was the real liberator of working-class power. His Reform Acts of 1884 and 1885 gave the vote to all adult males and secured fairer representation for the new towns.

The working man had become a full political shareholder in the state, but his economic stake was still unequal. The property qualification for Members of Parliament had been abolished in 1858, and with this Chartist dream come true there was no constitutional barrier to the election of working men. The London Working Men's Association (not to be confused with Lovett's earlier organization) was founded in 1866 and made little impression on national politics, but the Labour Representation League of 1870 launched a more determined and successful effort. Thirteen Labour candidates stood in the 1874 election and two of them – both miners – were returned.

At the same time the trade union movement lost sympathy through the 'Sheffield outrages' of 1866, outbreaks of violence during a strike which led to the setting up of a commission to inquire into trade unionism as a whole. The unions had suffered adverse legal judgements in their attempts to justify their function as friendly societies, and their activities had been held to be illegal as in restraint of trade. The new inquiry seemed to be a threat, but it ended as a triumph. A succession of union witnesses impressed the commission with their integrity and responsibility. The Sheffield outrages occupied only a small part of the final report, which was largely favourable to the unions. A consequent Act in 1871 made it certain that a trade union could be registered as a friendly society and was not illegal merely by being in restraint of trade.

The struggle was not yet over. While the industrial unions were gaining recognition, the shadow of Tolpuddle stretched over the agricultural worker. It was not until 1872 that the Warwickshire labourer Joseph Arch stood up on a pig-stool and 'spoke out straight and strong for union'. The new movement was soon, in Arch's words, 'flowing over the country like a spring tide',[1] but its supporters suffered victimization for many years. Nor was all well with the industrial unions, whose new success in imposing their collective will was an offence against the prevailing Liberal individualism. The National Association of Employers of Labour, formed to do battle with the unions, made use of such weapons as the prohibition of picketing during strikes. After the 1871 Act, however, union membership grew until it had passed two million by the end of the century.

New unions of unskilled workers, more conscious of their insecurity in times of depression, were concerned with direct industrial activity rather than respectable status. It was the hitherto inarticulate who now set the pace: the match-girls whose exploitation won them sympathy from the more privileged, and Ben Tillett's dock-workers whose strike attracted the mediation of Cardinal Manning. At the Trades Union Congress there were annual clashes between the old and the new unionism.

The new unionism had a name for its outlook, a name not new in British politics but one for which the previous generation of workers' leaders had shown little liking. The dread word 'socialism' was now heard freely not only from certain trade unionists but also from those who, in the opinion of their families and friends, ought to have known better. The capitalistic basis of society was being questioned and the demand for the assumption of greater powers by the state was growing. The Paris Commune of 1871 and the French Socialist movement which followed it, the foundation of the German Democratic Party in 1875, stimulated the ideas already fostered by foreign refugees in London, of whom Karl Marx was one. Whereas Lovett had offered support and encouragement to distressed brothers in other countries, the current was now beginning to flow the other way.

Henry Hyndman was full of demands for both immediate and distant reforms when he helped to found the Democratic Federation in 1881. As well as reviving some of the unfulfilled Chartist aims he also wanted to do away with the House of Lords and to get state action to aid education, housing and

[1] Henry Pelling, *A History of British Trade Unionism* (Harmondsworth, 1963), p. 80.

employment. Land nationalization was something with which earlier thinkers had dallied. The Trades Union Congress voted for it in 1882, while Hyndman went on to ask for nationalization of the mines and railways.

Socialism split on the rocks of internal dissension and conflicting ideals, as Chartism had split a generation before. In 1884 some members of Hyndman's organization – by this time called the Social Democratic Federation – broke away to form the Socialist League. While the Federation became ever more political in its aims, the League was disinclined to Parliamentary action and nursed a vision of a utopian society built on trade and craft organizations. Members of the Federation worked among the unemployed and were involved in such direct action as the Pall Mall riots of 1886 and the 'Bloody Sunday' meeting in Trafalgar Square in 1887 when one of the demonstrators was killed. The League passed under Anarchist influence, and in 1890 William Morris sadly led a few of his supporters off to form the idealistic Hammersmith Socialist Society.

An earnest and intellectual group with socialism in their hearts founded the Fabian Society in 1884. Their desire was to remould society by slow, peaceful action, infiltrating into existing groups, winning parliamentary representation and gathering facts to prove their case. The names of Sidney Webb and Bernard Shaw as yet meant little, but it was they and their friends who set the pattern for the advance of socialism in the next century.

Labour power in Parliament became stronger when the formation of the Independent Labour Party in 1893 made it no longer necessary to take refuge under the Liberal wing and run the risk of being crushed in its fond embrace. In 1900 the Labour Representation League was formed at a meeting representing the SDF, the Fabians, the TUC and the ILP. The SDF wanted a definite declaration of socialist aims. The day was carried instead by Keir Hardie with his demand for immediate practical legislation on the problems of labour. Not many people had heard of the first secretary of the Labour Representation League; his name was Ramsay MacDonald.

Such were the affairs of the nation at home, where the interests of the majority were centred. Foreign policy did not impinge much on everyday life until the end of the century; for the greater part, people were content with a vague patriotism and xenophobia, a belief that Waterloo and Trafalgar had settled for ever the question of which was the best country in the world. More intelligently, the Liberal spirit tended to be sympathetic to foreign nationalist movements and to look for peace and prosperity through international understanding. If there was conflict, Britain would keep her old role of maintaining the balance of power; and for a large part of the period one of the main questions was whether it was France or Russia that most needed to be checked. The setback given to Russia by the Crimean War was only temporary but that war helped to focus public opinion more clearly on events abroad and to increase agitation about the muddle and mismanagement of the administration. Out of it grew various army reforms, including the setting up of a Staff College in 1858 and the formation of the Volunteers.

For many years foreign policy was dominated by Palmerston, as Foreign Secretary and later as Prime Minister. Favouring non-intervention where British interests were not affected, he pounced like a tiger on every threat to his country's supremacy. Victoria hated his casual attitude to crowned heads, including her own. She was able to secure his dismissal in 1851 but could only fume ineffectively nine years later when he supported the Sardinian rising against Papal and Neapolitan domination. He was not always right: it was his alienation of Russia over the Polish question in 1863 that prevented any firm joint opposition from Britain, Russia and France to the wave of Prussian aggression which began with the annexation of Schleswig-Holstein in the following year.

By this time Britain was no longer strong as a European power. Her only influence in the Franco-Prussian War of 1871 was in making a treaty with both sides to guarantee Belgian neutrality. For the rest of the century she managed to remain on reasonable terms with Germany during the ascendancy of Bismarck. She improved relations with the United States, having overcome her previous unpopularity in that country by accepting with a good grace the damages awarded against her by arbitration on the *Alabama* case. During the American Civil

War, British sympathies had tended to be with the South, on the principle of supporting endeavours for self-expression and independence.

The growing tension between Britain and Germany which followed the fall of Bismarck in 1890 was due mainly to clashes over colonial expansion. The Empire was now a popular and exciting theme, after the years which had seen responsible government granted in turn to Canada, Australia, New Zealand and Cape Colony. Canada, the first to demand freedom from direct British control over all her affairs, won dominion status in 1867. India had come under firmer rule since the Mutiny of 1857–8. The Indian Army was given a higher proportion of British troops and a fixed garrison; many of the native states were annexed to the Crown. In 1876 the wily Disraeli pleased many of the important interests by having the Queen made Empress of India.

This was not enough, and Britain joined with a will in the scramble for Africa and other developing areas of the world. Between 1875 and 1900 nearly five million square miles were added to the Empire, to make a total of some thirteen million square miles with 320 million people. The expansion had popular support: the concept of an empire so much bigger than the Mother Country and yet obedient to her appealed to the familial mind of the Victorians. A new romanticism grew up, as the desire to escape to Tartary or Xanadu could be fulfilled in Hong Kong or Nigeria. Some went away, as administrators or as missionaries, while the majority obtained vicarious delight by staying at home and reading about them. If administration and missioning sometimes got mixed up with each other and with commercial profit, it is also fair to say that the growth of indirect rule and the movements towards self-government owed at least as much to the men on the spot as they did to Whitehall. Men like Lugard in Africa and Hamilton-Gordon in Fiji, knew the people they were sent to govern and served their interests well.

Gladstone was no friend to Imperial expansion, but the later Liberals mostly followed the contrary view of Joseph Chamberlain. Under Disraeli, expansion became a positive feature of Conservative policy. Since their leaders were largely agreed, the people were happy to follow. John Seeley's book *The*

Expansion of England sold eighty thousand copies within two years of its publication in 1883. The Empire Theatre in Leicester Square was given its significant name in 1884. The Imperial tributes at the Diamond Jubilee in 1897 suggested that there was no corner of the world lacking loyal and devoted subjects of the Queen. The nineties were a decade of patriotic songs and poems, of *Soldiers of the Queen* in the music hall and Kipling in the drawing-room. The Empire provided the image of unity which was being vainly sought in society at home.

Only South Africa spoilt the image, as the Boers resisted British rule and asserted the right to govern newly-annexed territory. When the century ended they were at war, a war that was not going well for Britain and was making her disliked in many European countries. The champion of minority struggles and nationalist movements found herself in a new and uncomfortable position. The cheers of the Diamond Jubilee closed an age: the khaki uniforms that replaced the traditional red in the dust of the veldts ominously opened a new one.

2

Victorian Ideas

The Industrial Revolution was only one of many things of which the Victorians inherited the reality, struggled with the effects and were afterwards blamed for the consequences. The Victorian image which presented itself to the succeeding generation was a plump man in a frock coat, with a gold watch-chain over which he clasps his hands and a contented expression showing his belief that everything is good and is getting better. Today the image is a rather thinner man with a worried face, trying to absorb a quantity of new information and decide what it tells him about his duty. Mr Podsnap has given way to Robert Elsmere.

Both literary figures had numerous counterparts in life, with the Elsmeres coming to the fore in the second part of the reign. It was a period of growth and change; the same is true of many other periods, but the Victorian problem was that the changes were taking place in so many different aspects of life and were affecting each other so deeply. A new sense of the inter-dependence of sections of society set them looking for a unifying factor. There was passionate adherence to theories, each one claiming to have the whole answer to industrialism and poverty and class-conflict and religious doubt and . . . the list seems endless. For real complacency, for a general refusal to face the growing fragmentation of society, we have to look back to the years immediately following Waterloo.

The Victorians lived in the midst of changes that threatened stability, and they came to be frightened of much that was new. Chartism caused terror because it might overthrow law and establish mob-rule. Universal suffrage seemed almost as bad, and the secret ballot struck at the integrity of the individual. The emancipation of women would mean the end of family life. Agnostics feared that a general retreat from faith would remove all moral standards and reveal the beast in man.

Orthodox churchmen feared that the loss of belief in eternal punishment would make it hard to teach people to lead good lives. All through the period, people were earnestly canvassing something as the great panacea, while others were warning that the same thing would lead to total ruin, or at least to 'drink and huppishness in workin' men'.[1]

What frames of thought did they inherit at the beginning of the reign, within which to view the human situation? There were principally two, one old and the other new in form though with a long philosophic ancestry. The old was Christianity; the new, with little respect for the old, was the Utilitarian philosophy. Its chief exponent, Jeremy Bentham, died in the year 1832 with which our period opens. The school of thought often called after him changed a great deal with the passing years, moving from opposition to state control of economic and social affairs into a platform for reform through legislation. The change was inherent in its claim that the purpose of government was to assure the greatest happiness of the greatest number. This claim itself was based on the axiom that men are prompted in their behaviour by the pursuit of pleasure and the avoidance of pain.

The Benthamites were too impatient of inefficiency and waste to abide for ever by the *laissez-faire* doctrine of Adam Smith with which they had begun. The Philosophic Radicals, who formed a group in the House of Commons after the First Reform Act, were confronted by a system of government which had happened rather than been planned. The eighteenth-century idea of government had been essentially amateur, the permanent administration small and riddled with sinecures. Industrialism and the population growth overtook it and left it gasping behind.

The Philosophic Radicals had faded out of prominence by the time the hungry forties brought new problems, but they had left their mark. It was their onslaught on inefficiency which began the pattern already noted: of private conviction, unofficial publicity, governmental inquiry and eventual legislation. They had little idea of being able fundamentally to change human nature, but a strong faith that human beings could be manipulated and controlled.

[1] G. B. Shaw, *Candida* (1895), Act 1.

The strong new reforming spirit was weakened by disagreement about underlying principles. While the Benthamites did not expect to change human nature, the more utopian reformers like Robert Owen proposed to do just that. The utopian faith shows itself in many ways, all looking to a general 'change of heart' rather than to more practically enforceable measures. Its appeal to many of the writers, Dickens among them, perhaps explains the common literary image of the Benthamites as smug, callous and ultra-individualistic. The truth was that a great many things needed to be changed and that the reform of Parliament, insufficient though it was, proved change to be possible.

Although Christians and Benthamites had little love for each other, it was often a combination of their forces that initiated and carried through reform. Shaftesbury was a devout Evangelical, Chadwick was devout in his following of Bentham: neither of them was inclined to the mildest of socialism. They were both autocratic, with little respect for the voice of the majority. Yet both of them disliked the turn which society had taken and believed that it could and should take a different one. Chadwick in particular showed no wish to change the structure of the society which he was trying to make tidy and clean. Schemes for improving the working class were always strong on cleanliness. Washing was the accompaniment to so many reforming activities as almost to suggest a large guilt-feeling about the whole situation.[1]

That there was no single motive for reform is shown by the way in which the humanitarian spirit came to stand above party politics. The Whig Melbourne and the Radicals Cobden and Bright supported the Tory Government over the Factory Bill of 1844; Shaftesbury could find backing from Whigs like Macaulay and Palmerston. Neither party imitated the rival groups in many European countries by asserting that all good things depended on its own survival and the extinction of the other. Each of them claimed to stand for progress to the golden future and offered its leadership along the road.

In this they held a belief that was fundamental to the nine-

---

[1] A rich man was moved to give £1000 to the Salvation Army on discovering that the converts had washed their necks and ears. R. Collier, *The General Next to God* (London, 1965), p. 89.

teenth century, though not without doubt and depression from time to time. History was seen as a sequence of events, passing along a linear scale from the worse to the better. Tennyson, afflicted as he was by inner problems, could still join in the expectation:

> I the heir of all the ages in the foremost files of time.[1]

An heir would be more reasonably following the file than leading it, but Tennyson seems to have been having problems with his imagery. A few lines later his supposition that railway trains ran in grooved tracks leads him to extol 'the ringing grooves of change'.

The roots of the belief in progress are many. The French Revolution had seemed to some English Radicals to be the herald of a glorious future. Wordsworth, who lived long enough to change his mind, had written:

> Bliss was it in that dawn to be alive,
> But to be young was very Heaven![2]

The optimistic tradition leading from Locke had found new encouragement in the ideas of Condorcet. The faith in 'human perfectibility' held by William Godwin and shared by some of the young Romantic poets kept its hold on others in the next generation. The possibility that the Golden Age might be, not some poetic memory of a lost innocence, but a time which each age could strive towards achieving, was an inspiration to many Victorians who disagreed with each other about exactly what form it would take.

We shall see how in the second half of the period philosophical positivism and scientific evolution gave a new turn to the belief in progress. We shall see how William Morris expressed a distinctive brand of utopian socialism. There were many others who had their own intellectual or emotional interpretations of what progress meant. The ordinary man who had little idea of philosophy but who kept his eyes open might have more existential reasons. A man who was born in the years between Waterloo and the death of George IV might live to see the vote given to all men, without the bloody revolution that

[1] *Locksley Hall* (1842), line 155.
[2] Wordsworth, *The Prelude*, Bk. 2, lines 108ff.

had been prophesied. He would see the hungry forties give way to greater prosperity and contentment, with a contrast great enough to veil the real sufferings of the later years. He would see life becoming longer and healthier as disease retreated before the advance of medicine and hygiene. He would see communications improving, the railway giving new mobility to men and materials, the steamship and the telegraph linking nations in a new understanding.

So at least it seemed to those who lived through the changes. Many of them became complacent and a little self-righteous about the past while they looked with more confidence towards the future. To discover and fulfil one's duty, as individual or as nation, was necessary not only for the present but also for the right ordering of posterity. The blend of duty and optimism is a feature of the age, backed by the Benthamite proof that society could be improved by legislation and the scientific proof that man was now the master of his environment. There seemed to be an essential goodness in created things, but a goodness that needed to be fostered, organized and tidied.

Yet the optimism was not unshaken, the faith not absolute. Those concerned with social and political reform were more worried about their failures than elated by their successes. They suffered in the search for a unified solution to problems which were complex and irreconcilable. The Great Exhibition of 1851 may seem to be the apotheosis of the belief in progress, with material prosperity as its prop and symbol. Yet in that year Prince Albert wrote of the Queen's fear that there were coming:

Most dangerous times in which Military Despotism and Red Republicanism will for some time be the only powers on the Continent, to both of which the Constitutional Monarchy of England will be equally hateful.[1]

If such fears could be felt three years after the collapse of Chartism, the tension was to grow rather than decline as the century went on. How was the extension of the state's protection of the individual to be reconciled with that same individual's freedom? Could Christianity still be a vital force in an age of scientific theories apparently contradictory to the Bible? Did

[1] Quoted in *Ideas and Beliefs of the Victorians* (London, 1949), p. 53.

the liberating power of agnosticism mean a loss of moral standards? It was not a later critic but a contemporary who wrote this sober judgement in 1900:

The outlook at the end of the year which closed the nineteenth century could hardly fail to arouse misgivings as to the future in all except the imperviously self-satisfied.[1]

Strong individualism is another aspect of Victorian thought which has aroused both contemporary and later criticism. In its crudest form it could lead to the justification of ruthless competition in business, the assertion that only lack of initiative and hard work stopped anyone from making a fortune, the opposition to schemes of reform which collectively affected any part of society. Particularly in the first half of the period, there was insistence on the virtues of the self-made man and the iniquity of those who would interfere with the free flow of endeavour. The Industrial Revolution had raised men of ability and insight, as well as men of dishonesty and cruelty, from poverty to riches. The new inventions and their application had been the work of individuals. Why should the state now encroach on their freedom – the state which itself lagged behind in speed and efficiency of administration?

In the later years of Victoria's reign, when the state had done something to reform its own machinery as well as the working of society, this attitude was modified. Public reforms had not produced a rebellious mob demanding to be 'fed on turtle soup and venison, with a gold spoon'[2] but a more responsible and dignified working class. The early reformers were few in number but some of them had devoted their lives to reform as if to a vocation. Consequently the idea of reform became respectable: 'good causes' were fashionable things to support, but the principle of self-help remained strong. The sacred scripture of personal betterment, *Self-Help* by Samuel Smiles, sold 130,000 copies in the thirty years following its appearance in 1859.

The bad aspects of individualism in business, together with some of the good, declined after about 1870. Business itself was no longer such a cut-throat affair, and to make concessions did not mean that an employer would be ruined by the competition

---

[1] *The Annual Register*, 1900, p. 246.
[2] Dickens, *Hard Times* (1854), Ch. 11.

of others less conciliatory. The tendency now was towards united rather than individual capitalism. It was the age of the bigger combine, consolidating the successful survivors of the breathless speculation which had gone on in the previous generation. Legislation on limited liability and jointstock companies had changed the face of the business world. The trade unions had won the right of collective bargaining, and industrial negotiations were now beginning to take place between expert representatives rather than between those directly involved. It was no longer a question of facing the mill-owner himself across his own table but of dealing with a manager who was himself employed, and of being required to consider shareholders who had never come within a hundred miles of the factory.

Individualism declined in business and industry, but in other respects it remained part of the basic creed. Over the period from 1846 to 1874, during which no Conservative ministry stayed in power for much more than a year, Liberalism was more than the name of a single party. John Morley spoke for a widely-accepted view when he claimed that hope of a better society lay in:

Limiting the sphere of authority, extending that of free individuality, and steadily striving after the bestowal, so far as the nature of things will ever permit it, of equality of opportunity.[1]

This ideal could be reconciled with the need for social reform through John Stuart Mill's tenet that men are accountable to society only for actions which affect other members of it.[2]

Individualism was challenged by supporters of the General Will theory and by those who were coming to admire the challenging efficiency of the new Prussian state. Mostly, however, the Victorians held that ultimate responsibility lay with the individual. The Regency cult of indifferentism in personal behaviour was over: there was as yet scarcely a hint of theories of conditioned behaviourism. It was the golden age of belief that the way a man behaved was the outward sign of his

[1] *On Compromise* (1885).
[2] 'The only part of the conduct of any one, for which he is amenable to society, is that which concerns others. In the part which merely concerns himself, his independence is, of right, absolute. Over himself, over his own body and mind, the individual is sovereign.' *On Liberty* (1859), Ch. 1.

personal character – and that both character and behaviour were under his own conscious control.

The old-fashioned Tories could counter such demands as Morley's for 'equality of opportunity' with the traditional idea that the nation was composed of different and necessarily separate 'estates'. Class-consciousness was not confined to one political group, however, but kept nagging at almost everyone. A fear of losing the distinctions between classes lay beneath a great deal of the theoretical planning for improvement, and a great deal of the genuine compassion as well. Many reformers were concerned with doing good to a section of society represented as the 'working class' or the 'labouring population' or the 'lower orders'. It was this collective view that made the more individualistic creative writers distrustful of systematic schemes for reform.

Most people accepted the existence of social classes as naturally as the Sentry in *Iolanthe* accepts the birth of little Liberals or little Conservatives. The class-structure of Victorian society was a reality, but it was a changing reality. One phenomenon was the decline in the power and prestige of land-owning, beginning with the new strength of the manu-facturing interests and increasing sharply from the years of agricultural depression after 1873. The other feature of the age, connected with the first, was the great spread of the middle class. Linked neither by aristocratic tradition nor by the common dependence of those whose wealth was in their manual strength and skill, the members of the huge, disparate middle class became a strong social force. At the beginning of the period they were trying to ape the gentility of the upper class; by the end of it they represented the aspiration of the working class.

The Parliament which met in 1832 after the First Reform Act was in a mood to go on reforming in all directions. One of the targets was the Church of England, still entrenched and established but also seriously embattled for the first time since the 1660 Restoration. For nearly two centuries outward conformity to her teaching and practice had been the passport to higher education and to official positions. For the majority, conformity had presented no problems. In the eighteenth century, the general distrust of religious extremes had kept a reasonable harmony of Church and State, broken occasionally by those who took Christianity seriously and fell into the ungentlemanly error of being 'enthusiastic'. Most influential of these was John Wesley who, although he had not intended to start a new sect, was the founder of Methodism which made religion a vital thing for thousands who regarded the established Church as remote and alien.

In 1832 the Church of England might seem to be as stable as she had ever been. Its clergy were not always inwardly loved but they were generally outwardly respected, and the higher dignitaries were important members of society. Yet, although both clerical and lay Anglicans had already taken part in the work of social reform, there was a tendency for the ranks of the Church as a whole to be closed against change. There were many to agree with John Sterling's bitter accusation that the parson was 'a black dragoon' in every parish,[1] to remember that the Bishops in the House of Lords had voted, with only two exceptions, against the Reform Bill.

The episcopal bastion had been shaken by the removal of civil disabilities on Protestant dissenters in 1828 and the much more controversial Catholic emancipation in the following year. The Nonconformists, kept out by the Test Acts from the normal channels of social success, had thrown their ability, their industry and their integrity into other activities. They had helped to maintain the understanding of faith as a personal commitment and had won respect for their patience under difficulty. Nonconformity became a powerful force in Victorian life, an inspiration to many of those who fought against the Corn Laws, to the moderate Chartists and to many trade unionists.

The Roman Catholic population was a mixed one: the old families whose allegiance to Rome had been maintained since the Reformation; an increasing number of immigrants from Ireland and the Continent; and, few at first but more as the time went by, converts from the Protestant churches. The old fear of persecution lingered on, and the Catholic Emancipation Act was passed only after fierce debate and prophecies of impending doom. As late as 1850, the restoration of the Roman

[1] In a debate at Cambridge; the phrase 'ruffled the young imagination with stormy laughter', Carlyle, *Life of John Sterling* (1851), Ch. 4.

Catholic hierarchy in England was greeted with cries of 'Papal Aggression'.

To return to the Church of England, which Jeremy Bentham had joyfully regarded as 'ripe for dissolution'.[1] The new Parliament admitted Members who did not belong to the established Church. Not only Protestant dissenters but also Unitarians, Deists and freethinkers were willing to take the oath, and over the next few years there appeared a group whose common hostility to the establishment was stronger than their differences. The power of the Church of England was severely shaken by a number of measures affecting revenues and jurisdiction; the cathedrals came in for particular attention. A commission was set up, with power to abolish certain prebends and use their revenues to endow poor livings and set up new parishes. The latter work was particularly urgent, since the growth of new industrial towns had left the distribution of parish churches as unequal as that of Parliamentary seats.

Some Churchmen saw in these measures the shadow of Armageddon. While the Bishops were fulminating in the House of Lords, a small group at Oxford was murmuring things like 'National Apostasy' – the title of John Keble's Assize Sermon in 1833. As so often happens in history, the occasion was trivial compared with the underlying cause; the minor affront that Parliament had reduced, by amalgamation, the number of Irish bishoprics. The many Anglicans for whom 'Liberalism' in religion was a dangerous word began to urge their Church to return to primitive integrity, to be aware of her essential catholicity, to recognize that her sacraments were valid and her priesthood apostolic. In Oxford itself the group led by John Henry Newman expressed these ideas in the polemical *Tracts for the Times* which gave them the name of 'Tractarians'. They appealed to the Bible and to personal devotion as fervently as any Evangelical, but they were soon reeling under accusations of Romanism. There was indeed no surviving pattern for the outward demonstration of catholicity except the Roman. So vestments and incense began to appear in churches, rosaries were found in the boudoirs of pious young ladies and there were shocked whispers of such things as private confession.

The Oxford Movement, as it came to be called, proved a

[1] Quoted in Norman Sykes, *The English Religious Tradition* (London, 1953), p. 74.

revitalizing force in the Church of England. Some of its leaders, including Newman, read and prayed their way over into the Roman obedience. Others remained, to enter into unedifying quarrels about the minutiae of public worship, sometimes to undergo persecution and even prosecution for ritualism. Though the opposition of bishops and patrons denied them advancement, many of the younger clergy in the movement found their destiny in the squalid parishes of the new towns and served them with the same loving care as the dissenters with whom they outwardly seemed to have little in common.

It would be misleading to oppose the Oxford Movement diametrically to the Evangelical Movement. Evangelicalism was an attitude rather than a party, an attitude to be found most strongly among the dissenting churches. Yet it became increasingly important within the Anglican Church, where the Evangelicals linked up with the formerly antagonistic Low Church group to become the most influential section.[1] The Evangelicals looked for their doctrine to Calvin, by way of Wesley's contemporary George Whitefield.

Perhaps this helps to explain why the Evangelical outlook suited the Victorians so well. Calvinism meant a strong emphasis on the individual, on personal piety and good works, marred too often by a rigid insistence on pre-election for salvation or damnation. On the credit side, it inspired men like Wilberforce and Shaftesbury; on the debit, it played in too easily with the tendency to assume superiority through the possession of good fortune. It helped to foster that sense of duty and earnestness which is typical of even the agnostic Victorians. At the same time, it sometimes cared too much about the consequences of actions – in this world or the next – and too little about the action itself and the purity of its motivation. Social reforms could be held up for fear of the long-term results, and the doctrine of man's total depravity and inability to save himself could be made an excuse for doing nothing.

It would be unfair to blame the Evangelicals exclusively for

[1] Though not always the most favoured by the Establishment; the strong Evangelical tended not to reach high office. In 1868 the Queen wrote to Disraeli: 'It will *not* do merely to encourage the ultra-Evangelical party, than which there is none so narrow-minded, and therefore destructive to the well-being and permanence of the Church of England.' L. E. Elliott-Binns, *English Thought 1860–1900: The Theological Aspect* (London, 1956), p. 314.

the negative side of Victorian religion. The Puritan spirit is an interesting thing, manifested in many ways. A distrust of secular learning and a flight from worldly pleasures fitted in well enough with certain middle-class attitudes in a country never distinguished for popular admiration of culture. The emphasis on Sabbath observance had its good side in maintaining a day of rest but its bad side in keeping places of interest and amusement closed on the one day when working people had any chance of visiting them.[1]

Victorian Puritanism showed itself most strongly in the attitude to sex. The scandals of the Regency years had not reflected a general libertinism, but they had given to the aristocracy an unsavoury image to be countered by the assertion of more rigid standards. A certain constriction set in, ably led by the Prince Consort and manifested in matters as diverse as clothing and the subjects of fiction. The eccentricity for which the British had been famous abroad, and on which they had prided themselves, notably diminished. Only towards the end of the reign, when criticism of the age was growing, did tolerance of unusual views and behaviour begin a tentative return.

The results of the taboos on sex were sometimes bizarre, such as the suppression of information about birth-control in an age haunted by the theory of Malthus. In 1860 Lord Amberley was vilified for taking part in a discussion on the subject; a few years later Annie Besant and James Bradlaugh were prosecuted for publishing a pamphlet about it; in 1887 a doctor was struck off the register for issuing a sixpenny edition of *The Wife's Handbook* – it was the cheapness and therefore easy availability which created his worst offence.

Sexual scandal which had caused little comment in the first thirty years of the century could now ruin a man, as Sir Charles Dilke in England and Parnell in Ireland were ruined by being concerned in divorce cases. Yet prostitution flourished to a degree that shocked foreign visitors; in the eighties, the Haymarket was given up almost entirely to soliciting and brothels. It was unsafe to disturb the calm surface of life and show what lay beneath. In 1885 W. T. Stead shocked the nation with his exposure of the organized prostitution of young girls.[2] He carried

---

[1] London museums and art galleries were not open on Sundays until 1896.

[2] 'The Maiden Tribute of Modern Babylon', in the *Pall Mall Gazette* (1885).

out the procuration of a child to prove his case, and was sent to prison for the technical offence.

While the Puritan spirit remained strong, the hold of orthodox religion was weakening; and as so often, the House of Commons was involved in the controversy. The refusal of Lionel Rothschild to take the usual oath 'on the true faith of a Christian' kept him for several years from the Parliamentary seat to which he was elected in 1847. Although Jewish disabilities were removed in 1858, the militant atheism of Charles Bradlaugh clashed with the same problem in 1880 and it was six years before he was allowed to take his seat after a modified form of the oath.

Bradlaugh was the most notorious figure in the challenge to orthodoxy which was becoming stronger. Like many features of the age, it grew from various sources that were originally independent of each other. The legacy of eighteenth-century scepticism, which had already produced the offshoots of Deism and Unitarianism, found new philosophical backing from such thinkers as Auguste Comte. The Utilitarians had little time for religion, which they regarded as a rotting prop of inefficient sectional interests. The association of established religion with the forces of tyrannical government – the theme in different modes of Shelley, Paine and Owen – had filtered down into an assertive atheism among some of the more articulate workers. After the collapse of Chartism, George Holyoake found willing supporters for Secularism (the name which he coined for it in 1846) directed against the interference of religion in national life through such things as Sabbatarian restrictions.

The retreat from belief brought moral problems. Belief without intellectual assent would be dishonest, so belief must go if new ideas successfully challenged it. Since morality had traditionally been linked to belief, there seemed to be the danger that free thought would be followed by moral anarchy. The agnostics (the name given by Thomas Huxley) strove to find an ethical system not based on revelation. Their faith for life in this world had to rest on the greatest probabilities in the current state of knowledge, and leave the possibility of future life out of account as something not to be known and therefore not to form a working hypothesis.

What were these new ideas that threatened to end nearly two thousand years of Christianity? Some of them must be examined more specifically in later chapters and need be only briefly mentioned here. There was the new 'higher criticism', spreading from Germany and examining the Bible by the same tests as any other book. The revealing of improbabilities and inconsistencies had an alarming effect in a country where Protestantism was the main religious attitude, with the Bible both as its source of belief and its ultimate appeal.

Then there was the changed status of science and of its experimental method. Freed from the last accusations of black magic which had continued to harry it long after the foundation of the respectable Royal Society in 1662, science came to be accepted as a way of reaching conclusions after proper inquiry. Science had won respect largely through the changes which it had wrought in the material world. Appreciation of increased comfort and prosperity made men more ready to accept the conclusions of geologists that the earth was much older than Biblical chronology suggested – and if the Bible was wrong in one thing, could it be trusted in others?

The controversy may now seem feeble and laughable, whether watched through the eyes of whose to whom the allegory of *Genesis* was a prop to support the whole Christian faith, or of those who asserted that the awkward fossils had been planted at the Creation to test the present generation.[1] On top of geology came the impact of Darwin's interpretation of evolution, seeming to destroy Man's unique place in creation and superiority to all other creatures. Darwinism supported the optimistic belief in progress for some, while others found in it only the hopelessness of blind chance.

The churches were partly to blame for their losses. The contrast between nature and revelation so often made in the eighteenth century had caused science and religion to part company; science tended to become more mechanistic and quantitative, neither seeking nor being offered any close association with religion. The Evangelical insistence on the sufficiency of faith alone and on the literal truth of the Bible gave monolithic strength to the faithful which often disintegrated when a single part was broken.

[1] Philip Gosse in *Omphalos* (1857).

The Victorian Debate

The Victorians found themselves gazing into vast stretches of time which science had suddenly revealed; they were confronted by some very strange ancestors; they were challenged by that process of growth and improvement in which they had taken pride. If they sometimes seem to have been complacent, it was in the face of great waves of doubt and dismay.

3

Books and Readers

How widely were these conflicting ideas disseminated? Were the moral dilemmas and the arguments over principles the prerogatives of a minority? It has to be remembered that, for the greater part of human history, the educated few made little effort either to inform or to seek the opinion of the inarticulate many. The authentic voice of the common man only occasionally breaks through, like a flash of lightning that leaves the main expanse dark again. It is not until the nineteenth century that the voice becomes significantly frequent, better informed and more often heeded. Opportunities of doing more than work and sleep gradually increased as hours of work grew shorter, as real wages rose and as the retail distribution of necessities reduced the burden of housekeeping. It became possible for more people to read. What facilities did they have, and how did they use them?

Victorian self-congratulation on progress was justified in the matter of education. At the beginning of the period, though schooling was not strictly confined to the children of the rich, there was little chance of a full-time education unless one happened to be born into a fairly prosperous family. The grammar schools continued to be bound by their foundation statutes until the Grammar Schools Act of 1840 allowed some re-interpretation. Lord Eldon's judgement in 1805 had ruled it illegal for an endowed grammar school to teach anything but Latin and Greek, and it took many years before the 'modern' subjects could establish themselves.

A few of the grammar schools had obeyed the letter of their founders' statutes but departed far from their spirit by developing into the so-called 'public schools'. Until Thomas Arnold became headmaster of Rugby in 1828, these schools were more remarkable for their social status than for their scholarship, combining harsh physical discipline in school hours with anarchy outside. Arnold, with his insistence on socially-conscious Christianity as a proper faith for English boys, set an example of moral improvement and better teaching which other schools gradually followed. For those who could pay, the reign saw an extensive range of possibilities from the Eton extolled by Disraeli in *Coningsby* to the horrors like the Yorkshire schools which Dickens attacked in *Nicholas Nickleby*.

For the majority, however, the winning of education was a slow struggle. In the early part of the period, the reluctance of the state to interfere in educational matters had two main causes, one social and the other religious. The years of fear that the class struggle was bringing a real danger of revolution did not inspire much enthusiasm for teaching the poor to read. It was likely to give them ideas above their station and aid the spread of inflammatory doctrines. There were few as clear-sighted as Sir John Herschel, who frankly acknowledged the need to escape from the depression of overcrowding, insecurity and monotony.[1] Yet even those who were willing to provide education, whether for escape or as a means of improvement, were torn by religious strife in which the Government had no wish to be involved. Most of the free or very cheap schools were controlled either by the Protestant nonconformist British and Foreign School Society or by the National Society for Promoting the Education of the Poor in the Principles of the Established Church.

Both societies did their best under difficulties, but their teachers were not properly trained and were eked out by the monitorial system which allowed older children to learn a lesson and then pass it on to the others. A similar production-line for young parrots, at an even lower level of competence, was often to be found in the day and Sunday schools attached to particular churches and in the 'dame schools' where children were dumped in the care of an old person considered to be unfit for any other work. Similar schools were set up at factories, where the law was gradually making it compulsory for children to receive a certain amount of education during their working

---

[1] 'Address to the Subscribers to the Windsor and Eton Public Library and Reading Room', printed in *Essays from the Edinburgh and Quarterly Reviews* (1857), pp. 1–20.

hours. Two measures in 1833 pointed the way to better things: the provision in the Factory Act that children in certain textile industries should receive two hours' schooling daily, and the first Government subsidy to aid the two big educational societies in building schools.

Hampered by religious disputes, often made ineffective by lack of proper inspection, elementary education moved on its slow course towards the Education Act of 1870 which made at least the rudiments of education compulsory for all, administered by that balance of central and local authority which was increasingly becoming the way of dealing with national problems. There were still controversies to be settled and anomalies to be removed, but each step now tended towards the achievement of a good standard of free education.

Thus the chance of learning at least to read was better at the beginning of Victoria's reign than it had been earlier, and it improved all through the century. Opportunity and appetite grew together: for William Lovett and those Chartists who shared his ideas, education was to be the panacea for all ills. There were earlier precedents of 'mutual improvement societies' and private subscription libraries formed by groups of workmen, but the new enthusiasm for education was strong and sudden. The self-taught workman is a familiar figure during the period; there was no shortage of real-life prototypes for Kingsley's Alton Locke and George Eliot's Bartle Massey.

It was an enthusiasm which no difficulties could quench. If the local church gave a few reading-classes, even those who disliked the parson and his doctrine would take advantage of them. On a secular basis, men like Henry Brougham and George Birkbeck aimed at spreading the useful knowledge that would make better workmen, helping them to understand the new industrial techniques and incidentally keeping them out of mischief after working hours. The Mechanics' Institutes, foundations for adult evening education in a wide range of subjects, varied a good deal in their amenities. Some were badly housed, with libraries consisting of unwanted books from private collections. There were others like the People's Instruction Society founded in Birmingham in 1846, which offered lectures, debates, games, a good library and a reading-room, for the weekly subscription of a penny. There were also the less

ambitious and less successful Lyceums, a scheme which started
in Manchester in 1836 to offer more elementary adult education. At the other end of the scale, there were places like the
London Working Men's College founded in 1854 by the
Christian Socialist leader Frederick Denison Maurice.

There were 702 Mechanics' Institutes in Britain by 1850.[1]
They had been successful, but it was success gained at the price
of change. Their membership was moving towards the black-
coated worker and away from the artisans for whom they had
been intended. Even their modest fees could be too much for
the very poor, who were in any case usually too exhausted to
make any intellectual effort after the day's work. The trade
unions were claiming the time of many of the most alert
workers, who distrusted the Institutes which were often under
the patronage and control of local employers. With the change
in membership, the Institutes tended to teach more literary
and cultural subjects, and also to offer pure entertainment at a
more socially respectable level than the theatre. Dickens began
his brilliant and fatal course of public reading at the Birmingham and Midland Institute in 1853. The universities entered
the field with extension classes, pioneered by Cambridge in
1873, presumably raising the intellectual level of adult education but certainly not adding to the popular image. The old
Institutes slowly declined, though enduring in some places
to the end of the century. They had done a good service; many
of them eventually became polytechnics or grew into the new
civic universities.

They did good in a more indirect way by increasing the
ability to obtain books and stimulating the desire for them. It is
not easy to attain precise literacy figures for the period. The
official estimates were based on the number able to sign the
marriage register, a method which did not include those who
could read but not write or the large number who learned to
read later in their adult lives.[2] Yet even this inadequate source
shows an increase in the number of literate males from 67.3%
in 1841 to 97.2% in 1900, and of females from 51.1% to

[1] J. W. Hudson, *The History of Adult Education* (1851), p. vi.

[2] The present writer's great-grandfather was unable to sign his name when the
birth of his son was registered in 1845, but at the end of the century his grand-
children saw him reading the Bible.

96.8% over the same period. On this and other evidence it is safe to say that the totally illiterate were in the minority by the middle of the century.

There was thus a steadily growing number of potential readers, a group to be nurtured, discouraged or exploited according to different contemporary views. The new readers came at first largely from that section which was edging its way even more forcefully between the poor and the middle class: the skilled workers, clerks, those employed in retail trade and the 'upper' domestic servants. They led the way, but the desire for books was not confined to them. There are stories of people gathering in small shops to hear the reading aloud of the latest part of a Dickens novel, borrowed from a local library at two-pence a day.[1] There were small workrooms where the sewing-girls gave up a portion of their meagre wages to pay one of their number to read to them.[2] Wilkie Collins recognized the importance of 'The Unknown Public', still ignorant but learning to read books and get ideas from them,'[3] soon to be a force worth reckoning with.

The Utilitarian approval of the spirit of inquiry looked favourably on these tendencies but was anxious to divert them into safe channels. The Society for the Diffusion of Useful Knowledge was mainly concerned with spreading the principles of political economy, and similar appeals to the right use of reason; its supporters were usually as impatient of pure imagination in their way as the Evangelicals were in theirs. What to one group was a waste of time in a hard and serious age was to the other a breeder of lying fantasies that drew men away from the one truth. The Benthamites and the Evangelicals were both zealous for control of the newly literate, each wanting to fill the gap of which working people were becoming aware. Even those who disapproved of all this reading by the lower orders had to concede that worse damage might be prevented if the reading was of sound political or religious doctrine.

Consequently the stream of free or very cheap tracts was expanded from its previous steady flow into a torrent. Many of

[1] Edgar Johnson, *Charles Dickens: His Tragedy and Triumph* (New York, 1952), Vol. 1, p. 155.
[2] R. D. Altick, *The English Common Reader* (Chicago, 1957), p. 250.
[3] 'The Unknown Public', in *Household Words* (1858).

them, whether religious or secular, were foolish in the extreme, ignoring the physical wants and degraded environment of those to whom they were directed. The visit of Mrs Pardiggle to the brickmaker's family describes the utter lack of communication which too often existed.[1] Yet such misapplied efforts did their part in stimulating reading and giving material on which to practise the new skill.

The Evangelical spirit, and the cult of home and family which it fostered, helped in the spread of reading. There was a great deal of Bible reading in the home, and indulgence was not refused to all secular literature provided it had a good moral tone. The prejudice against such worldly forms of entertainment as the theatre, coupled with the strict limits imposed on Sunday activities, gave a strong if negative stimulus to reading. Even on Sundays, Milton was generally acceptable; and many a Victorian child was saved from Sabbath boredom by the spectacular woodcuts in Foxe's *Book of Martyrs*. Ruskin recalled in his autobiographical *Praeterita* how he suffered such restrictions and heard the Bible continually read through from beginning to end, but he also remembered a home where good secular literature was enjoyed. There were not many who went as far as a speaker at a Brethren meeting in the tercentenary year 1864, who referred to 'A blasphemous celebration of the birth of Shakespeare, a lost soul now suffering for his sins in hell'.[2]

There were growing possibilities of supplementing a home library which might consist only of the Bible, Foxe and an old almanac. The popular education centres, from the large Mechanics' Institute to the village Sunday school, usually had some kind of library attached to them. The Methodist classes to which Wesley had attached so much value encouraged reading and discussion, sometimes passing books round from one meeting to another. In some places a religious or secular body might subscribe towards an itinerating library, the collection spending a certain time with one group and then being sent on to the next. These were usually very small, but not inconsiderable. In 1846 the Artisans' Library at Edwinstowe in Nottinghamshire owned five hundred volumes which could be

---

[1] *Bleak House* (1853), Ch. 8.
[2] Edmund Gosse, *Father and Son* (London, 1907), Ch. 12.

borrowed for one shilling enrolment fee and one penny weekly subscription: a tiny but honourable rival to the 15,300 volumes owned in 1850 by the Liverpool Mechanics' Institute.[1]

The private circulating libraries were well established by the beginning of the period, ranging from those who sent out books to the country gentry at a high subscription to the penny-a-week shelves in barbers' and tobacconists' shops. The whole library business took on a new look from 1852, when Charles Edward Mudie opened his premises in New Oxford Street. He came to operate a nation-wide service at an annual subscription of a guinea, and to exercise almost dictatorial authority over publishers. A generation of writers had to keep a wary eye on the prejudices of Mudie and his rival W. H. Smith.

The public libraries were caught up in the mid-century enthusiasm for reform. A House of Commons Committee in 1849 found that the old endowed libraries were neglected and little used, that the British Museum collection was out of date and difficult to enter. The inquiry led to an Act empowering town councils to finance public libraries out of the rates. The permission was seldom accepted at first, and, even when it was, the result might be an inadequate building, or a splendid structure with no money left to buy books. The position gradually improved, but it is probable that even at the end of the century the public libraries were used by only a small percentage of the population, and that drawn mostly from the elusive group of newly-literate between the unskilled workers and the middle class. For the very poor, the libraries were uncomfortably official and disciplined; for the middle class they were all too public.[2]

It was of course possible to buy books if one could afford them. There were bookshops in all the large towns, as well as street stalls and the trays of hawkers. The country pedlar often included books in his pack, and the carrier would bring orders from London for those who already knew what they wanted. Book prices had risen during the early years of the century, when the general increase in the cost of living due to the

[1] Altick, op. cit., pp. 198–200.

[2] As late as 1891 letters were being written to newspapers about the demoralizing effects of public libraries. Including the case of a young man in Brighton who 'asserts that the library ruined him'. Thomas Greenwood, *Public Libraries* (4th ed. 1894), p. 82.

Napoleonic War had coincided with a demand for high wages by compositors. From 1832 onwards there was a slow but continual decline in the cost of books, with a rise in the purchasing power of money. Although Mudie and others founded rich empires, there was more buying and less borrowing of books than formerly.

The new novel usually appeared in three volumes, at the total price of one and a half guineas. Editions were fairly small, the first edition seldom numbering more than 1,250 copies until the last years of the century. Although the big circulating libraries were sometimes a restrictive force, they also helped the publisher and the novelist by agreeing to take a fixed number of every new novel from well-known houses. Many readers found it more exciting, and economically easier, to buy a novel in monthly parts. Serial publication, either alone at the average price of one shilling or as part of a magazine, became the common practice for new novels. It helped to stimulate the reading and purchase of new books, though the total cost might amount to more than that of the complete first edition.

Books gradually became cheaper, as the potential readership increased with the rise both in literacy and living standards. At the beginning of the period, however, even a cheap book cost a day's wages for a skilled artisan in London and almost a week's wage for a handloom weaver in the north.[1] More money for books came with increased wages, and the demand was not always met with motives as pure as those of the Evangelicals or the Benthamites. There was a spate of cheap, sensational literature which seemed to confirm the gloomy prophecies of those who opposed teaching the poor to read. The old tradition of the ballad, the chapbook and the broadside was caught up in modern methods of production to give lurid accounts of crime, crude pornography and the general exploiting of the starved urban imagination. There were many adventurers like Thomas Tegg, a kind of literary hyaena who prowled in search of bankrupt stock or expiring copyright. He worked to a close calculation of profit; if a classical novel was too long for his allocation of paper, so much the worse for the novel – it would

[1] G. M. Young, ed., *Early Victorian England* (Oxford, 1934), Vol. 1, pp. 104–8, 126–34.

be cut off in mid-sentence if necessary.[1] Yet even such mutilations helped to bring good work into competition with bad, and the eighteenth-century novel reached a new popularity. Modern novels still protected by copyright were blatantly imitated, so that the unwary reader might be offered a cheap edition of *Oliver Twiss* or *Martin Guzzlewit*.

The good publishers deplored these monstrosities and remained conservative in the economics of their own business. By the middle of the century, however, the success of the adventurers could not be ignored. The question of book prices became a public issue in 1852 when, following an argument about discounts given by booksellers, a committee of inquiry decided against the publishers' desire to keep up the fixed price of books. The principle of free trade thus continued to operate, to the customer's benefit, until 1899 when most booksellers accepted an undertaking to give no discount on books published at six shillings or more.

Falling prices were aided by improvements in the techniques of book production. The steam-driven press was used for *The Times* as early as 1814 and was in general use for books by the end of the forties. Soon after 1860, the introduction of the high-speed Hoe press from the United States made great savings in the production of newspapers, magazines and the cheaper types of book. Stereotypes were in common use by the beginning of the period. Cheaper bindings were introduced, and the cruder but quicker and simpler method of 'casing' was adopted for the majority of books. The size of books was reduced, the old quartos giving way to convenient 'pocket editions' for travelling or outdoor reading. The high cost of composing continued; machines were used by a few newspapers from the late sixties, but most books were set by hand throughout the century. The cost of paper dropped as esparto grass replaced rags as its raw material, and wood-pulp came into use for cheaper publications. The official tax on paper was halved in 1837 and abolished in 1861.

The railway keeps appearing as a factor in many nineteenth-century changes, and its effect on publishing and reading was

---

[1] Tegg did, however, keep up a respectable side in his business. For instance, he was the part-publisher of a fine (and un-cut) edition of Cruden's *Complete Concordance* in 1830.

considerable. Not only were books carried more quickly to remote parts of the country; there was a new opportunity of reading during the enforced idleness of a journey. The early railways were not notably comfortable, especially in the cheaper classes, but they offered a peaceful haven compared with the stage-coach and the carrier's cart. The practice of commuting to and from the suburbs in the later years of the reign gave a further impetus to reading and to the production of light literature. In 1852 W. H. Smith, who later became First Lord of the Admiralty under Disraeli and was satirized by Gilbert as Sir Joseph Porter in *HMS Pinafore,* started his railway book-stalls. The sales-concessions on railway stations, given to retired or disabled servants of the company, often included a few cheap books among their refreshments and miscellaneous wares. W. H. Smith extended the scope of casual bookselling and it was his growing empire which provided a market for the 'railway novel'. Large, cheap editions at one or two shillings each began to appear, some of authors who are still household favourites while others are only names in bibliographies of the period. The yellow-backs, as they came to be known, brought solace to the bored traveller and profit to the novelist. They included some non-fiction too, chiefly popular slices of contemporary history such as the Crimean War and the Indian Mutiny.

The railway novel was a catalyst in the steady cheapening of books. New novels were still expensive, but a reprint at not more than six shillings was likely to appear between three and five years after the first publication. Earlier writers, not subject to copyright, could be bought much more cheaply. For instance, the Parlour Library which started in 1847 offered books at a shilling in boards and one-and-six in cloth.[1] The vexed question of copyright was the subject of a Royal Commission in 1876–7 whose final opinion, as might have been expected in the heyday of Liberalism, was that a long period of copyright was not in the general interest. There were, however, no immediate practical results. International copyright was not dealt with until 1891; previously, a steady two-way traffic of pirated editions flowed between Britain and the United States. The British were not always the losers, for American novels were

[1] Altick, op. cit., p. 299.

becoming increasingly popular. Not all had the sales of *Uncle Tom's Cabin*, which reached 150,000 copies within six months of its appearance in 1852,[1] but many American authors were showing themselves more alert to the needs of the new reading public than were their British contemporaries.

The power of the circulating libraries was challenged by Henry Vizetelly, who brought out George Moore's *A Mummer's Wife* in a cheap one-volume edition in 1885, with the announcement that 'this book has been placed on the Index Expurgatorius of the "Select" Circulating Libraries of Messrs Mudie and W. H. Smith & Son'. Eventually, Smith and Mudie were mainly responsible for the end of the three-volume novel; in 1894 they declared that they would not pay more than four shillings per volume, less discount, for any new novel. The tradition which had lasted from Scott's *Kenilworth* was over, but the old libraries themselves were passing from their greatest years, their subscribers slowly being lured away by cheap editions and cheaper new libraries.

By the end of the century, cloth-bound recent novels could be had for as little as half-a-crown, older ones for sixpence. There were even cheaper condensations such as the Penny Novelist abridgements edited by W. T. Stead and labelled by Punch 'Penny Steadfuls'.[2] The 'Aldine' edition of the poets cost five shillings a volume in 1844 and had fallen to one-and-six by 1870.

It was all very good business for the novelist, perhaps less so for his art. The fifteenth serial part of *Pickwick* had sold 40,000 copies and been hailed as a publishing triumph. In 1900 Marie Corelli's *The Master Christian* had a pre-publication printing of 75,000. A longer run was achieved by Lytton's *Pelham*, which started as a three-volume novel at the customary one and a half guineas in 1828 and went on through ever-cheaper editions to sell 66,000 in a sixpenny reprint between 1879 and 1890.[3] It was the steady stayers that did best in the economics of nineteenth-century publishing.

Yet there are facts to be put into the opposite side of the

[1] Clarence Gohdes, *American Literature in Nineteenth-century England* (New York, 1944), pp. 29ff.

[2] Altick, op. cit., p. 314.

[3] Q. D. Leavis, *Fiction and the Reading Public* (London, 1932), p. 306, n. 86.

scales, to correct the image of a golden age for fiction and its readers. It should be recalled that religious books made up the biggest single category in publishing throughout the period. Marie Corelli becomes insignificant beside the 1,326,000 copies of tracts issued by the Methodist Book Room in 1841.[1] The *Publishers' Circular* for 1880 listed 580 new novels but 975 'theology, biblical, etc.'[2]

Nor was religion the only competitor of good fiction. The newly-literate working man, encouraged by the prevailing fashion for self-improvement, was more likely to be found reading the *Penny Cyclopaedia* issued between 1833 and 1844 by the Society for the Diffusion of Useful Knowledge; or perhaps Cassell's *Popular Educator* also at a penny a number. The latter was started in 1852 on a machine bought for printing tea-labels and went on to perform such services as helping Thomas Hardy to teach himself German. On the other hand, the trashy, sensational literature of the time was not bought by only one class. Successive reports on education commented on the poor or non-existent reading of those who were receiving education to a supposedly high level. The English classics were subordinate to those of Greece and Rome until they suffered the worse fate of becoming a 'subject' for the competitive examinations, which were being required as the old privileged entry was abolished.

Later in the century, the reading of imaginative literature had to contend with a new foe. The distrust of the Evangelicals and the Utilitarians was replaced by the scorn of the new scientism. First-hand knowledge and observation were the watchwords of a country conscious of the need to compete technically with others. The 'higher grade' public secondary schools which were opened had little time for the arts; English literature was often no more than a source of examples for English grammar.

Yet all this being said, the Victorian age was a time when the chance of getting books and of being able to read them increased on a scale never known before. The author reached a new height of popularity and influence, a readership whose size seemed

---

[1] H. F. Mathews, *Methodism and the Education of the People 1791–1851* (London, 1949), p. 172.
[2] *Journal of the Statistical Society*, 44 (1881).

more impressive before the arrival of mass-media. Nor was the author ignorant of his new followers: from Alton Locke striving to inform himself about the political issues of the forties, down to Mr Polly with his gaily catastrophic adventures among words, there is the recognition of a popular involvement with language and literature deeper than this country had known at least since the sixteenth century.

4

Magazines and Periodicals

Nineteenth-century critical opinions, on society and politics as well as on literature, must often be sought in the reviews and magazines. The growth of periodicals helped to establish responsible judgement of new writing, on criteria which gradually became free from political bias. Although the great early reviews helped to form the standards which made such assessment possible, yet partisan feelings tended to make both reviewers and their readers far from objective. The anonymity which was the rule in the first years of the century did indeed give the illusion that judgements were not personal opinions but reflected the general ethos of society: it also allowed vituperation and scurrility.

While the reviews in the first half of the century suffered from being too few and exclusive, with a monopoly of serious criticism, the later ones were affected by the Victorian problem of over-production in their attempt to capture an ever-increasing public. The potential readers were there, as we have seen. Those who were too poor to buy even the cheaper books might manage to buy or to share a more ephemeral publication. Nor was there room to amass books in the average worker's dwelling, nor yet the security of tenure which would make it desirable to invest in possessions even when they could be afforded. The factors which increased reading in general increased the demand for periodicals even more steeply than for books.

Criticism at the beginning of the period was still dominated by two great papers. The *Edinburgh Review,* founded in 1802, had increased its early Whig sympathies as the years went by, even to the extent of being bound in the Whig colours of buff and blue. The *Quarterly Review,* dating from 1809, was similar to the *Edinburgh*[1] in most respects except that its political allegiance

---

[1] In this and subsequent chapters, magazines and newspapers will generally be referred to by short titles after their first mention.

was Tory. They were both severe in their judgements, generally conservative and unwelcoming in their attitude to new writers, and strictly reviews in the sense that even their longest articles were based on the notice of new books. Their power slowly declined during the reign of Victoria as some of the acerbity went out of politics and as the power of the great editors declined with increasing competition from new papers. The *Edinburgh* became more narrowly political in its content, although Jeffrey, its editor for many years, was a strong admirer of Dickens; Macaulay became one of its leading contributors. The *Quarterly* kept up its bitter opposition to Romanticism, retaining the services of J. W. Croker who had already dealt harshly with the young poets. The opposition was a matter of politics more than of pure literature; Keats had suffered for his association with the 'cockney Radical' Leigh Hunt, and the early work of Tennyson received similar treatment for similar reasons. The two old giants kept their power long enough for Browning to be inspired to name his two pet geese 'Edinburgh' and 'Quarterly'.

There were other well-established papers in 1832, some of them already past their great days. One of the oldest was the *Gentleman's Magazine*, which lasted from 1731 to 1868 but was no serious rival to more recent enterprises. A Tory rival of the older reviews was *Blackwood's Edinburgh Magazine*, founded in 1817 as a somewhat lighter and more varied production than the *Quarterly*. It joined in the attack on Keats, but its critical opinions were not always contemptible; although it lost some of its influence and quality as the years went on, it had the distinction of printing some of George Eliot's early work. The *Westminster Review* (1823) was the organ of the Philosophic Radicals; dedicated to strict Benthamite views, it tended to regard imaginative literature with a mixture of distaste and amused condescension. It is perhaps not surprising to learn that 'The literary and artistic department had rested chiefly on Mr Bingham, a barrister (subsequently a police magistrate), who had been for some years a frequenter of Bentham'.[1] It was in decline by 1835, when the *London Review* appeared in a bid to capture the Radical readership, but after only four issues the two papers amalgamated as the *London and Westminster Review*.

[1] J. S. Mill, *Autobiography* (1873), Ch. 4.

Under John Stuart Mill, this took on a broader and less rigidly Benthamite outlook. It reverted to the name of *Westminster* alone in 1840 and became the *Westminster and Foreign Quarterly Review* after another amalgamation in 1851. Never a great commercial success, it was influential in representing informed Radical and progressive opinion. George Eliot was its assistant editor from 1851 to 1854, at a time when one of its main concerns was the new outlook in theology. It became increasingly more didactic and less concerned with the arts, and was one of the main channels through which the philosophy of Comte came to be known in Britain.

As well as these heavy and infrequent reviews, there were also a number of weekly magazines. Leigh Hunt's *Examiner* (1808), which had carried on a running fight with the *Quarterly* and *Blackwood's* on the side of Radicalism in politics under the guise of disputes about Romantic poetry, continued to be published until 1881. Other weeklies were more inclined to literature than to politics. There was the *Literary Gazette* from 1817 to 1862 when it amalgamated with the *Parthenon,* and the more important *Spectator* and *Athenaeum,* both founded in 1828. The *Spectator* was political in so far as it stood for an educated and perceptive Radicalism; it was independent and responsible in its attitude to the arts but tended to judge them on Utilitarian lines. From 1861 it came to reflect the political and religious ideas of R. H. Hutton, then editor. It had a distinguished band of contributors until the end of the century, including Swinburne, John Morley, Edmund Gosse and George Saintsbury. The *Athenaeum* got off to a slow start until Charles Wentworth Dilke became editor in 1830; he steadily increased its success – raising sales sixfold by halving its price – and its reputation for honesty, avoidance of partisan influence and support of proposals for reform. *Fraser's Magazine* (1830) shared with *Blackwood's* both its jovial Toryism and some of its writers; it helped to spread the ideas of Coleridge. On its acquisition by J. W. Parker in 1847, it became more of a Broad Church organ. It was edited by J. A. Froude from 1861 to 1874, and came to an end in 1882 when it was replaced by *Longman's Magazine.*

These were some of the periodicals which the Victorians inherited from the previous generation. The second half of the century saw the launching of a very large number of new papers, weekly, monthly or quarterly. The characteristics of the more serious reviews changed: they were no longer confined to the convention of hanging a review-article on a new book, but contained original material and even new fiction. Anonymity gradually came to be the exception and not the rule, but only after long controversy in which the question to sign or not to sign provoked hot passions. The supporters of anonymity declared it to be a safeguard of honesty and independence and of an objective criterion for the common good – a rather odd attitude in an age which tended to oppose the secret ballot on the grounds that everyone should be prepared to state his opinion openly. Yet the pressure against unsigned criticism mounted; the great reviews had gone too far too often and there was now a demand that personal responsibility should be accepted for articles. Trollope observed that, 'If the names of the critics were demanded, editors would be more careful'.[1]

A herald of the new custom was the rejection of anonymity by the *Leader*, founded in 1850 by Edward Pigott under the management of Holyoake and the editorship of Lewes. Like the early *Westminster*, it avoided commitment to either of the main parties, allowed free discussion and encouraged new ideas. Conceived in the old Radical spirit of Hunt and Place, it urged the brotherhood of man, supported Continental revolutionary movements and praised American republicanism. In 1852 it published Herbert Spencer's important essay on evolution, 'The Development Hypothesis'. It included an 'Open Council', suggested by John Stuart Mill, for the expression of readers' opinions.

Perhaps the most brilliant of the Victorian weeklies was the *Saturday Review* (1855) whose arrogant assumption of authority earned it the sobriquet of the 'Saturday Reviler'. It made a serious attempt to be the leading organ of culture and partly succeeded; its scholarship was unquestionable, its style usually impeccable.

The movement towards printing new fiction in periodicals – as distinct from the established convention of novels in monthly parts – gained strength from the middle of the century. In 1859

[1] Trollope, *Autobiography* (1883), Ch. 10.

Dickens began *All the Year Round,* which brought out his own *Tale of Two Cities* and *Great Expectations,* as well as new novels by Lever, Lytton, Reade, Collins and Mrs Gaskell. In the same year *Macmillan's Magazine* started, and went on to print work by Trollope, Arnold, Kingsley, R. D. Blackmore, Mrs Humphry Ward and Hardy. It was not, however, intended to be a predominantly literary paper, but rather to reflect the theological and social interests of its founders Thomas Hughes, J. M. Ludlow and Alexander Macmillan. From 1883–5 it was more politically orientated by the ubiquitous John Morley, whose name keeps recurring in any survey of Victorian periodicals and their editors.

One of the most successful combinations of critical reviewing with serial fiction was the *Cornhill Magazine,* which started under Thackeray's editorship in 1860 and published his own work as well as fiction by Trollope, George Eliot, Mrs Gaskell, Reade, Collins and Hardy. To this galaxy must be added most of Arnold's *Culture and Anarchy,* and a start on Ruskin's *Unto This Last* which was cut short by readers' opposition. Indeed, the *Cornhill* tended to be over-careful of Victorian sensitivity: Thackeray refused a poem by Elizabeth Barrett because it contained the word 'harlot',[1] and some of Hardy's work was thought unsuitable. It was popular from the start, and though it declined from its early peak of nearly twenty thousand copies it continued to do well, reaching its greatest critical influence under Leslie Stephen in the seventies. The new vogue for fiction brought less brilliant competitors such as *Temple Bar* and *Longman's Magazine,* as well as cruder compilations which pleased the taste for reading of 'high life' – a flicker from the moribund 'silver fork' novel. The last decade of the century saw the growth of papers devoted largely to short stories and 'true life' experiences. Their very titles reflect the new age of reading with its metropolitan culture and imperial vision: *Strand* (1890), *Pall Mall Magazine* (1893), *Windsor* (1895), *Royal* (1898), *Wide World* (1898).

The other outstanding name in the second half of the period is the *Fortnightly Review* (it soon became a monthly, but kept its title). Its prospectus before the first number in 1865 stated its intention of giving to Britain something comparable to the

[1] E. M. Everett, *The Party of Humanity* (Chapel Hill, 1939), p. 11.

French *Révue des Deux Mondes,* so much admired by Arnold.[1] It broke the insularity which was limiting critical opinion, by reviewing European and American writers and encouraging foreign contributors – Kropotkin and Mazzini among the latter. Committed to no party, it was intelligently questioning on most political and social issues. It came to express the good and the ill – and there was plenty of both – in Victorian liberalism as a total philosophy. Its rigid honesty refused anonymous work. It shared much of the current faith in progress, yet claimed the contemporary freedom to doubt the rightness of things as they were. It looked forward with those who had an eye to future changes, including Arnold, Ruskin and Gladstone among its contributors. Lewes brought his experience from the *Leader* as its first editor and was succeeded by Morley, who from 1867–82 made it a focus of liberal, rationalist and positivist opinions.

Every interest was finding a periodical to represent it. The *Contemporary Review* (1866) reflected the arguments and debates of the Metaphysical Society. A quarrel between its founder and its editor resulted in the latter's starting the *Nineteenth Century* in 1877, a venture rewarded by a high degree of influence in a few years. The *National Review* (1883) stood for the new imperialist Conservatism. On the lighter side, with the inevitable Victorian serious undertone, *Punch* started in 1841. It spoke up for the under-privileged, with a hatred of 'political economy' and *laissez faire,* and urged humanitarian principles in a humorously sentimental manner.

There were many papers devoted to religious themes, or at least based on overtly religious presuppositions. The Evangelical prejudice against the arts was declining, and the reading of fiction was not so widely condemned. The diehards, however, yielded very little ground. The religious magazine *Good Words* was attacked by the more extreme *Record* for proposing to serialize Trollope's *Rachel Ray. Good Words* did in fact publish fiction by Trollope, Kingsley and, with an irony worthy of the author himself, Hardy's *Trumpet Major.* The contemporary *Leisure Hour* not only published fiction but went so far as to carry illustrations by the fashionable du Maurier. Gladstone was one of the group of churchmen who founded *The Guardian* in 1846,

[1] 'The Function of Criticism at the Present Time', in *Essays in Criticism,* 1st series (1865).

which dealt with politics, social problems and literature as well as theology.

One of the features of the latter part of the century was the appearance of good periodicals for children. The breakthrough came in 1879 when the Religious Tract Society started *The Boy's Own Paper* and proved that it was possible to have juvenile fiction that was morally respectable and had literary merit. It included work by Conan Doyle and Jules Verne. In the Thomas Arnold tradition, it gave prominence to sport and received contributions from the already legendary W. G. Grace.

The growth of the popular weekly and daily press takes us back to the beginning of the period, to look at the economic background. The great increase in periodicals later in the century was made possible not only by more general prosperity but also by a lifting of restrictions. In 1834 the *Edinburgh* and the *Quarterly* each cost six shillings: a price far beyond most people, but the desire for a cheap press was hampered by the 'taxes on knowledge'. There was a duty on paper, and a tax-stamp had to be bought for all periodicals costing less than sixpence. This two-edged weapon – for it penalized cheap paper and put the others beyond the reach of the poor - was one of the repressive Six Acts of 1819. There had been a newspaper tax since Queen Anne's reign, but the new and more severe measure was directed against the Radical papers which were criticizing the Government. In addition, there was a tax on advertisements. In 1832 Lytton, pressing for repeal of the taxes, estimated that of the sevenpence paid for a copy of *The Times* fivepence-halfpenny went in various duties.[1]

The beginning of the fight for a cheap press belongs to earlier years, when Cobbett was bringing out his twopenny *Political Register*. It went on with papers like the Chartist *Northern Star* – the regular reading of Margaret's grandfather in *Mary Barton* – which either evaded the stamp-duty or paid it and tried to win a wide readership in other ways. The hiring of newspapers was illegal but was practised; papers could be read in coffee-houses and newsrooms. In addition, a stamped paper was free from postage and could be sent through the mails until it fell to pieces. By the time that Hetherington won the three-year fight

[1] *Cambridge History of English Literature*, Vol. 14, p. 174.

for the exemption from tax of his *Poor Man's Guardian* he could claim a circulation of twenty thousand copies:[1] the number of the actual readers must have been many times more.

The general attitude of the upper and middle classes towards a cheap press was similar to that on the wider question of increasing literacy. The success of the Radical papers, against many difficulties, was encouraging to its supporters and alarming to its opponents. Ebenezer Elliot, the 'Corn Law rhymer', was more exclamatory than most but perhaps not more optimistic:

> 'The Press!' all lands shall sing;
> The Press, the Press we bring
> All lands to bless;
> Oh, pallid want! oh, labour stark!
> Behold, we bring the second ark!
> The Press! the Press! the Press![2]

To cater for this appetite there was, on the one hand, a flood of crudely sensational periodicals, aided by the exemption from duty of matter previously published in book form. The interest in crime, particularly the more sexual and sanguinary cases, was not, however, limited to these. The *Police News* and *The Times* could find common ground in lurid and detailed accounts of trials, but with *The Times* costing sevenpence there was an eager demand for such things as the *Terrific Register*, which Dickens remembered as a boy:

Making myself unspeakably miserable and frightening my very wits out of my head, for the small charge of a penny weekly; which, considering that there was an illustration to every murder in which there was always a pool of blood, and at least one body, was cheap.[3]

On the other hand, the poor were offered papers designed for their self-help and improvement, to elevate their taste and keep them from drink. Charles Knight, whose *Penny Cyclopaedia* has already been mentioned, also produced for the Society for the Diffusion of Useful Knowledge the *Penny Magazine* from 1832 to 1845. The publisher Chambers started his *Edinburgh Journal* in the same year and on the same lines, with more lasting success. It was popular all through the reign of Victoria; but, like the

---

[1] Boris Ford, ed., *From Dickens to Hardy* (Harmondsworth, 1958), p. 218.
[2] 'The Press', in *Poetical Works* (1844).
[3] John Forster, *Life of Charles Dickens* (1872–4), Vol. 1, Ch. 6.

sponsors of the Mechanics' Institutes, Chambers found himself catering for a higher social class than he had intended and being read mainly by clerical, retail and skilled manual workers.

The readers in this 'superior' working class, now beginning to take more pride and pleasure in their homes, were attracted by such magazines as *Eliza Cook's Journal* and *Household Words*. The latter was started by Dickens in 1850 and sold at twopence; his prestige and the quality of his leadership did something to break the prejudice against cheap papers. Unlike Knight and Chambers, Dickens did not confine himself to the task of improvement but included fiction and poetry and issued the editorial injunction 'Keep *Household Words* Imaginative!'[1]

By this time, the first phase of the battle for a cheap press had been won. The stamp duty was reduced to a penny per sheet in 1836. This lowered the price of *The Times* to fourpence but did not greatly help the humbler papers which still had to bear the expenses of stamping and the loss on every unsold copy, since stamps were not redeemable. The next decade brought more urgent problems; although the Chartists continued to campaign for a cheap press, it was once again the respectable Anti-Corn-Law League which proved more effective. Its members needed papers to disseminate their views, and they continued to pursue the issue even after winning repeal. Speaking at the Manchester Athenaeum in 1850, Richard Cobden declared that:

> As a rule, grown-up men, in these busy times, read very little else but newspapers . . . I doubt if a man with limited time could read anything else that would be more useful to him.[2]

In the following year, the House of Commons set up a select committee on newspapers, and a proposal to abolish the stamp duty was passed in 1855 after long and heated debate. The main victory was won, to be followed by the abolition of the advertising tax in 1858 and the duty on paper in 1861. Now came the growth of popular newspapers, for which the demand had been rising ever since the Napoleonic War had quickened the concern of ordinary people for what was going on in the wider world. There was already a fair selection of daily papers for

---

[1] P. A. W. Collins, 'The Significance of Dickens's Periodicals', in *A Review of English Literature*, Vol. 2, No. 3, p. 58.

[2] *The Times*, 30 December 1850.

those who could afford them. The *Morning Chronicle,* which finished publication in 1862, had the distinction of employing the young Dickens as a Parliamentary reporter and the young Thackeray as an art critic. The *Morning Herald* (1780–1869) started as little more than a sensational sheet of police court news but grew into respectability. It prospered greatly – as did other papers – on the revenue from advertisements and public announcements during the railway boom of the forties. The more staid and fashionable *Morning Post* supported protectionism and a strong foreign policy as exemplified by Palmerston. The *Morning Advertiser,* started in 1794 as the organ of the licensed victuallers, continued to foster their trade interests but won a wider circulation. It was a leader in the attacks on the Prince Consort for his over-zealous interference in affairs of state.

Dominating the whole scene was *The Times,* the property of the Walter family, which had started in 1785 as the *Daily Universal Register* and taken its more familiar name three years later. It was a law to itself, sometimes foremost in innovation and sometimes the last stronghold of reaction. It was the first London paper to be printed on a steam-press, but one of the last to take up the campaign against stamp duty. It opposed the repeal of the Corn Laws for many years, but was strong for reforming the Church of England and curtailing ecclesiastical privileges. In the latter connection it was depicted by Trollope as the redoubtable *Jupiter* – a name derived from its popular appellation of *Thunder.* It was a pioneer in two notable journalistic developments: the 'leading article' and the use of special correspondents abroad. It sent W. H. Russell to the Crimea, whence his despatches helped to stir popular indignation at administrative mismanagement. It had its enemies of course, among them the *Saturday Review* whose declared aim was to break its influence:

> No apology is needed for assuming that this country is ruled by *The Times.* We all know it, or if we do not know it, we ought to know it.[1]

The Times suffered less from these attacks than from the competition of new, cheaper papers in the second half of the century.

[1] First Issue of *The Saturday Review,* 3 November 1855.

The launching of the *Daily Telegraph* in 1855 set the pattern for what came to be known as the 'new journalism'. It was the first London paper to cost only a penny and soon won a large circulation by the popular vitality of its reporting and comment; its first editor was Thornton Hunt, a son of Leigh Hunt of the Radical *Examiner*. It was never shy of bringing itself into prominence. Two of its more sensational efforts came in the seventies, when it commissioned the researches of George Smith at Nineveh which gave new material for biblical archaeology, and joined with the *New York Herald* in sending H. M. Stanley to Africa in search of Livingstone.

This was the most immediately successful, but neither the first nor the last of the new papers. The *Daily News* had started in 1847 and was edited by Dickens for seventeen issues before he retired exhausted and handed it over to his future biographer, John Forster. It was prominent in the campaign against the 'taxes on knowledge' and continued to support the Liberal cause in politics. One of its most popular phases came when Forbes was acting as its correspondent during the Franco-Prussian War.

In *Pendennis*, Captain Shannon draws up the prospectus for a paper to be written 'by gentlemen for gentlemen'.[1] This satirical aim was taken as a serious one when Francis Greenwood founded the *Pall Mall Gazette* in 1865. Greenwood had been sub-editor of the *Cornhill* under Thackeray and his aim was to combine news-reporting with the deeper quality of the best reviews, in a paper Liberal in outlook. After a phase of editorship by Morley, the *Pall Mall Gazette* came under W. T. Stead, who used it to present his disclosures on juvenile prostitution. Other popular papers were the Conservative *Standard* – later to have the doubtful distinction of Alfred Austin as a leader-writer – and the Radical *Morning Star* which supported Cobden and Bright. The Liberal *Daily Chronicle* was started by an amalgamation of smaller papers in 1877.

The beginning of even more popular daily journalism came in 1896 with the *Daily Mail*, 'written by office boys for office boys' said Lord Salisbury[2] in parody of Thackeray. Its founder Alfred Harmsworth was not troubled by gibes; he saw that

---

[1] Thackeray, *Pendennis* (1850), Bk. 2, Ch. 11.

[2] David Thomson, *England in the Nineteenth Century* (Hamondsworth, 1950), p. 176.

there was a new public to be reached, and he intended to reach it. News was written up in more palatable and easily-digested stories, with special attention to its sensational aspects. The paper soon achieved a huge circulation and drew its income largely from advertisements. In short, Harmsworth set the pattern for modern popular newspapers, followed by others such as the *Daily Express* (1900).

The new spate of publication was not confined to morning dailies. Both the *Morning Star* and the *Standard* had their evening counterparts; their price was a penny, halved by the *London Echo* (1888) and by the *Evening News* and the *Star*. Sunday papers had tended to specialize in sensationalism, obscenity, and scandalous 'revelations' sometimes combined with blackmail; they were also more generally popular in tone and Radical in politics. Some of them improved their image later in the century but others continued, in modified terms, the pursuit of sensationalism. Provincial papers, with an existing tradition of freedom and independence, were encouraged to begin a daily issue by the removal of taxes and the establishment of news agencies which, aided by the railways and the telegraph, enabled them to get news before it became history. By 1900 the *Manchester Guardian* was the leading organ of informed Liberalism.

The revolution in journalism combined, like most revolutions, good things and bad. There was a decline in the vicious scurrility and open obscenity which had been common. The job of being a journalist became less hazardous than it had been in the thirties when an author, angered by a bad review in *Fraser's*, assaulted the paper's proprietor and fought a duel with Maginn the editor – the original of Thackeray's Captain Shannon. The kind of journalism which Dickens satirized in his story of the Eatanswill election[1] slowly faded out. Imagination fails at the idea of *The Times* today emulating its attack on 'Mr Babbletongue Macaulay', described as 'hardly fit to fill up one of the vacancies that have occurred by the lamentable death of her Majesty's two favourite monkeys'.[2]

The improvement in journalistic manners and morals was accompanied by such descents to triviality as George Newnes's

[1] *The Pickwick Papers* (1837), Ch. 13.
[2] *Cambridge History of English Literature*, Vol. 14, p. 170.

75

Tit Bits (1880) which, as its name implied, offered a collection of scraps and snippets from books and journals. The competition for the new readership brought tempting Christmas numbers and supplements to replace the old, expensive gift-books; lotteries thinly disguised as contests of skill offered large prizes. There was no total decline in journalism, but there was evidence of the fragmentation that was affecting society by the end of the century.

The working class had less aspiration to follow the path of the privileged few, nor was there so much pressure from above for their 'improvement'. Middle-class papers tended to sponsor schemes for material relief rather than moral guidance, acknowledging such gifts from readers as 'Men's clothes, mended . . . very nice box of clothes'.[1] The worship of knowledge which had inspired the old Radicals was replaced by the pleasure of reading for pure relaxation. It was not that Newnes and Harmsworth got the better of Stead and Morley but simply that their aims and audiences were different. The result of the cheap press was not the atheism, revolt and immorality that had been feared, but triviality. Matthew Arnold's view of the 'new journalism'[2] was proved right:

> It is full of ability, novelty, variety, sensation, sympathy, generous instinct; its one great fault is that it is feather-brained.

Throughout the Victorian period, the various aspects of journalism are of the greatest importance in the study of the literature. Many writers saw the first publication of their work in reviews and magazines, a practice which helped them to reach a larger number of readers and thus to increase the demand for books. Some papers were founded with the intention of profiting from the reputation of an author who would edit or write for them: this is true of Dickens and *Bentley's Miscellany* and to a large extent of Thackeray and the *Cornhill*. At the beginning of the period the novelist, the serious essayist, the literary promulgator of new ideas, were the helpless targets of the magazines and their anonymous reviewers. By the end, the better type of journalism was part of their domain and ruled by their authority.

[1] *Longman's Magazine*, August 1891.
[2] *The Nineteenth Century*, May 1887.

5

Thomas Carlyle

Victorian literature yields more self-criticism than self-congratulation. Most of the great writers in the first half of the
reign were troubled by problems inherited from the past which
were now showing their full seriousness. They were not complacent about poverty, disease, starvation and premature
death: these were not new to life or to literature, but they
were no longer being accepted as part of inevitable human
destiny. The years of repression following Waterloo had
brought a new bitterness between classes, in which Chartist
demonstrations and revolutions abroad seemed to threaten
open conflict. The young Carlyle saw the Yeomanry riding out
to put down discontented gatherings and the young Charles
Kingsley saw the Bristol riots of 1831 when the mob burned and
looted in agitation for the Reform Bill which afterwards seemed
to have accomplished so little.

The sense of corporate guilt was to find eloquent expression
in such passages as Dickens's indictment of society for the death
of Jo.[1] While Shaftesbury and Chadwick campaigned for
ameliorative legislation, the writers tended to plead for a
'change of heart'. They attacked the attitude of mind which
tried to justify prevailing conditions more often than they
demanded public action. The Utilitarian philosophy came
under their fire, in its changed and somewhat self-contradic-
tory form which was agreeable to commercial and industrial
interests. There was scant literary praise for Malthus and Adam
Smith, or for David Ricardo who had conflated and developed
their ideas into the 'iron law of wages', with such dicta as 'Like
all other contracts, wages should be left to the fair and free
competition of the market, and should never be controlled by
the interference of the legislature'.[2]

[1] *Bleak House* (1853), Ch. 48.
[2] *The Principles of Political Economy and Taxation* (1817).

The hatred aroused by these doctrines and their results is understandable enough to any sensitive mind. The writers were troubled less by the fact that times were hard – though this did trouble them too – than by the fear that the nation was losing its soul of compassion. The individual seemed unable to hold his identity; the 'fear of meaninglessness' which Paul Tillich named as the ontological fear of the modern age[1] was already strong in those who protested against *laissez-faire* theories and the apparent determinism of the new 'dismal science' of economics. Dickens indicts Gradgrind and Mrs Gaskell blames Carson not so much for deliberate wickedness as for the sin of not caring to know that people had feelings to be fed as well as stomachs. Even when the Utilitarian spirit of efficiency tried to tidy up society by legislation, the motive seemed to be without soul, and not to touch the real problems of relationships and attitudes.

The writers shared and developed the contemporary tension between extremes which can be over-simply described as optimism and pessimism. The belief that a general change of heart would put everything right brought them into conflict with the growing faith in legislative and administrative measures and caused them to distrust institutional remedies. At the same time they rejected the eighteenth-century faith that there was basic justice and goodness in society, which literature could and should make explicit. They looked more deeply, and saw a worse reality than the previous age had generally admitted. The reality is documented beyond doubt; imagination touched but did not invent it. Podsnap and Bounderby, Plugson and Bulstrode, are creatures of fiction but not monsters of fable.

Out of their worry over the state of society came the type of pessimism about the times which Trollope described as 'Carlylism'.[2] Certainly Thomas Carlyle inspired many writers very different from himself in temperament and literary method. Dickens dedicated *Hard Times,* his most polemical novel, to Carlyle. Disraeli expressed Carlylean ideals in the 'Young England' manifestoes and in fiction. Carlyle detested

---

[1] *The Courage to Be* (London, 1952), pp. 30–59.
[2] *Autobiography* (1883), Ch. 20; see also the satire on Carlyle as 'Dr Pessimist Anticant' in *The Warden,* Ch. 15.

Disraeli the successful Tory politician and in 1865 had the satisfaction of being elected Rector of Edinburgh University against him. It says much for the magnanimity of Disraeli that he offered Carlyle a title – which was refused. Another reminder that the Victorians were not all narrowly intolerant is the story of Carlyle's reception by the Queen, when the old republican found himself in company with Grote the Whig and Utilitarian, Lyell whose *Principles of Geology* had upset some theologians, and Robert Browning. It must have been an interesting occasion, especially when Carlyle put the needs of old age before protocol, and insisted on sitting down.

This was late in a lifetime of judging contemporary problems as a phase in an eternal conflict, and a long way from Ecclefechan where he was born in 1795. The same year saw the birth of Keats, who was dead when Carlyle was still struggling to be heard. It is hard to think of them as contemporaries; Carlyle seems so much our idea of the typical Victorian, earnest, anxious, critical of society, voluminous in output. His early years were an experience of poverty, surrounded by the even worse poverty of spinners and handloom weavers suffering from the effects of mechanization. They were years when the repressive Government might have seemed like a magnification of the Carlyle home. The image of his stern, uncompromisingly Calvinist father hovered over his adult life, to be sought in various human substitutes and eventually in the idealization of the Hero.

Carlyle was not quite fourteen when, according to common Scottish practice then and later, he set off to walk to the University at Edinburgh. His student days were followed by school-teaching and private tutoring, and in writing a few articles for the *Edinburgh Encyclopaedia*. His emergence into the man for posterity began in 1826 when he married Jane Baillie Welsh. There is no marriage better documented, since the correspondence of each of them is vast even by Victorian standards. We can learn it all – the digestive troubles, the insomnia in separate rooms, the jealousies, the strange prevailing need of each other; it is the stuff of fiction, with factual truth.

By this time, Carlyle had left the faith of his father and undergone the mystical experience which he described as his

'Spiritual New-birth or Baphometic Fire-baptism'.[1] Whatever this may have been, it apparently led him to a position of strength and affirmation, from the 'Everlasting No' through the 'Centre of Indifference' to the 'Everlasting Yea'. Goethe was chosen as type and herald of the new age whose vision now spread before him. Carlyle had already translated Goethe and Schiller, with an enthusiasm for German Romanticism not shared by many of his contemporaries. He himself was somewhat baulked by their extreme aestheticism, but he always had a talent for finding what he wanted in other writers and for making the points which they had regrettably forgotten to make. Goethe, whose fame had not yet spread far beyond his own country, was gratified by this foreign admiration. Gifts were exchanged, including what sounds like a singularly hideous present for Jane of a black wrought-iron necklace with the head of Goethe cut in coloured glass and set in gold.[2] It is unlikely, however, that the first minister of Weimar shared the young Scot's fervour for revolutionary change.

With the money for his translation of *Wilhelm Meister*, Carlyle took a trip to London. His old friend Edward Irving was now minister of the Scottish Church in Hatton Garden, where he drew fashionable congregations and denounced them for their indifference to poverty and unbelief. Irving's apocalyptic vision was to lead him to insanity; Carlyle's vision was so far attracting less attention. Some of the frustration went into his unfinished *Romance of Wotton Reinfred*, a work aptly described as 'sired by *Rasselas* out of the French *Philosophes*'.[3] It is interesting as fictional autobiography, with Carlyle as the brilliant but bullied schoolboy.

After this jaunt, Carlyle endured a period of poverty in isolation with his wife at Craigenputtock, where he wrote a few articles for the *Edinburgh Review*. In one of them, an essay on Burns, appeared his first use of the image of the tailor who clothes reality with appearance. With a fuller treatment of this idea in his pocket, he came again to London and ended his search for a publisher with serialization in *Fraser's*. The new

---

[1] *Sartor Resartus*, Bk. 2, Chs. 7–9.
[2] Julian Symons, *Thomas Carlyle: The Life and Ideas of a Prophet* (London, 1952), p. 113.
[3] Symons, op. cit., p. 106.

work, *Sartor Resartus* had to wait until 1838 for publication in a single volume.

The graceful style of his *Life of Schiller* was now abandoned for the idiom which, he said, sprang from his father's speech and his mother's humour, and which seems also to derive something from his knowledge of Fichte and of Sterne. It is discursive, allusive, stressing the Germanic element in English with its scope for compounding and neologisms. The flexibility of English syntax is exploited to the full, as parts of speech change functions or are omitted altogether, and sentences develop into a mass of parentheses. Carlyle won a hearing, but he did something more: he broke classical diction in English prose as surely as the Romantics had broken it in poetry, and brought to polemicists and novelists a new freedom of expression.

Sartor Resartus is presented as the work of Diogenes Teufelsdröckh, Professor of Things in General at the University of Weissnichtwo. A good deal of the book is occupied with the Professor's early life of physical hardship and Romantic agony very like Carlyle's own, and with an account of how his manuscript came to be printed. The 'clothes philosophy' itself is Carlyle's handling of Kant's transcendentalist theory of imperceptible essences behind the appearances that we perceive. The clothes are the impressions which hide the nakedness of reality; we have obscured the truth with outworn symbols of experience. Current society must be destroyed before it can revive, and a great heroic leader must control its future.

This of course is the basis of 'Carlylism'. It is on the individual that the duties of society ultimately rest. He must overcome doubt by affirmation, train his mind and not just his mechanical skills, seek an experience of the divine not constricted by theology. In fact, Carlyle's own 'Baphometic Fire-baptism' is just what everyone needs. Though the readers of *Fraser's* did not know it, a great deal more was to be heard of this new visionary with his burning sincerity, his fierce humour, his hatred of cold reason.

In 1834 the Carlyles settled in Cheyne Row, Chelsea, where they spent the rest of their lives, and Thomas got down to the hard toil of writing a history of the French Revolution.[1] He was

---

[1] 'The Mind is Weary, the body very sick', he wrote after finishing the second volume in April 1836. Emery Neff, *Thomas Carlyle* (New York, 1932), p. 165.

helped by the loan of books from John Stuart Mill, with whom he had begun an uneasy friendship on his previous London visit and who had himself thought of writing on the same subject.[1] Mill hindered more than he helped, for his servant lit the fire with the manuscript of the first part of the history; Carlyle took the misfortune patiently and soothed Mill's anguished feelings.

In spite of these hazards, *The French Revolution* appeared in 1837 and was generally well received. Thackeray gave it a good notice in *The Times*, though some of the more timid readers were alarmed by Carlyle's clear enthusiasm for violence and the need to overthrow a government that has gone wrong. The Revolution seemed to him a judgement which one society had passed on itself, and which his own might repeat. He saw it as a portent, but did not fully consider its actual consequences in the politics and thought of its own and other countries; nor did he look very deeply into its sources. His concern was with the event itself, and his imaginative gift of projection into a past age was fully exploited. He was sometimes inaccurate through lack of available sources, and sometimes through such preference for effect above reality as appears in his account of the Flight to Varennes. Yet British interest in the Revolution derives a great deal from Carlyle.

He followed the current mode of literary-historical writing which had gained inspiration from Romanticism and particularly from Scott. Contemporary novelists were both feeding and stimulating the appetite for history, and Carlyle had a novelist's art with his vivid pictures of people and events, his emphasis on the great man as the maker of history. The early Victorian historians told history as a dramatic story, by no means excluding the bias of personal belief or political controversy. Only later in the century did Britain absorb the scientific approach to history, already pioneered by Niebuhr in Carlyle's admired Germany. From Mommsen, Ranke and others, our historians learned to look at evidence totally and objectively, through legal, cultural and linguistic knowledge. The new discoveries of geology and archaeology gave a longer perspective, and the theory of evolution a new way of looking.

Carlyle's method, however, suited his contemporaries. He was

[1] John Stuart Mill, *Autobiography* (1873), Ch. 4.

no longer obscure, and never again knew serious poverty. In his new fame, he gave a number of lecture-series between 1837 and 1840, after which he seldom spoke in public. He was a nervous but successful speaker, popular enough to charge a guinea for admission to six lectures. The only set which he printed, *On Heroes and Hero-Worship*, developed his doctrine of the great man who is humanity's only hope, in an odd assembly ranging from Odin through Mahomet, Shakespeare, Luther, Rousseau, Napoleon and others. He made Mill jump up and shout disagreement by praising Mahomet above Jeremy Bentham.[1]

Carlyle was now turning to more immediate questions. His *Chartism* (1840) was the first serious analysis of the movement which was exciting some members of society and terrifying others. He saw it as a symptom of deeper unrest, not to be crushed by panic measures or soothed by general suffrage and economic remedies. He attacked the reformed Parliament, and politicians in general, for not heeding the warnings of 1789. He reproached the upper classes for failing truly to help the poor by taking refuge in the palliatives of organized temporary relief. Against Malthusian fears, he opposed the remedies of education and emigration. Above all, he called on the 'collective wisdom of the Nation' to meet the challenge.

It was in *Past and Present* (1843) that Carlyle coined the phrase 'Condition of England'[2] to express his anxiety about the state of the nation. He wrote it after a visit to East Anglia, where workhouses increased his dislike of the present, and ruined churches inspired that nostalgia for an idealized medieval England which Burke had uttered and which was often to be heard again. The second part of the book develops this theme with an imaginative history of the rule of Abbot Samson at Bury St Edmunds, but the main concern is with present not with past. Without making any concessions to democracy, Carlyle champions the poor and exposes the absurd fears of over-production while so many are in want. The paradox of unused goods and unprovided people is an indictment of the

---

[1] Michael St John Packe, *The Life of John Stuart Mill* (London, 1954), p. 265.

[2] 'The condition of England, on which many pamphlets are now in the course of publication, and many thoughts unpublished are going on in every reflective head, is justly regarded as one of the most ominous, and withal one of the strangest, ever seen in the world'; opening sentence of *Past and Present*.

laissez-faire development from Utilitarianism. It is wrong for the Government not to control the national economy, but the followers of Bentham have over-stressed the reform of particular institutions and failed to see the necessity of a general spiritual revival. The answer is not universal suffrage, or any other 'Morrison's Pill for curing the maladies of Society',[1] but national leadership by a great man. For all its idiosyncracies, *Past and Present* is Carlyle's finest work, more controlled in style and imagery and marking the end of his first period. The burning radicalism is simmering down into a growing vexation with the whole idea of Parliamentary democracy.

The next hero to be tried out was Oliver Cromwell, whose *Letters and Speeches, with Elucidations,* Carlyle edited in 1845. Cromwell had been neither understood nor admired by most recent historians, and was now raised to the high repute which he has generally kept. The history of the Civil War and Commonwealth is made to reflect that of the French Revolution and also of Carlyle's own time. Cromwell is the man of clear, direct vision, adaptable to people and circumstances. The picture is left incomplete, since Carlyle did not admire, and therefore largely ignored, the seventeenth-century origins of the struggle for popular representation.

The events of 1848 delighted him but also made him feel guilt at his own lack of action. On the day of the last Chartist assembly, his attempt to reach Kennington ended with rain and an ignominious return to Chelsea by omnibus. Jane was becoming more difficult, and in the following year he was still further depressed by a visit to Ireland, where the usual poverty was being made hideous by famine. His *Latter-Day Pamphlets* reflect his mood, now savage to the edge of cruelty. The role of pessimistic prophet with a touch of the Romantic outsider now governed his relationship to society, plus a certain sado-masochistic satisfaction for himself and for many of his guiltily privileged readers. Again he berates the Government and calls for a search outside the despised Parliament for the nation's leaders. The Hero is now Peel, in whom Carlyle put more hope than in any other English politician, and with whose death in 1850 the pamphlets ended. In spite of the almost hysterical tone, Carlyle in these essays touched on some of the

[1] Bk. 1, Ch. 4.

issues which were to become dominant in later political thinking: problems like the growing power of the state, the need for coercion and control for the improvement of society, the direction of labour into more productive channels.

The early enthusiasm for Germany had not gone; failing to find an adequate successor to Peel, Carlyle wrote *Frederick the Great* (1858–65). The violence of his tone is now almost pathological in dealing with his old hates and some new ones. The uneasy feeling of the book may come partly from his lack of certainty about the latest Hero. Frederick is praised as the strong leader and the opponent of *laissez-faire* tendencies, but it is an idealized portrait with the facts sifted and adapted to suit a previous conception. In spite of the escapist secondary hero-worship of Voltaire as Frederick's 'spiritual complement', Carlyle probably finished his work with some relief. Less readable and more disagreeable than *The French Revolution,* this biography has passages of uniquely Carlylean brilliance. It is the climax of his historical moralizing, insisting more strongly than ever that a people makes its own destiny and that the great man is essential for good leadership.

He lived on after the sudden death of his wife in 1866, writing little and becoming more dyspeptic, more bigoted, more philistine. The Second Reform Act of 1867 produced *Shooting Niagara – and After?* In this new attack on the principle of government by 'counting heads', the new franchise was seen as merely extending the *laissez-faire* principle. A lifetime of attacking political and economic problems had left him seeing the old foes in every new venture. He died in 1881, having never spared himself or others.

Carlyle's influence was great: Dickens, Kingsley, Ruskin, Morris, Browning, Meredith – these and many others were able to draw something from his genius. He inspired and stimulated rather than guided, raging like an Old Testament prophet to arouse the nation from slumber and make men aware of the practical urgency of problems which until then had seemed theoretical. He taught the Victorians lessons for which they were apt pupils: that life is real and earnest; that work has a moral value; that social change must begin with a new attitude towards individual responsibility. Some of this Carlyle initiated and some he simply made more explicit. He is most Victorian in his failure to reconcile consistently the extremes within himself. He praised action and despised rhetoric, but his practice was the reverse of his preaching; he hated the idea of democracy and demanded a Hero to lead the multitude incapable of foresight or self-sacrifice, but he championed the cause of the poor; he wrote against patched-up measures of relief but he gave freely to beggars.

He is hard to label; Russell calls him one of the 'soft-hearted liberals',[1] in the tradition of Fichte and Byron which led through to Nietzsche. A Romantic in his contempt for cold reason, he yet attacked the real problems of society and had no time for the lachrymose sensibility which ignored immediate cases of suffering. He had little sympathy for Liberalism as it came to be understood and admired in his later years. He was consistent only in his dissatisfaction with the state of the times and in his own sense of personal responsibility. Although his attacks on industrialism may seem short-sighted and reactionary, he was not in fact wholly opposed to the age of machinery about which he had written an early essay in the *Edinburgh* called 'Signs of the Times'. He did not share the agricultural vision, common among romantically-minded Victorians, which saw industrialism only as a disruptive and divisive force. What he hated was the assumption that more machinery meant general social improvement, and the failure of the industrialists to accept the total responsibilities of their new power.

Carlyle led the revolt against materialism that became stronger before the end of his own life. He taught the Victorians to look again at the ideal, non-material part of human existence, which had been obscured by the different but equally limited visions of Fourier and Bentham and Owen. He shamed the Gradgrinds who were calling for 'nothing but facts' into facing the reality of the imagination. His urgent pessimism challenged easy optimism and laid bare the dread beneath prevailing calm. His 'clothes philosophy' took off the garments of smug respectability and showed the naked violence which lurked in social organizations and threatened their overthrow.

The Calvinism of his boyhood kept its hold, replaced by no cheerful humanism but by the stark need to make his own gospel. In other lands and in later years the demand for the

[1] Bertrand Russell, *History of Western Philosophy* (London, 1946), p. 667.

Hero took sinister turns. In his own day, Carlyle made articulate what many people were feeling about prevailing political and economic doctrines. There was much injustice and inhumanity in the 'condition of England' when he began to write. He explained to the reading public what the issues of Chartism and electoral reform really meant, and he showed his fellow-writers that such things were deeply their concern.

The other most popular historian of the early Victorian years is an interesting contrast to Carlyle. Thomas Babington Macaulay emphasized the essential goodness of the age, as Carlyle its badness. The fact that both were widely read and praised is an indication of the Victorian quest for a principle of unity to reconcile difficult extremes. Carlyle's life was long, devoted mostly to study and writing; Macaulay's was comparatively short, prolific in writing but also full of public action. He entered Parliament as a Whig in 1830 and, as a member of the Indian Supreme Council, helped to adumbrate later reforms. His adult brilliance followed a precocious childhood, which had early shown prodigious powers of memory and produced a 'Universal History'. His upbringing was as Evangelical as Carlyle's – his father was a leader of the Clapham Sect – but Cambridge was a different nurse from Edinburgh and sent him out full of Whig principles. Fame came with his article in the *Edinburgh* on Milton, which praised Cromwell before Carlyle's rehabilitation and began his lifelong antipathy to the Stuarts. His early essays attacked the Tory view of history. Where Carlyle looked to France and Germany, Macaulay stuck mainly to his own country. However, his time in India gave him leisure for the majority of the ballads which appeared in 1842 as *Lays of Ancient Rome*.

He shared with Carlyle the gift of making history alive for the ordinary reader. His great *History of England*, urbanely bright and easy to read, did in its own way as much as Carlyle's *French Revolution* to free historical prose from remoteness and the reader of serious books from virtuous resignation to being bored. It was planned to go from the Restoration to the death of George IV, but had not got beyond William III when Macaulay died in 1859. He had won public recognition and financial reward since the first two volumes had appeared in

1848, and made the first effective Whig challenge to Hume's history.

Macaulay's work is more orderly, a more organic structure, than Carlyle's. He researched thoroughly, including what was then almost the novelty of using literature, letters and diaries as sources. The famous third chapter on England in 1685 opened a new vista of historical writing: the total background treated with imagination. Yet there are gaps, suppressions, utter failures. He had little interest in religion and speculative philosophy and thus neglected some seventeenth-century preoccupations. He had no strain of mysticism, whereas Carlyle had too much.

The historian and the politician in Macaulay were inseparable. He set out to justify contemporary Whiggism, and he worshipped the spirit of 1832 as much as Carlyle hated it. William III was his hero, who had made the world safe for the nineteenth century and from whose time society had grown by detectable laws towards its present excellence. In the turmoil of 1848 he could write of the expulsion of James II, 'Its highest eulogy is that it was our last revolution'.[1] It was to him acceptable as a defensive move, which had established the rule of law and brought security. Where Carlyle denounced the age, Macaulay believed that all classes were better off than formerly and that 'the deliberate pursuit of progress was the rightful monopoly of the Whig party'.[2] Speaking on the Anatomy Bill in 1832 he said that nowadays any bricklayer who fell off a ladder got better treatment than a nobleman in the past.[3] The assumption that progress in some things meant progress in all, and the false optimism that because better possibilities existed all would benefit from them, reflected the kind of complacency against which Carlyle fought.

Imaginatively understanding of some aspects of past and present, blind to others, Macaulay seems sometimes to love theories more than people and an epigram more than either. For Carlyle education was a general right, for Macaulay a defence against 'the gross ignorance of the common people', which was a 'principal cause of danger to our persons and

[1] *History of England,* Ch. 10.
[2] Hugh Trevor-Roper, 'Lord Macaulay', in *The Listener,* 14 October 1965.
[3] Quoted in *Ideas and Beliefs of the Victorians* (London, 1949), pp. 49ff.

property'.[1] Carlyle saw the past as a refuge: 'The element of fear is withdrawn from it . . . the present and future are all so dangerous'.[2] Macaulay saw it as a time of growth and suffering towards the golden age of his own life. A great deal of Victorian thought was developed between those two extreme views.

[1] Speech in the House of Commons 19 April 1847; quoted in E. A. Baker, ed., *The Reinterpretation of Victorian Literature* (Princeton, 1950), p. 102.
[2] Carlyle's Journal for 1835; quoted in J. A. Froude, *Carlyle's Life in London* (London, 1884), Vol. 1, p. 20.

6

The Progress of the Novel

The early-Victorian novel began by struggling unconfidently in the void left by the deaths of the younger Romantic poets and the slow decline of the older ones who lived on. It finished in triumphant possession of territories hitherto unclaimed by imaginative literature. The devotees of Shelley and Byron looked upon the novel as an earthbound form, dealing with the immediate and transitory. As late as 1848 de Quincey was waging the old battle by grumbling at the poor type of person who habitually read fiction and scorning the novel as inferior to the 'grander passions of poetry'[1] but he was already out of date. Walter Scott, with his reputation as both poet and novelist, had gone far towards elevating the novel and overcoming prejudice against it; although regard for him declined for a while after his death, his achievement helped to determine the course of writers in the next generation.

The theatre offered no effective challenge until the last years of the century. 'To say that the novel is the modern substitute for the drama is only to repeat one of the commonplaces of criticism' commented the *Westminster* in 1867.[2] It was a fair observation, not only of what the novelists were producing by that time but also of the social response. The novel was not only enjoyed in private reading but was read aloud in the home and in the public hall. It was praised or blamed for its moral influence; its characters could inspire fashions of dress and patterns of behaviour.

Yet what was a commonplace of criticism by the sixties was far from being one in the thirties, when the novelist was still trying to get a serious hearing. His popularity was increasing

[1] Reviewing Forster's *Life of Goldsmith* in the *North British Review*, ix (1848) pp. 193ff.
[2] *Westminster Review*, October 1867.

but he was still likely to suffer from the contempt of the intellectual and the suspicion of the moralist. Disapproval was certainly less strong than it had been at the beginning of the century, when the *Evangelical Magazine* had placed 'love of novels' on the same level of its 'Spiritual Barometer' as scepticism and a degree lower than adultery,[1] but it was vigorous enough. The opposition has a familiar sound: we have heard it raised against the Elizabethan theatre and against television. The novel was said to inflame the imagination with sensual thoughts, to make humble folk discontented with their station in life, to cultivate falsehood and pretence. Though many Evangelicals kept up their attack throughout the reign, the better religious papers often became more liberal than the bulk of their readers. By 1867 an Evangelical magazine could praise George Eliot and commend the novel as combining the best of the poetic and dramatic forms.[2]

In 1838 the London Statistical Society made the following analysis of the contents of ten circulating libraries in the capital:[3]

Novels by Walter Scott, and novels in imitation of him, Galt, etc.	166
Novels by Theodore Hook, Bulwer Lytton, etc.	41
Novels by Captain Marryat, Cooper, Washington Irving, etc.	115
Voyages, Travels, History, and Biography	136
Novels by Miss Edgeworth, and Moral and Religious Novels	49
Works of a Good Character, Dr Johnson, Goldsmith, etc.	27
Romances, Castle of Otranto, etc.	76
Fashionable novels, well known	439
Novels of the lowest character, being chiefly imitations of Fashionable Novels, containing no good, although probably nothing decidedly bad	1008
Miscellaneous Old Books, Newgate Calendar, etc.	86
Lord Byron's Works, Smollett's do., Fielding's do., Gil Blas, etc.	39
Books decidedly bad	10

This list may leave much to be desired in its method of classification, but it shows up the very high proportion of novels

---

[1] Richard Stang, *The Theory of the Novel in England* (London, 1959), p. 4.
[2] *British Quarterly Review*, XLV, pp. 141ff.
[3] *Journal of the Statistical Society*, I (1838), p. 485.

among the books that were going the rounds. It shows also the typical contemporary inclination to combine moral judgements with factual records. It confirms that the prevailing taste in fiction was for the sensational and escapist: the themes of Romanticism lingered in prose when their creative power in poetry was almost extinct. Although the 'Gothic' novel was no longer engaging the talents of the leading writers, the taste for supernatural thrills was still strong. There were enough writers to produce and readers to lap up the kind of thing that had delighted Catherine Morland – 'Are they all horrid? Are you sure they are all horrid?'[1]

Production of the novel by the beginning of Victoria's reign was already so prolific, and so lacking in outstanding figures, that the historian is faced with an unenviable task of selection, and shares the fear that George Saintsbury felt in dealing with the minor novel of the previous period. 'The contents of the present chapter may seem at first sight, and that not merely to ill-informed persons, like those of a badly assorted omnibus box'.[2]

However, selection must be attempted; and it may begin by looking again at the list made by the LSS and noting the overwhelming proportion of 'Fashionable Novels' and their imitators, of varying moral quality but not 'decidedly bad'. The 'Silver Fork' school was still very popular, with its tales of aristocratic life, its characters liberally endowed with titles, its pages strewn with dinners, balls and parties. The aristocracy was still familiar enough as an institution, but remote enough in detail, to be the setting for the kind of escapism that seeks identification with the just-possibly attainable rather than in complete fantasy. The governess could dream of marrying a lord, and the self-improving clerk could reflect that prevailing conditions might reward enterprise with fortune. The fashion in fiction was on the wane, but it lingered on for at least two more decades despite its premature obituaries in the critical reviews. It had its effect on the early Disraeli and was parodied by Dickens and Thackeray before passing into the sub-literature of cheap magazines.

The popularity of novels about high life was at least rivalled

[1] Jane Austen, *Northanger Abbey* (1818), Ch. 6.
[2] *Cambridge History of English Literature,* Vol. 11, Ch. 13.

by that of novels about low life. The interest of the socially respectable in criminality is perennial; dishonesty is a literary theme from Chaucer to the latest thriller. In the 1830s the law and its administration came under frequent scrutiny. The Benthamites were pressing for codification, for a solution of the muddle resulting from the long development of different systems and courts. The criminal law was still biased more towards the protection of property than the rights of people, with capital punishment prescribed and sometimes carried out for trivial cases of theft or malicious damage. In spite of savage penalties, detective methods were still inefficient and the amount of crime was causing concern. The old Bow Street Runners were the only detective force in London until the Metropolitan Police set up its investigation department in 1842. Crime and punishment were sufficiently in the foreground of real experience for them to interest the growing middle-class readership of novels.

The less privileged class of reader found a different sort of allure in the crime novel. The years of repression after Waterloo had built up a sense of general opposition to authority and a degree of admiration for those who profitably defied it. The cult of highwaymen and master criminals, which caused much distress to the moralists, often became curiously linked with demands for social reform. Typical of this approach was the weekly *Annals of Crime, or New Newgate Calendar, and General Record of Tragic Events*, which ran from 1836 to 1838 and interspersed reports of crime with such articles as 'Slavery in England – the Factory System'. The criminal could be included in general sympathy for the submerged, the victim of an unjust system.

It was the extremes of society which fascinated readers, whether moved to envy, emulation, compassion or moral disapproval. Middle-class settings did not always satisfy the demand for sensation of one kind or another, as Harriet Martineau discovered when her novel *Deerbrook* was rejected in 1838:

People liked high life in novels, and low life, and ancient life; and life of any rank presented by Dickens, in his peculiar artistic light ... but it was not supposed that they would bear a presentment of the familiar life of every day.[1]

[1] *Harriet Martineau's Autobiography* (London, 1877), Vol. 2, p. 115.

Charlotte Brontë had similar trouble with *The Professor* eight years later. The vogue for 'middle life' in fiction came only when the middle class had gained more stability and self-confidence.

The sensational novel of the thirties was not lacking in moral judgements, but it tended towards vague compassion rather than particular reform. The attitude was of course largely shared by Dickens, and it issued in the melodramatic treatment of problems in the novel and the drama. Judgement is based on the immediate aspects of the situation and not on abiding principles or deeper motivation. It reflects the unwillingness of the time to face the fact that life was becoming more complex and more challenging: the urgency of the individual choice between equally unwelcome alternatives was not yet a theme of fiction. Yet throughout the thirties, the novel was expanding its scope, passing from light escapism towards the search after a unifying principle in society. The novelist's imagination was beginning to touch ideas and subjects not previously treated.

The development of the novel over these years can be seen in the literary career of Bulwer Lytton (1802–75), who combined a successful political life with prolific authorship, showing in both careers the ability to assess what would be acceptable to the majority. After early attempts at the fashionable type of novel, tinged with regard for the philosophy of William Godwin, he found the source of his immediate and lasting success by turning to historical material with *The Last Days of Pompeii* (1834). We have seen how Carlyle and Macaulay in their different ways found a wide readership for historical writing. The same appetite was fed by fiction; Lytton carried on what Scott had begun, bringing to his craft a genuine feeling for the past and a gift for detail which may not always be faultless as fact but which wins conviction in the reading. His inferiority to Scott needs no argument, but it is inferiority in degree rather than in kind. He dealt with fourteenth-century Rome in *Rienzi* (1835), took a run at the supernatural element with *Night and Morning* (1841) and added the historical thrills of the Spanish Inquisition in *Zanoni* (1842). The following year saw a return to straight historical fiction with *The Last of the Barons*.

The vogue for crime in fiction did not defeat Lytton's versatility. *Eugene Aram* (1832) rises above the stock 'Newgate novel' in its penetration of the criminal mind. For *Lucretia* (1846) he took the more recent doings of Wainwright, the forger and murderer. He went back to the historical novel with *Harold* (1848), set in late Anglo-Saxon England. By this time, however, the demand for quieter fiction in a familiar domestic setting was gaining strength. Its greater results must be deferred to another chapter; Lytton, never disobliging to his public, met it with *The Caxtons,* first published anonymously as a serial in *Blackwood's* (1848–9). It owes something to Sterne, particularly in its early episodes, but the hero – with the improbable name of Pisistratus – is a child of his own time. The spirit of the minor early-Victorian novel is epitomized in his return from success in Australia, rich and full of pious reflections. Pisistratus reappears as the imaginary author of *My Novel* (1850–3), in which the cult of domesticity is even more marked, and the virtues of the upper stratum are defended against radical criticisms. After another 'Pisistratus' novel of the same type, *What Will He Do with It?* (1857–9), Lytton proved himself to be still in touch with popular taste by writing a novel in which horrific sensation is based on the new realism rather than the old supernaturalism – *A Strange Story* (1861–2). After a pause for political activities he came back to write a weird vision of the future in *The Coming Race* (1871).

Lytton spans the course of the English novel from the Romantics to anticipation of H. G. Wells. He took his themes from current fashions, and helped in shaping those fashions too. He achieved greatness in no type but competence in all. He helped to raise the crime novel from the lowest rank of sensationalism to something which could appeal to the more discerning reader, even though he was often blamed for exciting unhealthy interest in the criminal. There is a Byronic element to his youthful enthusiasm in admiration for the grand villain, and in revolt based on personal protest rather than on plans for definite reform.

Romantic certainly: but true Victorian in the serious mind that always lay behind the mask of fiction. Lytton loved good sales, but he was willing to court unpopularity by referring openly to the growing problem of prostitution and laying blame on the limited social view of current morality.[1] He fought

[1] *England and the English* (1833), edition of 1874, pp. 190ff.

for the freedom of the writer to express things as he sees them, not to be forced to suppress subjects distasteful to the majority of readers. 'It is the treatment that ennobles, not the subject.'[1] He took the novel seriously and planned it with care, even in his earlier work; the preface to *The Last of the Barons* has a strikingly Jamesian analogy between the novelist's and the painter's art. Lytton seems always striving towards something a little better than he achieved, to be on the verge of writing a really fine novel. Perhaps if he had developed along one line he would have succeeded better in the verdict of posterity. As it is, his care in construction is sometimes too obvious, his style lacking in force, his eye for the changing fashion a little too acute.

Lytton and Harrison Ainsworth (1805–82) are linked by the irony that their historical novels have come to be regarded as good reading for children. Ainsworth mingled the sensational with the historical even more liberally than Lytton did, though his personality would seem to have fitted him even more for the 'Silver Fork' school. He gained success early and was already known as a fashionable and well-dressed young man when he began to attract the type of reader who looked to history for escape rather than enlightenment. He was at one time regarded as a serious rival to Scott; like Lytton, he made the best of the market by cramming history, melodrama, romance and crime between the same covers. The secret of his greatest success was discovered when he had been writing for some years; he may well have derived it from Victor Hugo but he turned it to good account in his own way.

It was the use of an ancient building as his centre of unity around which the complex story could revolve. He developed it first with *The Tower of London* (1840), where the structural setting was so reassuringly familiar to his readers. To read of places still extant, places that could be visited on family excursions, gave satisfying reality to the past and a veneer of safe respectability to its shadier aspects. The trick worked again and again – with *Old St Paul's* (1841), *Windsor Castle* (1842–3) and *Saint James's* (1844). Not only did he write about familiar places; he also shared the attitude of most of his readers to the ancient feuds and controversies. He stood as acceptably for the

[1] 'A Word to the Public', appended to the 1853 edition of *Lucretia*.

Protestant succession and the development of Parliamentary democracy as did Macaulay himself. Despite his errors in points of detail and his rough though admittedly lively style, Ainsworth commanded success and is still not quite forgotten.

The popular taste for history gave success, though less deserving, to G. P. R. James (1801–60). He was the most smoothly professional of the school, turning out two or three books a year over a long period and following the routine of a set number of hours and pages each day like Trollope after him. He had indeed a genuine historical sense and William iv made him historiographer-royal although the settings of his novels were more often foreign than British. Today his work seems coldly pretentious, lacking both in characterization and in humour, indulging in coincidences more wildly improbable even than those of Lytton and Ainsworth. Yet his popularity in his own day illustrates, more aptly than the work of better novelists, what the new type of reader was asking for and enjoying. James offered escape into distant times and exotic scenes where the pressures of the present could be forgotten in long and involved plots that were unravelled at last without demands on the intellect. He took advantage, as did Lytton, of the taste for high life and the taste for low life, notably in exploiting the Robin Hood type who is a perennial favourite in English fiction. He was not undone by the great advances in the novel but was still popular enough in 1847 for Thackeray to attack him with the wickedly shrewd parody *Barbazure*.

Some novelists romanticized the criminal world; others were moving in the direction of the newer realism while meeting the popular demand for sensation and violence. The union of the startling and horrific with social criticism made a best-seller out of G. W. M. Reynolds (1814–79), a Chartist and for a time the editor of a radical paper, who took full advantage of the new trend. His satires came out in penny parts, bought by those who could not afford the more expensive monthly parts of better writers. After Gothicism had almost disappeared from the English novel, it continued to thrill the unsophisticated in such effusions as *Wagner the Wehr-Wolf* (1857). Reynolds knew exactly how far to go in mild eroticism flavoured with sadism, and he trod the delicate line in *Mysteries of London* (1845–6), which was inspired (if that is the right word) by Eugène Sue's *Mystères de Paris*. He added to the familiar mixture attacks on the rich and the clergy, making social protest by those who just kept abreast of respectability more genuine in his lurid pages than it was in many better books.

At the same time there were novelists who used themes less distinctive of their age and derived from an earlier tradition. Frederick Marryat (1792–1848) had a successful naval career before his criticisms of the service made it necessary to seek another source of income. His novels fulfilled the demand for excitement and escapism, in the form of stories of the sea which are always dear to the British reader. He is of his age in his ability to sustain interest in an exciting, though often loose plot and in his frequent introduction of a conventionally sentimental love story. Yet he looks to both past and future in his best work, done in a very few years from *Peter Simple* (1832–3) to *Snarley-Yow* (1836–7). He looks to the social-problem novel of the next decade in his sympathy for the ordinary seaman. It is, however, a sympathy quite opposed to the egalitarian and levelling spirit, as indeed was the sympathy of most of the novelists who followed him. He has some hearty though rather heavy-handed fun with egalitarian theories in *Masterman Ready* (1841–2); Marryat's satire is not his strong point and compares badly with his exercise of more robust humour.

There is nothing Victorian, however, about the freedom with which he can describe coarser episodes and make fun of genteel evasions. It is a freedom that flourished in the Regency years when he was young and did not last very long into Victoria's reign. Peter Simple's encounter with the West Indian girl who was affronted by being invited to eat some 'breast' of turkey and insisted on calling it 'bosom'[1] was still amusing to readers in the thirties; a few years later sympathy would have been with the delicate maiden and Peter would have appeared a very coarse young man.

It is easy to see in Marryat the tradition of Smollett, who also knew seafaring life at first hand. The familiar ingredients are there – the episodic plot, the strong incidents, the lively, rough humour – as they appear again in the more sophisticated art of Dickens. There is another tradition as well, the cult of the odd,

[1] *Peter Simple*, Ch. 31.

eccentric character in which Sterne was the master. Marryat was to be outdone by Dickens in this as well, but none of his immediate contemporaries comes so near the greater novelist. After the first rush of success Marryat's writing flagged, to revive only when he set out to produce stories specifically for boys. He did not keep pace with the changing style of the adult novel; but in his best days he could arouse the kind of interest that made an American ship signal to a British one in mid-ocean to ask about the latest serial part of *Japhet in Search of a Father* (1836).[1]

R. S. Surtees (1803–64) satisfied the interest in sport which was spreading to a wider range of the population, an interest that did not need to be sustained by gambling or cruelty. His intimate knowledge of the countryside and his sharp eye for detail set him in tune with the realism in fiction. These qualities appear in *Jorrocks' Jaunts and Jollities* (1831–4), together with shrewd social observation of the commercial vulgarity that was beginning to raid sections of life hitherto reserved to privilege. The cockney huntsman is dissected without mercy, yet with the good-humoured tolerance that the Regency had extended to eccentricity and the Victorians were to lose. The change of temper becomes apparent in *Mr Sponge's Sporting Tour* (1849–50) where the sense of social hierarchy is stronger and 'specious, promiscuous acquaintance' is frowned upon. By the middle of the century, the landed class was on the defensive and the need to preserve moral influences had become a prevailing theme of fiction. Fortunately for the modern reader, Surtees could not suppress the exuberance which gives a pleasant lightness to the misdeeds of his principal character.

Amid all the guffaws and comic tumbles, Surtees reveals more than many more serious writers about the changing state of English society. It was a time when social divisions were still considered important but were becoming less easy to define. A man might rise from poverty to riches in the rush of industrial competition, and all doors would open to him as surely as they would shut if he were ruined. Yet the aristocracy and their admirers were still contemptuous of the money acquired through 'trade' even though they were forced increasingly to acknowledge its power. Thus Jorrocks, in the

[1] Lionel Stevenson, *The English Novel* (London, 1960), p. 231.

flush of self-confident snobbery, backs his opinion of a fellow-traveller at an inn:

'I'll lay you a hat, a guinea one . . . that he's a man of dibs and doesn't follow no trade or calling, and if that isn't a gentleman, I don't know what is.'[1]

Alas, poor Jorrocks! The 'gentleman' turns out to keep a commercial hotel in Liverpool. The point is that the mistake could so easily be made. Previous generations had known and portrayed the upstart in society, but he was generally easily identifiable and open to satire. The quiet-spoken, knowledgeable man of business was a new phenomenon, one who stood for much that was to be distinctive of the new age.

Diverse though they were in style and talents, the novelists who were already established at the beginning of the Victorian era were reaching towards a firmer purpose and a finer achievement. Inferior in many ways to the best of their predecessors, they were yet developing a more conscious understanding of the novel as a literary form and were opening new aspects of life as its subjects. Literary society already had lost the closeness of Johnson's time but it was still coherent enough for novelists to know each other, to meet and talk about their art. When Bentley the publisher gave a dinner-party in 1836 he included Ainsworth, Marryat, Moore, Lever, Barham and Dickens among his guests.[2] It was a fair sample of popular literature at the time; no one foresaw how far one of the party was to surpass the rest.

[1] 'A Week at Cheltenham', in *Jorrocks' Jaunts and Jollities*.
[2] Una Pope-Hennessy, *Charles Dickens* (London, 1945), p. 82.

7

Dickens

No Victorian writer has equalled Charles Dickens in holding popularity as well as critical esteem. The names and features of his characters are part of our cultural ambience; we hesitate whether to use a capital letter for *wellerism* or *pecksniffian* and never think of using one for *gamp*. The absorption of literary fancy into social communication began early, and *Punch* was basing political cartoons on his novels while they were still appearing in monthly parts.[1] When Dickens made his last visit to America in 1867, he was depicted in another magazine being seen off by John Bull surrounded by characters from Pickwick onwards – characters familiar enough to be recognized from a simple drawing.[2] His own age loved him as an entertainer, while acknowledging his attack on social problems; the next generation hailed him as a pioneer of reform; more recent criticism has analysed his creative genius and probed the depths of his symbolism.

Dickens was born in 1812 at Portsea, where his father was a government clerk. His first years were unsettled, with moves to and from London, until poverty culminated in his father's imprisonment for debt. At the age of twelve, Charles was cut off from the meagre schooling which he had so far received and was sent out to work. He lived alone in lodgings while his mother and the younger children moved in to join his father in the Marshalsea prison according to the custom during confinement for civil debt. It was not long before a legacy solved the family's immediate problem, but the misery of those few months of separation and rejection haunted him ever after. His novels have many examples of hard parents, step-parents and other

---

[1] For example, *Martin Chuzzlewit*, Vol. 7, p. 48; *Dombey and Son*, Vol. 13, p. 75; *David Copperfield*, Vol. 18, p. 135.
[2] John Proctor in *Judy*, 13 November 1867.

tyrants over the helpless young. For the time being, however, he had to remain silent. He taught himself shorthand and worked as a reporter in the law courts, tried without success to be an actor and worked for a newspaper reporting debates in the House of Commons.

Meanwhile he wandered and explored, until the London of his adolescence and early manhood grew deeply into his awareness and remained part of him for ever. Most of the novels pass all, or most, of their action in London; the characters who wander off on their travels return there in triumph or weary defeat. Almost every area has its associations with Dickens, from the eastern docks through the city and out into what were then the villages of Hammersmith and Twickenham. He knew London as few men can have known it even in the days before it grew to the modern giant, following its streets and alleys on foot as anyone must who aspires to understand the congeries of small communities that lives under the single name. It remained for him the city where stage-coaches began and ended their journeys to distant parts. Even towards the end of his life there was a tendency for his love of London to overrule his intellectual acceptance of the changes which had taken place. Other towns remained provincial, slightly inferior by the very fact of their apartness from the capital; he has few developed studies of industrial workers and none of agricultural labourers.

The first fruits of his effort to become a creative writer were some short stories and descriptive pieces which appeared pseudonymously in 1836 as *Sketches by Boz*. They showed humour, acute observation, and a gift for recording odd characters; they attracted some attention, even the august *Edinburgh* deigning to prophesy – correctly for once – that:

> If he will endeavour to supply whatever may be affected by care and study – avoid imitation of other writers – keep nature steadily before his eyes – and check all dispositions to exaggerate – we know no writer who seems likely to attain higher success in that rich and useful department of fiction which is founded on faithful representations of human character, as exemplified in the aspects of English life.[1]

In the same year, the publishers Chapman and Hall were

[1] *Edinburgh Review*, October 1838.

looking for someone to write a brief narrative for a series of plates by the popular artist Robert Seymour, illustrating the doings of the 'Nimrod Club', a Surtees-type group of townsmen trying their skill at country sports and meeting with various comic mishaps. Full of assurance, Dickens took on the assignment and insisted on widening the idea to include other aspects of contemporary life: it was on this basis that the first monthly number of *The Posthumous Papers of the Pickwick Club* appeared. Seymour committed suicide after two numbers, and the publishers engaged in his place an unknown youngster called Hablot Knight Brown, who as 'Phiz' was to illustrate many of Dickens's novels.

With this new collaborator Dickens was able to develop his narrative from long captions to full episodes. At first, however, the series went slowly; there was no great demand for what seemed to be just another display of stock incidents and characters. Then the irruption of Sam Weller in the fourth number brought a wider readership and eventually the monthly sales rose to forty thousand copies. The partnership of Pickwick and Weller, an early-Victorian descendant from the comic-pathetic lineage of Don Quixote and Sancho Panza, had revealed a new master of fiction.

Dickens was being discussed as a successor to Scott, but he did not confine himself to the novel. He wrote a little for the theatre, and he took on the editorship of a new popular magazine, *Bentley's Miscellany,* in which *Oliver Twist* began to appear serially in 1837. He seemed now to have joined the 'Newgate novelists', though his attitude to the criminal held little glamour. Nevertheless, Thackeray thought poorly of his treatment of the underworld and was not prepared to allow him more veracity than Ainsworth,[1] and the *Quarterly* chided him for 'a series of representations which must familiarize the rising generation with the haunts, deeds, language, and characters of the very dregs of the community'.[2]

The modern reader is more inclined to regard the tale as too highly moral, almost glib in its assignments of reward for virtue and punishment for vice, distasteful in such scenes as the confrontation of Oliver and Fagin in the condemned cell under

[1] *Catherine,* 'Another Last Chapter'.
[2] *Quarterly Review,* June 1839.

the tutelage of the supposedly philanthropic Mr Brownlow.[1] Yet it increased Dickens's reputation, not merely by transient sensationalism. Here was clearly a writer with something to say to society, arousing its compassion, indicting general cruelty and indifference through the exposure of specific abuses.

Nicholas Nickleby (1839) again champions the innocent against whom selfish interests are arrayed. Most people think first, when this book is named, of the attack on the 'Yorkshire Schools' where unwanted children were dumped by parents or guardians who stopped short of the moral offence and legal risk of direct murder. In fact Squeers and Dotheboys Hall occupy a comparatively small place. Nicholas is a natural victim, as much as Smike whom he rescues, and the plot reveals that they both owe their tribulations to the same man. Smike dies, but Nicholas survives to prove that virtue can make its way in a wicked world. His sister Kate passes unscathed through the perils threatening a young woman trying to earn her living in a society that still had little time for the middle-class woman outside her own family circle. Her situation in the Wititterly household foreshadows the intenser passions yet to simmer under subordination in Charlotte Brontë and later to burst into revolt in Olive Schreiner. Dickens, to whom the lot of the unattached woman was inevitably a matter for objective sympathy only, shows not so much the bitterness of the spirit as the practical drawbacks of dependence:

> Still worse and more trying was the necessity of rendering herself agreeable to Mrs Wititterly, who, being in low spirits after the fatigue of the preceding night, of course expected her companion (else wherefore had she board and salary?) to be in the best spirits possible.

Having expressed this much understanding, Dickens then embarks on a parody of the 'silver fork' novel. *The Lady Flabella* from which Kate is required to read aloud hits off the style admirably and is reminiscent of Disraeli's earlier and less happy effusions:

> 'At this instant, while the Lady Flabella yet inhaled that delicious

[1] As Steven Marcus reminds us, such a scene would not have seemed out of place to readers who accepted the gruesome treatment of children in *The Fairchild Family – Dickens from Pickwick to Dombey* (New York, 1965), p. 69.

fragrance by holding the *mouchoir* to her exquisite, but thoughtfully-chiselled nose, the door of the *boudoir* (artfully concealed by rich hangings of silken damask, the hue of Italy's firmament) was thrown open, and with noiseless tread two valets-de-chambre, clad in sumptuous liveries of peach-blossom and gold, advanced into the room followed by a page in *bas de soie* – silk stockings – who, while they remained at some distance making the most graceful obeisances, advanced to the feet of his lovely mistress, and dropping on one knee presented, on a golden salver gorgeously chased, a scented *billet.*'[1]

The Old Curiosity Shop followed in 1840 with a more sombre and minatory tone appropriate to the alarms of the coming decade. The wanderings of Nell and her grandfather cover a greater geographical and social range than Dickens had hitherto attempted, and the grosser sentimentality only thinly covers a deeper menace. The dread of violence from a mob driven by desperation and led by demagogues appears more strongly in *Barnaby Rudge* (1841) where the Gordon Riots of the eighteenth century barely disguise fears of militant trade unions and 'physical force' Chartists.

The eponymous hero of *Martin Chuzzlewit* (1844) is the innocent at large once again but with a less pleasing personal character. He shares in the selfishness which motivates others of the leading characters and his reclamation owes much to the optimistic and selfless example of the untutored Mark Tapley. It is a version of the old moral tales of degeneration after a misspent youth, but the great sin here is not physical dissipation: it is the persistent selfishness of Pecksniff the hypocrite which leads to his ruin and disgrace when truth overtakes him. The book had a slow start in the sales of monthly parts until the departure of Martin for America, which the author himself had recently visited, gave the necessary boost.

Dombey and Son (1848) shows Dickens's growing ability to hold a consistent central theme and take a look at the whole basis of a society in which the more blatant wrongs were being gradually righted. Its story of the outward strength and inward weakness of a rich man foreshadows the preoccupation with financial power that characterizes his later work. Next, however, he had to purge some of his personal bitterness in writing

[1] *Nicholas Nickleby*, Ch. 28.

David Copperfield (1849) which, in autobiographical form, retraces some of his own early struggle and his rise to fame. Years later he wrote to Forster, 'I read *David Copperfield* again the other day and was affected by it to a degree you would hardly believe'.[1]

The later novels are stronger and more confident in plot, richer in symbolism and more artistically planned. Dickens turns his anger less against such specific issues as the Poor Law and more against the total acquiescence in a society that is basically corrupt. The vein of comedy is still beating strongly, but it is more controlled and less exuberant. Society stands indicted over its whole range and not merely in the person of particular villains. A sustained denunciation of administrative neglect and muddle is woven into the melodramatic plot of *Bleak House* (1853). Issues of trade unionism are examined in the short novel *Hard Times* (1854) to which we shall return. *Little Dorrit* (1857) revisits with maturer eyes the scene of his father's imprisonment in the Marshalsea, but the prisoners are no longer all inside the walls. Mr Pickwick had suffered temporarily in the Fleet but emerged as a free man; now the rich are slaves of the same system as the bankrupt. Dorrit becomes rich but is still imprisoned in his own weakness; Arthur Clennam becomes a prisoner where once he had been an envied visitor; the rich and feared Merdle is ruined and escapes only into self-inflicted death.

Next came a second excursion into the previous century with *A Tale of Two Cities* (1859), back to the French Revolution which was still a symbol of hope or warning for the mid-Victorian world. Where Carlyle had rejoiced, Dickens saw mainly the recurring fear of violence and anarchy. He returned to the theme of tainted money in *Great Expectations* (1861). Pip, who discovers that the wealth which has brought about deterioration in his character comes from a convicted felon, carries some of the anxiety and guilt which his creator had not fully purged in *David Copperfield*. Further, he shows that the values of society are false when they rest on the show of prosperity and fail to judge the man for himself. The theme becomes obsessional in *Our Mutual Friend* (1865) in the person of Boffin the newly-rich refuse collector, clinging to his fortune

[1] John Forster, *Life of Dickens*, edited by J. W. T. Ley (London, 1948), p. 49.

founded on 'dust-heaps' in a society that is as foully based. *Edwin Drood*, left unfinished when Dickens died in 1870, is in the fashion of the new type of crime-novel, the detection of mystery rather than the feeding of sensationalist appetite.

Although he thus became increasingly critical of his age, Dickens was no rebel outsider who had to wait for recognition until after his death. To consider how he won and held contemporary esteem may be to learn more about those for whom he wrote. He approached them as an actor comes before an audience; and he did this for a public that longed to be entertained but lacked the outlet of a flourishing and meaningful drama. He himself loved the theatre, poor enough though most of it was during his lifetime. His frustrated early efforts to go on the stage found some later satisfaction in amateur productions and in the dramatic readings from his own work which took him on tour in England and America, ruined his health and helped to kill him. He maintained a long friendship with Macready, for whom he once wrote a prologue 'to get the curtain up with a dash'.[1] Some of his novels were adapted, legally or illegally, for the theatre. Henry Crabb Robinson saw a version of *Martin Chuzzlewit* in the very year of its appearance in volume form; he was not impressed:

> I went to the Lyceum where I had lost an evening by the sitting out a miserable drama founded on Dicken's *Chuzzlewit*, and a poor parody of Aladdin. In the first Keeley as Mrs Gamp was however delightful and Mrs Keeley very good as the boy Bailey – but nothing else during the whole evening to compensate.[2]

Dickens's histrionic tendencies yield both good things and bad: our quick acceptance of his characters as well as some very stilted set-pieces:

> 'Wretch!' rejoined Nicholas fiercely, 'Touch him at your peril! I will not stand by and see it done; my blood is up, and I have the strength of ten men such as you. Look to yourself, for by Heaven I will not spare you if you drive me on!'[3]

Vincent Crummles himself, in the same book, could not have

---

[1] Una Pope-Hennessy, *Charles Dickens* (London, 1945), p. 194.
[2] *The London Theatre 1811–1866: Selections from the Diary of Henry Crabb Robinson*, edited by Eluned Brown (London, 1966), p. 173.
[3] *Nicholas Nickleby*, Ch. 13.

produced more sensational heroism than this. It is melodrama, but melodrama which is successful in its almost Brechtian purpose of forcing the audience (or readers) to take sides, to share in a moral judgement arising from a specific situation.

Dickens was a man of his time, neither fighting against its conventions nor being mastered by them. He made the best use of what came to his hand, as did Shakespeare with the Elizabethan theatre; and was likewise sometimes constricted by it but more often transcended it. He knew what the growing novel-reading public wanted because he was involved in its world and had shared many of its experiences. He felt both the fascination and the complexity of the changing contemporary scene, striving to understand and not always succeeding. He was not highly educated in the formal sense; he had learned much through observation and reading, by many boyhood hours with the eighteenth-century novelists whose work was appearing in new cheap editions. He had learned how to indulge the popular taste for the picaresque, the sensational and the occasionally sordid. He recalls his own early reading, with pride tinged by a certain apologetic concession to the censorious morality of a later decade, through his fictional other self:

> From that blessed little room, Roderick Random, Peregrine Pickle, Humphrey Clinker, Tom Jones, the Vicar of Wakefield, Don Quixote, Gil Blas, and Robinson Crusoe, came out, a glorious host, to keep me company. They kept alive my fancy, and my hope of something beyond that place and time, – they, and the Arabian Nights, and the Tales of the Genii, – and they did me no harm; for whatever harm there was in some of them was not there for me: *I* knew nothing of it . . . I have been Tom Jones (a child's Tom Jones, a harmless creature) for a week together.[1]

He competed and triumphed in the struggle for the new and expanding readership. As a largely self-taught man with a serious purpose, he could find favour in the days of the Society for the Diffusion of Useful Knowledge. As one who knew the seamy side of London life, he could offer something to the addicts of crudely sensational fiction, without losing the middle-class reader by excess. The hardest task indeed was to woo the large section of this class that was still uneasy about the moral right-

---

[1] *David Copperfield*, Ch. 4.

ness of the novel but was at the same time very willing to be entertained. It was his own generation that accepted him most readily and remained most loyal. There is the ring of truth in *Cranford* where the younger people acclaim the new work of 'Boz' while the older Miss Jenkyns tries to refute them by a stately reading from *Rasselas*. Captain Brown, the chief supporter of the new novelist, is later killed by a train a moment after being 'deeply engaged in the perusal of a number of *Pickwick* which he had just received': a confrontation of the worlds of the stage-coach and the railway which is perhaps more symbolically effective than Mrs Gaskell herself realized.[1]

A public whose taste for fiction was but little developed, and whose acceptance of the novel as a work of art in its own right was still grudging, needed to be humoured and given an occasional shock. The extravagance and sensationalism in some of Dickens's early work had the effect of bringing him attention. It was an impact comparable to that of the Salvation Army later in the century. Booth demanded why the devil should have all the best tunes, and Dickens did not see why Egan and Reynolds and the anonymous hack writers should monopolize the most profitable element of the new fiction. He was willing to give sensation and sentimentality; he was child enough of his own times to feel as deeply as those whom he moved to tears – and they were not the most stupid or the most neurotic. Certainly not all his contemporaries shared the lachrymose tendencies which won him the nickname of 'Mr Popular Sentiment' from Trollope[2] and moved R. H. Hutton to write of his 'unctuous sentiment'.[3] He could, however, speak to an age that was uncertain of its verities and welcomed the reassurance of a situation to which the emotional response was familiar, ready-made and unequivocal.

He pleased the conventionally pious, and he pleased those who were feeling intellectual doubts about faith but feared perhaps to pursue them to the depths of their own commitment. He depicted plenty of bad and inadequate clergymen, but not too precisely. Everyone must deplore the abuse of true religion

---

[1] *Cranford* (1853), Ch. 1 and Ch. 2. It is perhaps fair to add that the novel was appearing in *Household Words,* of which Dickens was editor.

[2] *The Warden* (1855), Ch. 15.

[3] R. H. Hutton in *The Spectator,* 2 April 1862.

and understand that Stiggins and Chadband belong to one of the other sects – one of those in error. Dickens shows little enthusiasm for the neo-Calvinist faith of the Evangelicals, particularly for the type which stressed personal conviction of salvation to the neglect of active charity. Deeper contempt than had lashed Bumble and Creakle is poured on Mrs Jellyby who neglects her family to write appeals for the natives of Borrioboola-Gha and Mrs Pardiggle on her visit to the brickmaker. The latter episode opens the frightening gulf of non-communication between the reality of suffering and those who thought that they could cross it with words. Here Dickens is at the height of his artistic power; we hear only the brickmaker's speech, and through it the echo of Mrs Pardiggle's pious clichés dropping like pebbles into an abyss:

'Now you're a going to poll-pry and question according to custom I know what you're a going to be up to. Well! You haven't got no occasion to be up to it. I'll save you the trouble. Is may daughter a washin? Yes, she *is* a washin. Look at the water. Smell it! That's wot we drinks. How do you like it, and what do you think of gin, instead! An't my place dirty? Yes, it is dirty – it's nat'rally dirty, and it's nat'rally onwholesome; and we've had five dirty and onwholesome children, as is all dead infants, and so much the better for them, and for us besides. Have I read the little book wot you left? No, I an't read the little book wot you left. There an 't nobody here as knows how to read it; and if there wos, it wouldn't be suitable to me. It's a book fit for a babby, and I'm not a babby. If you was to leave me a doll, I shouldn't nuss it. How have I been conducting of myself? Why, I've been drunk for three days; and I'd a been drunk four, if I'd a had the money. Don't I never mean for to go to church? No, I don't never mean for to go to church. I shouldn't be expected there, if I did; the beadle's too genteel for me. And how did my wife get that black eye? Why, I giv' it her; and if she says I didn't, she's a Lie!'[1]

Even the most extreme Evangelicals could hardly turn up texts to disprove Dickens's contention that true religion is marked by active love and kindness. As for the doubters and agnostics, his religion was vague enough in its dogmas – or lack of them – to give satisfaction. The break with orthodox faith in the nineteenth century seldom meant a loss of moral earnest-

[1] *Bleak House*, Ch. 8.

ness; the outlook, the language, even the imagery of agnostics often remained basically Christian. Like many Englishmen during the last four hundred years, Dickens could express a Protestant viewpoint without getting too deeply involved in the finer details of Christianity. The Protestant interpretation dominates his *Child's History of England* (1853), though in *Barnaby Rudge* his dread of mob-violence and his respect for individual freedom edged his sympathies towards the Roman Catholics.

Although he provided a generous allowance of thrills, sensation and criticism, he knew how far the majority of his readers would allow him to go. Like the rest of the early-Victorian novelists, he was prevented from writing freely about sex – prevented not only by the private censorship of the circulating libraries but also by his own tensions. The criminal world of *Oliver Twist* contains every kind of violence and brutality, but only a veiled sexual element. Nancy is pitifully faithful to Sikes and contrasts herself with the untainted Rose Maylie in a flood of tearful penitence. Dickens chafed under this constraint but accepted it, as appears in his rather querulous defence:

It is, it seems, a very coarse and shocking circumstance that some of the characters in these pages are chosen from the most criminal and degraded of London's population; that Sikes is a thief, and Fagin a receiver of stolen goods; that the boys are pickpockets and the girl is a prostitute.

I confess I have yet to learn that a lesson of the purest good may not be drawn from the vilest evil . . . I saw no reason when I wrote this book why the very dregs of life, so long as their speech did not offend the ear, should not serve the purpose of a moral, at least as well as its froth and cream.[1]

The acceptance was not complete, however; on the overt plot-level his novels obey the convention that sex could not in any circumstances be positively enjoyable and that its extra-marital indulgence must lead to disaster. Like other writers of the period, he had to cut some awkward corners and occasionally sacrifice psychological realism. The suppression took its revenge by breaking out under cover. On the level of related

[1] Preface to the third edition of 1841. By 1867 the pressure of euphemism was so much stronger that he omitted the words 'the girl is a prostitute'.

action, Steerforth ends his career of seduction drowned by the purifying sea and cast up on the beach from which he had plucked the innocent. Earlier in the same book there is ambivalence, to put it mildly, in the apparently domestic scene when David is discomfited in the presence of Steerforth and Rosa Dartle:

> While we were talking, he more than once called me Daisy; which brought Miss Dartle out again.
> 'But really, Mr Copperfield,' she asked, 'is it a nickname? And why does he give it you? Is it – eh? – because he thinks you are young and innocent? I am so stupid in these things.'
> I coloured in replying that I believed it was.
> 'Oh!' said Miss Dartle. 'Now I am glad to know that! I ask for information, and I am glad to know it. He thinks you young and innocent; and so you are his friend? Well, that's quite delightful!'[1]

There is an even more striking example of imagery in *Hard Times,* when Gradgrind is trying to persuade his daughter Louisa to marry the uncouth manufacturer Bounderby:

> 'Are you consulting the chimneys of the Coketown works, Louisa?'
> 'There seems to be nothing there but languid and monotonous smoke. Yet when the night comes, Fire bursts out, father!' she answered, turning quickly.
> 'Of course I know that, Louisa. I do not see the application of the remark.'
> To do him justice he did not, at all.[2]

To return to the Shelleyan fate of Steerforth: it would have seemed to many readers a judgement for offence not only against the morality of sex but also against that of class. A true Victorian in this, Dickens had no leaning towards a classless society, although the range of his sympathy grew in later years.[3] Most of his convincing characters are those of the class he knew in boyhood: the amorphous lower middle class and the poor who are not quite submerged in the towns. His aristocrats and his destitutes tend towards melodrama. The late novels show the rise from poverty to fortune, the fall from security to penury,

[1] *David Copperfield,* Ch. 20.
[2] *Hard Times,* Ch. 15.
[3] For instance, the marriage of Lizzie Hexam and Eugene Wrayburn in *Our Mutual Friend.* However, Lizzie can be regarded as 'low' only in her environment: her morals and manner of speech are unrealistically refined.

the wasting away of old estates – the problems both serious and comic of a capitalist society in transition. His anxiety about the situation was sometimes keener than his apprehension of it. Yet there is understanding and deep social comment in such a scene as the confrontation of Sir Leicester Dedlock and Rouncewell: the conservative aristocrat with wealth rooted in land meets the new power of industrial money in the iron-master, and they talk without real communication. It is, nevertheless, Rouncewell who represents the shifting of power and the triumphant return of the youth sent away in disgrace after 'constructing a model of a power-loom' to the remote and unheeded region of 'the iron country farther north'.[1]

Dickens was no great lover of the working people as a class. He could be severe about the rising trade unionism, as a tyranny little better than that of the employers. He truly hated oppression and injustice; and since it was the poor who suffered most from these things, he needed to become their champion. He could not share the Malthusian assumption that the lower classes ought to practise restraint and renunciation, accepting starvation of physical and emotional needs so that the national difficulties could be shrugged off. Micawber, feckless and unsystematic, cocks a snook at these principles and emerges triumphant. Gradgrind who approves of them is yet the father of five children, one of them named 'Malthus' and another 'Adam Smith'. Although Dickens found little good to report of his first visit to America, he was impressed by the self-respect and cultivated interests of the factory girls in Lowell. He describes their appearance, their thrift and their recreations and then turns on his British readers whose notions he is assaulting. In an indictment of the desire to keep the workers ignorant and degraded as well as poor:

> The large class of readers, startled by these facts, will exclaim with one voice, 'How very preposterous!' On my deferentially inquiring why, they will answer, 'These things are above their station.' In reply to that objection, I would beg to ask what their station is.
>
> It is their station to work. And they *do* work. They labour in these mills, upon an average, twelve hours a day, which is unquestionably work, and pretty tight work too. Perhaps it is above their station to

[1] *Bleak House*, Ch. 7.

indulge in such amusements, on any terms. Are we quite sure that we in England have not formed our ideas of the 'station' of working people, from accustoming ourselves to the contemplation of that class as they are, and not as they might be? I think that if we examine our own feelings, we shall find that the pianos, and the circulating libraries, and even the Lowell Offering, startle us by their novelty, and not by their bearing upon any abstract question of right or wrong ... I know no station which has a right to monopolize the means of mutual instruction, improvement and rational entertainment; or which has ever continued to be a station very long, after seeking to do so.[1]

All this may not seem today to be strikingly radical; the desire to elevate those in a certain 'station' does not go with any suggestion of abolishing those divisions which the concept implies. 'Station' seems to be a principle as unquestioned as 'degree' was in the sixteenth century. Yet the argument was not one calculated to increase a writer's popularity when it was first uttered; and despite his eye to the market, Dickens never feared to tell his readers where they were going wrong. Can he fairly be described as a social reformer? Like most of the great Victorian writers, he was willing to express himself freely about current topics whether or not he had any deep knowledge of them. It was a time when reform was in men's minds and on their lips, an ideal now made attainable through legislation.

Both in fiction and in journalism Dickens attacked a variety of abuses which were beginning to trouble the social conscience. He spread existing knowledge rather than revealing things hitherto unrevealed, and he left some areas almost untouched. For instance, he never followed the advice of a reviewer of *Oliver Twist* to turn his attention to the plight of children in factories.[2] David Copperfield among the blacking-bottles is not a typical working-class boy but one who, like his creator, had seen and accepted better times.

Yet to say that reform was a current topic and a part of the natural ambience for the new fiction does not explain away Dickens or suggest that his compassion was purely intellectual. He distrusted organized systems to bring about reform and had little faith in the sequence of inquiry, commission, debate and

---

[1] *American Notes* (1842), Ch. 4.
[2] *Fraser's Magazine*, October 1838.

legislation. His great achievement was not to be a pioneer in an age of indifference but to prevent the newly-awakened conscience from falling back into a complacent belief that all was now well. His sympathy told him that new wrongs could replace old wrongs. Whether the workhouse in *Oliver Twist* is conceived as under the old or the new Poor Law is less important than the fact that paupers were still being treated as less than human.

As a reporter in the House of Commons he must often have heard speeches from the Philosophic Radicals. Utilitarian principles, even though now tending towards practical reform, were abhorrent to him. He hated the cataloguing and codifying of people and was harsh in portraying those like Dombey, Gradgrind and the Smallweeds who order their lives on Utilitarian lines. How deeply he understood the real philosophy of Bentham's followers is doubtful, and we learn little from the casual parody of one tenet in *Edwin Drood*.[1]

He did not wish to change the whole structure of society, by revolution or by legislation. He greatly admired Carlyle, to whom he dedicated *Hard Times* and whose *French Revolution* he hyperbolically claimed to have read 'for the 500th time'.[2] But he did not apply himself to examining and fostering what was good in Chartism as the Christian Socialists did. His nightmare glimpse of the raging industrial mob is part, but only part, of the truth. It records an impression of what was indeed happening in the north, but takes no account of the quiet men in a London coffee-house earnestly considering how best to obtain a constitutional redress of grievances.

Night-time in this dreadful spot! – night, when the smoke was changed to fire; when every chimney spirted up its flame; and places, that had been dark vaults all day, now shone red-hot, with figures moving to and fro within their blazing jaws, and calling to one another with hoarse cries – night, when the noise of every strange machine was aggravated by the darkness; when the people near them looked wilder and more savage; when bands of unemployed labourers paraded in the roads, or clustered by torchlight round their leaders, who told them in stern language of their wrongs,

[1] Drood's should be, in the words of Bentham, 'where he is the cause of the greatest danger to the smallest number' (Ch. 16).
[2] *Letters,* Vol. 2, p. 335.

and urged them on to frightful cries and threats; when maddened men, armed with sword and firebrand, spurning the tears and prayers of women who would restrain them, rushed forth on errands of terror and destruction, to work no ruin half so surely as their own.[1]

It is worth noting that, when he wrote *Bleak House* thirteen years later and after the collapse of Chartism, he was able to be amused about Sir Leicester Dedlock's vague image of Rouncewell as:

One of a body of some odd thousand conspirators, swarthy and grim, who were in the habit of turning out by torchlight, two or three nights in the week, for unlawful purposes.[2]

Dickens's first visit to America made him sceptical of democracy expressed in a more direct manner than in Britain and made him afraid that too much political equality was a quick road to barbarous manners. (It ought in fairness to be added that he does not seem to have made much effort to get a fuller understanding of the Americans and that the pirating of his works rankled.) In his own country he cared too much for individualism and the delights of eccentricity to entertain thoughts of socialism. He hated whatever tended towards bureaucratic rule, though he hated waste and inefficiency more. He shows, for instance, a great respect for the quiet efficiency of the new police like Inspector Bucket in *Bleak House* and the anonymous Inspector in *Our Mutual Friend*. The beadle who had loomed so large and ominous in his early work comes to be seen through the eyes of the new constable as 'an imbecile civilian, a remnant of the barbarous watchmen-times, that must be borne with until Government shall abolish him'.[3]

From this we might learn, if we had not known it before, that no man is wholly consistent. In his books Dickens fulminated against systems and pleaded for a general change of heart. Compassion, honesty, candour and cheerfulness are the virtues which he extols most highly and offers as remedies to a sick society. Those who possess them seem to show them physically, to be rotund and childlike in the manner of Pickwick, the

---

[1] *The Old Curiosity Shop*, Ch. 45. It is interesting to compare the image of the chimneys here with its use in *Hard Times* quoted above.
[2] *Bleak House*, Ch. 7.
[3] *Bleak House*, Ch. 11.

Cheerybles, Wilfer. The fulness of living needs the abandonment of dignified social restraint: the gaiety of a Fezziwig to
exorcize the Benthamite Marley's ghost. Yet in his own dealings
Dickens could be rigid and severe, could even insist on the
prosecution of a girl who used bad language in the street.[1]

Paradoxically again, he could support practical schemes for
improvement. He shared the contemporary faith in education
and gave help to the 'ragged schools' founded by Angela
Coutts. A chance meeting with Henry Layard brought him into
the campaign for administrative reform stimulated by mismanagement in the Crimea campaign. His acceptance of the
general current faith in progress glows all through his *Child's
History of England,* which inclines in spirit towards Macaulay
rather than his admired Carlyle.

His acquaintance with Layard – also an enthusiast for
Carlyle – helped to make him more aware of the problems
facing society as a whole, not merely the ills of certain unfortunate groups. It was with the growing sense of general disquiet
that he followed *Bleak House* with a much shorter novel that is
the only real *roman à thèse* he wrote. Few critics have given it
much approval, though it is outstandingly important to those
who would interpret Dickens in the context of his age. From a
purely literary view it is not negligible, but shows that advance
towards a more controlled central theme which characterizes
his later work.

He began writing it in January 1854, but though the main
story went well enough he found it difficult to capture the
authentic industrial scene. He knew little in depth of English
society outside London; now the needs of the new book, as well
as the growing pressures that lay behind it, made it essential
to learn more. In search of this knowledge he set off for Preston,
where five textile mills had stopped work after the weavers'
demand for better wages had been refused. The owners had
replied, as was common enough in the bitter diplomacy of
contemporary negotiations, with a lock-out of all men who
belonged to the union. Dickens spent only a few days there, but
he returned with many things clearer in his mind. While he
worked on *Hard Times,* he continued his efforts through popular
journalism to make people more aware of the running fight for

[1] 'The Ruffian', *All the Year Round,* 10 October 1868.

power. He reported factually as well as fictionally on his Preston visit; and he warned workers against the machination of demagogic union leaders even while sympathizing with their struggle.[1] At no other time perhaps did his current preoccupations run so closely with his imaginative world.

The story of *Hard Times* is uncomplicated, at least by Dickensian and mid-Victorian standards. There are two main themes, frequently interwoven. Thomas Gradgrind has brought up his children on the strictest Utilitarian lines, starving their imaginations until they revolt under the stresses and temptations of adult life. Louisa is pushed into marriage with Gradgrind's friend the millowner Bounderby, nearly runs away with a smooth young man from London and is saved only by the intervention of her faithful maid (supported by the contemporary morals of the circulating libraries). Tom gets a job in Bounderby's bank, robs it and escapes abroad. Bounderby is the link with the second theme: the story of his workman Stephen Blackpool who is afflicted with a drunken wife and an acute conscience. He is ostracized by the other workers for refusing to join the union and sacked by Bounderby for speaking out. He falls under suspicion of the bank robbery and is eventually retrieved from the bottom of a mine-shaft in time for a noble and articulate death.

In looking at the industrial scene, Dickens showed some understanding of both sides. The collapse of Chartism had brought more urgency and mounting bitterness in the efforts of the trade unions to become an effective bargaining force. As usual, his main sympathy lay with the less privileged; at Preston he had been favourably moved by the restraint and good sense of the workers as a whole, and appalled by the town in which they had to live. The 'Coketown' of the novel carries his depression, breaking out into the humour that he never could resist for long. The first description is typical of his style, beating home its effect by repetitive syntactic constructions and strong visual images:

It was a town of red brick, or of brick that would have been red if smoke and ashes had allowed; but as matters stood it was a town of unnatural red and black like the painted face of a savage.

[1] 'On Strike' and 'To Working Men', in *Household Words,* 11 February and 7 October 1854.

It was a town of machinery and tall chimneys, out of which
interminable serpents of smoke trailed themselves for ever and ever,
and never got uncoiled.

It had a black canal in it, and a river that ran purple with ill-
smelling dye, and vast piles of building full of windows where there
was a rattling and a trembling all day long and where the piston of
the steam-engine worked monotonously up and down, like the head
of an elephant in a state of melancholy madness.   (*ch. 5.*)

From his usual compassion, Dickens can condemn the sins of
Gradgrind and Bounderby; but the condemnation is not for
wealth, not for their failure to anticipate reforms which Parliament had not yet passed, but for their attitude to life as a profit-
and-loss transaction. They fall beneath the deep contempt that
he kept for those who worshipped theories to the exclusion of
people. Gradgrind acts from what passed at the time for
benevolence and sets up a 'model school', but it is one which
starves the imagination and in which the aptly-named master
Mr M'Choakumchild is exhorted to 'teach these boys and girls
nothing but facts'. Sissy Jupe, whose father trains and rides
horses in a circus, is in disgrace for being unable to 'define a
horse' according to the book. Yet it is she who later saves
Louisa, and her father who helps Tom to get away. Bitzer, the
star pupil who can define with accuracy, refuses to help because
he stands to gain more from Bounderby than from Gradgrind,
whose training-system is thus turned ironically against himself.
Stripped of self-deceit and ruined by what he has built, Gradgrind is a figure of tragic quality who begins to learn through
suffering.

His crony Bounderby, on the other hand, is more of a comic
than a tragic creation. He is not the monster of wickedness that
some critics have thought; any employer of his type at this
time would have sacked a workman who acted as Stephen does.
The injustice was general, not specific. Bounderby is comic –
and anticipates a strong later tendency in society – in his
inverted snobbery that makes him pretend to have been
abandoned by his parents and risen from the gutter by his own
efforts. He likes to claim that any industrious workman could
do as much for himself and he plays a continual game of mock-
humility with his genteel housekeeper, Mrs Sparsit. At the end,
his mother comes up from the country and reveals that he in

The Victorian Debate

fact had a good start in life. His discomfiture then is in the humour of the deflated Falstaff – the clown of *The Merry Wives of Windsor*, not the semi-tragic reprobate of *Henry IV*.

Bounderby is not singled out for condemnation above the other millowners, who refer to the workers contemptuously as 'hands' and bitterly resent the growing interference of the state with the rights of private capital:

> Surely there never was such fragile china-ware as that of which the millers of Coketown were made. Handle them never so lightly, and they fell to pieces with such ease that you might suspect them of having been flawed before. They were ruined, when they were required to send labouring children to school; they were ruined, when inspectors were appointed to look into their works; they were ruined, when such inspectors considered it doubtful whether they were quite justified in chopping people up with their machinery; they were utterly undone, when it was hinted that perhaps they need not always make quite so much smoke. (*Bk. 2, ch.* 1)

Yet despite his new respect for legislative reforms, Dickens remained distrustful of the tyranny of the organization over the individual. He saw this tyranny in the trade union movement, which seemed to him to be often using the workers' misery to further selfish interests for a few.

Bounderby and Gradgrind get off lightly compared with Slackbridge, the fiery orator who promises Utopia to the Coketown workers and who may well have been based on the Chartist leader Feargus O'Connor. It is Slackbridge who turns the workers against Stephen, overriding their natural decency and tolerance by his oratory:

> But O, my friends and brothers! Oh men and Englishmen, the down-trodden operators of Coketown! What shall we say of that man – that working-man, that I should find it necessary so to libel the glorious name – who, being practically and well acquainted with the grievances and wrongs of you, the injured pith and marrow of this land, and having heard you, with a noble and majestic un-animity that will make Tyrants tremble, resolve for to subscribe to the funds of the United Aggregate Tribunal and to abide by the injunctions issued by that body for your benefit, whatever they may be – what, I ask you, will you say of that working-man, since such I must acknowledge him to be, who at such a time, deserts his post, and sells his flag. (*Bk. 2, ch.* 4)

The grandiloquence, the clichés, the incitement to discover a scapegoat – these are familiar still and not confined to any party or group. The specific issue continues to be fought out, often tragically for the individual as it is for Stephen (the proto-martyr?) in the novel. Like others in Dickens's later work, he stands for more than his own story and is more comprehensible as a type than as an individual creation. Both the masters and the unionists have a stereotype of what a worker should be like, and Stephen is condemned for failing to conform. It is irony of the kind often true in life that Slackbridge sees Stephen as a traitor and Bounderby sees him as a troublemaker. Neither of them wants to see the real man, who shakes his head and says sorrowfully ''Tis a muddle, and that's aw'. Only Louisa, made perceptive by her own unhappiness, can see that 'By the prejudices of his own class and by the prejudices of the other, he is sacrificed alike'. In the total conception of the novel 'sacrificed' is more than a merely emotive word.

The depth of symbolism coupled with a more radical criticism of society increases in the novels from this time onwards. Without making any detailed structural rethinking on socialist lines, Dickens came to see that the sickness of society was not to be remedied by discrete changes alone. The world of the later novels is outwardly more civilized than the jungle which threatens the innocence of Oliver and Nell, but its reforms only mask a deeper corruption. Its prosperity is like Harmon's fortune in *Our Mutual Friend* made out of 'dust' – which meant the human refuse that was troubling the minds of Chadwick and his successors. Thus all society can be indicted for the death of Jo the crossing-sweeper:

Dead, your Majesty. Dead, my lords and gentlemen. Dead, Right Reverends and Wrong Reverends of every order. Dead, men and women, born with Heavenly compassion in your hearts. And dying thus around us, every day.[1]

As the accusing *Dead* strikes again and again, none is exempt, and Dickens reaches towards the more sweeping condemnation of society that comes in the decade after his own death. The later novels are farther from the world of *Pickwick* than they are

[1] *Bleak House*, Ch. 47.

from that of William Morris and Samuel Butler; though Dickens would probably not have felt much sympathy for their views and Butler dismissed his work as 'literary garbage'.[1]

From beginning to end of his literary career, however, the imagination of Dickens seldom flagged in its great power to create characters that spring to life and compel the reader's acceptance. They are not often people with whom we can find full identification and whose experience seems to grow along with our own. They are known by description, through features distorted to the point of caricature, which ensure recognition as they stumble in and out of the plot. Some of the best-loved – Sarah Gamp, Mrs Jarley, Captain Cuttle – could fit into almost any of the novels or be removed from their own without greatly affecting the story as a whole. They are accepted through a series of impressions, as acquaintances come to be accepted in life; we should know them in the street where we might pass by the profounder creations of George Eliot and Thomas Hardy. George Orwell was right when he said, 'Tolstoy's characters can cross a frontier, Dickens's can be portrayed on a cigarette card'.[2]

There is weakness as well as strength. Too many of the 'good' characters are flat necessities for a hero or heroine rather than inspiring incident out of their very conception. Dickens was best when describing the kind of individuality and oddity that moved him most. The peril of drawing eccentrics is that they may become self-isolating; some of them are most delightful in soliloquy on their pet obsessions. They protest thus against conformity and assert the right to such inconsistency in the world as can make Micawber ultimately prosperous and respected. Yet there is a disquieting undertone to the comic-dramatic melody. The self-isolating eccentric may be a pleasant source of fun or melodrama, but his particularity means the breakdown of communication between man and man. The monologues and oddities foreshadow the vacuum of non-communication in the modern novel and theatre. Self-

---

[1] Pontifex 'had devoured Stanley's Life of Arnold, Dickens's novels, and whatever other literary garbage of the day was most likely to do him harm'. *The Way of All Flesh*, Ch. 53.

[2] George Orwell, 'Charles Dickens', in *Inside the Whale* (London, 1940).

isolation becomes self-destruction, the disappearance of Krook through 'spontaneous combustion' or the slower death by fire of Miss Havisham. A strong individualist in an age of individualism, Dickens yet shows that full identity is found only in the acceptance of society with its opportunities to exercise kindness and love.

The comparative weakness of Dickens's women has often been noticed, and perhaps overstated. Certain predictable types occur but even these are relieved, curiously enough, by the limitations of their creator. Agnes Wickfield, Rose Maylie and Esther Summerson are not quite the stock Victorian product, because they are women seen as by an intelligent adolescent. There are beautiful flirts like Estella and Dolly Varden; cold, remote creatures with a frightening sexual attraction like Rosa Dartle, Miss Wade, Edith Dombey; imperious battleaxes with the comedy of Betsy Trotwood or the macabre of Miss Havisham; or riotously comic and sexless like Mrs Gamp. A partial resolution comes with *Little Dorrit* where a man finds consummation with the child-woman and the fragmented feminine image is made whole. Little Nell saves her innocence by death; the maturer Dickens looks more boldly at the problem of growing up.

Yet the obsession with threatened innocence never quite faded. Evil hems in Pickwick, Oliver Twist, Nicholas and Kate Nickleby, Pip – all obliged to enter into the great shelterless world where only Grace operating through kindly mortals can save them. From the misery of his own boyhood he was able to utter the insecurity and guilt of a society that was trying to deal with problems but was hampered by repression. His readers knew the feeling of being rootless, abandoned, bewildered, cut off from the safety of established tradition. He shared their emotional instability and turned the handicap into a treasury of imaginative experience. Those who were born in the same decade as himself were overtaken by external developments and could lament a lost past by middle life, praising the stage-coach and regarding the railway with mingled excitement and trepidation.

He had not the intellectual power of Arnold or Ruskin, Browning or George Eliot. Where he has no master is in the scenes of childhood, where the world is paradise or nightmare.

He draws his characters with the candour and exaggeration of a child, in a setting where anything is possible. To accept his vision is to assume the vision of a child enriched by adult sense-experience, to enter a world of Bosch or Breughel. It is a world where one may live in an upturned boat, where a megalosaurus may loom out of the fog; a world where animate and inanimate continually dissolve into one another, where Pancks is a steam-tug and Twemlow a table to be extended with leaves; a world where a steam-engine is a mad elephant and snow goes into mourning for the death of the sun.

Yet the vision, wondering and innocent as it seems, is consummate in art. Few English writers come near him in the ability to make the physical setting of the novel something more than a scenic backcloth, to draw it into the dimension of characterization. Emily Brontë did it, less trammelled by realism and the need to write popular sellers. Hardy at his best did it magnificently, and in our own time Graham Greene has sometimes succeeded. Dickens can give breadth to his story through the natural phenomena that open a book or recur in it: as the sea in *David Copperfield*, the fog in *Bleak House*, the river in *Our Mutual Friend*. Nature at her kindest can appear too, but she seldom dominates. Dickens's settings are strongest when nature brings a touch of horror to urban surroundings, a reminder that the walls which society builds around itself are not impenetrable.

This treatment grows from the theatrical and poetic elements in his art. He was not really a lover of the rising cult of realism, though he described the familiar world in detail. In comparison with Trollope, and much more with lesser contemporaries, he can be seen to make the slimmest concession to the popular demand. His spirit was a Romantic one in an age of prose and 'facts', saved only by abounding talent and vitality from the submergence for which he pities Gradgrind's children and M'Choakumchild's pupils. At the height of his popularity he was bold enough to make the point explicitly: 'I have purposely dwelt upon the romantic side of familiar things.'[1] For him the Pre-Raphaelite painters were too literalistic; he launched a savage, and it must be said stupid, attack on Millais for the realism of the carpenter's shop in *Christ in the House of His*

[1] Preface to the first edition of *Bleak House*.

Parents – 'the lowest depths of what is mean, odious, repulsive and revolting'.[1]

His vision can be Blakean in its intensity, then suddenly collapse in hoots of schoolboy laughter or floods of sentimental tears. He has, supremely, the Victorian novelist's gift of sustaining interest despite particular faults, carrying on the belief of the reader from moment to moment. He has the wild prodigality of an age that feared over-production yet seemed unable to check it. His talent is extravagant, incapable of leaving person, place or incident without pressing out its last ounce of effect. Hammer-blows beat us into acceptance; yet there remains the sense of power still in reserve, genius yet untapped.

One contemplates the total achievement with a feeling akin to that of looking at Stanley Spencer's unfinished painting *Christ at Cookham Regatta*. So much of the conception has been carried out in splendid detail, but the outline strokes reveal how much more was envisioned and not brought to completion. Would more have appeared if Dickens's personal and contemporary problems had been less – or different? The critical spirit can be roused to exasperation, to the point of wanting to be able convincingly to deflate his reputation. The private reader is gratefully contented with his gift of delight.

[1] 'Old Lamps for New Ones', in *Household Words*, 15 June 1850.

8

The Social and Political Novel

The desire to propagate ideas is not always the companion of literary gifts. The record is strewn with the hulks of 'novels with a purpose', long since burnt out by the heat of sincerity that fed on a single and immediate issue. The qualities by which a novel survives are not limited to particulars, but they are rooted in awareness of what is temporary. The good novelist is unlikely to be either prophet or salvationist; his reaction to what is going on around him is more sensitive than that of his contemporaries, rather than different in kind.

Those novelists who concerned themselves with national problems during the early part of Victoria's reign had this sensitivity. The novel had come to be more widely read and more generally accepted than the previous generation could have foreseen; the sympathy between the novelist and his readers was firmer. The custom of publishing in serial parts no doubt had something to contribute to this greater immediacy, since readers could and did write to the author offering advice or remonstrance about the development of the story. There was no chance of a premature look at the ending, which was not always fixed even in the author's mind. Appearing like a periodical, the novel seemed more dynamic and more closely linked to current events.

The age was willing to take the novel seriously, permitting it to be relevant to problems still unsolved. The novelist was becoming as serious and explanatory about his own craft as other specialists were about theirs. The new fiction was ousting Romantic ideas of spontaneous inspiration, and proving that a work of literature demanded both free choice and hard facts. There was a crop of writing by men and women with more earnestness than talent, in sincere but often dreary attempts to draw attention to wrongs. A reviewer in 1848 grumbled:

Novels are not objected to as they were; now that every sect in politics and religion have (*sic*) found their efficacy as a means, the form is adopted by all.[1]

In taking Benjamin Disraeli, Elizabeth Gaskell and Charles Kingsley as three outstanding examples of novelists who combined social concern with literary talent, it is well not to press too far the likeness between them. They are at least as interesting for their differences in approaching problems which troubled them all. Those problems have already been described, and it needs no effort of imagination to understand how sensitive people were alarmed by the state of society in the forties. The legacy of industrialization that had been allowed to develop without care or control was a heavy enough burden, but it seemed intolerable when Parliamentary reform failed to bring about the millennium. The actual conditions were past their worst, but they were still bad enough to drive men to desperation when the possibility of improvement produced only piecemeal and inadequate measures.

These novelists expressed in fiction the sympathy, the indignation and the fear of revolt which Carlyle had seen as part of the 'Condition of England question'. 'After Carlyle the poetic, prophetic and visionary possibilities of the novel are fully awakened.'[2] Carlyle influenced them, although he himself had little patience with the contemporary novel and urged the writers to 'sweep their novel-fabric into the dust-cart and betake themselves with such facility as they have to understand and record what is *true*'.[3] Fortunately, there were novelists with skill and confidence to act on the second part of this advice and ignore the first, putting into fiction the spirit of *Chartism* and *Past and Present*. Lacking Carlyle's intellectual power, they surpassed him in imagination. Also in optimism, for their distress at the troubled times did not drive them into a Romantic defence of alienation from a society become too corrupt and

---

[1] *Blackwood's Magazine,* October 1848.

[2] Kathleen Tillotson, *Novels of the Eighteen Forties* (Oxford, 1954), p. 154.

[3] *Critical and Miscellaneous Essays* (1839).

ugly for the artist. (Disraeli does show signs of a backward-looking Romanticism, but keeps it in line with a shrewd sense of what is politically practicable.)

There is a certain optimism in the very attempt to deal with problems of contemporary society. It implies a belief that society as a whole is worth preserving if some abuses can be remedied. It places faith in the individual, who can do his part as a responsible member of the whole and whose right conduct is a positive contribution to social morality. In these respects the novelists were very much of their time and country. Dissatisfaction with the whole basis of society emerged after the middle of the century, but the disappointment immediately following the hopes of 1832 did not lead to the kind of sickness that was mounting in France: Flaubert's *muflisme* found no echoes here for many years. Rather was there hatred of certain things which disturbed the harmony of the whole, and a desire to make full use of the modes of reform which were already beginning to work. In an age of remedial legislation, the novelists sometimes anticipated the official process and sometimes followed it to sweep up the bits that had been overlooked.

The reports from commissions of inquiry had proved that people could be moved by what they read, and the novelists took their opportunity. They shared the current belief that knowledge was valuable and that reason would lead to solutions once the wrongs were known. The lives of Disraeli, Mrs Gaskell and Kingsley followed very different courses, but they all came into contact with extreme want and suffering. Having read the warning signs, they wanted to arouse the compassion of the country before it was too late. They told in fiction of what had happened to them in fact – the emergence from sheltered ignorance to distressed awareness of Egremont in *Sybil*, Margaret Hale in *North and South*, Lancelot Smith in *Yeast*.

These characters cross the gulf between what Carlyle called 'two contradictory, uncommunicating masses',[1] and what Disraeli described as 'two nations'. The passage which gives *Sybil* its sub-title is well known: the questing hero Egremont learns from Morley the Chartist that the Queen reigns not over one nation but two:

[1] *Sartor Resartus*, Bk. 3, Ch. 10.

'Two nations; between whom there is no intercourse and no sympathy; who are as ignorant of each other's habits, thoughts and feelings, as if they were dwellers in different zones, or inhabitants of different planets; who are formed by a different breeding, are fed by different food, are ordered by different manners, and are not governed by the same laws.'

        'You speak of – ' said Egremont, hesitatingly.

        'THE RICH AND THE POOR.'[1]

Disraeli supplied the rhetoric and the capital letters, but he did not greatly exaggerate. His phrase could have applied almost as well to the division which Mrs Gaskell suggested in her title *North and South*.

Morley is made to speak of the prevailing ignorance. Though there was indeed too often a refusal to see the facts, the novelists did not burst upon an unprepared readership. The revelations in the official reports and the popular press could not go unheeded. Communication was bringing people closer to each other's experiences, and the public conscience was stirred not only by new wrongs but by distress which had long existed but never before become widely known. Growing less parochial, the new readers could accept a novel covering areas which they did not know at first hand, and which substituted a precise topography for the vague setting of the fashionable novel. More precise dating also became possible and acceptable, as *Coningsby* is placed clearly in the years before and after the First Reform Act.

The earliest-born and longest-lived of the three, Disraeli became one of the great Victorian statesmen without ever fully catching the Victorian spirit. From his first incursion into Parliament with a white waistcoat and a proliferation of gold chains, to his last gifts of primroses to the widowed Queen, he has the air of a Regency buck troubled by a social conscience. Born in 1804 into a Jewish family of Italian origin, and baptized thirteen years later when his father was piqued by a dispute with the Hebrew Congregation in London, Benjamin Disraeli was successful as a novelist before he became a politician. His first book *Vivian Grey* (1822) was published anonymously; the story of a young man's swift rise in politics is interesting as a forecast of what the author himself was to do later. The success

[1] *Sybil*, Bk. 2, Ch. 5.

of this novel and of those that followed enabled him to travel and to gain an entry into fashionable society. He made more than one attempt to enter Parliament, but was eventually returned in the Tory interest at the election following the death of William IV. He came to a House which shouted down his maiden speech but which he was one day to lead, a House still far from representative of the nation but which had caught the spirit of reform and in whose counsels the popular voice was more and more being heard.

The greater confidence of *Coningsby* (1844) came from seven years of political experience. This story of the political education of a young man who grows to distrust the sort of life depicted by the 'silver fork' novelists, is a fine example of the English political novel. It was written by one who understood practical politics from the inside, with a political aim under the literary form which he saw as 'a method which, in the temper of the time, offered the best chance of influencing opinion'.[1]

Of influencing it to what end? By this time Disraeli was prominent in the 'Young England' group of Tories who were aware of the uneasiness of the times and impatient with the entrenched complacency of their leaders, but regarded the Whigs as tools of a mercantilism which was ruining the nation's integrity. Its members voted for factory reform, spoke to workers' meetings and were also in fashion at house-parties. Their aims were threefold: the restoration of the power of the monarch against the 'Venetian constitution' imposed by the Whigs; the strengthening of the national Church (with Disraeli urging a rediscovery of the Judaic roots of Christianity): an alliance of the landed interest and the working people. They wanted to calm popular agitation and achieve its just aims without revolution. Like many public figures of the nineteenth century, they combined self-interest with genuine compassion.

Coningsby is a great muddle of a book: indulging in long passages of political history that hold up the narrative; flashing between the aristocratic world of the fashionable novel and the realism of political life; all interspersed with the romantically symbolic course of Coningsby's love for the daughter of a Whig millowner. It is a novel of political ideals reactionary in their vision of society but progressive in their understanding of

[1] Preface to the fifth edition, 1849.

practical issues. It flatters Disraeli's aristocratic colleagues like Smythe and Manners by its Carlylean insistence on the need for great men as leaders. Yet its real hero is Disraeli himself; though Coningsby may be partly a portrait of George Smythe, he contains a great deal of his creator. Disraeli in fact has a dual role, as the young political aspirant and as Sidonia. This strange Jew who keeps riding into the scene like one of G. P. R. James's 'solitary horsemen' is more than a melodramatic creation. He speaks with the racial wisdom that Disraeli had inherited, a disturbing power which bursts in on complacency and warns that all is not well.[1]

As a political satire, *Coningsby* exposes the new corruption after the inadequate reform of Parliament: the cut-throat struggle of the two parties for power, made fiercer by the new system of registration of voters and the continuing lack of a secret ballot. The world of Lord Monmouth and his 'creature' Rigby, his agents Taper and Tadpole, is an eighteenth-century world. Rigby's election speech, crowned by 'plenty of ale and some capital songs'[2] is a fair summary of how far the nation had still to look for sound representation.

In *Sybil* (1845) another young hero plunges into the world of Chartism and industrial unrest. It was one of the boldest pictures of the sufferings of the northern poor yet attempted in fiction. It reflects the current belief that a complete readjustment of relationships between the classes was the only alternative to destructive violence. Disraeli grasped the real issues behind the Chartism of the miners and handloom weavers. There is again a symbolic love-story, between the noble Egremont and Sybil, the Chartist's daughter. Alas, Victorian class-consciousness will not be flouted, and she is proved to be really of high birth.

The religious side of Young England, interpreted in Disraeli's special way, dominates *Tancred* (1847). Yet another young nobleman, egged on by the indefatigable Sidonia, goes to Palestine in search of the origins of his faith. Of course, he falls in love with a beautiful Jewish girl. The central theme of the

---

[1] For example: 'That mighty revolution which is at this moment preparing in Germany, and which will be, in fact, a second and greater Reformation, and of which no tittle is yet known in England.' *Coningsby*, Bk. 4, Ch. 15.

[2] *Coningsby*, Bk. 5, Ch. 3.

importance of Judaism to Christianity is broken up by strange and improbable adventures; its truth is more alienated from reality than in the earlier books. Although Disraeli failed here, he had already shown exceptional qualities as a novelist. He knows how to build up to a climax and how to handle the set-piece once he has reached it – such as the steeplechase in *Coningsby* and the riot at the 'tommy-shop' in *Sybil*. His heroines may be artificial, their affairs contrived for a purpose, but they also have minds of their own which foreshadow the new emancipated woman. Sybil is a stage-figure among the Gothic ruins, a model of Victorian piety in her sick-visiting; but in her perilous search for her father in London she is a real young woman facing real problems.

These problems scarcely touched Elizabeth Gaskell (1810–65), although she saw some of the worst contemporary sufferings. She faced them not as the champion of new causes but as the compassionate wife and mother whose simple duty was to relieve distress wherever she could. 'To give some utterance to the agony which, from time to time, convulses this dumb people; the agony of suffering without the sympathy of the happy.'[1] As the wife of a Unitarian minister in Manchester, she met industrial conditions and the plight of the cotton workers battling against the ebbing tide of economic prosperity. Here she wrote her first novel in 1848, the year that brought revolution to several European countries and the unrealized terror of it to England.

Mary Barton tells a simple enough story of distress leading to violence, with melodramatic action and a love-interest that brings about reconciliation. Mrs Gaskell professed ignorance of 'economics and the theories of trade'[2] and this book does not prove her to have been too modest. Yet what it lacks in theory it supplies in observation and sympathy. It appeals for the workers without idealizing them, and has scant respect for the leaders who seem only to take political advantage of their misery. Mrs Gaskell shared the current basic optimism about the future: not through faith in any public programme, but in trust that the human heart is essentially good and can be moved to right action. It was perhaps too naive a proposition,

[1] Preface to the first edition of *Mary Barton*, 1848.
[2] Ibid.

yet we ought not to underestimate its influence when multiplied many times. The theories and plans for reform were necessary, but in the end the solution of the Condition of England question owed much to the simple goodness of people who saw that certain things were intolerable and had to be remedied.

Mrs Gaskell moved into the sphere of domestic fiction with *Cranford* (1851–3), an uneventful narrative based on memories of her own early life in Knutsford. Yet this is no world out of time and place like so many early domestic novels. Captain Brown may be a romanticized woman's conception, but he is an enthusiastic reader of Dickens and he is killed by that new symbol of potency, fear and progressive hope – a railway train.

She returned to sterner matter with *Ruth* (1853), the story of a 'fallen woman' befriended by a dissenting minister who gets his sister to look after her and her illegitimate baby. When offered marriage by her seducer, a man of higher social rank, she refuses because she considers him unfit to have the care of her child. The symbolism of alliance between the classes is here more telling and deeper than the romantic attractions in Dickens, Disraeli and her own first book. The ending is of the type dear to early-Victorian readers. After neighbours have discovered her secret and persecuted both her and her bene-factors, Ruth nurses them as well as her seducer through an epidemic in which she eventually dies. Here again, Mrs Gaskell offers no answer but compassion. She deals realistically with the problem of the seduced woman, avoiding dramatic remorse as surely as she had in dealing with Esther in *Mary Barton*. The reviewers were not all favourable to *Ruth*, which seemed to some a condonation of immorality, and a suggestion that a minister of religion could tell a lie.

Her best book, *North and South* (1854–5), has been under-valued because convention made her draw out her inspiration into a long novel. Yet even though the story is slight, there is a great advance in technique and a firmer integration of theme and action. Her ability to write episodes that contribute to the total effect, always one of her strong points, is here even more developed. The daughter of a clergyman has to migrate from the south to the north of England when his doubts make him give up his living. She is drawn into the unrest of the cotton industry, finding sympathy for both sides. Her final marriage to the millowner Thornton is more than an alliance of classes: it is an alliance of human attitudes out of which a new hope may be born. Mrs Gaskell had come to see that the problems were more complex than she had supposed and to tackle them with more informed sympathy. There is no work of the time that gives a better idea of the conflict between rival interests or a clearer view of the minutiae of life in an industrial town.

With *Sylvia's Lovers* (1863) and *Wives and Daughters* (1864-6) she returned to that quieter domestic fiction from which, in a sense, she had never far departed. There is a calm innocence in all her books, the innocence of the child who utters profound truth in over-simplification. She could deal with the 'fallen woman', and yet avoid the disturbance shown by her male contemporary novelists. She describes and understands her own sex without concession to masculine sentiment and romanticism; and if she fails to understand men in their motivation, she is a scrupulous observer of their external lives.

The problems of the age had need of a feminine as well as a masculine approach, of one who could perceive rather than analyse, who would be moved more by individual cases of distress than by grand theories about society as a whole. Mrs Gaskell brought such an approach to what Carlyle had uttered in his tumultuous prose. So did Dickens, but his delicacy of perception was often clouded by current inhibitions and by awareness of his own demanding masculinity. Yet although the power of Dickens's imagination and the range of his vision make him so much the greater novelist, she shares with him the passionate demand for a national change of heart. The very simplicity which makes her pass over important questions (what exactly *were* Mr Hale's doubts?) leaves her free of embarrassment when she wants to indulge her sympathy. The account of the 'knobstick' in *Mary Barton,* blinded by a striker who is later remorseful, is starkly moving and has the stamp of tragedy.[1] Two good motives have clashed – the loyalty to companions in adversity with the loyalty to dependants in want. By not totally condemning either, by referring all

---

[1] The *Shorter Oxford English Dictionary* gives 'knobstick' as an equivalent of 'black-leg' and as first recorded in 1826. An acquaintance has told me that, as a boy in Lancashire in the 1930s, he would run alongside men going to work during a strike and call 'Knobstick, knobstick, face like a knobstick'.

judgements to a faith not aggressively dogmatic or sectarian, Mrs Gaskell made herself the spokesman of many in the muddled society of the time.

Charles Kingsley (1819–75) was less reluctant to praise or to condemn. He too grew from a peaceful country childhood to an understanding of how the poor suffered. For him the revelation came when, after a period of religious doubt, he took orders and served in a Hampshire parish during the time of acute agricultural depression. The sufferings of the farm workers were receiving less attention in print than those of the industrial workers. Where Disraeli had written fictional manifestoes for Young England, Kingsley was moved by the ideals of Christian Socialism, a subject to be examined in a later chapter. The most imaginative though not the most intellectual of its leaders, Kingsley was able to put into fiction some of the things that F. D. Maurice was saying in more directly theological terms. From Maurice he learned that the needs of the time could be a pragmatic sanction for Christianity; from Carlyle, how to subordinate reason to emotion. The combination was, to say the least, a lively one. Like Samuel Butler, so different in other ways, Kingsley wrote best about those things which he had made into a personal grievance.

Yeast (1848) came out in *Fraser's* until irate readers started cancelling their subscriptions. Its hero Lancelot Smith – whose name seems to blend old ideals with present reality – is very much a projection of Kingsley. He has a similar experience of village sufferings, aided by a manly gamekeeper who, unlike Lawrence's Mellors, keeps his passion pure and puts it into robustly radical verse. The squires snorted over the instalments, but *Yeast* won general sympathy for its main idea; perhaps because more than one contemporary reader could have identified Smith's personal problems with his own.

Alton Locke, Tailor and Poet (1850) follows in fiction the career of Henry Cooper. This remarkable 'moral force' Chartist who started as a shoemaker's apprentice had educated himself to the extent of being able to lecture on Shakespeare and Milton. Cooper, who suffered imprisonment for his activities, was the essence of faith in the Charter and the political means of dealing with distress, Kingsley shows Locke reading himself into political understanding. Mackaye, the Scots bookseller who teaches him, derives something from Carlyle, while the faithful but broad-minded Dean Winnstay is unmistakably the author himself – who had in reality tried to convert Cooper from scepticism. Both these novels tend to incoherence, as Kingsley warms to his theme. *Alton Locke* succumbs to sentimentality in the deaths of the hero and heroine, and to coincidence in the fate of the rich man killed by typhus caught from an overcoat made by one of his own sweated workers.

Yet what he had done for rural poverty in *Yeast*, Kingsley here did for the London tailoring workers who were still unprotected by legislation. To compare his account of conditions with those that were beginning to appear in the papers is to understand how the imagination could work on facts, and act as a catalyst in getting something done. He expressed the new class-consciousness of the intelligent workers, the protest of those no longer content to be despised but not yet filled with the confidence of owning the future which was to appear later in the 'little man' heroes of Wells and Bennett.

Kingsley, like the other Christian Socialists, dealt sympathetically with Chartism, which was the chief attempt of the workers to solve their own problems in the forties. Disraeli in *Sybil* had shown some respect for Chartist principles, but also a desire to organize their exponents into the new Toryism and a strong distrust of the chances of universal benefit through their demands. The Trade Unions seem to him a dangerous force, using Chartism for their own ends and exploiting misery for the advantage of a few demagogues. Dickens, as we have seen, took a similar view. Mrs Gaskell had shown John Barton driven into trade unionism after his dismissal for attending a Chartist convention, and it is seen as a moral decline when he meets 'desperate members of trade unions, ready for anything.' Both she and Disraeli develop the feeling of mystery which still surrounded the rituals and oath-takings of the unions, and Disraeli has a lurid picture of such an initiation in *Sybil*. By the time of *North and South*, however, Mrs Gaskell could show Higgins the union leader exercising a moderating influence on the mob.

Kingsley went on to take the early Church as a warning for the age in *Hypatia* (1853). He looked at the problem of female emancipation with the eponymous heroine and gave a sly warning against the machinations of Cardinal Wiseman in the person of Cyril, Bishop of Alexandria. The author's own views colour the character of Synesius, a commonsense Christian keen on out-door activities and opposed to clerical celibacy. In *Two Years Ago* (1857) he made the recent Crimean War a peg on which to hang the things which angered him – and by this time they were plentiful. Some of his muscular faith found expression in his books for the young: notably in *The Water Babies* (1863), an over-excited farrago which yet manages to convey a good deal about child labour and social justice.

How well did they really understand the age, these novelists so preoccupied with its problems? Though Disraeli had a political vision and Kingsley a theocratic prescription, Mrs Gaskell shared something common to all three of them with her insistence on the need for a general change of heart. They all saw a society where the individual could preserve old values and influence the formation of new ones, where each man and woman had a personal responsibility for the public scene. In reality, the power gained by the individualistic middle class in 1832 was slowly tending towards a greater control by the state over the individual. They saw and hated the tyranny of economic forces, and the consequences of Utilitarian doctrines; but to combat these things they, and Dickens too, pinned their faith on the noble individual and the spirit of self-help. Disraeli lived to apply more political remedies.

Yet they spoke for their age as it appeared to many of those living in it. Christian principles could still be socially invoked, and a system that caused waste and suffering could be called morally wrong. Conscience was strong, but fear was equally strong – fear of revolt, of epidemic, of the destruction of class-divisions which were believed to be fundamentally desirable. It was to prevent these things, as well as in the name of simple compassion, that they tried to solve the Condition of England question. A later age can be thankful that it was solved at last, without feeling too superior about their confused motives. All three of them have scenes of riot and violence – even the gentle Mrs Gaskell, who falls rather flat on such occasions (compare her affrays with the election riot in George Eliot's *Felix Holt*).

Their voice was not universally echoed. The opposition to *laissez-faire* economics was the most imaginatively stated, but the very strength of the attacks shows that there was an enemy to be feared. They were sometimes criticized for lowering art to the level of propaganda. A reviewer dealing with *Alton Locke* among others sniffed at the new fashion for 'writing political pamphlets, ethical treatises and social dissertations in the disguise of novels'.[1]

They did not turn society upside down, nor did they wish to do so. What they did was to give flesh and blood to the debate which was raging. They could arouse sympathy for suffering through an immediacy which the official reports lacked. They could give imaginative understanding of social problems to those who were still cut off from the reality. By writing novels instead of tracts, they could present all sides and help to give their country the blessing of comprehension which saved it from the bitter conflicts of the Continent.

They brought the novel to a new phase, by applying realistic method to great public issues. Their insight into personal lives set against a national background gave a larger perspective to fiction. Far from being the mouthpieces of theories, some of their characters attained a rich inner life in which their readers could share. Above all they had a sense of human dignity which makes their best work endure after the immediate problems have faded into history.

[1] *Fraser's Magazine,* November 1850.

9

Thackeray

By 1840 the novel was established but not unchallenged. Arguments still raged about its nature, its purpose, its propriety as a literary form and its fitness for domestic reading. The novel-reading public was growing but was not yet fragmented as it became in later years. It was a time of opportunity for the novelist: a time to be bold in establishing relations with his readers, to accept his new status in a society still cohesive enough 'to meet the immortals in the streets, and to read them with added zest for the encounter'.[1] The writers who sold well at that time are mostly still respected today; a few have sunk in our estimation, but we have discovered no neglected genius – except for Emily Brontë.

If William Makepeace Thackeray has not held popular regard equally with Dickens, one reason may be his apparent exclusion of many topics which contemporary writers were treating at length. He says little or nothing about social reform, at a time when the novel at large was saying a great deal about it. He seems happier in the world of the eighteenth century and the Regency than in his own time. There is, too, a certain lack of vigour, a refusal to reach out and grab hold of the reader, which can make him unattractive to those who warm at once to the direct approach of Dickens.

Yet Thackeray proves to be a true child of his age – almost its victim. There is much that seems puzzling at first. He put up a show of casualness, almost of indifference, towards the craft of fiction about which in reality he pondered deeply. He avoided the most overt contemporary issues but saw himself as a realist, indeed as a calculated pessimist, who could say:

I want to leave everybody dissatisfied and unhappy at the end

[1] G. M. Young, *Portrait of an Age* (Oxford, 1936), p. 13.

of the story – we ought all to be with our own and all other stories.[1]

There were tensions in him that were never fully resolved; his early life may go some way towards explaining them.

He was born in 1811 at Calcutta, into a family well-established in the administration of an India where British power had not yet reached its imperial height, where fortunes were still to be quickly made and lost by the individual adventurer. Both his father and his maternal grandfather were in the service of the East India Company. The exotic and sometimes turbulent environment need not have meant insecurity; but his father died, his mother remarried, and he himself was sent off to the care of an aunt in England. It was in the following years that his characteristic attitude to the world emerged, growing through the unhappiness of private schools, to harden in his time at Charterhouse into the apparent toughness that he took up to Cambridge. Here he spent two years more interested in recreation than in academic work; like his later fictional hero Pendennis, he left without taking a degree.

Then followed a series of abortive attempts to make his way in the world: a spell of legal training, flutters in the new journalism, art studies in Paris and a sojourn in Germany. All these served him well in the writing of his novels, but for the present they brought little tangible reward. A small but useful inheritance from his father disappeared in various directions. Like many a penniless young man before and since, he decided to try his hand at writing.

The novel, which was offering the most substantial monetary returns, did not attract him at first. His early work came out under different pseudonyms in periodicals. His inimitable snobbish footman, James Yellowplush, began as a satirical mouthpiece in a book-review and burgeoned into a series of sketches ridiculing the new social pretensions. Indeed, most of his first publications were inspired by the wish to parody or expose some current fashion. As 'Ikey Solomons, Jr' he brought out *Catherine* serially in *Fraser's*, making scornful fun of the 'Newgate Novel' which was attracting such accepted authors as Lytton and Ainsworth, as well as the new favourite Dickens.

[1] *The Letters and Private Papers of William Makepeace Thackeray,* edited by Gordon N. Ray (Cambridge, Mass., 1945–6), Vol. 2, p. 423.

He set out to show crime in its sordid reality but found that the characters were beginning to please him as personalities instead of mere exemplars (Shakespeare had the same kind of trouble with Falstaff) and the story was never completed. Another work ended for more tragic reasons: *A Shabby Genteel Story,* dealing with life among the people who were struggling to attain middle-class status and security, was going along well in *Fraser's* in 1840 when it stopped suddenly. Thackeray's wife, whom he had married in 1836, had suffered the complete mental breakdown that had been threatening for some time.

For the second time in his life Thackeray experienced a broken household, a family dispersed, the need to adjust to a new way of life. Something of the anguish, together with a newer and more mature compassion, appeared in *The History of Samuel Titmarsh and the Great Hoggarty Diamond,* also serialized in *Fraser's* (1841). He started contributing to *Punch* in 1842, soon after its inception; he wrote lightly and easily enough in its humorous-critical vein. It was not until 1847 that he showed where his real genius lay, in the series of parodies called *Mr Punch's Prize Novelists.* His private reading, his work as a reviewer, his explorations into creative writing, all combined to produce some brilliant mockeries of the most popular novelists of the day. He had thought long about what the novel should and should not be; he was working out his own artistic belief as well as his jealousy. Here, for instance, he is sending up Disraeli's ubiquitous and omnicompetent Sidonia:

> During the boat-race, a gentleman pulling in a canoe, and smoking a Nargilly, had attracted no ordinary attention. He rowed about a hundred yards ahead of the boats in the race, so that he could have a good view of that curious pastime. If the eight-oars neared him, with a few rapid strokes of his flashing paddles his boat shot a furlong ahead; then he would wait, surveying the race, and sending up volumes of odour from his cool Nargilly.[1]

By this time he had produced *The Memoirs of Barry Lyndon, Esq.* (1844), a picaresque story reminiscent of Fielding's *Jonathan Wild,* in which the unprincipled anti-hero is allowed to tell his own story in autobiographical form. His first true excursion into the novel, however, began in January, 1847, when the first

[1] *Punch,* Vol. 12, p. 198.

monthly part of *Vanity Fair* appeared. What appeared at first to be just another series of satirical episodes, illustrated by the author's own drawings, soon developed into an extended work which showed that a new talent had entered the competitive world of fiction. Set in the years just before and after Waterloo, the completed book gave a picture of society in the fortunes of a variety of memorable and lively characters. Henceforth Thackeray did not lack for recognition, though fame did not bring an end to the problems that his early life had created.

The History of Pendennis (1848–50) was coming out in serial form at the same time as *David Copperfield*, and the coincidence extends further. Both Thackeray and Dickens were working out some of their own troubles under the guise of fiction, reliving the torments and uncertainties of young manhood. It is possible to trace even closer correspondences between episodes and characters in the two books.[1] Pendennis is, on the whole, a less likeable young man than even the rather priggish Copperfield; as we shall see, Thackeray was suffering tension not only from his own remembered experience but also from current pressures against his desire to show a young man's affairs with complete frankness.

Perhaps because of these pressures, more probably because he had recently been working and lecturing on eighteenth-century writers, Thackeray plunged back to the beginning of the eighteenth century with *The History of Henry Esmond* (1852), again using the autobiographical form but trying now to cast it in the idiom of a previous age. The result was possibly his finest work, creating a central character who is complex, profound, almost neurotically volatile and insecure, yet who engages interest and sympathy. In the background there lurked the author's affection for Jane Brookfield, a married woman who broke off their friendship on her husband's insistence. The difficulties and final resolution of Esmond's love gain new poignancy in this light.

When *The Newcomes* began its serial parts in 1853, it may well have seemed to be in the new vogue of domestic fiction. In fact it soon showed the same insecurity and general dissatisfaction as his earlier work: Clive Newcome relives some of Thackeray's youth, including an unhappy marriage. Once again wish-

[1] Lionel Stevenson, *The English Novel* (London, 1960), pp. 287ff.

fulfilment comes to the rescue and Clive is ultimately free to marry his beloved Ethel, a heroine who is more vivid than most of Thackeray's good women without showing the vices of his bad ones. The revival of Arthur Pendennis to tell the story and take a small part in it was not a happy device; the action often seems to drag.

In fact some critics have considered that Thackeray's talent was already starting to fail, and have cast colder eyes on *The Virginians* (1857–9). Here the New World comes, if not to redress the balance of the old, at least to irrupt into it and reveal some of its foibles. It is again the old world of the eighteenth century, into which the young Americans (grand-sons of Esmond) come with their innocence which so many are ready to corrupt. The political historical setting is taken up and dropped rather heavily, with a final swoop into a synopsized War of Independence, but the social history is delightful. Thackeray proved supremely his power to conjure up a lost world, to produce figures like Samuel Johnson in their believable persons.

Decline is indeed too visible, however, in Thackeray's later work, though his essays collected as *The Roundabout Papers* are still pleasant to read. The short novel *Lovel the Widower* (1860) sinks from serious purpose into farce. Arthur Pendennis is once more dredged up as narrator for *The Adventures of Philip on his Way through the World* (1861–2), which also brings in some of the characters from the unfinished *Shabby-Genteel Story* and revives the memory of Thackeray's own unhappiness in marriage – all things which he had handled better in the past. *Denis Duval* remained unfinished at his death in 1863: its four completed instalments show him back in the eighteenth century with autobiographical technique: developing an adventure that might have shown the old genius.

It is impossible to say; Thackeray was sick and old when he died, though his years numbered only fifty-two. It was the end of a life ill at ease with the world, a life in which his unusual height and his broken nose seemed to symbolize a standing apart from the cheerful society of the majority. Yet he had won fame and critical esteem, had come to be coupled in literary discourse with Dickens who at first had seemed to get such a start on him. He had shown his power to move so austere a critic as G. H.

Lewes, who had written of Amelia's separation from her son in *Vanity Fair*, 'one bit we must copy, though it is difficult to read it, our eyes are not dry enough'.[1] He had become a popular public speaker, despite the nervous sensitivity which he concealed under mockery of himself as 'Tight-rope dancer to the nobility'.[2]

The nervousness and insecurity are understandable enough when the story of his life is told. They produce in his novels a blend of cynicism, diffidence and extreme sensitivity which makes them uneasy reading for those who prefer the more robust and extrovert tradition in the English novel. It is a blend that appears in the work of Somerset Maugham, whose life-story was in some points similar. It is a blend appropriate to many of the keener minds of his own time, whose intellectual powers were upset by emotional problems and who felt a guilty impotence in face of the problems of society. Thackeray did not enter the stream of novels on social and political themes; he professed to be impatient with the committed novelist:

> This one writes with a Socialist purpose, that with a Conservative purpose: this author or authoress with the most delicate skill insinuates Catholicism into you, and you find yourself all but a Papist in the third volume: another doctors you with low church remedies to work inwardly upon you, and which you swallow down unsuspiciously as children do calomel in jelly.[3]

If the reader's image of the mid-Victorian novel is moulded in Dickens and Mrs Gaskell, he will find Thackeray seemingly detached from society, viewing it with a range from tolerance to faintly amused disgust. There is almost constant reference to its evasions of reality, its pretensions and its conformist pressures on the individual, but little analysis of the problems which caused these things to be. He seems to be above all the opponent of snobbery, a theme which becomes apparent with the series *The Snobs of England, by one of themselves,* which appeared in Punch (1846–7) and was reprinted as *The Book of Snobs* in 1848. The manner certainly is detached and uncommitted, but the matter is as firmly based in his own time as anything to be

[1] In *The Morning Chronicle,* 6 March 1848.
[2] Geoffrey and Kathleen Tillotson, *Mid-Victorian Studies* (London, 1965), p. 317.
[3] *Punch,* Vol. 20, p. 75.

found in those more overtly dedicated to reform. Thackeray shows up a society that is in flux and uncertain of where its fluidity is tending. Fortunes are made and lost, reputations rise and fall with them. There is a tempting vision of middle-class status and a frightening one of destitution. Society is competitive and those who do not press their claims ahead of their neighbours may go to the wall. We had a glimpse of it in Surtees, but it was Thackeray who revealed and flayed the new insistence on outranking others.

How can we help Snobbishness, with such a prodigious national institution [sc. the Peerage] erected for its worship? How can we help cringing to Lords? Flesh and blood can't do otherwise. What man can withstand this prodigious temptation? Inspired by what is called a noble emulation, some people grasp at honours and win them; others, too weak or mean, blindly admire and grovel before those who have gained them; others, not being able to acquire them, furiously hate, abuse, and envy. There are only a few bland and not-in-the-least-conceited philosophers, who can behold the state of society, viz., Toadyism, organised:- base Man-and-Mammon worship, instituted by command of law. – SNOBBISHNESS, in a word, perpetuated, and mark the phenomenon calmly. And of these calm moralists, is there one I wonder whose heart would not throb with pleasure if he could be seen walking arm-in-arm with a couple of Dukes down Pall Mall? No; it is impossible, in our condition of society, not to be sometimes a Snob.[1]

Thackeray may seem often to fancy himself one of the 'few bland and not-in-the-least-conceited philosophers', but he knew that he also shared their need to compromise with the pressures of society. The attack on snobbery was only a part of his total dissatisfaction with the hypocrisy in that same uneasy society, a trait which some of those who lived within it could show up more vehemently than any Lytton Strachey. Dickens attacked it with a burning zeal, passing from particular wrongs to an indictment of the falsity of a corrupt society. Thackeray seems to show little more than discomfort, but there is a feeling of underlying power that could have boiled into a Swiftian *saeva indignatio*. He held the power in check; the moments of anger flare up and die down, never mounting into a consuming fire. Much is amiss, but at last there is little to be

[1] *The Book of Snobs*, Ch. 3.

done and blame becomes pointless; there is a quiet, dismissive close, like the conclusion of *Vanity Fair*:

Ah! *Vanitas Vanitatum!* which of us is happy in this world? Which of us has his desire? or, having it, is satisfied? – Come, children, let us shut up the box and the puppets, for our play is played out.

Thackeray grew to maturity in a country where materialistic push and puritanical repressions were marks of the middle-class rise to influence. He liked neither half of the equation, but he did not look for a specific Benthamite, Malthusian or other scapegoat. The faults that he condemns are the faults shown by men and women in the social groupings that are seen to exist, not those of particular institutions or theories. He deplores and satirizes but seems to see little likelihood of improvement either through specific reform or general change of heart.

Yet much of what we find in Dickens we can find in Thackeray too if we choose to look. Both of them had risen to comparative wealth from poverty; both had personal experience as well as observation to tell them that social values rested a great deal on the possession of money; both felt the insecurity of their early years as a continuing threat that opulence might not last. They wrote in and for a society that was well aware of these pressures. Not a social reformer, and seeming to have little sympathy for the crippling poverty under which a large section of the population suffered, Thackeray has his own urbane way of showing total involvement in the affluent society and its hazards:

When we read that a nobleman has left for the Continent, or that another nobleman has an execution in his house – and that one or other owes six or seven millions, the defeat seems glorious even, and we respect the victim in the vastness of his ruin. But who pities a poor barber who can't get his money for powdering the footmen's heads; or a poor carpenter who has ruined himself by fixing up ornaments and pavilions for my ladies' déjeuner; or the poor devil of a tailor whom the steward patronises, and who has pledged all he is worth and more, to get the liveries ready, which my lord has done him the honour to bespeak? When the great house tumbles down, these miserable wretches fall under it unnoticed: as they say in the old legends, before a man goes to the devil himself, he sends plenty of other souls thither.[1]

[1] *Vanity Fair*, Ch. 37.

This kind of social comment may not have the vigour of Dickens's tirade on the death of Jo, but Thackeray understood well enough the total involvement of all members of a society that was becoming increasingly complex and economically interdependent. Admittedly he says little that could not have applied to conditions in the previous century, but he says it with a realism that cuts through the residual Romanticism which the contemporary novel was often showing. He was impatient of what tended away from the observable realities of life. The sub-title of *Vanity Fair* is worth thinking about – 'A Novel without a Hero'. It is not only a book in which no one man dominates the action, one in which the most lively of the sustained characters is female. It is also one which, like all Thackeray's work, has little time for the cult of the great and noble individual who can free himself from the restraints of society in the Byronic manner, or bend society to his will in the Carlylean.

Heroism, loyalty, sincerity, are rare and improbable virtues in his world; when they exist, they are often coupled with the stupidity of a William Dobbin and their recital makes dull reading. How much more lively are his successful scoundrels, his Becky Sharp and Costigan. How much more vivid than the heroism at Waterloo is the confusion and panic of the flight from Brussels: the cowardice of Sedley is more memorable than the conventionally heroic and tragic death in action of Osborne.

Almost all the hotels occupied by the English in Brussels face the Parc, and Jos wandered irresolutely about in this quarter, with crowds of other people, oppressed as he was by fear and curiosity. Some families he saw more happy than himself, having discovered a team of horses, and rattling through the streets in retreat; others again there were whose case was like his own, and who could not for any bribes or entreaties procure the necessary means of flight. Amongst these would-be fugitives, Jos remarked the Lady Bareacres and her daughter, who sate in their carriage in the *porte-cochère* of their hotel, all their imperials packed, and the only drawback to whose flight was the same want of motive power which kept Jos stationary.[1]

That is the kind of thing which shows Thackeray at his best: the laconic, uncommitted description of human frailty. The one

[1] *Vanity Fair*, Ch. 32.

detail is perfect; the image of the noble ladies stranded in the midst of their possessions is the epitome of old aristocracy made helpless in a time of change. Dickens would have pounded every bit of fun and pathos out of the episode; Thackeray lets it stand for itself. Yet in such strength lies also his basic weakness – the bitterness which is scarcely concealed by his urbanity. He sees a world where rewards go to parasites and time-servers instead of to the really meritorious, of whom indeed there are few enough. The nonentity whose temporary usefulness is over can be sent off to govern a distant colony, carelessly entrusted with the welfare of people for whom the great in London care nothing. Rawdon Crawley's posting stands for a great deal that is implicit in Thackeray's work.

The pleasure in satirizing follies and failings continually turns sour on him. By the end of *Vanity Fair* there is a sense of sterility. The characters who have survived are ageing without grace; they have failed to get what they want, or have got it only when the appetite has dulled as it has even in the faithful Dobbin. Critics have noticed the apparent lack of feeling for the passage of time, but it would be more accurate to say that Thackeray is acutely aware of the time-process in its dreariness and loss while he excludes its maturing and mellowing power. Even the irony – he loves to seem to compare his own age favourably with the eighteenth century – grows sour in his later work. From gently poking fun at Victorian gentility he becomes almost querulous:

In those homely times a joke was none the worse for being a little broad; and a fine lady would laugh at a jolly page of Fielding and weep over a letter of Clarissa, which would make your present ladyship's eyes start out of your head with horror.[1]

The irritable quality which appears in much of Thackeray's work, and particularly in the later, may be traced to an extreme degree of the anxiety which was beginning to afflict many writers and has grown stronger in succeeding generations up to the present day. What could one man do to reverse the degeneration of society? Even while the novel was reaching the height of popularity and influence, the social problems were coming to need the attention of divers experts rather than the healing that a single imaginative genius could give. For

[1] *The Virginians*, Ch. 70.

Thackeray, both vain and shy as he was, there must have been particular anguish in the knowledge. The assumption of bland, almost arrogant detachment and perception had served him well as a shield against early trials, but its failures were the more acute. That society should be so much in error and he could not manage to put it right!

Perhaps in acceptance of his inadequacy, he practically excludes some of the greater issues of his time. He does not tackle the struggle between capital and labour, the results of Benthamism as it was being applied, the popular demand for representation. He seems to accept the inequality of individual conditions, so that the negro slave Gumbo in *The Virginians* is depicted with affection but without any attack on the institution of slavery. Yet acceptance does not banish compassion, as appears in the passage from *Vanity Fair* quoted above, and in such sudden bursts as this:

If you are to be miserable, what is Colin Ploughman, with the ague, seven children, two pounds a year rent to pay for his cottage, and eight shillings a week? No: a healthy, rich, jolly country gentleman, if miserable, has a very supportable misery; if a sinner, has very few people to tell him so.[1]

This is the compassion and the social criticism which the sensitive in all ages have felt, and the articulate expressed; it does not get down to the particular and remediable troubles of the Victorian labourer.

The fact is that Thackeray, like the rest of us, did not always act as if his basic principle were true. He was willing to speak in support of the movement to establish free libraries and was so affected by the vision of 'the educational and elevating influences which would necessarily flow from the extension of the movement' that he was unable to finish his speech.[2] These glimpses are illuminating and moving; but the man who elects to perpetuate himself in writing must accept judgement based on what he sets down. On this evidence Thackeray dodged some of the main issues. For instance, he could be satirical about the railway mania in the forties,[3] but he did not develop in fiction the economic and social implications of the new power.

[1] *The Virginians*, Ch. 50.
[2] Richard D. Altick, *The English Common Reader* (Chicago, 1957), p. 226.
[3] He was one of the most prolific contributors to the many satires in *Punch*.

Again, he shows little sense of the new spiritual conflicts or the growing opposition between faith and doubt. The churches and the clergy enter his pages often enough. *Vanity Fair* has its conventional churchgoers (Bute Crawley), Evangelicals (Pitt Crawley, Lady Southdown), Dissenters (old Osborne). Country parsons tutor or censure the young Pendennis. The hero of *The Virginians* has experience of the fanatical Ward and the dissipated chaplain Sampson. The 'Clapham Sect' is satirically but tellingly delineated in *The Newcomes*. But there is little sense of spiritual struggle or the understanding of deep commitment in faith. Even those characters who are strongly religious are viewed mainly from the outside. Thackeray's attitude to faith seems to be the blend of eighteenth-century indifferent tolerance with traces of later ecumenism, which he puts into the mouth of the fictionalized Richard Steele:

'Howbeit, in our times, the Church has lost that questionable advantage of respites. There was never a shower to put out Ridley's fire, nor an angel to turn the edge of Campion's axe. The rack tore the limbs of Southwell the Jesuit and Sympson the Protestant alike ... 'Tis not the dying for a faith that's so hard, Master Harry – every man of every nation has done that – 'tis the living up to it that is difficult, as I know to my cost.'[1]

However, Thackeray can moralize when the mood is on him and the subject is of his choosing – can moralize as tediously and repetitively as his admired Fielding could in the same circumstances. His vision is acute and penetrating, but the conclusions which he draws are sometimes tame enough. In spite of all the satire and criticism, he falls back very often into the conventional expressions of his own age. There is something basically middle class about him and about most of his characters even though they bear titles. To suggest so much is not to impugn his quality as a novelist or to say that he was incapable of compassion. The moments of really seeming to care are the more striking for their comparative rarity; the attack is more telling for its sudden impact after pages of mild and unadventurous comment:

Virtue is very often shameful according to the English social constitution, and shame honourable. Truth, if yours happens to differ

[1] *Henry Esmond*, Bk. i, Ch. 6.

from your neighbour's, provokes your friend's coldness, your mother's tears, the world's persecution. Love is not to be dealt in, save under restrictions which kill its sweet healthy free commerce. Sin in man is so light that scarce the fine of a penny is imposed; while for woman it is so heavy that no repentance can wash it out. You proud matrons in your May Fair markets, have you never seen a virgin sold, or sold one? Have you never heard of a poor wayfarer fallen among robbers, and not a Pharisee to help him? Of a poor woman fallen more sadly yet, abject in repentance and tears, and a crowd to stone her?[1]

Realism, conventionality, satire, protest – they can all be found in Thackeray and illustrated by quotation. Yet what remains with the reader is not any of these in predominance, but rather the total impressionistic sense of a society which we can feel to be fully alive. He shows up the failures and weaknesses more than the virtues of the early-Victorian scene. The individual is caught up and carried along by the conventions of society, which are themselves revealed as imperfect as much by implication as by overt criticism. The family, on which middle-class and Evangelical ideals centred, is seen not as a secure refuge but as a source of bickering, spite and incomprehension: there is scarcely another writer before Butler who reveals so bitingly 'the isolation of the domestically intimate'.[2] The evolutionary struggle rages; habit and custom are more potent than intelligence. In this Darwinian world, no one makes a really disciplined effort to change his circumstances, and such repentances as come are brief and shallow. The effective individual adapts to the environment, goes along with its opportunities and survives like Becky Sharp. The man who imagines himself free has failed to learn the lesson of non-communication, that 'you and I are but a pair of infinite isolations, with some fellow-islands a little more or less near to us'.[3]

This despondent and apathetic outlook owes much no doubt to Thackeray's own essential laziness; it is, however, an outlook common in his generation, disappointed by the course of events after 1832, the year of promise when he himself was twenty-one.

[1] *The Newcomes*, Ch. 28.
[2] Tillotson, op. cit., p. 165.
[3] *Pendennis*, Bk. 1, Ch. 16.

To the prevailing optimism, there were many willing to oppose the unlikelihood of general improvement. He writes like a man who has come to terms with personal and public disappointment, attaining even a certain serenity but without basic security. He shows little faith in either specific reform or the general 'change of heart' on which some of his contemporaries in fiction were pinning their hopes.

Thackeray is most typical and most effective in reliving the years of early manhood. Dickens is magnificent in the world of childhood, portraying adult events through a child's eyes. Thackeray does not recapture the same wise innocence, when he attempts it for instance at the beginning of *Henry Esmond*. He is at home in the world of young men beginning to find their way about and learn what life is like. He has no rival in descriptions like the infatuation of young Pendennis for the actress. Under all the sophistication, there is always in Thackeray a very young man whose assumed cynicism masks his tenderness, his minor intolerances, his basic warmth.

His world therefore is, in its outlook, the world of the thirties when he was young, the time of the transition from Regency to Victorian life whose tension remained strong in him. The fact that his novels are often set in earlier periods does not conceal this fact. *Vanity Fair* is very clearly the world of his experience, not of history. A character like Wenham may be the 'creature' of a pre-Waterloo aristocrat, but is even more plainly the type of monster that the Victorian middle class was creating out of its patronizing attempts to 'improve' the poor while keeping them still in their place: like the Heep and Bitzer of Dickens.

No, Thackeray is not a historical novelist in the sense of Scott or even the inferior sense of Lytton and Ainsworth. He shows unusually detailed knowledge of eighteenth-century life and a skill in parodying the literary style of an earlier generation. Yet his plunge into the past is neither escapist nor utopian: he does not retreat as Carlyle and Morris did into a fancied Middle Ages from which anything can be argued. His withdrawal is akin to that of Mrs Gaskell, George Eliot and Hardy – taking the more recent past as a vantage-point from which to observe and criticize his own time. The distance is great enough to give satire a respectable cover, not too great to change the basic circumstances of life: the reader has the liberation of being abroad, together with the security of being at home. Thackeray both demands and yields more understanding of his own period than do many of his contemporaries in the novel.

He brought many things to the art of fiction. Some of his tricks were not new and had been done better. For instance, Fielding despite certain lapses keeps better control of the omniscient and commenting narrator. Thackeray's machinery sometimes works with a loud creak, as when Arthur Pendennis is called up to tell the story of *The Newcomes* or when George Warrington suddenly becomes the narrator of *The Virginians*. At his best, however, Thackeray can emerge triumphant from the comparison with Fielding. His guiding of the reader's emotions can be assured, as he assumes the second self who is neither fully protagonist nor fully creator, who moves between the fictional and the real worlds with the easy transitions of a classical chorus. It is something that Butler achieved in *The Way of All Flesh* by making the mature-self Overton tell the story of the emergent-self Pontifex. Thackeray carries off the same mingling of detachment and involvement, of domination over his characters and intimacy with them. The image of puppetry that closes *Vanity Fair* is well chosen.

It is this manipulative skill that enables him to turn up the same character under different names and guises, to repeat motifs and situations without losing credibility. It is a mark of his genius that the repeated characters remain quite individual and could not be bodily transported from one novel to another, as the livelier creations of Dickens often could be.[1] He seems, nevertheless, to study mankind as a species rather than a set of free individuals, to take in fact a position similar to that which Darwin expounded with such devastating effect. When we identify ourselves with his characters, we do so for their experiences of the human condition rather than for individually recognizable traits. For instance, everyone has felt in youth the tormented egocentricity with which Pendennis fancies that the whole country is aware of his failure in his degree:

Pen . . . skulked about London streets for the rest of the day, fancying that everybody was looking at him and whispering to his

[1] For a reasoned contrary argument see Simon O. Lesser, *Fiction and the Unconscious* (London, 1960), pp. 69ff.

neighbour, 'That is Pendennis of Boniface, who was plucked yesterday.'[1]

This episode may have evoked the unconscious fears of its first readers who believed that the eyes of the world were on the English middle class and would eagerly note any lapse from respectability.

Certain weaknesses and inconsistencies may be found in his work and explained, in part at least, by his own story. There is, for instance, his distinctly ambivalent attitude to women. His female characters tend to appear in dualisms of saving or destructive attraction – Amelia and Becky, Lady Castlewood and Beatrix, Laura and Blanche. The love of a young man for an older woman recurs too and its psychological complexity is recognized in 'that anxiety with which brooding women watch over their sons' affections . . . I have no doubt there is a sexual jealousy on the mother's part'.[2] The hostility is not surprising in one who had suffered the loss of his father and his mother's remarriage (though he regarded his step-father with respect and affection and based Colonel Newcome on him). Then there is the story of his own marriage and its tragic course, and his unfulfilled feeling for Jane Brookfield. It is not surprising that he can burst into remarks like this:

There are some meannesses which are too mean even for man – woman, lovely woman alone, can venture to commit them.[3]

The result of experience was often bitter to the point of savagery. He can become unusually animated in dissecting the follies of women and deploring the way in which men are taken in by them. The eager spinster, desperately concealing her age, can be a source of cruelly Gilbertian fun as in his account of the machinations of Maria in *The Virginians*. Yet this is not the whole story; Thackeray can offer the ideal vision too and make us accept it. His description of Esmond's meeting with Beatrix on his return has been many times quoted and deserves quotation yet again. Here is Thackeray at his most powerful; we share in the enchantment, even when we know what the rest of the story is to be – even when we are familiar with the

[1] *Pendennis*, Bk. 1, Ch. 21.
[2] *Pendennis*, Bk. 2, Ch. 3.
[3] *A Shabby-Genteel Story*, Ch. 3.

appalling picture of the aged woman in the later story of *The Virginians*. Here his style sweeps us away, as its tone of easy, fireside conversation swells into the panegyric:

> Esmond had left a child and found a woman, grown beyond the common height, and arrived at such a dazzling completeness of beauty that his eyes might well show surprise and delight at beholding her. In hers there was a brightness so lustrous and melting, that I have seen a whole assembly follow her as if by an attraction irresistible; and that night the great Duke was at the playhouse after Ramillies, every soul turned and looked (she chanced to enter at the opposite side of the theatre at the same moment) at her, and not at him. She was a brown beauty – that is, her eyes, hair, and eyebrows and eyelashes were dark, her hair curling with rich undulations, and waving over her shoulders; but her complexion was as dazzling white as snow in sunshine, except her cheeks, which were a bright red, and her lips, which were of a still deeper crimson. Her mouth and chin, they said, were too large and full; and so they might be for a goddess in marble, but not for a woman whose eyes were fire, whose look was love, whose voice was the sweetest low song, whose shape was perfect symmetry, health, decision, activity, whose foot as it planted itself on the ground was firm, but flexible, and whose motion, whether rapid or slow, was always perfect grace – agile as a nymph, lofty as a queen – now melting, now imperious, now sarcastic: there was no single movement of hers but was beautiful. As he thinks of her, he who writes feels young again, and remembers a paragon.[1]

The ambivalence and tendency to extremism in Thackeray's attitude towards women may indeed be part of a greater tension in himself and in his society. He could feel to a special degree the need to keep a respectable front turned towards a world based on externals and snobbery; a need pulling against the dangerous atavistic attractions of low life. Thackeray had known both extremes; he had known the public school and university, as well as the society of bankrupts and semi-criminals in his years of penury. Although he more than once attacked the literary glamorizing of the criminal, he never lost a fascinated interest in the possibilities of low life. His rascal Barry Lyndon speaks for him, for many of his characters, and for a large number of his contemporaries, when he recalls:

---

[1] *Henry Esmond,* Bk. 2, Ch. 7.

At least, thought I, if I am degraded to be a private soldier there will be no one of my acquaintance who will witness my shame; and that is the point which I have always cared for most.[1]

It is this same desire to cover up distasteful facts, to assume that all is well if it appears to be so, which even the warmest admirer of the Victorians has to acknowledge as having existed. It sometimes played havoc with the novel, as it did with individual lives. Viewed in the light of the realism which he professed, it does not make sense that Thackeray's young heroes should be so full-blooded, so 'dissipated' in respect of cards and drinking, yet so sexually chaste. Thackeray was troubled by the dilemma which troubled most writers of fiction at the time. How could the novelist fulfil the growing demand for realism, be truthful, frank, complete in his reporting, and yet draw a veil over some important aspects of human life? When he began to write, the freedom of the Regency years was not quite lost and the pressures of the circulating libraries had not reached their full strength. The sixties imposed more prudishness than the forties, when a good deal could slip through the net of social censorship.

However, the old notion that novels were liable to 'inflame the passions of youth'[2] was still held in some quarters, and from the middle of the century it began to link up with taboos spreading far beyond fiction. The growing difficulty of expression may partly account for the unease and frequent snappishness in the later Thackeray. The moralists were winning by the time his fame was established, though not without challenge even from the most respectable journals. A reviewer commented in 1851:

If we are to make a choice between prosy decent books and vicious books that are written with sprightliness and skill, we are, of course, bound to prefer the former . . . But we cannot help regretting . . . that our English novelists . . . should not be able to make [morality] a little more amusing.[3]

Thackeray, like many Victorians, was dragged between a natural vigorous zest for life and a fear that the beast in man

[1] *Barry Lyndon*, Ch. 6.
[2] Mrs Chapone, *Letters on the Development of the Mind* (1775), quoted in Frank W. Bradbrook, *Jane Austen and her Predecessors* (Cambridge, 1966), p. 25.
[3] *Fraser's Magazine*, October 1851.

could be released through the pleasures of the senses, and particularly through sex. His protest in the preface to *Pendennis* is well known: 'Since the author of "Tom Jones" was buried, no writer of fiction among us has been permitted to depict to his utmost power a MAN'. Yet in his lectures on *The English Humourists of the Eighteenth Century* (1853) he was more censorious of Fielding's morality. We have seen that he could speak in favour of free libraries, but he dreaded the bad effects of cheap literature – 'penny libraries for debauchery as for other useful knowledge'.[1] He could sneer at the 'pure and outraged Nineteenth Century' which would ban the eighteenth-century novel and 'order Mr Mudie never to send one of that odious author's books again'.[2] Yet where his own sales were in question, he could glide around the awkward corner as he does in his dealings with the question of Becky Sharp's relations with Lord Steyne:

> What *had* happened? Was she guilty or not? She said not; but who could tell what was truth which came from those lips; or if that corrupt heart was in this case pure?[3]

He himself did not escape rebuke for being too outspoken. Walter Bagehot found him 'close to the borderline that separates the world which may be described in books from the world which it is prohibited to describe'.[4] Before the end of his life he had to give in to contemporary pressures to the extent of cutting short the publication of *Unto this Last* in the *Cornhill*, of which he was editor. It is easy to sneer at a generation that could find Thackeray immoral and Ruskin a dangerous revolutionary, less easy perhaps to feel compassion for their tensions and repressions. It is salutary to remember that every age puts some restriction on its artists: what popular novelists today would dare to utter tender sentimentality or Evangelical piety?

In respect of sentimentality, Thackeray gave in less often than Dickens – whose temperament was indeed more apt for yielding. Thackery handles the final union of Dobbin and

---

[1] Altick, op. cit., p. 346.
[2] *The Virginians*, Ch. 41.
[3] *Vanity Fair*, Ch. 53.
[4] *Literary Studies* (1879), 2nd series, pp. 187ff.

Amelia in a very different vein from that with which Dickens marries off his faithful heroes:

> This is what he pined after. Here it is – the summit, the end – the last page. Good-bye, Colonel – God bless you, honest William! – Farewell, dear Amelia. – Grow green again, tender little parasite, round the rugged old oak to which you cling![1]

The 'tender little parasite' is Thackeray's protest against convention, so mild as to pass unnoticed by the reader enamoured of a 'happy ending', but so telling as to expose what is false in the great Victorian novels. When he indulges sentimentality without satire, as in the death of Colonel Newcome, he rises above the convention and makes it something that does not jar even on present-day sensitivity.

The warm enthusiasm of Dickens and the cool observation of Thackeray both found their expression in the developing novel. The literary form needed both of them, as the age needed both attitudes (not that either was consistent throughout his writing or his life). If Thackeray has sunk in popular esteem, he is the victim of a stereotyped view of the mid-Victorian novel rather than of his own weaknesses. He refuses the socio-political label but remains, under the achievement that is timeless, as fully a child of his age as any of those on whom it can be tied with assurance.

[1] *Vanity Fair*, Ch. 67.

10

The Brontës

Although research has documented the Brontë sisters more fully than many Victorian writers, the popular image of them remains somewhat vague and inaccurate. Dickens reading from his works in public, Trollope assiduous at his standing desk – these visions are clear and vital enough. But the Brontës – did they really exist, are they only creatures of a strange fiction? They seem to stand apart from the mainstream of society, outside the world of theological anguish, parliamentary reform and railway-shares. The little eyasses hover about their northern eyrie, cut off alike from the benefits and ills of a changing world. They are simple children of nature, wild creatures of the fells. All that they know of life comes from their imagination, or from old, romantic books.

It is a pleasing enough picture but it happens to be false. These young women earned their living in a hard and very real world, two of them going abroad to do it. They came to London, dealt with their publisher, met other writers. The place and conditions of their early lives influenced them, as these things must always do, but the limitations ought not to be exaggerated. To their contemporaries they were not shy innocents of the uplands; they were talented, cheeky and rather daring young women.

The controversy about the morality of the novel touched them as it touched most writers of the day. The influence of 'Georges Sandism' from France was being blamed for a decline in the purity of the English novel. Charlotte Brontë was not too sheltered to be acquainted with French writers, though she found them 'clever, wicked, sophisticated and immoral'.[1]

---

[1] *The Brontes: Their Lives, Friendships and Correspondence,* edited by Thomas James Wise and John Alexander Symington (Oxford, 1932), four volumes, Vol. 1, p. 215. These volumes are part of the 'Shakespeare Head Bronte'; later references to them are made as S. H. B.

However, she was herself attacked for departing from the highest moral tone; popular approval of *Jane Eyre* was tempered by dislike of the final happy marriage of the dreadful Rochester, 'a proof how deeply the love for illegitimate romance is implanted in our nature'.[1] Both she and Emily were censured for the blunt, unrefined speech of their characters: a trait which owed something to the Yorkshire environment and something perhaps to impatience with the genteel convention which most readers and reviewers shared:

It may be well also to be sparing of certain oaths and phrases which do not materially contribute to any character and are by no means to be reckoned among the evidences of a writer's genius.[2]

They were fully involved in the outer world; but it remains true that the inner world was stronger. The power of their imagination, as expressed in what they wrote, does not bring about a total withdrawal from reality. It continually touches and transforms the real world, not into fantasy but into a special abstraction where their own experience cannot be challenged. They speak thus for many who shared their condition but not their transforming imagination. They speak for those who were perforce living and moving in a changing society but were held back from active influence on the process of change: held back by temperament or circumstances, or by the prevailing disabilities of class or sex. They speak for the great areas of the country which were still remote and sparsely populated in that age of new communications, urban overcrowding and industrialization.

It is perhaps not surprising that their own story has become a legend, touching the fancy like one of their novels. Their father, who had changed his Irish surname Brunty, was perpetual curate of Haworth, in Yorkshire.[3] The death of his wife left him with six small children, whose upbringing was undertaken and influenced by his devout and gloomy Evangelical sister-in-law. Four of the five girls were sent to a cheap boarding-school, where two of them contracted tuberculosis

[1] *Quarterly Review,* December 1848. The (female) reviewer was one of many who refused to believe that 'Currer Bell' could be a woman.

[2] Review of *Wuthering Heights* in *The Examiner,* 8 January 1848.

[3] A perpétual curate was the incumbent of a parish without endowment of tithes. Trollope's Mr Crawley is a particularly depressed member of this generally depressed class. The title was changed to 'Vicar' in 1868.

from the Dickensian conditions and soon died. The other two, to the benefit of literature, were brought home and kept there with the remaining girl and the one boy. Their father became increasingly withdrawn, and they were thrown a great deal on their own resources.

Those resources were not meagre. They created their own world of imagination, writing down their invention in miniature books. Their 'Angria' was different in degree rather than in kind from the fantasy-worlds of many lonely children. The minute particulars of history and geography, the mingling of real public figures and fictional characters, the wish-fulfilment through tales of violence and excitement – these are not unique. But there are seldom four children equally sharing the enthusiasm, or with such talent for putting it into language. Charlotte (1816–55) was sent away to school again when she was fifteen; Emily (1818–48) and Anne (1820–49) created together the island of 'Gondal'. Their brother Branwell was left out of the new collaboration, though what influence he had then and later remains a subject for conjecture. He undoubtedly had talent and attempted to become a painter; but frustration and indiscipline made him unemployable, drove him to compulsive drinking and early death.

Charlotte and Anne worked for a time as governesses. Escape from that grim drudgery seemed to be possible only through opening a school of their own, and Charlotte went with Emily to Brussels for further study. Emily soon made her way home, Charlotte stayed as a pupil-teacher and fell unhappily in love with the school principal's husband. The result was her first book, though the last to be published, *The Professor*. She transformed herself into a Swiss girl and the man into an English teacher, bringing the affair at last to a happy marriage. Otherwise, the story is very much her own, both in the details and in the general background of Brussels and of Yorkshire in the early chapters.

She did not work alone or without sympathy. Back at home together, the sisters had discovered that each of them had been writing poetry; they paid for publication and sold only two copies. If poetry was not in demand, where could the fashion of the age lead them but to the novel? They set to work, and Charlotte was the first to finish. The rejection by several publishers, sometimes on the grounds that it was too short a book in the era of the three-volume novel, was tempered by some encouragement. Charlotte went on to finish and find a publisher for *Jane Eyre* (1847), the story of a girl who becomes a governess after unhappy schooldays, and who after various tribulations marries her Byronic employer.

In the same year Emily published *Wuthering Heights* and Anne published *Agnes Grey*. Emily's story has since come to be regarded as the greatest achievement of the three sisters, but at the time it seemed coarse, insensitive and poorly constructed. The influence of the childhood fantasies is clearer than in her sisters' books; the plot is woven around a strange love-hate relationship, against the background of Yorkshire scenery. *Agnes Grey* deals also with a governess who falls in love and comes to a happy marriage, in a tone more muted and wistful than Charlotte's. The similarity of the background when the three books appeared, under the pseudonyms of 'Currer, Ellis and Acton Bell' caused interest and conjecture whether they could all be in fact by the same author. The true story gradually became known, though all that had gone into the making of the novels remained waiting to be uncovered by later research.

Anne went on to write *The Tenant of Wildfell Hall* (1848), a more violent and stark treatment of experience based on the story of Branwell who was now near to death. Emily and then Anne died within a few months. Charlotte alone remained, forcing herself to go on writing until she had finished *Shirley* (1849), in which the two contrasting types of heroine make a focus for more realistic treatment of contemporary problems and controversies within the Church. Later she returned to her Belgian story for *Villette* (1853), now putting herself into the less opaque disguise of a young English teacher who falls in love with a foreign colleague. The ending is left more doubtful than in previous books of hers: does Paul come safely through the storm or not? Her own end was near when she wrote it; she married a young clergyman and died within a year. *The Professor* was published posthumously in 1857.

Like most great writers, the Brontë sisters made the best use of their outward experiences as well as their own imaginations. The loneliness of much of their lives turned them more violently towards the inner world when pressures became strong, and it is the power of imagination that strikes out again most strongly to the reader. For that reason perhaps we tend to see them as more alienated from their age than they really are. The very imagination was fed most richly not on ancient myths but on the literary fashions that were only just out of date. Romanticism is poured into prose fiction as the previous two generations had poured it into poetry – and indeed as Carlyle had survived to use polemically. Pantheism, the visionary exaltation of emotion, the strength of rebellion that sets a great man at odds with society – these themes linger on in their work among the attitudes and prejudices that are peculiarly of their own time.

It says much for the liberal appetite of the new novel-reading public, and indeed for the general tolerance that still remained in the forties, that their work could be published, read and praised. Censure was outvoted by approval; their work was seen to be important even in that decade of great novels. When their secret was known, it gave some impetus to the acceptance of the female novelist; they too had their part to play in the history of female emancipation, together with their more militant contemporaries and successors. Some may have thought that the example did more harm than good, as Trollope suggests in his tale of a young girl with aspirations to write:

'Currer Bell was only a young girl when she succeeded', she added. The injury which Currer Bell did after this fashion was almost equal to that perpetrated by Jack Sheppard, and yet Currer Bell was not very young when she wrote.[1]

Charlotte indeed did not see herself as a pioneer in the novel of social and political reform; 'I *cannot* write books handling the topics of the day; it is of no use trying', she protested.[2] Her attempts to deal with some of the more recent national problems in *Shirley* were not notably successful; her description of Luddite riots draws more from a sense of the atavistic violence in human nature than from a real understanding of the kind which Mrs Gaskell brought to industrial problems.

Where she is fully of her time, and often ahead of it, is in her

---

[1] 'Mary Gresley', in *An Editor's Tales* (1870).
[2] In a letter to the publisher George Smith; S. H. B. Vol. 4, p. 14.

assertion of the rights of women. The genius of *Shirley* is in the eponymous heroine who contains much of her sister Emily, but the contrasted Caroline is of no less importance when she sees even the condition of the governess as an escape from domestic subservience. Charlotte, who had earned her living in this way, knew what she was writing about and had a contribution to make to the debate on the question of the independent woman trying to make her own life in a male-orientated society. It had exercised Dickens in the person of Kate Nickleby and Thackeray in Becky Sharp. The year which saw the publication of *Jane Eyre* saw also Tennyson's *The Princess* and Frederick Denison Maurice's attempt to provide better education for women with the foundation of Queen's College. Charlotte's heroines, however, were of the type that seemed immodest and almost immoral in the general opinion. Nearly forty years later Olive Schreiner was to shock the reading public by her assertion that young women had minds and desires of their own.

Charlotte chafed against convention but was also limited by it. Her relationships between the sexes are usually of the pupil-master type, with the prepotent and experienced male dominating the young women. Did her youthful attraction to Héger in Brussels condition what her books reveal; or did that same attraction spring from the attitudes inculcated in early-Victorian girls? The interplay of social and personal forces is sometimes more easily observed than explained. What is certain is her brilliant handling of these limited and immature relationships. Rochester in *Jane Eyre* is, in realistic terms, quite incredible. We tolerate his impossibility because the author's passionate involvement suspends our disbelief: who can resist the battering force of that continual *I*? She writes with feelings too strong for arrest and analysis, pouring into the novel emotions which had previously found expression only in poetry. We tolerate her heroes as we tolerate her plots with their many coincidences and improbabilities. She makes us read on, though her style is often faltering, stilted in conversation, rhetorical over trivialities, bathetic at moments of tension; for instance:

What a consternation of soul was mine that dreary afternoon! How all my brain was in torment, and all my heart in insurrection! Yet in what darkness, what dense ignorance, was the mental battle fought! I could not answer the ceaseless inward question – *why* I thus suffered; now, at the distance of – I will not say how many years, I see it clearly.[1]

Yet tolerance soon warms to admiration, strengthened by the very trait which is given melodramatic expression in the passage just quoted. Like Dickens she suffered in childhood, and like him she is at her finest in the scenes where the young suffer and wonder. The time was now propitious for children to be seen with new understanding and sympathy: the Commissions on children's employment had revealed things that could move a society already feeling its way towards a more general compassion. Dickens had dealt with the threats to innocence; Marryat in *Peter Simple* with the cruelties which had been accepted as more or less incidental to a boy's upbringing; Frances Trollope in *Michael Armstrong* (1840) with the sorrows of the factory child.

It is of course possible to see something obsessional and masochistic in Charlotte's frequent references to the suffering and distress of childhood and young womanhood. The child is the sacrificial victim with whom she seems to identify her own losses and frustrations. But the achievement is unsullied by such views, the achievement of making coherent in words the misery of the lonely ones, the outcasts, the alienated. She has few rivals – the comparison with Dickens is again inevitable – in giving the child's view of a world which is grotesque, distorted, terrifying, and which adults see as ordinary. Horror lurks under the smooth surface of nineteenth-century domesticity. She uncovers the darker side: not only the physical discomforts and actual pain, but the insecurity which adult tensions could pass on to the young. Rochester's mad wife may be Gothic melodrama, but she is nothing to the perfectly realistic account of Lucy Snowe in Brussels during the summer vacation, alone in the school with the one imbecile girl, seeing the horror of mortality in the dormitory with its long row of empty beds.

She reaches here towards the anxieties that were seldom openly expressed until a later time. In doing so she creates a new type of heroine for the English novel. Her leading figures have a deep, neurotic egocentricity which makes the other characters seem to have identity only through the perception of

[1] *Jane Eyre*, Ch. 2.

the one observer. This singleness of vision is what gives her work integrity, despite her formal weakness and her startling juxtapositions of realism and fantasy. She has the vision of those who must live out their lives in their own worlds, whatever the shape of society may be. The way in which her characters are swept along by currents which they cannot control, but against which they oppose their own private desires, is sometimes reminiscent of Thackeray. For that author she conceived a strong admiration; and after her death he wrote movingly of his respect for her with 'the trembling little frame, the little hand, the great honest eyes'.[1]

Like Thackeray again, she gives little indication of deep spiritual commitment or understanding of theological controversy. Her Mr Brocklehurst is a terrible specimen of the worst type of bigoted Evangelical, a figure based on Carus Wilson at whose school she had suffered as a child. Poor Wilson perhaps did not deserve to be singled out from his many contemporaries who really believed themselves to be at war with the Devil for the children under their control. Her more charitable Christians are not strongly drawn: Helen Burns is a conventional model of piety and St John Rivers scarcely seems three-dimensional. Her father's attitude, and her own satirical spirit, gave her little sympathy for the extremes in religious faith and practice, whether of Protestant dissent or Anglo-Catholicism. The curates who appear in the novels get cavalier treatment (though she married a real-life one in the end). She spoke for many in her time when she distrusted the 'disciples of Dr Pusey and scions of the Propaganda', and when she made lively if slightly ill-informed sport with the ecclesiastical calendar:

> The first dish set upon the table shall be one that a Catholic, ay, even an Anglo-Catholic, might eat on Good Friday in Passion Week: it shall be cold lentils and vinegar without oil; it shall be unleavened bread with bitter herbs and no cold lamb.[2]

Yet she is of her age in her strong moral sense, her belief in a Providence which makes sense of human affairs.[3] She con-

[1] 'The Last Sketch', in *The Cornhill*, 1860, I.
[2] *Shirley*, Ch. 1.
[3] For a fuller discussion of this point see Barbara Hardy, *The Appropriate Form* (London, 1964), pp. 61ff.

tinually asserts, with the intolerant certainty of a child, that there is a right and a wrong and that she knows the right. Her heroines suffer from scruples as firm as those of Charlotte M. Yonge. They may be ridiculous, as when Lucy Snowe appears in an extraordinary costume because she refuses to wear men's clothes on the stage,[1] but they are convincing within the world which they inhabit. The Victorians owed much of their greatness and many of their mistakes to their ability to believe that they were indisputably in the right. Charlotte Brontë assumed the total authority of the narrator as Thackeray did, though with more involvement in her tale, and in a way that looks forward to the greater art of George Eliot.

Anne Brontë is overshadowed by her sisters, but she has quality in her own right. *Agnes Grey* has too much kinship with *Jane Eyre*, without its passion, but it has also some splendidly detailed writing about domestic life and an honest look at the perennial problem of the governess. She is frank about the reality of the situation, but more patiently and with a less waspish humour than Charlotte shows. Emily's novel influenced *The Tenant of Wildfell Hall*, even in the bolder technique of starting the story in the middle and using the flashback method. Against the background of the dark Yorkshire moors, she tells here a tale of violence and cruel relationships which was more shocking to its first readers than it can be today. She succeeds in her vivid portrait of a man degenerating through excess, made poignant by our knowledge that her brother Branwell followed that same path. Even Charlotte seems to have thought that she had gone a bit too far: 'I do not like it quite so well as "Agnes Grey" – the subject not being such as the author had pleasure in handling'.[2]

Emily Brontë, with her one novel, refuses to fit into any category. She writes of a conflict which it would be impertinent to call 'supernatural', since her characters seem so closely linked with natural forces. The human soul carries its survival of death into the present world: the 'ghost' is not an invasion but a part of the total situation. There are no Gothic intrusions

[1] *Villette*, Ch. 14. The whole episode is psychologically interesting: Lucy at first reacts with puritanical horror to the idea of performing on the stage, is locked in a fearful attic by the hero while she learns her part, and eventually finds that she enjoys the experience of acting.

[2] In a letter to Mary Taylor; S. H. B., Vol. 2, p. 250.

into reality, but one realm shades into another, one life into another. The moors that she loved so well are not merely a background but an integral part of the action, as the Wessex scene is in Hardy. Her vision is not to be tagged simply as 'pantheism' or 'pathetic fallacy' – it is not self-conscious enough for that. She takes it for granted that human beings and their natural environment must react together:

> The rainy night had ushered in a misty morning – half frost, half drizzle – and temporary brooks crossed our path, gurgling from the uplands. My feet were thoroughly wetted; I was cross and low, exactly the humour suited for making the most of these disagreeable things.[1]

Her technique reveals her as the most skilful artist of the three sisters and as a bold experimenter in the form of the novel. The story of conflict and tortured relationships through two generations is told by the remembered experiences of onlookers, whose detachment heightens the involvement of the main characters in the way that a Greek chorus does. The story is taken up near its end, when Lockwood becomes curious about his neighbour Heathcliff and begins to learn the strange story through the housekeeper at Wuthering Heights, Nelly Dean. The latter is an odd character in herself, articulate and shrewd, playing an ambivalent part in the tragedy. Is she an innocent onlooker, or does her interference make her the real villain of the piece? It is Emily's skill to make us uncertain yet able to feel the emotional effect of either possibility.

Emily makes her own values, without asking the moral questions that concern her sisters. She is neither for nor against the social norms of her time. She is dealing with affections and enmities that spring from primitive existence, not from any institutional grouping. The forces of calm and of storm, the wish for life and the wish for death, rage in a manichaean dualism that promises ultimate victory for neither. People react strangely on each other, not because one is bad and the other good, but because they are creatures of different psyches, almost of different species. Even an argument about the ideal way to spend a summer day can end by touching the depths of being:

> He wanted all to lie in an ecstasy of peace; I wanted all to sparkle

[1] *Wuthering Heights*, Ch. 23.

and dance in a glorious jubilee. I said his heaven would be only half alive; and he said mine would be drunk; I said I should fall asleep in his; and he said he could not breathe in mine.[1]

Yet, as her technique shows, Emily is no mere child of nature writing out of a wild stream of consciousness. When she writes of nature, it is in general rather than particular terms, imaging the broad sweep of human life more than the details. She can rise to a climax of natural and human tempest and still keep control. Her passion, stronger than Charlotte's, is also more disciplined: except when the thought of physical violence takes control of her pen and the frustrations of her own turbulent nature are set free in symbols:

The charge exploded, and the knife, in springing back, closed into its owner's wrist. Heathcliff pulled it away by main force, slitting up the flesh as it passed on, and thrust it dripping into his pocket. He then took a stone, struck down the division between two windows, and sprang in. His adversary had fallen senseless with excessive pain and the flow of blood that gushed from an artery or a large vein. The ruffian kicked and trampled on him, and dashed his head repeatedly against the flags.[2]

Yet in her greatest moments she is utterly realistic. There is nothing supernatural, nothing Gothic, in the description of Heathcliff dead, but all the terror of the story is here condensed:

His eyes met mine so keen and fierce, I started; and then he seemed to smile. I could not think him dead: but his face and throat were washed with rain; the bedclothes dripped, and he was perfectly still. The lattice, flapping to and fro, had grazed one hand that rested on the sill; no blood trickled from the broken skin, and when I put my fingers to it, I could doubt no more.[3]

Emily's recapturing of childhood is less naive than Charlotte's, and thereby somewhat less convincing. She does, however, look past the single vision of the lonely child and see the effects of heredity and environment in families – the two influences fused as they are in life. Her story is a sense outside time, but it continually locates itself surely in her own age. The Victorian

[1] Ibid., Ch. 24.
[2] Ibid., Ch. 17.
[3] Ibid., Ch. 34.

'two nations' are figured in the neat, comfortable, effete Thrushcross Grange and its master Linton, set against the tempests of Wuthering Heights and Heathcliff. For all its oddity and lack of conformity, *Wuthering Heights* could have been written only when the novel was an established and consciously artistic form.

Further, it could have been written only by a poet. Emily Brontë has some claim to be the best woman poet of Victorian literature. It is true that she never fully developed a poetic language that got away from the influence of Romanticism and made a new exploration of the medium. Yet her integrity of vision, her quest for a complete identity, raise her achievement higher than her prosodic and linguistic skill. In totality, Christina Rossetti may be her superior; but she has expressions of high, moving intensity which few can rival. For the imaginative escape that is more than escapism, the age needed pieces like *The Prisoner*:

> Still let my tyrants know, I am not doom'd to wear
>   Year after year in gloom and desolate despair;
> The messenger of Hope comes every night to me,
>   And offers for short life, eternal liberty.
>
> He comes with Western winds, with evening's wandering airs.
>   With that clear dusk of heaven that brings the thickest stars:
> Winds take a pensive tone, and stars a tender fire,
>   And visions rise, and change, that kill me with desire.
>
> Desire for nothing known in my maturer years,
>   When Joy grew mad with awe, at counting future tears:
> When, if my spirit's sky was full of flashes warm,
>   I knew not whence they came, from sun or thunder-storm.
>
> But first, a hush of peace – a soundless calm descends;
>   The struggle of distress and fierce impatience ends.
> Mute music soothes my breast – unutter'd harmony
>   That I could never dream, till Earth was lost to me.

Realism and Sensation

By the middle of the nineteenth century the novel had reached a height of popularity that would have seemed unattainable twenty-five years earlier. The novelists had passed from anxious protestations that they did not corrupt innocence to a more positive assertion of their merits. The prestige of Dickens and Thackeray encouraged other writers to take themselves and their art more seriously. The critics followed more slowly, accepting the novel as a branch of literature worthy of more than passing attention. The old diehards eventually succumbed, until the *Edinburgh* was prepared to allow that fiction could be 'in a very high rank among the achievements of the human intellect',[1] though the *Quarterly* still tended to accompany praise of a novel with a certain apology for its being a novel at all.

The growth of realism in fiction came partly from the desire of that serious-minded age not to waste time on triviality. If the novel taught something about the 'real' world, where problems were pressing hard from all sides, reading novels did not seem such a frivolous activity. The novel was expected to portray life as it was being lived – and for the majority of readers that meant a middle-class existence firmly grounded in domesticity. The spirit which looked for verisimilitude and 'subject' in painting required the novelist to hold up a looking-glass that should be mildly flattering but not distorting for good or evil. Such at least was the theory: in practice the prevailing tension and nervous reluctance to face the whole truth, faithfully served by the controls of the circulating libraries, tended to give the novel a restricted view. As we have seen, the personal vision of writers like the Brontë sisters could win admiration when interpreted with technical skill. But as the reading of novels

[1] *Edinburgh Review*, April 1853.

increased, and the writing of them became a lucrative profession for the talent which fell short of genius, there came a levelling-out of attainment. The terrain of fiction showed smoother contours; its explorers were more assured but more accepting of their limitations, essaying fewer peaks and falling into fewer crevasses.

The concentration of fiction on limited and mainly externalized description was not universally commended. John Stuart Mill considered that avoidance of the inner conflict branded the novel as an inferior form.[1] In 1862 the young T. H. Green was patronizing about the kind of novelist who showed 'merely the outward and the natural, as opposed to the inner and ideal'.[2] At least the novel was being taken seriously by the minds who would not long before have dismissed it as trivial and incompetent. The question of why fiction was read and what role it should play in society was discussed in the leading periodicals.

The novel had to win over not only the philosophers but also the type of reader who 'on the strength of a number of manuscript sermons, and a pretty good library of divinity, considered herself literary'.[3] It sometimes succeeded too well: in 1860 a reviewer commented sadly, 'It is well if sitting up to your reading desk with Lemprière and the *Encyclopaedia Britannica* within reach, you can fathom the depth of your author'.[4] That the novel could inculcate principles had not been doubted by the authors of *Caleb Williams* and *Hermsprong* many years before, but the acceptance of the idea by the Victorians was bemused by controversy about how didacticism and fiction could be mingled. Should the novel be a reflection of society at which people might look to see familiar things in their profounder reality, or should it be more like a telescope to present new and hitherto unknown aspects of life? The bolder claim accorded well with the ideals of useful knowledge and helped to gain approval for the novel from the new class of readers, the educated artisans and servants for whom reading was a skill painfully acquired, rare and precious, not to be squandered.

[1] 'Thoughts on Poetry and its Varieties', in *English Critical Essays*, edited by Edmund D. Jones (London, 1947), p. 344.
[2] Quoted in Richard Stang, *The Theory of the Novel in England*, 1850–70 (London, 1959), p. 9.
[3] Elizabeth Gaskell, *Cranford* (1853), Ch. 1.
[4] *Fraser's Magazine*, August 1860.

Those who came to learn often stayed to be entertained by novelists of less ambitious theory.

The religious temper of the age helped where previously it had hindered. A tendency to sermonize came naturally to authors who had been brought up on weekly homilies, and their readers easily responded to doctrinal and ethical themes. From being feared as the instigator of vice, the novelist came to be approved for his power of making virtue attractive and showing the sad results of vice. Either way, the novel was held to affect behaviour; the guardians of morals remained vigilant for any lapse. Nor did the erring writer have to account only to one narrow sect; it was no Evangelical but the agnostic John Morley who said that French realism was 'only another name for a steady and exclusive devotion to a study of all the meanest or nastiest elements in character and conduct'.[1]

Domestic realism and didactic purpose were not enough to ensure the novel's success. Sensationalism was driven out of the door and flew back through the window, as it has a habit of doing in all ages. The old, crude tradition of writing about crime and low life was given a new respectability by the approval of realism and by the fact that the novel had proved itself a powerful medium for social criticism and reform. The adventurous novelist could get away with a great deal by paying lip-service to the ideal of the family and by claiming to expose abuses. His most respectable readers could swallow sordid episodes so long as the underlying ethos was 'decent'. Despite the acrimony of many critics, the sensation novel became increasingly popular.[2]

It brought success and reward to Charles Reade (1814–84), who crammed a great deal of writing into a generally crowded life. A Fellow of Magdalen College, Oxford, he managed to take a business interest in herrings and antique violins as well as writing novels and plays. His life was made more eventful by his engagements in litigation arising from his work as an author. Like Ainsworth and Lytton, he is remembered today mainly for

---

[1] *Macmillan's Magazine,* August 1866.

[2] In 1863 the *Quarterly* published an article on 'The Sensation Novel, which alleged that this type of fiction was forming the outlook of the new generation. Cheap periodicals, libraries and railway bookstalls were all blamed for its popularity and profusion. See Q. D. Leavis, *Fiction and the Reading Public* (London, 1934), pp. 159ff.

a historical novel that has come to be considered good reading for children. For *The Cloister and the Hearth* (1861) he researched hard on the fifteenth-century setting; the period was congenial to his involvement in the intellectual curiosity and social ferment of his own time.

For it was as a stark realist and an exposer of abuses that Reade became famous. He attacked the penal system in *It is Never Too Late to Mend* (1856), the cruelties of private lunatic asylums in *Hard Cash* (1863), the scuttling of ships for insurance money in *Foul Play* (1868), the unjust aspects of the new trade unionism in *Put Yourself in his Place* (1869–70). He came to the novel after writing for the theatre, where the extreme realism demanded by his stage directions was too much for some of the critics.[1] His experience as a dramatist may explain some of the strongest and weakest features of his novels, with their highly-charged and often effective scenes, their spaced climaxes and their episodic structure.

In his quest for realism Reade collected facts with the assiduity of a Gradgrind, talked to people with experience of the things he wanted to describe, amassed cuttings from news-papers. He drew on recent events as Trollope drew on them for the first of his Barsetshire novels, but there the resemblance ends. If Trollope's treatment of the popular novel is at times over-cautious, Reade's is frequently outrageous. He omits no trick of coincidence, melodrama, strategic sentimentality, facts concealed from the reader for most of the book. Why were both Trollope and Reade popular when one of them played scrupulously fairly with the reader and the other did not?

Trollope soothed his readers with a generally happy picture of the life that they cherished. Reade worked on their complacency in another way, by giving them sensation and appealing to the social conscience without calling on them to run out into the streets and demand immediate reform. To say this is not to impugn his sincerity; for all his mountebank's tricks he had a genuine passion for justice and a desire to right what was wrong. But there had been changes since the 'condition of England question' had been the theme of novelists. Although Reade pulls out every stop in his attacks, one does not feel the

[1] Sheila M. Smith, 'Realism in the Drama of Charles Reade', in *English*, Vol. 12, No. 69, pp. 94-103.

sense of direct involvement and personal responsibility that comes from the unsensational pages of Mrs Gaskell. Nor is there the disquieting alienation and private vision of the Brontës. Beneath the tirades, justifiable as they were, there is a new faith that discrete reforms can and will put things right. The great cry for a general change of heart is muted.

By the sixties, the machinery of reform was working fairly steadily. A campaign against a particular abuse was likely to lead to its eventual amendment, and Reade was in fact influential towards the correction of some of the things which he attacked. The State has now added reform to its recognized functions, and the duty of the conscientious individual is to put pressure on authority rather than to change his relations with every one of his fellow men. Reade's failure to move the modern reader is not entirely a mark of his weakness as a novelist. Whereas the novels of the forties had reflected Carlyle's unease, that of Ruskin and Arnold was ignored in the sixties; the novel no longer held this dissident role in Reade's time.

Wilkie Collins (1824–89) has found more lasting favour. In his own time he owed some of his success to his own merit and some to his association with Dickens, who found in the younger man a congenial companion and perhaps a happier extension of his own youth. Certainly he was willing to collaborate with Collins in some shorter pieces, and he made him the assistant editor of *Household Words* in 1856. Less polemical than Reade, Collins resembles him in showing how the demand for sensation was met when the worst social conditions were passing and the treatment of crime was becoming more efficient if little more enlightened.

He started in the fashion of historical romance with *Antonina* (1850), a story influenced in style and setting by *The Last Days of Pompeii*. A more individual talent began to appear with *Basil* (1852), where an eighteenth-century story is put into a contemporary setting, with full attention to the new demand for realistic detail and a generous allowance of crime, sensation and mystery. The mingling of mystery with the setting of quieter domestic fiction appeared in *Hide and Seek* (1854). All this was largely experimental work, where he was feeling for his own style and also apparently getting free from oppressive memories of his early life. His association with Dickens helped him, and there is stronger writing in *The Dead Secret* (1857). What is interesting about the early Collins is the way in which he took up the novelist's career deliberately and methodically, working to perfect his art along the lines which were most popular: it is a phenomenon much more common after his time than before it.

It was with *The Woman in White* (1859–60) that he really broke through into individual achievement. The theme of the desperate, fleeing woman had a counterpart in his own life and the idea of mistaken identity was also one which he drew from his reading and from personal contacts. Out of it all he created a story which still absorbs the reader's attention even while the intellect protests. His device of telling the story through several characters who take part in it gives a sense of being present at the actual investigation of the crime. The minor details of premonition and anxiety add up to a disturbing verisimilitude.

Collins continued the novel of sensation with *No Name* (1862) and *Armadale* (1864–6). In the latter he touches scenes such as an abortion den which reveal a criminal world less grossly violent but more distasteful than the earlier one of the 'Newgate novel'. The respectable veneer of the sixties covered a sordid world which research has still not fully explored. For Collins the realization of these depths was made more acute by a growing morbidity in his own nature, connected with excursions into drug-taking. There is, however, no falling of power in *The Moonstone* (1868), where the story is again told through different characters. Murder, drugs, mysterious foreigners, combine to build up sensation which is set against the plain realism of a police investigation. Sergeant Cuff is a model of the new detective, a more developed study of painstaking method than Dickens's Inspector Bucket. The old, melodramatic encounters of highwaymen and Bow Street Runners have yielded to the logical following of clues by a trained mind. Yet the sinister East Indians link up with an older tradition and may be seen as mid-Victorian substitutes for the wicked monks of the old Gothic novel.

The decline in Collins's later books comes from his unsuccessful attempt to enter the field of social criticism and reform. He had not the feeling for it, and his attitude remains coldly detached and without true sympathy. Further, he bases his attacks too obviously on his own experiences and prejudices; our knowledge of his own domestic arrangements gives less universal point to the attack on the marriage-laws in *Man and Wife* (1870). There is still power in the examination of prostitution in *The New Magdalen* (1872), but the novels that appeared in the last fifteen years of his life are mostly forced and overstated to the point of boredom.

The women novelists, no longer masked by masculine or epicene pseudonyms like the Brontës, but rather stressing their respectability by the use of their married names, came to new popularity with the spread of domestic realism in fiction. They got away with a great deal by giving a conventional background to sensationalism that could titillate without openly offending. They were accused of immorality in their writing, but they had their staunch defenders as well. Mrs Henry Wood (1814–87) started writing novels when her husband failed in business and the family needed money. Her first novel, *Danesbury House* (1860) was written for a prize offered by a temperance league for a novel showing up the evil of drink; an example of how the didactic power of the novel had come to be accepted. She won the prize, with a story that shows remarkably detailed knowledge of contemporary drinking habits, and went on to greater success with *East Lynne* (1860–1). Here she took the story of a wife estranged from her husband who comes back under the guise of a governess to her children. It is improbable, melodramatic, sentimental; and it contains such matters as bigamy and adultery – but it is based on the most firm moral presuppositions. The Victorians loved it, as a novel and in an adaptation for the stage.

Mrs Braddon (1837–1915) became Mrs Wood's great rival, even to the extent of their each acquiring control of a fiction magazine. The younger writer makes even more free with adultery, illegitimacy and the like, with a more mocking and less openly didactic tone. In spite of attacks, however, she managed to maintain an aura of respectability by assuring the ultimate triumph of conventional virtue. She could even get away with a tale of bigamy and murder in *Lady Audley's Secret* (1862). It would be otiose to claim any great interest for the modern reader in the women novelists who were so popular a hundred years ago – for example in the exotic and improbable debaucheries of the characters of Louise Ramé–Ouida (1839–1908), in whom the 'silver fork' novel flickered into life again before descending into the brittle pages of the cheap magazine. She was already out of date before the end of the century, as the more discerning critics realised:

> Perhaps the modern realism has made novelists desert the world where Dukes and Dowagers abound. Novelists do not know very much about it; they are not wont to haunt the gilded saloons, and they prefer to write about the manners which they know. A very good novel, in these strange ruinous times, might be written with a Duke for hero; but nobody writes it, and, if anybody did write it in the modern manner, it would not in the least resemble the old fashionable novel.[1]

Yet the old tendencies kept their hold on the novel. Under the truly great, under the popularly competent, there were writers who continued to turn out reading-matter with very few concessions to changing times. The heroine of *Northanger Abbey* would not have been short of books to her taste from the circulating libraries of the sixties. An American journalist who visited London in 1869 reported the conversation of an artist who was commissioned to illustrate the latest work of a 'great female London novelist'. Even if there were some exaggeration by the reporter, his informant or both, it is clear that the Gothic tradition was still very much alive. The lady had apparently demanded:

> 'I want two Convent scenes in the sixth chapter; a rocky pass, with a skeleton standing in the middle of the gap, his grisly arms outstretched, for the ninth chapter; and in the fifteenth chapter you must give me a powerful tableoo (*sic*) where the chief butler is discovered in the room off the banqueting-hall poisoning his mistress's wine.'[2]

The cult of domesticity, a liking for being mildly shocked and the general popularity of the novel all help to explain the overpraising in her own time of Elizabeth Barrett (1806–81). She was well esteemed as a poet before she was hauled out of Wimpole Street to become Mrs Browning. Her long poem

---

[1] Andrew Lang, 'The Last Fashionable Novel, in *Essays in Little* (1891). He goes on to discuss 'the ingenious lady who calls herself Ouida'.

[2] Daniel Joseph Kirwans, *Palace and Hovel*, edited by A. Alan (London, 1963), p. 61.

Aurora Leigh (1857) is in effect a novel in verse, with a theme pertaining to sentimental and sensational melodrama. The hero passes from one disaster to another, including the loss of his house in a fire and of his own sight like Charlotte Brontë's Rochester, until he finds happiness with his cousin who had originally refused him. It is heavy going for the modern reader, though at the time it seemed to deal with themes which it was inappropriate for a woman to handle.

Where the Brontës had put into the novel emotional experiences which had previously been mainly confined to poetry, Elizabeth Barrett used poetic form to tell a story that would have been better expressed in a novel. There are episodes that can still move us, but the language too often becomes stiff and pretentious. She lacked Browning's ability to create and sustain characters through the medium of poetry. Whatever her weaknesses may be, there is no doubt of her sincerity in appealing to those who were taking the novel seriously as a social phenomenon: those who were unhappy about many things in their society but fundamentally assured that it was on the whole the best of all possible worlds. She could make more direct attacks with short pieces like 'The Cry of the Children' which she wrote in the forties, and now she turned against the more subtle complacency that masked the cruelties of a world outwardly less brutal. She is of value for background information on the life of the age – and it is not often the best poetry which lends itself easily to such reading. Virginia Woolf put the point truly and fairly:

> The aunt, the antimacassars, and the country house from which Aurora escapes are real enough to fetch high prices in the Tottenham Court Road at this moment. The broader aspects of what it felt like to be a Victorian are seized as surely and stamped as vividly upon us as in any novel by Trollope or Mrs Gaskell.[1]

Her gifts fell short of her aspirations and she stretched them in that over-production which was the curse of Victorian literature as well as of other aspects of the age. Her *Sonnets from the Portuguese* (1847–50) have warmth, and a gentle humour that breaks through the frequently stilted diction. Her contemporaries were able to accept more readily the prevailing tone of

[1] 'Aurora Leigh', in *The Second Common Reader* (London, 1932).

her poetry. A mixture of the oracular and the domestically intimate jars on the modern reader, but it was a mixture to which they were well accustomed in their own homes. Perhaps after all her reputation has taken too deep a plunge; she wrote things which speak out not to one century alone, for instance:

> If thou must love me, let it be for nought
>   Except for love's sake only. Do not say
> 'I love her for her smile – her look – her way
>   Of speaking gently – for a trick of thought
> That falls in well with mine, and certes brought
>   A sense of pleasant ease on such a day' –
> For these things in themselves, Beloved, may
>   Be changed, or change for thee, – and love, so wrought,
> May be unwrought so. Neither love me for
>   Thine own dear pity's wiping my cheeks dry, –
> A creature might forget to weep, who bore
>   Thy comfort long, and lose thy love thereby!
> But love me for love's sake, that evermore
>   Thou may'st love on, through love's eternity.

12

Trollope

The fashion of domestic realism as the setting for popular fiction contributed to the success of Anthony Trollope (1815–82). Its decline helped in turn to reduce his reputation, a loss that started in his own lifetime when the novel was already crossing new frontiers, and was sharply increased by the posthumous publication of his *Autobiography* in 1883. His workmanlike approach to his craft offended lingering Romantic views of the artist. His revelation of set periods of work, with a calculated number of words to be put on paper, made his readers feel that they had somehow been cheated. They were irritated by the casual manner in which he described novel-writing as if it were a skill to be acquired by the steady application of certain techniques.

They ought not to have been surprised, since Trollope had managed to produce over fifty novels in the course of an active working life. His childhood had been wretched: he was the fourth and supposedly dull son of a mother who was continually dragging the family out of debt with her pen. Frances Trollope (1780–1863) was a well-known novelist in her own time and it is a pity as well as an irony that her least promising son should have come to overshadow her. She had a biting wit which she used to satirize middle-class pretensions and to expose social abuses. *The Widow Barnaby* (1839) held its popularity all through the century.

Like Dickens, Trollope found himself at school when the family fortunes were high and out of it when they were low. For him, the schools included Harrow and Winchester; he remembered them not as havens of culture in the midst of insecurity, but with misery which the urbane irony of age can scarcely conceal:

I feel convinced in my mind that I have been flogged oftener than any human being alive. It was just possible to obtain five scourgings in one day at Winchester, and I have often boasted that I obtained them all. Looking back over half a century, I am not quite sure whether the boast is true, – but if I did not, nobody ever did.[1]

At the age of nineteen he became a clerk in the Post Office, a profession in which he eventually reached high rank after a poor start. It was a turn of duty in Ireland starting in 1841 that seemed to release his personality and give him the impetus to start writing novels. His first books made little impression and it was back in England that he began a rapid rise to success. With *The Warden* (1855) he began the novels of 'Barsetshire' which are still his chief claim to readers' affection, though in fact they form only a small part of his output.

The list of his novels and stories is formidable and threatens to make a mere catalogue out of any short study. The Barsetshire novels proper are six in number, though settings and characters sometimes cut across into other books. *The Warden* was followed by *Barchester Towers* (1857), *Doctor Thorne* (1858), *Framley Parsonage* (1860–61), *The Small House at Allington* (1862–4) and *The Last Chronicle of Barset* (1866–7). The sequence was, however, interspersed with novels on different themes such as *The Three Clerks* (1858) in which he wrote out some of the bitterness of his early life in London. He continued all his life to write stories of the familiar domestic type, but his later years saw a movement from the quiet provincial life of Barchester to the world of public affairs and politics. In 1867 he left the postal service, stood unsuccessfully for Parliament, and began *Phineas Finn, the Irish Member*. This proved to be the first of several political novels, including *The Prime Minister* (1875–6) and *The Duke's Children* (1880). The last-named shows how far politics and their treatment in fiction had moved since *Coningsby*: the former Prime Minister suffers loneliness and self-doubt, his children marry outside the accepted circle of society in which he had moved.

Trollope's early struggles and domestic insecurity might well have made him a neurotic or a rebel – both familiar products of the age. He turned out in fact to be one of the most urbane and apparently contented Victorian novelists, sharing his readers'

[1] *Autobiography*, Ch. 1.

assumptions about life and taking them into his confidence instead of lecturing them about their failings. That is, as we shall see, not the whole story. To take his work at a broad sweep, however, it is reasonable to say that his outlook is essentially middle class: admiring the gentry without feeling awestruck, willing to be kind and helpful to the poor but preferring not to see too much of them.

His fictional world is consequently a world of many omissions, excluding some of the most disturbing features of the age as indeed many ordinarily comfortable people were inclined to exclude them. There is little mention of the problems of capital and labour in the new phase of industrialization that was going on during his most productive period. A character like Roger Scatcherd is indeed a typical figure of the 'rags-to-riches' saga, but he lacks the significance of Dickens's Rouncewell or Mrs Gaskell's Thornton. He is an oddity, an interesting 'sport', rather than a portent.

Trollope indeed is strangely silent about the real challenges to this society which he depicts mainly with approval. Even his famous feud between the old-fashioned and the newly-arrived clergy in the Barchester books does not penetrate far into theological controversy or spiritual ferment. The real strengths and weaknesses of the Evangelicals are hardly considered; the tormented consciences of the Oxford Movement have no place among these inheritors of the eighteenth-century 'high and dry' churchmanship. It would make little difference to the realism of the story if the Proudies were Tractarians and the Grantly faction were Evangelicals.

Bishop Proudie, his wife and his creature Mr Slope are seen as unsympathetic because they tend to upset the pleasant balance of life in which most people are as happy as the human condition allows. This acceptance of the *status quo* is characteristic of Trollope's early work; it accorded well with a large area of contemporary thought, kindly about particular suffering but unwilling to admit the need or the possibility of general change. In *The Warden* he set himself on the side of tradition, though with the right to criticize specific abuses, and he continued to hold that basic position for most of his career as a novelist.

The Warden shows how a tale of quiet, provincial life and

domestic realism could be combined with awareness of public events. The Church of England, still entrenched but now embattled, was more newsworthy than she had been for a long time. The story which Trollope tells is simple enough. Mr Harding, a gentle and devoted clergyman, is the Warden of an almshouse for old men – a sinecure given to him by his friend the Bishop. The endowments of the almshouse have appreciated in value over the years, a fact which arouses the reforming zeal of a young doctor, John Bold. The latter's campaign to let the bedesmen profit from the money which goes to the Warden works up into a national controversy. The chief protagonist of the established order is Archdeacon Grantly, whose wife is Harding's elder daughter; Bold is in love with the younger. When the crisis is at its height, with legal action and the intervention of the National press, Harding quietly resigns; the almshouse falls into decay.

Could there really be so much fuss about a minor ecclesiastical appointment? *The Warden* has to be read against the background of controversy that had been going on since the new Parliament assembled in 1832. Church dignitaries were trembling, some with fear and some, like Grantly, with indignation:

> He is a personal friend of the dignitaries of the Rochester Chapter, and has written letters in the public press on the subject of the turbulent Dr Whiston, which, his admirers think, must well nigh set the question at rest. It is also known at Oxford that he is the author of the pamphlet signed 'Sacerdos' on the subject of the Earl of Guildford and St Cross, in which it is so clearly argued that the manners of the present time do not admit of a literal adhesion to the very words of the founder's will.[1]

Grantly is in the very midst of two real controversies which recent inquiries had brought to light. The foundation of St Cross at Winchester had been involved in attacks similar to those made on the administration of Hiram's Hospital. At Rochester, the new head of the Cathedral School, Dr Whiston, had quarrelled with the Chapter over the question of endowments and had gone on to a wider issue with his pamphlet *Cathedral Trusts and their Fulfilment*. The dispute had been raised

[1] *The Warden*, Ch. 2.

in Parliament, and Whiston had eventually been reinstated after his dismissal.[1]

Grantly is, then, no old-fashioned clergyman clinging to privileges that he does not understand, but a man of the time. He is full of outward confidence that the world will continue to revolve steadily around the established order, but he is secretly insecure and fearful that all change will be for the worse. Against him stands John Bold, the early-Victorian 'new man':

Bold is a strong reformer. His passion is the reform of all abuses; state abuses, church abuses, corporation abuses (he has got himself elected a town councillor of Barchester, and has so worried three consecutive mayors, that it became somewhat difficult to find a fourth), abuses in medical practice, and general abuses in the world at large. Bold is thoroughly sincere in his patriotic endeavours to mend mankind, and there is something to be admired in the energy with which he devotes himself to remedying evil and stopping injustice; but I fear that he is too much imbued with the idea that he has a special mission for reforming. It would be well if one so young had a little more diffidence himself, and more trust in the honest purpose of others – if he could be brought to believe that old customs need not necessarily be evil, and that changes may possibly be dangerous; but no, Bold has all the ardour and all the self-assurance of a Danton, and hurls his anathemas against time-honoured practices with the violence of a French Jacobin.[2]

There indeed is the type of the reforming spirit, seizing the new possibilities of social change through legislation. It was indeed a type frequently brash in its methods, sometimes arrogant and even callous in its regard for principles above individuals. The shadow of the French Revolution continued to loom over cautious men in the middle of the nineteenth century who had lived through Chartism and were witnessing the growing strength of organized labour. What needs to be added is that the John Bolds were those who were gradually making British society more just and tolerable for all classes; without them, 'the violence of a French Jacobin' might indeed have been felt in this country.

Yet although he did not follow the line of radical reform, Trollope's achievement is not to be undervalued merely by

[1] See *The Whiston Matter* by Ralph Arnold (London, 1961).
[2] *The Warden*, Ch. 2.

contrast with those who did follow it. He may be able to write at length about rural society with scarcely a hint of what the agricultural labourer was enduring; he may seem to suggest that all the new capitalists need is to be absorbed into the higher classes and refined by them. The omissions do not negate his world, which is an imaginative model of contemporary England. It is conceived not with the imagination of Dickens or Charlotte Brontë, but with the inspiration of a good researcher who can breathe life into his sources. His novels are a guide-book to the age – a guide-book of the lively, idiosyncratic type that bears the distinctive imprint of its author. He does not fail in fancy, but he gives his fancy the backing of verifiable facts; his view of life is narrow by choice, not through ignorance.

Nor is that view quite so narrow as has sometimes been supposed. He lays out in his novels a panorama over which the reader can range from the rural scene of Barsetshire to the spa of *Miss Mackenzie* (1865), the small town of *Rachel Ray* (1863), the metropolis of the later political novels. The sight that he allows us is comprehensive rather than close: a bird's eye view with occasional swoops on the details of particular scenes. The swoops give a great deal of information about the life of the time – its meals, its social events, its offices and clubs, its churches, its travelling conditions.

His characters cover a wide area of society. Some, like the Duke of Omnium, link one series of books with another and increase the sense of complex but interwoven relationships which is given by Trollope's work as a whole. Whatever their social status, the characters are seen in relation to the structure of society; they are aware of the market value of property and of family alliances too. They are not allowed to become portentous, but are depicted with tolerance and amusement at their mixture of good and bad. There are no sudden conversions, no acts of wild inconsistency through the rebel spirit. There are scarcely any heroes or villains in the conventional sense, only people notably capable of noble or mean actions. This was no chance oversight, no lack of strength, but an essential part of Trollope's attitude to the novel:

When I declare that he [Harry Clavering] had not come to any firm resolution, I fear that he will be held as being too weak for the rôle of hero even in such pages as these. Perhaps no terms have been so injurious to the profession of the novelist as those two words, hero and heroine. In spite of the latitude which is allowed to the writer in putting his own interpretation upon these words, something heroic is still expected; whereas, if he attempt to paint from nature, how little that is heroic should he describe![1]

Trollope has no melodramatic setting of total good against total bad. He has no illusions even about his beloved clergymen; he can show up the pluralities, the indifferentism, the worldliness. A character like Mark Robartes in *Framley Parsonage* is no vehicle for anti-clericalism, nor is he a pious hero out of a church novel – still less from one of the 'false little dialogues between Tom the Saint and Bob the Sinner'[2] with which Trollope had even less patience. Robartes is a well-meaning enough young man whose convictions are honest but not deep enough to withstand the temptations of fashionable life. He is typical of what was likely to happen so long as holy orders conferred social status or financial advantage. Even Archdeacon Grantly, who grows into a dominant figure, is first introduced with the very faint commendation, 'Dr Grantly is by no means a bad man'.

Trollope's main weakness as a creator of character is a tendency to be verbose about emotional problems, without the deep analysis of motivation that can make us tolerate such fictional exercises. Yet though his balance and refusal to take matters to serious extremes can be infuriating, it nearly always wins some grudging admiration at his skill in spinning out a plot smoothly towards the conventional happy ending. He gets there without engaging the reader's full imaginative sympathy, but he gets there also without the excess of sentimentality which was rife in the novel at the time, although serious criticism was reacting against it. His satire on the way 'Mr Popular Sentiment' (almost certainly Dickens) would have treated the events narrated in *The Warden* is shrewd as well as amusing. His right to satirize is vindicated by his own quiet treatment of Mr Harding's farewell to the old bedesmen.

When Trollope is obstinate and goes against the popular demand for a romantic ending – as he did in refusing to let Lily Dale marry John Eames – the rebellion is the more

[1] *The Claverings* (1866–7), Ch. 28.
[2] 'Mary Gresley', in *An Editor's Tales* (1870).

exciting for its rarity. It gives him an illusion of depth and courage about human relations which is not borne out by his work as a whole – yet even the conjuring-trick is a tribute to his artistry. He pulls it off more than once; he is brilliant in his way of suggesting that he is being very frank and daring, when really he is saying almost nothing. An entirely virtuous girl refusing a proposal of marriage can seem to become a rather dubious character about whom the boldly realistic author withholds nothing:

> This was not quite ingenuous on Katchen's part, seeing that she had found herself obliged to refuse him long before he had spoken those harsh words. I am sorry to have to record it, but I am trying to describe her as she really was.[1]

He can rise to greater heights than this, however. The character of Crawley in *The Last Chronicle of Barset* touches the realms of obsession and psychosis without losing the realistic sense of participation in suffering. Crawley's pride in his poverty, his genuine piety, his humble acceptance of his own mental confusion, add up to a greater conception than the beginning of the Barchester series had promised. In his uncertainty when the accusation of stealing a cheque is added to former trials, he rises to tragic greatness as he preaches his final sermon to the congregation that he has served. The squabbles of the cathedral seem far away; the pluralities are forgotten as another side of Victorian established religion rises starkly before us:

> 'I have always known my own unfitness, by reason of the worldly cares with which I have been laden. Poverty makes the spirit poor, and the hands weak, and the heart sore, – and too often makes the conscience dull. May the latter never be the case with any of you.'[2]

Another study of mental obsession, this time of jealousy leading to madness, is the character of Louis Trevelyan in *He Knew he was Right* (1868–9).

The Trollope of the quiet cathedral town is indeed harder to find in the later novels of public and political life. He seems to disappear in *The Way we Live Now* (1874–5), which dissects and exposes the corruption of private and public behaviour in contemporary society. It is not his best novel, if judged by

---

[1] 'Katchen's Caprices', in *Harper's Weekly*, Nos. 521–6.
[2] *The Last Chronicle of Barset*, Ch. 69.

artistry and the power to give enjoyment. It is too long, sometimes melodramatic, and not balanced enough to make its
effect with full conviction. It is, however, a most interesting
participation in the general unease with the basis of society
that was afflicting many Victorians in that decade. Dickens had
already dealt with the new power of money; his brilliance does
not make Trollope's achievement negligible, and the powerful
creation of Merdle does not eclipse that of Melmotte who also
kills himself after misfortune has overtaken him. The worthy
Roger Carbury who acts as the author's spokesman is less
memorable than the financier. Nor is this novel a mere red-
action of old themes. We are in the new world, the second
Victorian age, when British interests are expanding far beyond
her own shores. Melmotte is not insular in his machinations but
is engaged in such projects as the 'manipulation of the shares of
the Mexican railway'.[1]

There is considerably more to Trollope than the gentleman
who enjoyed hunting foxes, who acquiesced cheerfully in the
wealth and fame that his writings brought him. There is more
to him than the novelist who gave his readers the complacent
image of society that accorded with their desire. He inherited
some of his mother's astringency, and it becomes more marked
in his later books. Yet criticism of injustice is not absent from
his first attempts. There is understanding of the harsh plight of
Ireland under English rule in *The Macdermots of Ballycloran*
(1847) and *The Kellys and the O'Kellys* (1848), and a stern attack
on tyranny in *La Vendée* (1850). He had little time on the whole
for gloomy warnings about the state of the nation, and could
ridicule Carlyle in *The Warden* as 'Dr Pessimist Anticant', but
all this may conceal a degree of guilt and anxiety. The almost
hysterical note in parts of *The Way we Live Now* is the voice of a
man who has lived too long at odds with his conscience.

If he seldom attacked the middle-class ideal of the family,
he did not fail to see its tensions. Pressures are shown to build
up in all social strata: marriages are opposed because the
alliance would not be of advantage to the wider family interest.
Relatives find themselves awkward or estranged, as when the
Archdeacon's daughter passes into the great world of the
nobility. The expectations of Crosbie are disappointed so that

[1] *The Way we Live Now*, Ch. 73.

he finds himself with a well-connected wife but forced to struggle to save his financial pledge from being dishonoured. The aristocracy emerge from the pages of Trollope as inadequate to deal with the realities of life, and his distrust of the traditional solutions becomes more open as his experience grows. In the early novels the rural scene is dominant and seems to enshrine the truly abiding life of the nation: London is a place of discomfort and vague menace, to be visited as seldom and as briefly as possible. In his later books, the point of balance has shifted to the capital; clergy and farmers are replaced by politicians, lawyers and financiers. It was in truth the way that things were tending.

The impression that Trollope is no more than a competent journeyman of the novel was once seemingly confirmed by his deceptively easy style. His novels generally flow smoothly, dealing with trivialities in a manner than avoids bathos, playing lightly with imagination but never losing touch with sober reality. How splendidly recorded is the moment when Mrs Proudie lapses into the melodrama of inferior fiction, and how well Trollope shows her as ridiculous against the realism of his narrative. Bertie Stanhope has just torn her elaborate train and is trying to disengage it from the sofa in which it is caught:

'Unhand it, sir!' said Mrs Proudie. From what scrap of dramatic poetry she had extracted the word cannot be said; but it must have rested in her memory, and now seemed opportunely dignified for the occasion.[1]

Or he can catch the subtle undertones of feminine conversation, with just enough comment to show that the honeyed words cover venom:

'You're getting on famously, my dear,' said the lady from Barbados.
'Pretty well, thank you, ma'am,' said Miss Viner.
'Mr Forrest seems to be making himself quite agreeable. I tell Amelia' – Amelia was the young lady to whom in their joint cabin Miss Viner could not reconcile herself – 'I tell Amelia that she is wrong not to receive attentions from gentlemen on board ship. If it is not carried too far' – and she put great emphasis on the 'too far' – 'I see no harm in it.'

[1] *Barchester Towers*, Ch. 11.

'Nor I, either,' said Miss Viner.

'But then Amelia is so particular.'

'The best way is to take such things as they come,' said Miss Viner – perhaps meaning that such things never did come in the way of Amelia. 'If a lady knows what she is about she need not fear a gentleman's attentions.'

'That's just what I tell Amelia; but then, my dear, she has not had so much experience as you and I.'[1]

There is a whole chapter of social history in the subtle insult of the last sentence as spoken by a mid-Victorian married woman to an unmarried one. We have come to understand that Trollope's daily industry did not deceive him into banality; he writes with the artlessness that conceals art.[2]

He shows some of the symptoms of hack-writing though his genius overcomes them. He often draws out a slight theme to the length of a novel, brilliantly giving it full life by his richness of character and incident. It is true that he was writing when the demand for novels was great and increasing, but that very fact was bringing strong competition. The new fiction magazines were offering a serial novel as well as other matter for a shilling, and cheap reprints of earlier novelists were attracting a large section of the new reading public. It was a sign of the times that the serial parts of *The Last Chronicle of Barset* were published at sixpence instead of the customary shilling; 'the enterprise', Trollope commented later, 'was not altogether successful'.[3]

Trollope regularly made the best of his talent by not attempting to beyond what he could do well. He conformed to what the age demanded in respect of morality and restraint, though not without some brushes with those who were even more cautious, as when his publisher raised questions about the vulgar character of Signora Neroni in *Barchester Towers*.[4] His accommodation to the moral demands of the time is usually brilliant and allows him to produce young men neither heroic nor demonic but thoroughly credible. John Eames kissing the

[1] 'The Journey to Panama', in *Lotta Schmidt and others Stories* (1867).

[2] See 'Trollope's Style' in Geoffrey and Kathleen Tillotson, *Mid-Victorian Studies* (London, 1964), pp. 56–61; 'Trollope and his Style', by Hugh Sykes Davies, in *A Review of English Literature*, Vol. 1, No. 4, pp. 73–85.

[3] *Autobiography*, Ch. 15.

[4] Michael Sadlier, *Trollope: a Commentary* (London, 1945), pp. 170ff.

landlady's daughter when he is in love with Lily Dale is truer
to life than the stop-go morality with which Thackeray makes
young Pendennis warm-blooded and amorous but entirely
chaste.

Later on he was prepared to go further, as the urge for the
novelist's freedom of expression was growing and giving a
double edge to the concept of 'realism'. If the novelist was to be
true to life, were there any areas that he ought to exclude? The
question that was to become more controversial before the end
of the century was already being asked. Trollope, in his later
work, did not lack courage in dealing with moral problems. His
treatment of the misfortunes of the 'fallen woman' in *The Vicar
of Bullhampton* (1869–70) was compassionate and honest. He
was prepared to defend it in the published preface and in
private correspondence:

> Of course one's sympathies are with the fathers and mothers and
> brothers, – and should be so; but not the less should one have mercy
> on the most terrible sufferers of this age; – on a class who suffer
> heavier punishment in proportion to their fault than any other, and
> who often have come to their ineffable misery almost without fault
> at all. It would be quite against the grain with me to represent such a
> woman as interesting, charming, fit for diamonds, and a thing to be
> adored.[1]

This was a fair view at the end of the decade which has come to
be regarded as one of the murkiest in the sexual conduct of
British society. It was only a few years since Mayhew had given
factual evidence of the huge number of prostitutes, ranging
from the romanticized companions of the rich ('fit for dia-
monds') to the pathetically degraded streetwalkers and camp-
followers.[2]

Far-seeing and myopic; compassionate and complacent;
there is much in the paradoxes of Trollope that helps us to
comprehend the paradoxes of his age. To return in the end to
his early work – what happened to Mr Harding after he had
resigned from the wardenship of the almshouse? He is given
'the smallest possible parish', with a tiny church close to the

---

[1] In a letter to Anna Steele dated 25 May 1870; *The Letters of Anthony Trollope,*
edited by B. A. Booth (Oxford, 1951), p. 461.

[2] Henry Mayhew, *Those That Will Not Work,* volume 4 of *London Labour and the
London Poor* (1862).

cathedral. He is a good clergyman, humble, devoted, un-ambitious, and 'here he performs afternoon service every Sunday and administers the Sacrament *once in every three months*'.[1] It was because men as good and intelligent as Anthony Trollope could not see anything wrong in this kind of situation that the Church of England had to suffer attacks from without before she could reform herself within and begin once more to be a living force in English society.

[1] *The Warden*, Ch. 21; my italics.

13

Tennyson and Browning

The Victorian period produced no poetic movement comparable in vigour to the two generations of the Romantics, and at no time after 1832 were the majority of the leading writers making poetry their chief preoccupation. In the early years there was a hiatus in English poetry as the trails of Romanticism died away and no new signpost confidently showed the way ahead. Other types of writing had been quietly gaining ground, and poetry henceforth had to compete with the novel and the essay, the treatise and the pamphlet – with forms that were not new but were now attaining a new dignity and significance. Poetry was no longer the acme of literary composition, nor was the poet the most honoured of writers, the one genuine 'maker'.

Most of the Romantic poets were dead when Victoria came to the throne, though Wordsworth lived on until 1850 and Southey until 1843, but they had impressed their pattern on poetry and on the popular notion of what poetry should be. Of them all, Keats ironically left the strongest influence: ironically, because his life had been the shortest and his recognition the most grudging and belated. Tennyson started under his spell, and Browning came early to him from Shelley by way of *Adonais*.

Tennyson and Browning both lived to commit faults typical of the first-generation Romantics, writing too much and trying to force poetry out of events and experiences that would not readily yield it. They did, however, revive social respect for the poet and help to correct the image created by the escapades of Shelley and Byron. A generation imbibing the ideas of Carlyle and Thomas Arnold was inclined to see effeminacy in the writing of poetry and probable immorality in the claim to be a poet. Two men who could devote their lives to poetry without being any less virile or respectable than their fellows did something to reinforce Pope's satirical claim that 'a poet's of some weight, And, though no soldier, useful to the state'.[1] They were the most important poetic voices of their time, but it is erroneous to think of them as identical, or antithetical, or even complementary. To compare them is valid only if we start from a recognition of their individuality. Born within a few years of one another, living through the same public events and feeling the impact of many of the same ideas, what poetic expression did they give to experience?

The elder of the two, Alfred Tennyson, was born in 1809 at Somersby in Lincolnshire where his father was Rector. The darker side of his poetry was perhaps rooted in memories of that frustrated, almost embittered priest who neither knew nor communicated the blessing of personal peace. The mother gave, more gently, the Evangelical piety which was becoming dominant in many families, both clerical and lay. At Cambridge, Tennyson won the Chancellor's prize for verse with his poem *Timbuctoo,* and fell in with the group who called themselves 'the Apostles'. The fact that students like to argue about everything under the sun, and beyond it, was no new thing then, and is happily in no danger of disappearing. The Apostles, however, were more thorough than most such groups, and with better-defined intentions. They acknowledged the philosophical influence of Coleridge and dedicated themselves to inquiry, with the belief that all things could be properly investigated with due reverence. New truths might be found, without the loss of all the old – a forward-looking view in contrast to the appeal to antiquity of the Oxford Tractarians.

Here Tennyson began his friendship with Arthur Hallam, who became engaged to his sister and with whom he travelled abroad after taking his degree. Then came quiet years at Somersby and, after his father's death, at High Beech in Epping Forest. They were years of poverty too, years when the melancholy ate more deeply and was not dispelled by the gradual coming of fame as a poet. Hallam died in 1833, leaving him to mourn for the first real understanding and sympathy that he had known. Yet despite – or because of – all this, his poetry continued to appear; volumes of it in 1830, 1833 and 1842 each attracted much favourable attention. He was,

[1] *Epistle to Augustus,* lines 203ff.

however, at a low ebb of health and money in 1845 when Peel granted him a small civil pension. His reputation was increased by *The Princess* (1847), and 1850 was the golden year when he was made Poet Laureate in succession to Wordsworth and was at last able to marry.[1] It was also the year of *In Memoriam,* the elegy for Hallam which he had started in 1833 and now published as a thematic whole.

Acknowledged now as the premier British poet, with the personal and official approval of the Queen and the Prince Consort, he went on writing with Victorian prodigality. *Maud* appeared in 1855 and *Idylls of the King* started in 1859. He wrote for the theatre too, managing to do better with poetic drama than had men like Talfourd and Henry Taylor. He had the distinction of Irving for *Queen Mary, Becket* and *The Cup,* of the Kendals for *The Falcon.* He was made a baron in 1883, and his death in 1892 was followed by a state funeral and a tomb in Westminster Abbey.

Robert Browning did not win a peerage or the Queen's personal regard, but he shared with Tennyson the respect of society. He was born in 1812 in Camberwell, a district which was then scarcely part of London but which grew in his lifetime into one of the most populous metropolitan suburbs. His father, a clerk in the Bank of England, had faced the frustration of early hopes with a serenity denied to Tennyson's. His mother contributed the Evangelical strain without the puritan narrowness of the mid-century. It was a happy family, far from any stereotype of the nineteenth-century home, establishing a security which never entirely forsook him. After leaving school at fourteen, he spent a brief time at the newly founded University College, London, and an even briefer one at Guy's Hospital. At the age of twenty-two, the influence of an uncle gave him two months in Russia, and four years later he made his first visit to Italy. Then, and when he went to Naples and Rome in 1844, the country captured his imagination and his love. He spent many of his later years there, used Italian settings in poetry and became such a staunch friend of resurgent

---

[1] He had been engaged to Emily Sellwood, whose sister Louisa was married to his brother Charles. The break-up of the latter's marriage had caused the breaking of the engagement as well but both marriage and engagement were restored in 1849.

Italian patriotism that Mazzini could encourage his fellow-exiles in London by reading aloud to them from *The Italian in England.*

An aunt paid for the publication in 1833 of *Pauline,* which failed to sell a single copy. At the height of his fame Browning was inclined to disown his firstborn; he felt some embarrassment at the querulously Shelleyan tone of this young man's poem of soul-searching and conflict with elders.

> I am ruined who believed
> That though my soul had floated from its sphere
> Of wild dominion into the dim orb
> Of self – that it was strong and free as ever!
> It has conformed itself to that dim orb,
> Reflecting all its shades and shapes . . .[1]

He did better with *Paracelsus* (1835), which won him kind words from John Forster: 'Without the slightest hesitation we name Mr Robert Browning at once with Shelley, Coleridge, Wordsworth'.[2] The critic's hindsight can see an anticipation of later work in this tale of an alchemist who learns that knowledge without love is barren. It brought him into literary society. He was a guest at Talfourd's dinner to celebrate the first performance of *Ion,* when Macready turned to him with the proposal, 'Write a play, Browning, and keep me from going to America',[3] – a request which shows the difference between the aspirations of an early-Victorian actor and a modern one. Browning did in fact write several plays, starting with *Strafford* (1837), but they brought him neither profit nor much satisfaction. However, his association with the theatre served him well in poetry, as it served Dickens in the novel.

Browning's reputation for obscurity was established by *Sordello* (1840), a long study of an idealist who finds himself still held within the hard world of sense. The gift of projection into a poetic character had not yet matured, and our impatience with *Sordello* is due perhaps less to its difficulty than to its obviously literary inspiration. It smells of the lamp, though it

---

[1] *Pauline,* lines 89ff.

[2] 'Evidences of a New Genius for Dramatic Poetry', in *The New Monthly Magazine,* March 1836.

[3] Mrs Sutherland Orr, *Life and Letters of Robert Browning* (rev. ed. London, 1908), p. 82.

attempted things which no other poet at the time could have done so well. Browning's father paid for the publication, in shilling numbers, of *Bells and Pomegranates* (1841–6). Meanwhile there began the correspondence with Elizabeth Barrett which led to their meeting, elopement and fugitive marriage in 1846. They lived in Italy until her death in 1861. These middle years brought Browning's greatest work, with the poems collected as *Men and Women* (1855), *Dramatis Personae* (1862) and *The Ring and the Book* (1868). There came at last such public homage as the formation of the Browning Society in 1881, and the social success which made the young Henry James unable to equate the noble poet with the man who was always dining out and enjoying himself with such enthusiasm.[1] But it was in his beloved Italy that Browning died in 1889; like Tennyson, he was buried in Westminster Abbey.

Although serious criticism has been more penetrating, there is still a popular image of Browning as a super-optimist, reflecting the heartiness of a complacent age devoted to the cult of muscular Christianity. Tennyson is seen as a rather vapid neo-Romantic, turning out odes on royal birthdays and pandering to the jingoistic patriotism of the age whenever he was not lost in medieval mists. Browning is too often associated with the one line 'God's in His heaven, all's right with the world', which is in fact put into the mouth of a dramatically-conceived character on a particular occasion. One might as well sum up Shakespeare's philosophy in the vituperation of Thersites. As for birthday odes, the Laureate was no longer obliged to produce them by the time Tennyson held the office.

These are light answers to weightless criticism. It is true that Tennyson could show almost the insularity of a Podsnap: he seldom travelled out of England, and he once turned back from Italy without reaching Rome because he could not get his favourite tobacco.[2] He could voice national patriotism while saying little about social conditions. Critics have noticed that in *The Princess* the poet is the guest of a prosperous magnate and seems happy enough about the profitable alliance between the old aristocracy and the new industrialism.

[1] L. Edel, *Henry James: The Conquest of London* (London, 1962), pp. 330ff.
[2] Gertrude Reese Hudson, ed., *Browning to his American Friends* (London, 1965), pp. 279ff.

More important than outward acquiescence is the theme of inner conflict and divided personality which recurs in his poetry from the suicidal thoughts of *The Two Voices* to the anguish of *In Memoriam*. Tennyson often tried to come to terms with the new age and equally often retreated into the comfort of idealized medievalism – a retreat shared, in divers ways, by many Victorian writers. *The Palace of Art* anticipates the 'Byzantium' poems of Yeats, with desire to leave the world of nature for the static peace of artifice; but the earlier poet is drawn back to the real world by disturbing awareness of sin.

The agonizing often ends with a weary resignation, a sad acceptance that things must be as they are. The desire for withdrawal and its accompanying guilt may be covered by sensuous imagery as in *The Lotos Eaters* and *The Lady of Shallott*. In *Locksley Hall*, and with finer effect in *Maud*, the soliloquizing hero rages at circumstances before resigning himself to life without happiness. A sickliness in the protagonist of *Maud* reflects the sickliness of a whole society. It is a study of a basically weak and insecure personality trying to assert himself within conflicting pressures: and that is one truth, though not the whole truth, about Victorian England. Tennyson had almost an obsession with sickness, medicine and hospitals.

Browning, however, has little mention of sickness and bodily decline. The Bishop ordering his tomb is remarkably vigorous and seems, like most of the people in the poems, to be bursting with energy. When Browning's creations suffer, they suffer more often from blows and violence than from illness. When one of them is roused to anger he is liable to express it in physical terms, as the unspeaking auditor roughly handles 'Mr Sludge'. While Tennyson wilts and withdraws before the threats of the age, Browning expands his muscles and shakes his fist at them. His famous optimism is more truly the tolerance which a vigorous man can afford to show. It is not the optimism which is blind to evil, but the objectivity of the artist who sees all and portrays what he sees. Like his own Fra Lippo Lippi, Browning painted a huge fresco crammed with characters of all kinds – the good and the bad, the imaginary and the recognizable contemporaries. The bad have a Chaucerian gusto; his rogues speak up for themselves and make their defences.

Ugliness, of body or of character, yields grotesque interest and amusement.

There must be a reservation here. Browning is a master at showing human frailty, but does he comprehend the deepest evil? His indignation is strongest when aroused by what touches him directly, as *Mr Sludge the Medium* expresses his wrath at his wife's leanings towards spiritualism and the pretence of Home, the American medium. He could indeed touch the degree of horror which Tennyson touched more often, as in the dreamlike dread of *Childe Roland* where the challenge is willingly accepted. It is true that, here and elsewhere, Browning is a little vague about what the acceptance entails, that he seems to find justification in action itself rather than in its motives or consequences, and to be satisfied with such affirmations as, 'I was ever a fighter, so one fight more'.[1]

Where Browning looked most deeply into his age was in recognition of a society no longer whole. All his major characters have failed to express the total vision of truth, while grasping at a facet of it. Both poets could still write in terms of generally-accepted presuppositions, but Tennyson is inclined to surrender when these threaten to lose their validity. Browning fights on, the liberal Victorian who can take his ease among his peers but still see the battlefield of a fragmenting society not far away.

Neither of them now seems to be a great philosopher, in the sense of having a system of thought about the nature of being. It is unlikely that a modern history of literature would entrust the chapter on Browning to a Professor of Moral Philosophy.[2] The poet does not make a model of the world from which he can explain it, but rather selects from apparent experience and finds there a pattern for what is universal. Browning's flashes of insight and sympathy illuminate our own less vivid experience. We seem to be directly addressed in our own situations; we become the silent listener to the dramatic monologue or the recipient of the poetic letter; we share not by observation but by participation. What we share is not particularly new or striking: the need for love, compassion,

---

[1] *Prospice,* lines 13ff.
[2] *Cambridge History of English Literature,* Vol. 13, Ch. 3.

honesty, and above all the need to keep striving and aspiring. It is not new, but it is not therefore obsolete.

Tennyson offers these values too, but with less emphasis on perseverance in striving. His morality seems more facile than Browning's, lacking the sense of discovery after a long and hard quest. Meredith saw Tennyson as a great poet spoiled by 'The Curate's moral sentiments, the British matron and her daughter's purity of tone'.[1] Others have accused him of reducing the great Arthurian themes in *Idylls of the King* to the conventions of mid-Victorian morality. Judgements like these presuppose that such conventions are to be deplored. They were imperfect certainly, and they often won only lip-service and were secretly broken, but in themselves they were not contemptible.

To Victorian society as a whole, morality seemed inseparable from the Christian religion, though some were questioning this and seeking for a humanist substitute. There were doubts in plenty, and religion was becoming a matter of open debate, but there were few who assumed atheism or agnosticism with indifference. Neither Tennyson nor Browning wrote much religious poetry in the narrow sense, but they kept within the bounds of orthodoxy while being aware of the storms that were shaking it. Tennyson tended to seek escape from the shortcomings of modern religion into a fancied age of faith. Browning also became impatient with many of the outer signs of religion, perhaps from dislike of their narrowness and unaesthetic quality as much as from problems of belief. It was he who showed the better historical perspective, ready to satirize what is amiss in any age without condemning the whole.

In *Bishop Blougram's Apology*, Browning makes a Roman Catholic bishop (probably based on Wiseman) defend himself to an agnostic journalist. The tone is one of reason, of casuistry made necessary by the problems of the age. Acknowledging the difficulties of orthodox belief, Blougram challenges his opponent with the folly of changing uncertain faith into equally uncertain scepticism. He speaks frankly, and with a sense of history:

'Had I been born three hundred years ago

[1] *Letters of George Meredith*, ed. W. M. Meredith (London, 1912), Vol. I, p. 197.

> They'd say, "What's strange? Blougram of course believes,"
> And, seventy years since, "Disbelieves of course".
> But now, "He may believe; and yet, and yet,
> How can he?" '[1]

The arguments are forceful; yet, and not here alone, Browning seems to pass lightly over things that were troubling his contemporaries. There is too much desire to be all-inclusive, a willingness to accept cheerfully the old and the new, like the juxtaposition of pagan and Christian images planned by that other bishop ordering his tomb in St Praxed's Church. The challenge of science seems to have been little challenge to Browning. The evolutionary idea appealed to him as a symbol of striving hopefully, years before *The Origin of Species* appeared. *Paracelsus* lauds Man as the summit of the evolutionary process, but the later *Cleon* is more doubtful and follows the hope of advancement with the comment, 'Most progress is most failure'.

Browning's faith rests less on intellectual conviction than on trust and love. The doubts that he expresses are seldom those distinctive of his time, but rather those which flow directly and perhaps inevitably from living Christian experience. Human love seems a reflection of divine love, its very existence revealing God who gives it life and scope. Yet under this teleological faith there is fear – what if our sense of the divine be only a wishful projection of the human?

> Only, heart's utmost joy and triumph, terror
> Sudden turns the blood to ice: a chill wind disencharms
> All the late enchantment! What if all be error –
> If the halo irised round my head were, Love, thine arms?[2]

Further, where does evil stand in relation to divine love? To this oldest of theological questions Browning gives an answer more satisfactory to his day than to ours: evil is a necessary part of the struggle towards better things. Men must know evil and suffering if they are to develop free will and are not to be carried along helplessly in the tide of evolutionary change.

> No, when the fight begins within himself,
> A man's worth something. God stoops o'er his head,

---

[1] *Bishop Blougram's Apology*, lines 415ff.
[2] Epilogue to *Ferishtah's Fancies*, lines 25ff.

Satan looks up between his feet – both tug –
He's left, himself, i' the middle: the soul wakes
And grows. Prolong that battle through his life!
Never leave growing till the life to come![1]

While Browning thrashed out his faith through creatures of his imagination, Tennyson carried on the dialogue with himself. His knowledge of science was greater than Browning's; from his youth, he showed the typically Victorian blend of fascination and worry about new discoveries. He was early aware of the evolution question; the subject of embryonic development interested him especially, as it was later to interest James Joyce. The scientific writings current when he was a young man were well calculated to swing the pendulum between hope and despair. He knew Herschel's *Preliminary Discourse on the Study of Natural Philosophy,* a cheerful interpretation of the new problems posed by geology, but he was also worried by the way in which Lyell's discoveries upset biblical chronology. He was somewhat more cheered by Robert Chambers's *Vestiges of Creation* (1844), which pointed out that if events are indeed governed by scientific laws the latter may be expressions of divine will.

Tennyson came to believe that Christianity would win the battle with new ideas, but he was haunted by fear that the pure spiritual light of former times would be partially dimmed by scientific and philosophical positivism. This fear runs through *In Memoriam,* and is resolved only by an appeal to personal experience:

If e'er when faith had fall'n asleep,
    I heard a voice, 'Believe no more'
And heard an ever-breaking shore
    That tumbled in the Godless deep;

A warmth within the breast would melt
    The freezing reason's colder part,
And like a man in wrath the heart
    Stood up and answer'd, 'I have felt.'[2]

In fact, both Tennyson and Browning ultimately stood by the subjective experience of faith as the answer to criticism. There is a vagueness in their belief which is common enough in the

[1] *Bishop Blougram's Apology,* lines 693ff.
[2] *In Memoriam,* canto 124.

religious writing of the nineteenth century outside the work of trained theologians (and sometimes within it). The agonizing debate ends in a desire to accommodate all possibilities, leaving retreat open in several directions if new knowledge brings more certainty. To compare the subjectivism of Tennyson and Browning with that of their contemporary Kierkegaard is to realize its inadequacy.

One of their achievements was to teach people to look afresh at the natural world, which was shrinking under the observations of science and being occluded by urban expansion. No major English poet after them could write so freely and so unself-consciously about nature. They both combined a love of rural beauty with that curiosity about the phenomenal world which had been steadily increasing for two centuries. Tennyson's nature-poetry is more within the Romantic tradition, drawing much from his early years in Lincolnshire. He knew rural scenes and rural life better than did Browning, the townsman and creator of town-dwellers, but the latter could still appreciate the countryside which came near to the town's edge. Browning's dynamic, throbbing world of sense owes at least as much to art as to natural observation; it is full of changing shapes and colours. For him, art and music were vital things, participants in the great struggle, rather than the colder means of escape that they often were for Tennyson.

They were true Victorians also in the length of their best work, rescuing the long poem from the pre-Victorian depths to which it had sunk with versifiers like Pollok and Montgomery. Browning poured out the sum of his belief in *The Ring and the Book,* telling from different points of view the story of a murder in Renaissance Italy. Few readers who have persevered to the end can have failed to admire his skill in showing the complexity of motives, the need to see all sides of the case and be compassionate to them all. Like Dickens in the novel, he can show the involvement of all society in an apparently isolated case of injustice. But again, few readers can have failed to note wearily how Browning goes on and on, often becoming tedious and then suddenly waking the drowsy attention with a fine flash. He gives an inner unity to the long poem; nothing is unimportant within the total scheme. He can evoke and populate a distant scene, not perhaps with the historian's accuracy but with the air of an entertainer who sets up a sensational trick.

While Browning carries on a dialogue with fancied opponents or with the world in general, Tennyson follows the stream of his own mind. He builds up a mood rather than creates a dramatic situation in pieces like *Ulysses* and *Tithonus*. Browning's people give a monologue in the concert-hall sense, but Tennyson's are talking to themselves. The setting and incidental details in Tennyson, sensuously lovely as they may be, show the ambience of the central character but not a dynamic background for conflict. It may well be that our own introspective and existentially-minded age finds his distress the more compelling for not being externalized.

Both of them learned early to develop away from the Romantic imagery and phrasing which lesser poets carried on to a final decadence. Tennyson indeed is the more conventional of the two, saved from mere imitation by his own fine ear and ability to control linguistic patterns in a perfect combination of sound and sense. He was sometimes carried away by the pattern, as Browning was sometimes carried away by his own verbal cleverness. At his best, Browning made poetic language take a step forward, mastering the colloquial strain without losing discipline of form. In an age that was having problems with language in all fields and searching for more precise, objective expression of new concepts, he showed that poetry could still deal with metaphysical themes and did not need either padding or artificial turns of phrase to remain poetical. His contemporaries often found him obscure, a charge which he repudiated; but this charge is made less often by the modern reader who has learned to find his way through Joyce, and through Pound and Eliot, who both owed something to Browning. He wrote to Ruskin, who was puzzled by sections of *Men and Women:*

> You ought, I think, to keep pace with the thought, tripping from ledge to ledge of my 'glaciers', as you call them; not stand poking your alpenstock into the holes and demonstrating that no foot could have stood there:- suppose it sprang over there?[1]

The vigour of this 'springing over' makes Browning succeed with his eccentricities, his abrupt, broken turns of phrase, his

[1] Quoted in John Bryson, *Browning* (London, 1959), p. 8.

daring and sometimes outrageous rhyming: successful except when he misjudges and drops into the 'glacier'.

Without either of them, English poetry would lack some of the qualities which have come to seem distinctive of its tradition. Tennyson and Browning impressed poetic order on a wide variety of themes and attitudes, in a society already suffering fragmentation and doubt. For that reason, our knowledge of their age, and our understanding of its consequences, would also be the poorer.

14

Ruskin

Although the dread of impending revolution and class-warfare receded after the middle of the century, other anxieties about the relationships within society increased. The majority of the middle class might feel that a threatening situation had passed away and that the Great Exhibition of 1851 had opened a new era of peace and prosperity. They were encouraged in their optimism by Prince Albert himself, who observed in the official catalogue:

> The progress of the human race, resulting from the common labour of all men, ought to be the final object of the exertion of each individual. In promoting this end, we are accomplishing the will of the great and blessed God.[1]

The pious aspirations based on material success did not seem unfounded. The Crystal Palace was crammed with evidence that this was the new age of machinery, of ever-increasing production, of the subjugation of the natural world to human skill – and of course Britain was leading the way.

The nation was indeed beginning to benefit from the investments of earlier years and the application of new inventions. There were plenty of hands to manage the new machines, as the high birthrate at the beginning of the reign now yielded ample cheap labour. Prices were rising, but there were enough jobs to employ all the members of large families. Free trade and the open market were becoming the watchwords of commercial philosophy, pointing towards the end of international strife and the spread of general prosperity. Not for the first or the last time in history, ideas which suited the few were accepted without much question by the majority.

Yet the spirit of protest was not dead, even among those who

[1] C. H. Gibbs-Smith, *The Great Exhibition of 1851* (London, 1950), p. 26.

stood to gain most from material expansion. There were some who refused to be satisfied, who suggested that it was no good to rescue people from physical starvation and then to starve them of self-respect. The true self could die from spiritual and cultural short rations as surely as the body would perish without food. The cult of material prosperity seemed ugly both in its visible manifestations and in its unseen effects.

There were other problems too in a society which was extending the individual's political power but at the same time bringing his life more under control by the state. He had the shadow of influence, but the substance of his life was often dull, mechanical work, relieved only by narrow and barren leisure activities. Would such a mass-society result in a kind of democratic tyranny worse than what had gone before? The fear expressed in De Tocqueville's *Democracy in America* (part 2, 1840) was increasingly felt in Britain.

These public anxieties engaged the attention of one whose private anxieties were unusually acute. John Ruskin (1819–1900) seems to confirm and almost to caricature a popular image of Victorian England. His tone was prophetic, outwardly full of assurance but inwardly trembling towards the collapse that eventually overtook him; his appearance was inspiring, completed in later life by a fine beard, but the eyes in his portraits are sad, longing, uncertain; the size of his collected works is intimidating, yet much of what he wrote was fugitive – in pamphlets, magazines and the texts of lectures. Like Carlyle, he was always most fervent about the latest problem.

He shared with Carlyle also the frequent inconsistency, the lapses into near-incoherence and, in more severe degree, the personal lack of adjustment. Nevertheless, his thought is more unified and his basic view of society develops rather than changes. He too was of Scots parentage, but born in London and brought up in circumstances that were materially much more comfortable than those of Carlyle's childhood. The deprivation from which he suffered was not physical, but it proved in the end more harmful. His possessive parents made it hard for him to develop his own personality apart from theirs, to work out his sense of rights and duties beyond those laid down in the family version of Evangelical religion. The Bible was read doggedly through from beginning to end, with the learning of large portions by heart. The study which gave Bunyan the direct simplicity of narrative gave Ruskin, especially in his early writing, an emotional rhetoric which at its worst is turgid but which can be sonorously impressive:

Since first the dominion of men was asserted over the ocean, three thrones, of mark beyond all others, have been set upon its sands: the thrones of Tyre, Venice and England. Of the First of these great powers only the memory remains; of the Second, the ruin; the Third, which inherits their greatness, if it forget their example, may be led through prouder eminence to less pitied destruction.[1]

His mother took lodgings at Oxford when he was an undergraduate and he spent every evening with her until his health broke down – probably a psychosomatic retreat from an intolerable situation – and he left without taking a degree. Even after his marriage to Effie Gray his parents were never far from the scene; it is perhaps not surprising that she won a decree of nullity in 1854 and married the painter Millais a year later. Yet despite all, Ruskin came to be the most influential art critic of his time, returned to Oxford as Slade Professor and wrote voluminously about the problems of society. Like many earnest Victorians he was sometimes driven too far by the attempts to reconcile extremes and find a central principle. His writing and his more active organizational work can show the frenetic energy of neurosis, which becomes more marked after his attack on Whistler and the ensuing libel action. Yet there is an abiding sanity, as the love of art passes to admiration for the craftsman, thence to detestation of the conditions which make pride in craftsmanship impossible. His concern with social problems never obscured his aesthetic sense; he has none of Carlyle's philistinism.

Ruskin's effective life as a writer starts with the first volume of *Modern Painters* (1842), in which he came to the defence of the aged Turner. Lacking profound knowledge of the old masters, he compares them unfavourably with the modern artist who paints with more fidelity to nature. He takes the subjective, Romantic view that it is through full experience of nature that art may be assessed and appreciated. It is fairly slim as criticism, but it makes a point that he never abandoned: art is not merely

[1] *The Stones of Venice*, Ch. 1.

an artificial recreation, but a reflection of life. His first enthusiasm for Turner did not wane with the passing years: mentally ill in 1878, he fretted, 'What will become of my Turners?'[1]

Further volumes of *Modern Painters* continued to appear until 1860. Ruskin became more and more engaged in the struggle which was to occupy most of his intellectual life. Here was an age in which science was coming to be the dominant mode, with undoubted benefits to the comfort and security of daily existence. The pursuit of factual knowledge about the real world seemed both profitable and laudable. What then was to become of artistic creation: was it to be left behind in the rush of progress and become an antique survival, or was it to remain important only at the cost of the private vision? Could the sense of wonder be maintained in these pragmatic days? It was a problem that he never really solved, but he kept on asking questions for which our later age may well be grateful. He welcomed attempts to revolt against the cult of anecdotal and minutely factual painting. In 1851 he wrote a spirited defence in *The Times* of the Pre-Raphaelite Brotherhood, then suffering from attack in terms similar to those which he himself applied to Whistler years later.

His concern in these years was not solely with painting. It was a time when architecture tended to be an explosive subject among those who were concerned for the visual appearance of town and country. The second Gothic Revival had developed at the beginning of the century, a part of the general Romantic outlook which was rediscovering medieval culture and finding in it an expression of direct, 'natural' creation untrammelled by Classical rules. The outstanding neo-Gothic architect was A. W. N. Pugin (1812–52), whose *Contrasts* (1836) became a manifesto of the movement. The medievalism of the Tractarians and their immediate successors gave additional impetus to the Gothic style for ecclesiastical building: there were Catholics of both the Roman and the English obedience who could condemn, as pagan-looking, such churches as Inwood's beautiful St Pancras. The greatest public triumph of the Gothicists came when the Houses of Parliament were rebuilt in their style after the fire of 1834.

---

[1] *Dearest Mama Talbot: A Selection of Letters from John Ruskin to Mrs Fanny Talbot,* edited by Margaret Spence (London, 1966), p. 87.

Although a new 'free Classic' style developed and became strong after about 1870, the Gothic mode proliferated in the most unlikely places. Pugin's work was carried on by George Gilbert Scott (1811–78) who was guilty of some sweeping 'restorations' as well as egregious original work on the Albert Memorial in 1864. In the following year he spread himself more widely – the classical St Pancras Church could not be undone, but the new St Pancras Station soared up in neo-Gothic pinnacles.

In all this activity, Ruskin was distinctly on the side of the Gothic Revival. *The Seven Lamps of Architecture* (1849) was influential in practical matters of design. *The Stones of Venice* (1851–3) contained the essay 'On the Nature of Gothic' which excited and influenced the young William Morris. There were other implications too: the discerning reader might have seen that Ruskin was neither simply an art-critic who happened to have views about society, nor a social thinker who was interested in art. He was already making clear his belief that the good or bad health of art and society must affect one another and be revealed in their outward forms. His work on architecture, with its combining of beauty and utility, was symptomatic of his refusal to treat art as a retreat from the world. *The Seven Lamps of Architecture* showed that, for him, art and morality were inextricably connected.

In 1845 John Ruskin's parents had ventured to let him travel abroad without them, accompanied only by two servants. He saw much to delight him, but he also felt uneasy about his own luxurious travel in the midst of so much poverty. Back at home, he found himself more aware of the squalor through which he had to pass from his suburban home into London. Earlier writers like Disraeli and Mrs Gaskell had been moved by conditions in the newly-grown industrial towns; Ruskin was distressed by the ugly sprawl of London, the steady deterioration of areas as the fashionable parts moved ever away from the centre. This centrifugal tendency was a symptom of the sickness in society, expressed in the tolerance and open encouragement of ugliness. The railway, for some a blessed portent of progress, seemed to him sinister:

At this time when the iron roads are tearing up the surface of Europe, as grapeshot to the sea; when their great net is drawing and twitching the ancient frame and strength of England together, contracting all its various life, its rocky arms and rural heart, into a narrow, finite, calculating metropolis of manufacturers.[1]

The ugliness of London and its suburban railways became an obsession with him. As late as 1881 he was dragging it unreasonably into an attack on George Eliot:

It is very necessary that we should distinguish this essentially Cockney literature, developed only in the London suburbs, and feeding the demands of the rows of similar brick houses, which branch in devouring cancer round every manufacturing town – from the really romantic literature of France. George Sand is often immoral, but she is always beautiful . . . But in the English Cockney school, which consummates itself in George Eliot, the personages are picked up from behind the counter and out of the gutter; and the landscape, by excursion train to Gravesend, with return ticket for the City Road.[2]

For Ruskin, then, good art was the product of a healthy society and its neglect or debasement must be seen as a social evil. Yet not all could be artists, though he would praise the heroes of art in almost Carlylean manner in *Sesame and Lilies* (1868). His lectures at the Working Men's College put him in touch with a different section of society and gave new drive to the thoughts about the dignity of the free craftsman which he had already set forth in *The Stones of Venice*. In the medieval Gothic buildings he found a vision of happiness and social balance: to restore this creative pride among working men would surely improve the national sense of values. Some of these ideas he expressed in *Unto This Last* (1862). When these essays appeared in the *Cornhill* they seemed to many readers to be outrageous, subversive, tending towards the class-conflict that had been averted in 1848, and Thackeray as editor was forced to cut off the series after four numbers. Similar themes had the same effect and the same abrupt end when *Munera Pulveris* appeared in *Fraser's* under the editorship of Froude.

Ruskin's appointment as Slade Professor of Fine Art at Oxford in 1869 seemed to some a dangerous move and to himself a barrier to social criticism. In fact he now entered on the time of his greatest activity and influence: undergraduates

[1] *Works*, edited by E. T. Cook and A. Wedderburn (London, 1903–12), Vol. 4, p. 31.
[2] *The Nineteenth Century*, October 1881.

sampled the dignity of toil by street-cleaning and road-making; the Guild of St George was started in 1871, an endeavour to teach and practise the good life without economists and politicians. At the same time he was addressing monthly pamphlets to working men under the title *Fors Clavigera*. He became a national figure, widely though not universally revered. To the critical eye of a young girl at the Academy exhibition in 1884 he appeared 'one of the most ridiculous figures I have seen. A very old hat, much necktie and aged coat buttoned up on his neck, humpbacked, not particularly clean looking.'[1]

Until his death, even through the last years of clouded intellect, he continued to question accepted economic doctrines. He insisted on a basic respect for human beings: the rich might be greedy and stupid, the poor undisciplined, but he had a better opinion of their rights and potentialities as individuals than Carlyle ever had. He led the protest against the belief in inevitable progress, as equated with technical advance and greater production; and against the reformers, who were content to achieve full employment and full stomachs without going farther. 'Sure good is, first in feeding people, then in lodging people, and lastly in rightly pleasing people, with arts, or sciences, or any other subject of thought.'[2]

He had no sympathy with the results of Utilitarian doctrine. That which was slick, convenient and cheap was utterly wrong if it led to human degradation. 'We are not one whit the richer for the machine, we only employ it for our amusement. For observe, our gaining in riches depends on the men who are out of employment consenting to be starved, or sent out of the country.'[3] He arraigned those who cared more for profits than for people, who denied the importance of beauty and the imaginative life. Mill's 'economic man' seemed to him a false abstraction, a mere rationalization of the tendency in an industrial society to neglect the full human being. 'There is no wealth but life,' he announced, printing the whole phrase in capital letters.[4]

[1] *The Journal of Beatrix Potter*, transcribed and edited by Leslie Linder (London, 1966), p. 70.
[2] *Sesame and Lilies*, lecture 3, para. 135.
[3] *The Crown of Wild Olive*, lecture 4, para. 156.
[4] *Unto This Last*, 4, para. 77.

Ruskin shared the dilemma of many Victorian intellectuals who had pulled away from orthodox religion without entirely breaking its hold, and who felt committed to the advance of science without entirely surrendering to it. His parents had intended that he should be ordained, following the dream of many middle-class families to whom the medieval status of the clergy still seemed a reality. The Church kept something of its pre-Reformation social importance, holding the keys to higher learning through its clerical dons and headmasters. The Evangelical discipline left him with an obsessive sense of the sin in himself and in society; the philosophy of art took on the sanctions and mystique of religion, and he uttered his fiats in pulpit tones. He kept the Evangelical regard for self-denial as a high, almost the supreme, virtue, with self-indulgence as the deepest sin. The visions of his madness accused him of such failures, and even as a young man he felt the need to deny his harmless desires in order to strengthen his power as a teacher. He wrote to his father:

I am going to preach some most *severe* doctrines in my next book, and I *must* act up to them in not going spending on works of art.[1]

He was well acquainted with science in several of its branches, but he scarcely allowed it to be an independent discipline. He looked rather for its inner poetry as something to be applied to social theory. His lecture on 'Crystal Sorrows' is a fair example of his ability to find tear-jerking but effective analogies between science and society:

Sometimes you will see unhappy little child-crystals left to lie about in the dirt, and pick up their living, and learn manners, where they can. And sometimes you will see fat crystals eating up thin ones, like great capitalists and little labourers; and politico-economic crystals teaching the stupid ones how to eat each other, and cheat each other; and foolish crystals getting in the way of wise ones; and impatient crystals spoiling the plans of patient ones, irreparably.[2]

The extreme cult of scientific method disquieted him, though it fascinated him as well. He was frequently critical of Darwin's theory, his outbursts being often unjustifiable: his reference to

[1] *Works,* Vol. 12, p. lxix.
[2] *Ethics of the Dust,* lecture 9.

'the Natural Selection of which we have lately heard, perhaps, somewhat more than enough'[1] is one of the milder examples. In fairness it should be added that he came to a greater appreciation of what Darwin had done and could speak of 'the theories which Mr Darwin's unwearied and unerring investigations are every day rendering more probable'.[2]

Ruskin has suffered, in common with other Victorian thinkers, from the fulfilment of many of his hopes. What was once a liberating and revolutionary voice now seems old-fashioned; he strikes the modern reader as a man portentously uttering the truisms which we have grown up accepting. Yet there was a time, not so long ago, when it seemed extremist and utopian to advocate minimum wages, general education and old-age pensions: a time when it seemed absurd to fear the coming of unemployment on a large scale. The next generation of Labour thinkers claimed him as a forerunner because he had seen the flaws in Victorian economic complacency. William Morris admired him and was influenced by him, but had qualities which he lacked – an essential optimism and a zest for life. Ruskin could analyse better than co-ordinate and his non-attachment to a single policy is distinctive of both his greatness and his weakness. He gave strength to the Fabians who aimed at planning for the correction of social evils. He helped to break the hold of Utilitarian philosophy on industrial life and to bring the scale of human values into economics.

All the same, a gulf lay between him and socialism, opening sometimes where the ground seemed firmest:

Not countenancing one whit, the common socialist idea of division of property; division of property is its destruction; and with it the destruction of all hope, all industry and all justice.[3]

The same opposition appears in varying guises: in the paternalistic hierarchy outlined in *Time and Tide* and practised in the Guild of St George; in the surprising burst of imperialism during his inaugural lecture as Slade Professor, uttered in terms that might have come from any Tory politician of the time who had an unusually good command of the English language:

[1] *A Joy for Ever*, para. 181.
[2] *The Queen of the Air*, note to para. 61.
[3] *Unto This Last*, 4, note to para. 79.

She [England] must found colonies as fast and as far as she is able, formed of her most energetic and worthiest men; – seizing every piece of fruitful waste ground she can put her foot on, and there teaching those her colonists that their chief virtue is to be fidelity to their country, and that their first aim is to be to advance the power of England by land and sea.[1]

These things must be remembered to counteract, or rather perhaps to counterbalance, the radicalism of his thought and such ideas as limited approval of the nationalization principle.

A partial explanation for the conflict may be found in his inability, as the result of childhood pressures, to form any relationship that was not in some way a filial one. The limitation ruined his private life, destroyed his marriage and continues even to his late-written autobiography *Praeterita* (1885–9). It also helped to make him a very successful lecturer to the young. The publication of his letters to Effie Gray can show how tragically the opportunities of fulfilment in marriage were to be lost. Even in the calmer phases of the correspondence, the authoritarian and possessive attitude shows through with devastating strength. Encouraging his fiancée to share his interest in church architecture, he could write:

You know I must go on with my *profession* and – while for a certain time of the day – I shall always be entirely *yours* – to go and be with you where you choose – yet for another part of the day, and that usually the largest – you will have to be mine – or to sit at home.[2]

It was the same in public life: he could not love society except upon conditions of his choosing, could not try to liberate the oppressed except upon his own terms. He came to understand this enough to hold his parents culpable, but he could never break from their hold and the passion in his nature warred with guilt. Drawn to the future and held by the past, he was typical of his age in this as well. Yet he understood well enough that present problems were urgent, and he did not shun them:

The words on the scroll of a crest must be always the declaration of the bearer's own mind . . . I changed on my seal the 'age quod agis' into 'To-day'.[3]

---

[1] *Works*, vol. 20, p. 42.
[2] W. James, *The Order of Release* (London, 1948), p. 59.
[3] *Praeterita*, 2.

15

Society and Personal Responsibility

In spite of his prophetic tone and his frequent bursts of insight into future developments, Ruskin tended to take an early-Victorian position in the debate about what power the state could and should have over the individual. He distrusted trade unions and the forces of collectivism as heartily as the novelists of the forties did. Yet the need for total involvement was being realized; the individual's duty was seen to go farther than changing his own heart. Even the staider sources of opinion were coming to new attitudes:

The Community should address itself to the great social questions which every day are knocking more loudly at our doors.[1]

Although many of those who were far from socialism could accept the need for more state control, individualistic liberalism remained the dominant mode of thought in the sixties and seventies. In a man like John Morley it could be an honourable and unselfish creed; it could on the other hand be stultifying and antagonistic to social reform. The tension troubled the second generation of Victorians as it had troubled the first; but it was hardest for those whose mature lives spanned the time of transition. Of these, one of the outstanding thinkers was John Stuart Mill (1806–73), the son of Bentham's friend and disciple James Mill. In his *Autobiography* (1873) he recalled his upbringing in the strict Utilitarian gospel, the cramming and forcing of his mind that led to a nervous collapse, and his winning through to freedom for his own opinions.

Mill developed and modified Utilitarian doctrine towards a more humane conception of society, some of which he set out in

[1] *Westminster Review*, 1887, p. 1063; quoted in M. Beer, *A History of British Socialism* (London, 1920), p. 265.

his *Utilitarianism* (1863), of which a modern philosopher has acidly remarked:

John Stuart Mill, in his *Utilitarianism,* offers an argument which is so fallacious that it is hard to understand how he can have thought it valid.[1]

Even a reader without philosophical training can see that Mill gets himself into logical and linguistic difficulties in his attempt to reduce the harshness implicit in Bentham's principle that 'actions are right in proportion as they tend to promote happiness, wrong as they tend to produce the reverse of happiness' (ch. 2). Nevertheless, the doctrine of the second generation shows more respect for human dignity than that of the first, and less inclination to reduce all choices and relationships to mechanistic terms. 'It is better to be a human being dissatisfied than a pig satisfied; better to be Socrates dissatisfied than a fool satisfied' (ibid.).

Ruskin looked and wrote like a prophet, but Mill like a disillusioned don. His place, and it is of the highest importance, is in the history of philosophy and political ideas rather than literature. He made the transition in economic thought from the permissive laissez-faire theories to a more exact and scientific idea of the scope of state regulation. His regard for scientific method is apparent in *A System of Logic* (1843) where he develops a theory of evidence in accordance with empirical philosophy. He had no time for the belief in truths known intuitively, independently of observation and experience, of the type suggested by William Whewell in his *History of the Inductive Sciences* (1837). Such ideas seemed to Mill to be dangerous, bolstering up false doctrines and bad institutions in defiance of reason. The later editions of his *Principles of Political Economy* (1848) show him moving towards the socialist position which he claimed for himself and for those who shared his ideas:

Our ideal of ultimate improvement went far beyond democracy and would class us decidedly under the general designation of socialists.[2]

His socialism, however, is not Marxist; it insists on the value of the individual and the ideal of human freedom within the structure of the state.

[1] Bertrand Russell, *History of Western Philosophy* (London, 1946), pp. 805ff.
[2] *Autobiography,* Ch. 7.

Mill wrote on many aspects of the human situation as it was developing in his time, always with the strong Victorian sense of duty, the faith in reason, the stress on the importance of individual conduct. Progress would come through slow development, as the individual learned to take his share in government. He pursues this theme in *Considerations on Representative Government* (1861), with the idea that good government must comprehend the rights of all classes. The extent and limit of the state's control over its members is dealt with in *On Liberty* (1859), with the well-known assertion of the right to eccentric behaviour which injures no one else – a right which is still disputed among lawyers and moralists today:

As soon as any part of a person's conduct affects prejudicially the interests of others, society has jurisdiction over it, and the question whether the general welfare will or will not be promoted by interfering with it, becomes open to discussion. But there is no room for entertaining any such question when a person's conduct affects the interests of no persons besides himself, or needs not affect them unless they like (all the persons concerned being of full age, and the ordinary amount of understanding.) In all such cases, there should be perfect freedom, legal and social, to do the action and stand the consequence.[1]

Brought up to despise religion, Mill came to a position that a number of his contemporaries shared. He agreed with Comte that Christianity had outworn its value and must be replaced by a new faith, but he was troubled about the loss of fundamental certainties which religion had traditionally guarded. The search for a new unifying principle in society led him towards a vague theism, suggested rather than formulated in his *Auguste Comte and Positivism* (1865) and the posthumously-published *Three Essays on Religion* (1874).

As a Member of Parliament from 1865 to 1868, he acted on his individualistic faith to the extent of getting seventy-three votes on an amendment to add female suffrage to the Reform Bill of 1867. Although his views on this subject were advanced – he set them out in *On the Subjection of Women* (1869) – he was not disposed to enfranchize those people – like paupers and illiterates – who could not play their full part in the

---

[1] *On Liberty*, Ch. 4.

responsibilities of government. He opposed the secret ballot, since voting was a public duty and not to be hidden.

He is worthy of remembrance also as a pioneer of the study of sociology in Britain. He did not share Macaulay's assumption that society was too complex for the extrapolation of general laws: still less Burke's denial of principles underlying change. His essay 'Of the Moral Sciences', which was published as the last book of the *System of Logic* though it was in fact the first written, is concerned with the study of human behaviour as it was then understood. He looked forward to the modern belief that thorough knowledge of social groups must precede any useful reform, and he grounded sociology firmly on the scientific approach. The latter assumption is of course still a point of dispute among sociologists. As an indication that the 'two cultures' were not yet felt to be in opposition, it is worth recalling that Mill had already found the poetry of Wordsworth to be 'the precise thing for my mental wants' at a time of nervous tension.[1]

The relationship between the individual and society also vexed the mind of Matthew Arnold (1822–88). He, like Mill, had a father who had been intellectually dominant in his generation. Both men had later problems of adjustment, though not to the same crippling degree as Ruskin. Arnold worked out some of his difficulties in poetry, for instance in *Sohrab and Rustum* with its fight between father and son. In the elegaic *Rugby Chapel*, where his own melancholy seeks justification from the past, the tension is scarcely hidden by the tribute. Here the opposite father-image, the menacing judge, may be seen in the mysterious old man who meets and questions the travellers:

> With frowning foreheads, with lips
> Sternly compressed, we strain on,
> On – and at nightfall at last
> Come to an end of our way,
> To the lonely inn 'mid the rocks:
> Where the gaunt and taciturn host
> Stands on the threshold, the wind
> Shaking his thin white hairs –
> Holds his lantern to scan
> Our storm-beat figures, and asks:
> Whom in our party we bring?
> Whom we have left in the snow?   (11. 105–116)

[1] *Autobiography*, Ch. 5.

Arnold shared the malaise of the best minds in a society which seemed to be degenerating. Like Ruskin, he appealed to a past aesthetic for its redemption; but his ideal was classical and literary instead of medieval and visual. His distress was more constructive, his personal life happier, partly through factors that made his father's benefits to him more than outweigh any difficulties. Thomas Arnold, seen as he would have been if he had lived to the age of 'thin white hairs', might continue to be a challenge to the son. More important was what the son gained, both in the family and as a boy at Rugby – the joy of classical studies, the sense of duty towards society, the deep moral earnestness. As a boy he was 'something of a disappointment to his father'[1] who did not have a very high opinion of his potential. However, it was largely his father's influence that stopped his personal admiration for Newman from developing into full Tractarian commitment. After all, it was something to be the son of the author of the article on 'The Oxford Malignants'.[2] So at Oxford Matthew contented himself with such achievements as winning the Newdigate Prize for poetry and getting a fellowship at Oriel.

He became an Inspector of Schools, and he has a place in educational history. His duties started him nagging at his countrymen to learn from the Continent, especially from France, a theme which he developed in his *Schools and Universities on the Continent* (1868). It was during the years of public service that he produced nearly all his poetry, and held the Chair of Poetry at Oxford (1857 to 1867). His habit of revising and reprinting poems has made the record of his poetry complex out of proportion to its extent, which is small enough by Victorian standards. Some early pieces, first published anonymously, appeared in the acknowledged *Poems* of 1853, a volume which was augmented in later editions. The second main collection, *New Poems* (1867), again contained work which had appeared previously, including his elegy for A. H. Clough entitled *Thyrsis*. With the rather dull verse-tragedy *Merope* (1858) and a few late poems, these make up his poetic output. Most of it is thus the work of a comparatively young man and ante-dates his main social criticism: the importance of poetry was firmly

[1] T. W. Bamford, *Thomas Arnold* (London, 1960), p. 112.
[2] *Edinburgh Review*, April 1836.

implanted in him by belief and practice before he began to apply it to immediate issues.

Ruskin began his attacks through the criticism of painting; Arnold began his through literature with *Essays in Criticism* (1865) and developed it in *Culture and Anarchy* (1869). The fact that his work is easier than Ruskin's to see as a whole is due partly to its much smaller volume and partly to his easy, persuasive style which offers the reader a familiarity and confidence that is not so readily found in either Ruskin or Carlyle. For instance:

> It is natural that a man should take pleasure in his senses. But it is natural, also, that he should take refuge in his heart and imagination from his misery. And when one thinks what human life is for the vast majority of mankind, how little of a feast for their senses it can possibly be, one understands the charm for them of a refuge offered in the heart and imagination. Above all, when one thinks what human life was in the Middle Ages, one understands the charm of such a refuge.[1]

With what urbanity, what bloodless dissection, Arnold lays bare the condition of all ages, not least his own and ours. In spite of occasional contradictions and failures to carry through to the logical conclusion, he surpasses most of his contemporaries in coherent and consistent thinking.

That he aroused less controversy and hostility than Carlyle or Ruskin is also explicable in part by this easy charm of manner. The content of his thought is forceful and aggressive enough, striking at the strongholds of the upper class whom he called 'Barbarians' and the middle class that he called 'Philistines', attacking their narrow religious dogmas and their stultifying morality, mocking their shallow literary taste. In classical manner, he would appeal to past authority, repudiating the cult of modernity which required the poet to 'leave the exhausted past and draw his subjects from matters of present import'.[2] In his own practice he drew on both past and present, caring less for subject-matter than for the fulfilment of poetry's moral duty.

Literature was for him a criticism of life, as for Ruskin art was

---

[1] 'Pagan and Medieval Religious Sentiment', in *Essays in Criticism,* 1st series.
[2] Preface to *Poems* (1853).

a symptom of the health of society. A proper regard for literature was what the English character needed, to save it from
being so dull, heavy and unreflective, so full of materialistic
values, so committed to the Gradgrind cult of facts. Arnold
loved his country and desired regeneration of the spiritual
depths which were being choked by the new materialism. He
imaged his longing in *Heine's Grave*:

> Yes, we arraign her [England] but she,
> The weary Titan, with deaf
> Ears and labour-dimmed eyes,
> Regarding neither to right
> Nor left, goes passively by,
> Struggling on to her goal;
> Bearing on shoulders immense,
> Atlantean, the load,
> Well-nigh not to be borne,
> Of the too-vast orb of her fate.

The Philistines were to be educated, given a taste of the best
that had been thought and written. He saw their great vice as
insularity: they needed the civilizing influence of French
culture and the formal influences of classical Greece. Arnold's
admiration for France was not widely shared at this time, when
such regard as could be spared for other nations was mostly
lavished on Germany. The Royal Family was German by
descent and connections, and the fear of economic rivalry or
military menace was yet to come. The French were generally
regarded as hysterical, immoral and rather absurd.

Arnold's classical ideals extend to his views on religion, where
he stresses the 'Hellenist' attitude to Christianity, as opposed to
the more constricting 'Hebraist';[1] a notable contrast to
Disraeli's call to Christians to rediscover Judaic origins. Arnold
shows himself no militant opponent of Christianity, but can
attack with fierce irony those of its followers who offend his
sense of balance and reason. He disliked Evangelicals, Anglican
as well as dissenting, but took some comfort from the fact that
their influence was declining:

The Evangelical clergy no longer recruits itself with success, no
longer lays hold on such promising subjects as formerly. It is losing
the future and feels that it is losing it. Its signs of a vigorous life, its

---

[1] *Culture and Anarchy*, Ch. 4.

gaiety and audacity, are confined to its older members, too powerful to lose their own vigour, but without successors to whom to transmit it.[1]

His assessment of the situation was shrewd enough, though his hostility tended to become an obsession. Four years after the prophecy just quoted he was writing to a French correspondent:

> From the first, French Protestantism had too much of the sectarian and narrow character which Protestant Dissent has with us, and this will probably in the end be fatal to your Protestantism as a religious organisation, as it will be fatal to Protestant Dissent in this country.[2]

More positively, Arnold spoke for those who were doubting the divine sanctions for belief but who feared to lose the spiritual content of life: a growing number, to whom he offered the comfort that religion was more valuable for its poetic than for its literal truth, and that conduct was the supreme test of validity. Yet conduct did not have to be fenced in by the cold, unemotional limits of puritanism:

> Religion, if we allow the intention of human thought and human language in the use of the word, is ethics heightened, enkindled, lit up by feeling; the passage from morality to religion is made when to morality is applied emotion. And the true meaning of religion is thus, not simply *morality*, but morality touched by *emotion*.[3]

The key to it all he finds in literature, particularly in poetry. The search for standards in literature is part of the same quest as the search for standards in life. A society cannot be judged apart from its expression through literature, and criticism should be applied to both. Arnold practised these precepts in his essay 'The Function of Criticism at the Present Time', making his readers study and reflect on the juxtaposition of political eulogies on the nation with newspaper reports of a brutal child-murder. A passage in a later work sums up what he meant:

> Poetry . . . is a criticism of life under the conditions fixed for such a criticism by the laws of poetic truth and poetic beauty . . . And the criticism of life will be of power in proportion as the poetry conveying

---

[1] Preface to *St Paul and Protestantism* (1870).

[2] Letter to M. Fontanès, 1 April 1874, published in *Letters of Matthew Arnold*, collected and arranged by George W. E. Russell (London, 1895), Vol. 2, p. 114.

[3] *Literature and Dogma* (1873), Arnold's italics.

it is excellent rather than inferior, sound rather than unsound or half-sound, true rather than untrue or half-true.[1]

There would seem here to be some begging of the question, between semantic and artistic truth, but Arnold does sometimes fail to define his language fully. Yet there can be no question of his contribution to literary criticism. He insisted on the need for valid standards to which assent can honestly be given, and feared that these were being lost in literature and in life. His influence on later critics has been through this emphasis on the search for standards rather than through detailed and particular analysis, though the latter was practised to good effect in *On Translating Homer* (1861) and *Last Words on Translating Homer* (1862). He exalted the place of poetry in human affairs, but without making it a means of escapism. The liberal, reforming faith of his father kept its hold, and he accepted the necessity of gradualism and the extension of state control.

The tension between individualism and the state is examined in *Culture and Anarchy*, where the English are urged to modify their claims to complete personal freedom irrespective of the rights of others. Such extreme individualism is seen to tend towards anarchy and must be corrected by 'the notion, so familiar on the Continent and to antiquity, of *'the State.'* (ch. 2). None of the social classes is fit to rule, so the State, as the 'best self' of the nation, must act for all: thus selfish individualism will be checked and social inequality reduced. He understood well enough the fears of his contemporaries:

What if we tried to rise above the idea of class to the idea of the whole community, *the State*, and to find our centre of light and authority there? Every one of us has the idea of country, as a sentiment; hardly any one of us has the idea of *the State* as a working power. And why? Because we habitually live in our ordinary selves, which do not carry us beyond the ideas and wishes of the class to which we happen to belong. And we are all afraid of giving to the State too much power, because we only conceive of the State as something equivalent to the class in occupation of the executive government, and we are afraid of that class abusing power to its own purpose. (ibid.)

[1] 'The Study of Poetry,' in *Essays in Criticism*, 2nd series (1888); first published in 1880 as the General Introduction to *The English Poets*, edited by T. H. Ward.

That is well said, and it goes to the heart of one Victorian problem which still looms large in our present-day politics.

Arnold, like Ruskin, has uttered things which were startling a century ago but now may suffer the indignity of being passed over as commonplace. His reputation as a poet, however, has risen, perhaps because themes which seem cold in the objectivity of prose can gain more immediacy in his poems. The shaking of faith seems more poignant, the recognition of social and political changes more disquieting. There is a trace of that desire to escape which is resisted in the prose works: but even in the more imaginative sphere of poetry the dream is not allowed fully to enter reality but is enviously assigned to ghosts as in *The Scholar Gipsy* or legends as in *The Forsaken Merman*. Arnold is willing to look forward, less verbosely than Browning but with more real understanding of what the future may mean, and will not soften the blow by clinging to a religion which no longer convinces him or by fading into a vague optimism. In *Dover Beach* he makes an earnest but tremulous assertion of the power of human affection between a disintegrating present and a doubtful future:

> Ah, love, let us be true
> To one another! for the world, which seems
> To lie before us like a land of dreams,
> So various, so beautiful, so new,
> Hath really neither joy, nor love, nor light,
> Nor certitude, nor peace, nor help for pain;
> And we are here as on a darkling plain
> Swept with confused alarms of struggle and flight,
> Where ignorant armies clash by night.

We recognize in Arnold, most clearly in his poetry, a tension still marked in European literature and in life. The Romantic attitudes that sprang from his early admiration for Sénancour and Georges Sand are at war with the classicism of his home and education – for once, those well-worn labels are meaningful. The solitary instincts of *Obermann* tug against the duties of the progressive, liberal humanist towards society: an almost morbid pessimism is opposed by urbane irony. We salute the struggle because we are still involved in it. We salute the restraint which forbids the sentimental excess that mars too much Victorian poetry, the tension that does not slacken into self-pity as it sometimes does in Tennyson.

Though Arnold knew well enough that times were changing, he did not foresee the full extent and depth of the change. He deplored the loss of standards for judgement, but he was in fact able to assume much that was soon to be disputed. Words like 'culture' and 'perfection' meant something more basically acceptable to the majority of his readers than to us today. They aroused argument, but no one suggested that they might be meaningless. He called for the adoption of Continental methods in education, but his aim was to reform rather than to innovate: 'he would call up memories of the old world to redress the balance of the new'.[1] The study of classical language and literature was still basic in education; Arnold wanted to increase knowledge of English literature, and was not caught up in the demands of men like Huxley and Spencer for a more scientific content. He saw and hated the falling of old standards and saw that coming years would bring worse fragmentation. Yet he remained essentially optimistic, unable or perhaps unwilling to comprehend what the new literacy would mean:

We are often told that an era is opening in which we are to see multitudes of common readers and masses of a common sort of literature; that such readers do not want and could not relish anything better than such literature, and that to provide it is becoming a vast and profitable industry. Even if good literature entirely lost currency with the world, it would still be abundantly worth while to continue to enjoy it by oneself. But it never will lose currency with the world, in spite of momentary appearances: it never will lose supremacy. Currency and supremacy are insured to it, not indeed by the world's deliberate and conscious choice, but by something far deeper, by the instinct of self-preservation in humanity.[2]

There is a courage in this which only prejudice can label complacency. It holds the faith which a technological age like ours needs if it is not to evolve into the inverted Utopia of a Huxley or an Orwell.

[1] Douglas Bush, *Science and English Poetry* (Oxford, 1950), p. 129.
[2] 'The Study of Poetry'.

16

Escape through Art

Both Ruskin and Arnold attacked the general ugliness of their time and the attitude of repression which it symbolized, but their attack had the reformation of society as its aim. They did not place the creative artist in a special caste, scornful of the outsider and withdrawn from society as a whole. The exaltation of art as the supreme activity, its own law and its own justification, begins its Victorian career with painting and grows into a wider revolt against accepted morality as well as against artistic canons.

The middle of the nineteenth century was a prosperous time for the artist with a popular appeal. The comfortable middle class – and those who aspired to join it – had generally more money than taste. The domestic display of original paintings was a sign of material stability; pictures were valued as a part of interior decoration, perhaps offering refreshment and regeneration to the tired spirit like a stroll in the country after a hard day. The deeper perception of a work of art as an entity in its own right, making its effect independently of external aids, was seldom considered.

There was a fashion for literary subjects, depicting a character or an episode in some well-known work: a demand which had been increasing since the time of Hogarth and now reached its peak. If the painting was not specifically literary, it might have a historical or anecdotal subject. The owner would enjoy answering the question, 'What's it all about?' The main point of a picture was a subject which could be explained and perhaps move the sentiments in the explaining. The love of sentimentality, with its quick, ready-made reactions to particular situations, did harm to the novel but could be partly swallowed up in the movement of the plot. It was much more pernicious in the static, synchronic art of painting.

In execution, the request was for accurate representation and fine detail. The passion for naturalism in painting came before the invention of photography, and artists took pains to be 'correct' in their historical and literary scenes. The century produced some fine technicians, not negligible in the history of British art. There are things of permanent value in the best work of Mulready, Frith, Leslie and Webster; there is good draughtsmanship in the pseudo-classical scenes of Leighton and Alma-Tadema. Even Landseer, who became the chief victim of the reaction against Victorian painting, had that sense of animal beauty which runs back to Stubbs in the previous century. These and others sometimes rose above the demand for a subject that could be verbalized and representation that could be judged as imitation. But on the whole, the artistic vision was contained within everyday life and did not transcend it.

The young painters who founded the Pre-Raphaelite Brotherhood in 1848 did so in conscious revolt against the prevailing trends.[1] They did not mean to commit themselves to the subjects or to the faith of the early Italian painters, but they looked for genuine artistic ideas drawn from the close study of nature and expressed in sympathy with what was direct and serious in human experience. They tried to recapture the light and colour of the Primitives: they loved the technique of painting on a wet white ground to give their pictures a special brightness.

Their protest was against the heaviness and darkness then in fashion, rather than against the cult of subject or the insistence on naturalistic detail. They illustrated scenes of history and legend; they painted so closely from nature that Holman Hunt sat for hours outdoors at night for *The Light of the World,* while the model who posed for Millais in *The Death of Ophelia* nearly got pneumonia from lying so long in a bath. What they disliked was the trend that could increase the value of a Constable by

---

[1] 'In 1848 Rossetti co-operated with two of his fellow-students in painting, John Everett Millais and William Holman Hunt, and with the sculptor Thomas Woolner, in forming the so-called Praeraphaelite (*sic*) Brotherhood. There were three other members of the Brotherhood – James Collinson (succeeded after two or three years by William Howard Deverell), Frederic George Stephens, and the present writer.' W. M. Rossetti's Preface to *The Poetical Works of Dante Gabriel Rossetti* (London, 1907), p. xvii.

covering it with dark varnish. They repudiated the idea of 'rules' in painting as formulated by Reynolds, whom they dubbed 'Sir Sloshua'.

The Pre-Raphaelite Brotherhood was not primarily a literary movement, but many of its members wrote as well as painted. Their poetry, like their painting, tended to pass over the contemporary realities and find refuge in an imagined purer world. The only joint literary effort of the Brotherhood as a whole was *The Germ*, which ran for four issues in 1850. It contained little that remains memorable except a story and some poems by Dante Gabriel Rossetti (1828–82), and early pieces by his sister Christina whose different line of development is considered in another chapter. The son of an Italian political exile, Rossetti made both himself and his ancestral literature better known in England with *The Early Italian Poets* (1861), a volume of translations. His first original collection, *Poems by D. G. Rossetti* (1870), was printed largely from manuscripts which he had buried with his wife Elizabeth who had died in 1862. Both the dramatic interment and the later exhumation had a touch of the morbidity which tinged Pre-Raphaelite eccentricities and became more marked in their successors. Rossetti's last volume, *Ballads and Sonnets*, appeared in 1881.

It is little enough on which to build a reputation. Rossetti wrote slowly and revised carefully; if he had given the same painstaking attention to the basic techniques of painting he might have been an outstanding artist instead of a pleasing one with flashes of brilliance. His importance is less in the intrinsic merit of his poetry than in his leadership of the revolt against poetic treatment of spiritual aspirations, moral values and the themes of contemporary debate. The Romantics, elevating poetry to supreme importance, had nevertheless written about these things which Rossetti almost entirely excluded.

Yet not totally: he is a poet of his time although he has been thought medieval in his blending of the religious and erotic modes. He is a long way from the lyrics written when the doctrines and symbols of Catholicism were an inescapable part of the social background and when all life seemed to be suspended between eternities of beatitude and damnation. The 'religious' language of *The Blessed Damozel*, like the imagery of his painting with the same name, fails to cohere with deeper exploration of the central themes. The details are precise, boldly materialistic, visually stimulating, but the mysticism and the sensuality are in conflict. His visual imagination and skill as a painter mark out both the achievement and the limitation of Rossetti as a poet. Out of the sensory experience of a mid-Victorian he creates a world of moonlight, strange colours, elaborate draperies stirred by the wind. His poems are sensuously delightful but yield few images that can be apprehended by the intellect. This fulfilled his own purpose, but the question remains whether there can be a full poetic experience borrowed from the visual sense alone.

Yet Rossetti is more versatile than his own declared aspirations would seem to permit, touching on the romantically supernatural in *Sister Helen* and *Rose Mary*, on the ballad style in *The White Ship* and *The King's Tragedy*. He shares with Elizabeth Barrett the distinction of bringing the sonnet back into favour after a period of neglect: in *The House of Life* he makes it express anew the sensuality of love, writing of deep physical experience in light word-music. Nor is the contemporary debate always excluded, and his desire to flee into an idealized past does not prevent him from making a positive contrast with the present. No great satirist, he could be ironically aware of what was going on around him, in poems like *The Burden of Nineveh* and *On Certain Elizabethan Revivals*. In *The Paris Railway Station* he is entirely of his time and succeeds in startling through naturalism.

There is in Rossetti a broad vision not entirely subordinated to his theories of art. He may be too much a verbal trickster to be a really great poet, too much concerned with the verbalization of magic numbers and emblematic flowers. An autumnal, lotus-eating dreaminess, too languid even for melancholy, drifts through much of his work. The musical lilt of his language goes with it, the Romance element emphasized as if he wished that he wrote always in Italian. Nor is this dreaminess a matter only of sensory response: he offers generalizations, making seemingly portentous propositions which neither develop nor consort with the central theme. Yet he stands for something at the heart of the age – the sense of guilt and inadequacy which made the Podsnap of fiction and the Samuel Smiles of life fly to a blatantly optimistic assertion that all was well. He sees the shadow behind the substance, the selfishness and remorse behind the fullest giving of love. There is a sickness in his beauty; not quite an evil, which was yet to come.

What can be said of Rossetti is largely true of other poets associated with the movement. Arthur O'Shaughnessey (1844–91) was a personal friend of Rossetti and something of an imitator, but with an original quality within his haunted dream-world. His 'We are the music-makers' was included in Palgrave's *Second Golden Treasury* and has appeared in many later anthologies, but he has other things that deserve reading. James Collinson (?1835–81) wrote at least one memorable poem with *The Boy Jesus,* an imaginative description of the Passion foreshadowed in the early life of Christ which reminds us that a similar spirit animated certain aspects of both the Pre-Raphaelite Brotherhood and the Oxford Movement. Thomas Woolner (1825–92) was a better sculptor than poet, but there are good things in his love-poems *My Beautiful Lady.*

The Brotherhood tended to become more dreamily detached from reality as time went on; but if society was lulled into thinking that art and literature were gentle recreations, it woke up with a start in 1866. Its awakener was Algernon Charles Swinburne (1837–1909), a little man with red hair, green eyes, small hands and feet, excited movements like a child. He was neither a painter nor a member of the Pre-Raphaelite Brotherhood, but he was well acquainted with Rossetti and others who now found themselves sharing his sudden notoriety. He came to the writing of poetry already enthusiastic about a variety of literatures, especially the Greek and the Elizabethan. His attempts to revive blank-verse drama, like most such attempts in the nineteenth century, were of little value either to the theatre or to poetry. His first plays, *The Queen Mother* and *Ronsard,* were dedicated to Rossetti when they were printed in 1860. His trilogy on Mary of Scotland spread over many years with *Chastelard* (1865), *Bothwell* (1874) and *Mary Stuart* (1881).

He was poetically happier with Greek themes and styles as in *Atalanta in Calydon* (1865) and *Erectheus* (1876). The fine choruses in the former aroused some favourable notice; the underlying atheism could easily be ignored by readers whose education had been in studying and imitating the verbal expression of classical writers without going too far into their moral implications. But the first series of *Poems and Ballads* was not veiled by the decency of the past. Here was revolt in earnest: atheism openly chanted in the cadences of the Bible and the Anglican liturgy; sensual experience praised; the suggestion that pain could be pleasant, cruelty justified – that both were inherent in the pursuit of beauty. John Morley, reviewing before publication as was common at the time, attacked the volume so fiercely in the *Saturday* that Swinburne's publisher grew alarmed and withdrew the whole edition. People of course wanted to read the wicked stuff, and a less timid publisher took over.

It was many years since poetry had caused such excitement. Suddenly it seemed to have shot back into the prime literary place from which the novel had driven it. Tennyson and Browning had respect and large sales, but they had not aroused passions like these. Some were delighted by the idea that the pursuit of experience was noble and should be uninhibited. Undergraduates, enchanted by the notion of revolt untainted by socialism or democracy, linked arms to chant the poems in street and quadrangle. Their elders were perhaps thrilled, certainly horrified so to find themselves, by the praise of strange cruelties and delights:

> Ah that my lips were tuneless lips, but pressed
> To the bruised blossom of thy scourged white breast!
> Ah that my mouth for Muses' milk were fed
> On the sweet blood thy sweet small wounds had bled![1]

Nowadays this kind of thing is wearisome: we have seen too much striving for sensation, too much glorifying of cruelty. A century ago it was like a release from a conspiracy of repressive silence. W. M. Rossetti, the poet's brother, wrote a brochure in defence of Swinburne; George Meredith declared:

> It has done the critical world good by making men look boldly at the restrictions imposed upon art by our dominating, damnable bourgeoisie.[2]

There was no such storm again; though Swinburne's later work is not short of passion, the old, defiant force is too often overlaid with rhetoric. The spirit of revolution which he learned –

---

[1] *Anactoria* (poem significantly preceded by an epigraph from Sappho).
[2] *Letters of George Meredith*, ed. W. M. Meredith (London, 1912), Vol. 1, p. 189.

always in strictly literary experience – from Landor, Shelley and Hugo, made him a vocal supporter of nationalist movements and particularly that for Italian unification. Out of this came *A Lay of Italy* (1867), *Songs Before Sunrise* (1871) and *Songs of Two Nations* (1875). He wrote a great deal more, including the second and third series of *Poems and Ballads* (1878 and 1889), a number of unactable dramas and some lively but over-subjective literary criticism.

What was the startling impact of Swinburne's poetry? Keats had made as impassioned a plea for the recognition of physical beauty in a pagan sense, and Rossetti had been frank about what men and women could enjoy together. But Swinburne made the anarchic suggestion that things considered painful might be pleasurable, that the traditionally unnatural might be better than the natural. The Victorians did not mind being shocked so much as having their basic assumptions attacked and their stability threatened.

Perhaps we know too much of Swinburne the man to take his poetry seriously. We know Max Beerbohm's cartoon, we know of his confinement by his admiring nurse-warder Theodore Watts-Dunton, we know how rebellion turned to Imperialism by the time of the Boer War. His paganism, his blasphemy, his perversions, seem childish and slightly comic. In fact one thing that Swinburne could not do with sex was to see anything comic in it. He has the seriousness of D. H. Lawrence, a dedication to restore the joys of abandoned passion which society had repressed.

In technique he shows more versatility than any other Victorian poet. His verbal management is brilliant even when it outstrips the sense and becomes rhetorical, as it does increasingly in his later work. He can give, by the juxtaposition of common words, a complexity and ambiguity of meaning that commends him to modern critics, who have little patience with most of his contemporaries. The very pattern of metre, rhyme and alliteration is sensually stirring. The recurrent sea-imagery – fitting for an admiral's son as he was – makes his work dynamic and potent. The first effect is exciting, but re-reading brings boredom and a realization that here is little to develop along with personal experience.

What was the source of these notions which so upset Victorian equilibrium? Here, as the old stage-directions said, the scene shifts to France, where things disagreeable to bourgeois morality had been brewing for some time. Many of the artists and writers, disillusioned by what seemed to them the stultifying materialism of French society after 1830, had come to see themselves as a society against society. The concept of the 'Bohemians', living for delight in the appreciation and making of art, refusing conformity to the social norm, had developed. Murger with his rose-coloured description of the life of poor but free young intellectuals; Daumier with his savage caricatures of the respectable citizenry; Gautier who coined the phrase 'L'Art pour l'Art' – these were leaders of the new movement, if movement it can be called.

In France more than in England, the more extreme notions of Romanticism were pursued into paths hitherto forbidden.[1] Where the Pre-Raphaelites only whispered, the French shouted that all sensations were to be sampled, experienced, made the sources of art irrespective of moral codes. Art was the sole authority and the final appeal; that which was true in the artistic sense could not be questioned or forbidden by other criteria. Painters like Delacroix scorned the notion of agreeable or morally improving subjects which dominated fashionable English paintings, finding their concepts of beauty in scenes of suffering, vice, and cruelty. Edgar Allen Poe was a hero to them, his Roderick Usher a type of the ideal.

England as a whole inclined towards admiration of Germany; if some like Matthew Arnold saw great virtue in Gallic culture, it was not in that of the *Société des cafés*. The tidings of new and surprising things were brought back to England by those who had gone to study art at one of the popular *ateliers*. They included such future pillars of the artistic establishment as Thomas Armstrong and E. J. Poynter, as well as fashionable illustrators like George du Maurier. They included also a young American called James Macneil Whistler.

Whistler (1834–1903) is as insignificant a writer as he is important a visual artist, but he had considerable influence on the world of letters. He met Swinburne in Paris and this gave him an introduction to Rossetti which began an improbable but firm friendship lasting many years. As Whistler became

[1] See Mario Praz, *The Romantic Agony* (Oxford, 1933).

prominent in the artistic and fashionable society of London, a new word came to be often heard – aestheticism. The study of aesthetics had generally been regarded as a German prerogative, so much so that in 1832 the *Penny Cyclopaedia* had described aesthetics as:

The designation given by German writers to a brand of philosophical inquiry, the object of which is a philosophic theory of the beautiful.

What Whistler had in mind, and what others took up from him, went a great deal farther than philosophical inquiry.

The Pre-Raphaelites had not completely broken away from the prevailing idea that art was morally significant. They reverenced Ruskin, who had said a great deal on this subject and on the sterling quality of hard work, and links with such responsible thinkers became apparent in some of their paintings.[1] They might paint flowers for their own sakes rather than as part of a story, but the flowers would often have an emblematic meaning which gave significance beyond themselves. Whistler painted flowers purely for their decorative effect. He found in Japanese art an example of his ideal – art purely for the visual sense, unrelated to morality, social commitment or 'subject' that could be verbalized.

Whistler challenged the establishment and his challenge was returned. In 1877 Ruskin saw one of his *Nocturnes* at the Grosvenor Gallery and rushed back to accuse the artist of 'ill-educated conceit'. His attack, in *Fors Clavigera*, went on to say:

I have heard and seen much of Cockney impudence before now but never expected to hear a coxcomb ask two hundred guineas for flinging a pot of paint in the public's face.

Whistler, always ready to quarrel, brought an action for libel. Ruskin was too ill to appear but the theories of art were thoroughly, not to say rhetorically aired in court. The success of Whistler's case, despite his derisory farthing's damages, was

[1] A good example is the painting *Work* by Ford Madox Brown, now in the Manchester City Art Gallery, which shows Carlyle and F. D. Maurice as types of mental work, in company with manual labourers. Brown was not formally a member of the P. R. B. but was very sympathetic to its aims and contributed to *The Germ*.

a moral victory for aestheticism. But the cost of the action made him bankrupt; the butterfly with which he signed his paintings acquired a barbed tail, and he continued on his aggressive way with attacks on his opponents in conversational epigrams, private notes and letters to newspapers. The whole farrago of malignancy, occasionally brilliant but more often hysterical, was published in 1890 as *The Gentle Art of Making Enemies*.

By the late seventies, all this publicity was having its effect. The general public, assaulted first by Pre-Raphaelites backed by the revered Ruskin, scandalized by Swinburne, entertained by Whistler, lumped them all together into 'aestheticism' and rendered Gautier in the crisp monosyllables of 'Art for Art's sake'. There was a spate of 'aesthetic' fashions in dress, decorations, furniture; touches of frivolity became permissible even in the suburban villa.[1] The fashionable thing was to be 'intense'; a satirical French observer noted:

> To be in good form, one had to . . . appear to be dying of decline; therefore to be lean and pale, to have one's eyes encircled with black and lost in ethereal regions. The supreme object was to look consumptive. Walking was abandoned for a kind of crawl; ordinary meals were suspended, a little sustenance was taken; voices became deep and hollow; the face was made to express disgust for the reality of the world's pursuits.[2]

Blue and white china, as a symbol of 'pure' Oriental art, was in great demand and even affected the poetasters to the extent of volumes like *Ballades in Blue China* (1873) by Andrew Lang and *Proverbs in Porcelain* (1877) by Austin Dobson.

The British public was having a holiday from the idea that art was full of moral seriousness. It was encouraged by Walter Pater (1839–94), a Fellow of Brasenose College who was making himself a hierophant of art. He was an oddity even for Oxford: an ugly man who admired physical beauty; an admirer too of Ruskin and Arnold but opposed to their views on art and society; a solitary who exiled himself from both the euphoric port-drinking, inherited from the eighteenth century, and the

---

[1] George and Weedon Grossmith, *The Diary of a Nobody* (1892), Ch. 9. 'Our new enlarged and tinted photographs look very nice on the walls, especially as Carrie has arranged some Liberty silk bows on the four corners of them.'

[2] 'Max O'Rell' (Paul Blouet), *John Bull and his Island* (N. D., c. 1885), pp. 41ff.

theological debate that was occupying the more earnest dons and undergraduates.

Pater was in fact a new and alien figure – a man who assiduously cultivated his sensations. His ideas and attitudes came to be thought of as distinctive of aestheticism, notably those in the essays called *The Renaissance* which appeared in collected form in 1873. Stressing the pagan richness and emancipation of the European Renaissance, he urged his readers to enter fully into its spirit, to shun no sensation that could lead to richer appreciation. Some of his more extreme remarks were withdrawn from the later edition, perhaps partly because of the parody of his views by W. H. Mallock in *The New Republic* (1877), where he appears in a modern Platonic dialogue as 'Mr Rose'. For all his flouting of convention, Pater was a timid soul and hated the suggestion that he might be a bad influence on the young.[1] *Marius the Epicurean* (1885) is, in spite of some fine passages, marred by a tendency to caution and by the mannerisms of his later prose style. As a serious critic, Pater was probably more influential than has generally been supposed. His idea that 'all art constantly aspires towards the condition of music'[2] is indicative of the new thinking. Form and rhythm, not subject, were the aims; the old theory of art as imitative of nature was challenged.

A great deal of the essential Pater came to be known, both to his contemporaries and to posterity, through Oscar Fingal O'Flahertie Wills Wilde (1854–1900). After a childhood which sowed the seeds of his later disaster, after a brilliant period at Trinity College, Dublin, where he absorbed classical ideals from Mahaffy, Wilde went to Oxford. He attended Ruskin's lectures and even worked on the Hinksey Road project, but it was Pater who touched the deepest chord and whose ideas he soon launched upon London society. Elegant, witty, charming, a great talker, Wilde was just the man to spread new ideas. A lecture-tour in the United States helped to increase his fame at home; he was shown in *Punch* and Gilbert put him on the stage in the person of Bunthorne in

---

[1] In a note to a later edition of *The Renaissance* Pater explains his omission of the famous 'Conclusion', 'as I conceived it might possibly mislead some of those young men into whose hands it might fall'.

[2] 'The School of Giorgione' (1877), included in the third edition of *The Renaissance*.

Patience. The latter representation aggravated the general confusion about who stood for what, since Bunthorne 'a fleshly poet' clearly referred to Buchanan's attack on the 'Fleshly School of Poetry' in the *Contemporary* in 1871, into which Rossetti, Swinburne and even Morris had been drawn.

The young Wilde made a new synthesis out of the muddle, appearing rather paradoxically as an aesthete with social commitment. His distinctive dress was a protest against conventional fashion and derived something from du Maurier's drawings; his cult of flowers was vaguely Pre-Raphaelite; on top of all there were gems culled from Gautier, Pater and others. Then it changed: the new pose, owing something to his semi-friendly sparring with Whistler, was that of the dandy – impeccably dressed, detached from commitment, examining and savouring sensations.

The eclecticism was still amusing, but sinister implications were entering. *The Picture of Dorian Gray* (1891) tells the story of a young man who transfers age and corruption to a portrait of himself, retaining his appearance of innocence through a lifetime of vice until he and the portrait change places again in the end. It sounds a mild exercise in the supernatural, in the manner of Stevenson or M. R. James, but in fact it sums up what aestheticism was becoming. Its theme of building up an artificial life of the senses from the exquisite in every age owes something to *Marius the Epicurean* and more to *A Rebours* by J. K. Huysmans – the book that sets Dorian Grey further on the downward path.[1] The idea of the portrait taking on a man's sins is a perfect parable, conscious or not, of the corruption and cruelty at the heart of beauty and of the power of art to liberate the individual from both conformity and consequences.

Wilde's plays are discussed in another chapter. The *Poems* of 1881 and later pieces are unsatisfying, so languid as to be tedious. Their conscious detachment from life and their cult of sensation through sound and imagery give them some of the quality of a painting by Whistler; to say as much of poetry reveals both its beauty and its limitations. Wilde carried the

---

[1] 'It was the strangest book that he had ever read . . . Things that he had dimly dreamed of were suddenly made real to him. Things of which he had never dreamed were gradually revealed.' *The Picture of Dorian Gray* Ch. 10. In cross-examination during the Queensberry case Wilde admitted that he was thinking of *A Rebours*.

belief in the special status of the artist beyond what society would tolerate. He was forced into a libel suit by his evil genius Alfred Douglas whose father, the Marquess of Queensberry, had made an accusation of homosexual behaviour. The action was withdrawn, but enough had been heard to bring prosecution and imprisonment.

It was the revenge of a society that had been taunted for too long by the artists. Wilde's cross-examination by Carson was the beginning of the end for aestheticism, as Whistler's action nearly twenty years before had been the beginning of its triumph. After his release, broken and in exile, Wilde produced his long prose apologia *De Profundis* (1905) and his poem *The Ballad of Reading Gaol* (1898). The posing is still there, the self-pity, the mannerisms. But there is also an acknowledgement that the artist is not above all rules. Wilde never lacked generosity and charity; he learned to add true compassion without a sideways glance for the effect.

The *Ballad* has won much esteem for its indictment of capital punishment and cruelty in prisons. Looked at more critically as a work of literature it is less satisfactory. Vague images evoke sensations without clear connection to the theme: moonlight, roses, violins, wander in and out. The syntax is often clumsily distorted by the prosody. Yet at its best the poem shows the achievement of aestheticism brought back into relationship with life.

> With yawning mouth the yellow hole
>   Gaped for a living thing;
> The very mud cried out for blood
>   To the thirsty asphalte ring;
> And we knew that ere one dawn grew fair
>   Some prisoner had to swing.

The images of colour, the ugly things admired dispassionately for their effect as pictures, the extreme poeticism of the penultimate line, and then the crash into brutal slang – all this makes something memorable.

The last decade of the nineteenth century may seem overshadowed by the fall of Wilde and all for which he stood. It was also the decade when Shaw and Wells were rising to maturity, the decade of Henley, Kipling and the loudest expressions of imperialism. Yet the decline of aestheticism is its distinctive mark. The nineties used to be given the epithet 'naughty', though in general naughtiness they were rather better than the sixties before the work of Stead, Booth and others. Decadence was the cult of only a few, but the few made it notorious and completed the distrust of modern art. The idea of decadence came from France as the logical conclusion of the aesthetic dream. The aesthete had come round in a circle; from saying that questions of morality did not enter into artistic calculations, he was now urging the artist to experience sin and corruption, imposing a firm if inverted moral standard.

The literary society of the nineties was less cohesive and less attractive than that of the Pre-Raphaelite Brotherhood, with artists who despised not only bourgeois society but also each other. A satirical view of it was given by Robert Hichens in *The Green Carnation* (1894). George du Maurier's *Trilby* (1894) also touches the artistic world, with memories of his art-student days in Paris in a story of para-psychology and a malignant mesmerist. Du Maurier (1834–96) had come late to the novel with *Peter Ibbetson* (1892) which also gives some pleasant glimpses of France though its central fantasy is rather tiresome. *The Martian* (1896) is a type of science-fiction in piquant contrast to what Wells was starting to write.

A reputation disproportionate to its quality and quantity alike was acquired by *The Yellow Book,* which appeared as a quarterly between 1894 and 1897. It reached no literary heights; its best achievement was to introduce the work of the young Aubrey Beardsley, who became its art-editor. Beardsley (1872–98) was associated in the public mind with Wilde, although the two did not much like each other and their only professional contact had been with Beardsley's drawings for Douglas's translation of *Salome*. Nor did Wilde ever contribute to *The Yellow Book;* he seems to have taken a discerningly poor view of its merits, though his story of vain attempts to get rid of a copy probably owes more to his imagination than to fact.[1] Nevertheless, Beardsley was dismissed after Wilde's fall, and Arthur Symons approached him on behalf of a new publication by the rather shady Leonard Smithers (who did at least have the courage later to publish *The Ballad of Reading Gaol*).

[1] Hesketh Pearson, *The Life of Oscar Wilde* (London, 1946), p. 231.

Beardsley served this new periodical, *The Savoy*, until his death aged twenty-five.

'Mr Danby Wierdsley' as *Punch* called him was largely responsible for the reception of *The Yellow Book*, which *The Times* summed up as 'a mixture of English rowdyism and French lubricity'.[1] His illustrations have affinities with the Japanese art that Whistler loved, with a viciousness of his own. They are filled with dwarfs, deformities, epicene figures, all seeming to act out fantasies of perversion. It is the world of falling aestheticism, still protesting its supreme importance but sterile and exhausted. Beardsley was a brilliant draughtsman and created a convincing but anti-natural world. His eerie romance *Under the Hill* echoes in prose the world of his drawings, as the Pre-Raphaelites in their gentler way had connected paintings and poems.

The few poets who came to brief fame in this decade mostly handled their language and imagery wearily, as if they knew them to be already dying. Poetry was becoming a cult rather than an art, with its trivial, sensuous, derivative productions printed in small editions with artistic bindings. For most of them the last affinities with society had been thrown aside; they made images from their own sensations and systems from their own moods.

J. A. Symonds (1840–93) is typical of them. His inspiration seems purely literary – not merely detached from reality, but repeating with verbal skill the outworn attitudes and symbols. It is in this literary sense that the word 'decadent' may truly be applied to the poetry of the nineties, though some of its practitioners did carry their inverted principles through drugs and degradation to suicide. Such was Ernest Dowson (1867–1900), who wrote little but became part of the legend. Despair, abandonment, misery, are the keynotes of his poetry. The sense of regret which he captures in 'I have been faithful to thee, Cynara' has made this be remembered as a typical poem of the age when other and less mannered pieces are forgotten.

Lionel Johnson (1867–1902) seldom wrote badly in the technical sense, though much of his work is lifeless. He has music, a softness like that of the early Yeats – he loved Ireland and made a study of her history and literature – and an ability

[1] Quoted in William Gaunt, *The Aesthetic Adventure* (London, 1945), p. 140.

to write nature poetry which at its best is comparable with Hardy's. He in fact wrote a study of Hardy, a perceptive and appreciative one although he himself was a Roman Catholic. John Davidson (1857–1909) was admired in his own time. His dramatic poetry had little sense of theatre and his panting tones of rebellion are too plainly derivative from Swinburne. Yet he has originality too, sometimes producing a blend of aestheticism and realism which looks forward to the next generation of poets.

The revolt which began with young painters backed by the moral authority of Ruskin ended between the pseudo-luxury of the Café Royal and the benches on the Embankment. It continues to make itself felt: the notion of criticism based on subject-matter or moral worthiness has never returned to its former power. The British public has retained a certain admiring distrust of artists in general and painters in particular, a tendency to giggle at the word 'Bohemian' and a belief that to regard any form of art as really important in life is slightly effeminate. As for the poetry, it has found its nadir in certain types of popular sentimental songs. It is all there – the moonlight, the roses, the exaltation of the immediate personal emotions. Mr Ruskin would certainly not have approved.

17

Socialism

The word 'socialism' has been emotive ever since its first appearance early in the nineteenth century. It has engendered hope and fear, praise and abuse; it has meant different things to different people; it has created division as well as unity. In essence, it describes the wish for communal rather than private control of natural resources and productive power, with the aim of improving both the material position and the political status of those with no bargaining power beyond their own strength and skill. Socialism was not a feature of Chartism and was distrusted by many Chartist leaders. It won no sympathy from most of the more privileged who pressed social reforms through Parliament or advocated them in literature. Its growth was aided, paradoxically enough, by the Benthamite Utilitarianism which Carlyle, Dickens and others attacked as the worst enemy of the poor.

The doctrine of the general good underlies much of the social thinking and action of the Victorian age. The old-guard Benthamites had no patience with any socialist application of their ideas, but looked to self-help and personal enterprise which the forces of government should foster towards the harmony of the whole. Others used a different logic and believed that society would benefit more from state initiative than from state encouragement: the government should be the producer of the show rather than the compère.

After the collapse of Chartism there was an attempt to develop in contemporary terms the socialism implicit in the early Church.[1] Victorian Christianity with its strong Evangelical bias tended to regard personal salvation as more important than social welfare; too often the expected justice of the next world was made an excuse for failing to act in this one.

---

[1] *Acts*, ii, 44ff.

Yet there were fine exceptions, such as the members of the 'Clapham Sect' with their passion for justice and the redress of social grievances at home and abroad. The Tractarians quarrelled with the materialism and self-interest of the capitalist system. Hurrell Froude admired the French Christian Socialists and Newman denounced the political economy of wealth and gain. More often, however, the bitter anti-clericalism of men like Robert Owen discredited socialism in the eyes of orthodox Christians, although the Trade Union movement drew much strength from Protestant dissent. The movement known as Christian Socialism was associated mainly with 'Broad Church' Anglicans, shunning extremes of doctrine and practice, and trying to find what was relevant to the actual situation.

Their leader was Frederick Denison Maurice (1805–72) whose theological writing has become more highly regarded in recent years. It was as a theologian that he joined in the mounting attack on laissez-faire policies, preaching the brotherhood of man and castigating society for creating false divisions. Men ought to be living not in competition but in co-operation. Out of the family and the nation there could grow that universal community to which the best in the Church was already witnessing. For him it was no utopian vision but an ideal that such realities as monastic communities had proved to be attainable. *The Kingdom of Christ* (1842) was written to demonstrate that the Kingdom was not to come in a vague future time but was already among men.

Maurice, however, was neither a leveller nor a democrat. A pamphlet which Lord Goderich wrote for the 'Christian Socialist Tracts' series in 1852 was rejected by him, after gaining the approval of Kingsley, for advocating democracy.[1] The notion of brotherhood did not lead to egalitarianism; to abolish the hierarchy of society would mean anarchy, or a new and worse despotism. Maurice accepted the need for monarchy and strong maintenance of order, and even his sympathy with Chartism did not prevent his offering his services as a special constable during the last demonstration in 1848.

Maurice took the lead in the movement, the others nearly always bowing to his will as they did over the Goderich affair. Yet Christian Socialism might not have developed as it did

[1] H. G. Wood, *Frederick Denison Maurice* (Cambridge, 1950), pp. 158ff.

without J. M. Ludlow (1821–1911), who made its supporters aware of foreign ideas and brought in the sense of solidarity with struggles abroad which Lovett had already introduced to the working-class movement. If Christian Socialism can be traced to a single origin, it might be in the letter which Ludlow wrote to Maurice from Paris, stating his conviction that socialism 'must be Christianized or it would shake Christianity to its foundation'.[1]

Another prominent member of the movement was Thomas Hughes (1822–96) who idolized Thomas Arnold and enshrined his image in *Tom Brown's Schooldays* (1857). This is a valuable document of the transition of the public schools from lawless freedom mingled with savage discipline into their self-appointed role of equipping English gentlemen for their duties in the world. It is old-fashioned in its nostalgia for stage-coaches, its robust action and its almost picaresque structure, but of its age in its priggishness and its clear division of human beings into the good and the bad. That Christianity should be the heart of British citizenship was an idea of which Arnold would have strongly approved, though he would not have been prepared to go so far as his earnest disciples in some of the implications.

The most talented and imaginative of the leading Christian Socialists, though not the most intellectual, was Charles Kingsley, whose contribution to the novel has already been considered. He was not a systematic thinker, but produced a muddled, honest and typically British synthesis, owing more to a warm heart than to a cool head. He drew something of his politics from Carlyle and most of his theology from Maurice. He sympathized deeply with the Chartists but was no more wedded to democracy than was his leader; he found his ideal in an alliance of the Church, the gentry and the common people against the machinations of the traders and the political economists. In fact, his aims approximated to those of the 'Young England' group, though with less seeking for personal advantage and much less competence in practical politics.[2]

The literary energies of the movement went mainly into

[1] Quoted in Alec R. Vidler, *The Church in an Age of Revolution* (Harmondsworth, 1961), p. 96.

[2] It should be remembered that Disraeli's *Sybil* deals with the first phase of Chartism 1838–43, whereas Kingsley's *Alton Locke* describes the last struggle and collapse 1845–8.

pamphlets and journalism. As a young man Maurice produced a novel, *Eustace Conway* (1834), in which he skirmishes with the Benthamites for their selfishness and disregard of moral principles – though the episode of a character justifying abduction and betrayal by reference to Utilitarian doctrine takes opposition too far to be convincing. Maurice's mature thought is foreshadowed in his attack on the commercial principle which he sees as governing the country and even tainting its religion. In spite of his attempts at a real alliance with the workers, in spite of his talks with Chartist and co-operative leaders, Maurice remained a visionary to the end. His own attempts to set up co-operative enterprises failed through being too small to compete with the capitalist market. He fell outside the mainstream of the new socialism with his distrust of trade unionism and collectivism, indeed of any firm party organization. At length he turned his energy to education, and here he left his mark more clearly in such enterprises as the foundation of the Working Men's College.

The aims of the movement were set forth in the series *Politics for the People,* starting in 1848 and running for only four months. Yet in that short time it attracted contributions from church dignitaries, including Archbishops Whateley and Trench, while at the other end of the social spectrum it gave an opportunity for working men to express themselves through published letters. It also contained some lively pieces by Kingsley as 'Parson Lot'. The 1850 series *Tracts on Christian Socialism* was also short-lived; it was in this title that the name of the movement was first officially used. At the end of that year began the weekly *Christian Socialist,* which ran to the end of 1851 and then changed its name to *The Journal of Association.* The change was significant; the attempt to sanctify and rebuild the ruins of Chartism was abandoned for the new faith in co-operation.

The attempt to combine socialism and Christianity was not agreeable to all. J. W. Croker, still going strong after all the Romantic poets were dead, wrote a bitter attack on Maurice and Kingsley in the *Quarterly,* accusing them of every kind of infidelity.[1] In spite of their plea that socialism meant no more than the principle of partnership and brotherhood inherent in

[1] Wood, op. cit., p. 95.

Christianity and was tied to no secular party, they failed to convert either the nation or the national church. The Christian Socialist movement as led by Maurice was finished by 1854, though its effects were to be felt again later in the reign. It had been more forward-looking than the Oxford Movement in theology or the Young England group in politics, not to mention a considerable section of the Chartism with which it had flirted so passionately.

To move forward in the strength of the past was the ideal of William Morris (1834–96). His boyhood enthusiasm for the Middle Ages never left him: it was a medievalism not of escape but of challenge. By all theories of environmental influence Morris ought to have been a perfectly complacent Victorian. Born into a solidly respectable middle-class family, he was sent to Marlborough – one of the first new Victorian public schools – where he hated the cult of games so much belauded by Thomas Hughes. He liked work better than play, starting his life's dedication to the value of good and beautiful toil. The child was father to the man also in his hatred of the ugliness of the commercial system; at the 1851 Great Exhibition he went into the first hall, took one look at the plethora of products witnessing to the cause of the open market, and refused to go any farther because it was all so 'wonderfully ugly'.[1] Soon afterwards he struck an adolescent blow for socialism by refusing to go to the funeral of the Duke of Wellington.[2]

At Oxford his early inclinations were confirmed when he read Ruskin's essay 'On the Nature of Gothic' in *The Stones of Venice;* he abandoned his idea of ordination and vowed to devote his life to art. In 1861 he founded the firm of decorative artists in Red Lion Square, Holborn, which was the main practical concern of the rest of his life. He was a good employer, who carried his principles into his business affairs. He became increasingly involved with the new socialist organizations which began with Hyndman's Democratic Federation and the history of which was outlined in the first chapter. By his death, he had been exploited and thrown over by one splinter-group after

[1] Marjorie and C. H. B. Quennell, *A History of Everyday Things in England* (London, 1934), Vol. 4, p. 1.

[2] J. W. Mackail, *The Life of William Morris* (World's Classics edition, Oxford, 1950), p. 27.

another; he died worn out with the strain of lectures, street-meetings and internal dissensions – worn out but not disillusioned. He kept his optimism to the last.

Morris expressed things which other Victorians expressed as well or better, but no one else combined them in quite the same way. Influences which took different channels through other people found a unique outlet in his ability to hold a total vision. He comes near to being one of the greatest Victorians; and though he neither fully interprets his age nor fully transcends it, he helps us to understand some of its strongest pressures. His denunciations of commercial civilization link him with Carlyle, Dickens, Disraeli and all those who had similarly fulminated in the forties, but more directly with Ruskin from whom he learned to hate the world of the classical economists which placed a premium on large-scale production and immediate profits. He saw the coming extinction of the craftsman by machines, and feared that choking over-production would mean the loss of the beautiful in life.

His contemporaries took different views about the social value of beauty. While the Pre-Raphaelites were building a mystique of beauty which had strange results before the end of the century, the younger Plugsons and Gradgrinds were still dismissing beauty and imagination as irrelevant weaknesses which were likely to interfere with smooth and efficient production. The Romantics had left their mark on society as a whole, and the connection between beauty and goodness was agreed by many who accepted the most desperate visual ugliness in their surroundings. It was an age of bad taste, deriving less from indifference than from an over-anxious attempt to produce something impressive, from the unintelligent mingling of styles by Victorian opulence which saw the whole world as its market-place.

The backwash of the 'Condition of England question', touched by a late Romanticism, grew into the philosophy of William Morris. Ruskin taught him, both directly and through the Pre-Raphaelites, that a healthy society ought to make beautiful things; he took the message further and desired to refashion society in the name of beauty. While the Pre-Raphaelites were drifting towards aestheticism and eccentricity, Morris was plunging into the realities of the world and holding a cheerful sanity in the midst of his disgust. For all his participation in politics, he remained a visionary. He kept his ideals in the maelstrom of rival socialist groups by looking to the future of his dreams, in which the best of the past would come to life again.

Poetry was his first love, and despite his attachment to practical needs he remained faithful to her. Political action drew him away from the writing of poetry, partly through negative difficulties and partly through conscious renunciation, but poetry was nevertheless for him a part of the good life towards which all activity should be striving. He did not, like Arnold, look to it as a way of refining sensibilities and deepening total understanding. These things he did not deny, but counted them as implicit in the life where the production and enjoyment of poetry would be as natural as breathing.

He was a poet from his undergraduate days, and some of his earliest poems appeared in *The Defence of Guenevere* (1858). This volume seemed to set him squarely among the Pre-Raphaelite Brotherhood, in a world culled from Malory and Froissart, a world light and dream-like, capturing moments of reality like the illuminations of medieval manuscripts. In spite of their self-conscious archaisms of manner and vocabulary, parading obscure names of architecture and armour, some of these pieces have the true lyrical voice. They are written with the ease of manner which makes Morris a fine poet but ultimately stops him from being a great one.

This lack of intensity, the failure to communicate with the complexity of which language is capable, becomes more marked in *The Life and Death of Jason* (1867), where a classical subject is caught up in the tradition of medieval romance. The love of telling tales in the manner of the Middle Ages brought Morris back to a medieval setting in *The Earthly Paradise* (1868–70), with poetry that is more cunning than before in skill and craftsmanship. Yet it is somehow less human than the pseudo-ballads of *Guenevere*: its seekers towards the ideal seem a parable of his own increasing urgency to reach Utopia. The tales are lively enough, varied in subjects and sources, vivid in narrative and colour, but they seem unable to touch the real world that was pressing so hard on him.

A visit to Iceland stimulated interest in the Norse Sagas and

led to *Sigurd the Volsung* (1877) and various translations including a version of *Beowulf* and a practical share in the new *Saga
Library*. The growing interest in philology, which was causing
controversy with the exponents of 'pure literature' in the
honours schools of English, roused him to enthusiasm which did
not have entirely happy results. His attempts at writing in
English freed from the taint of Romance words cause stiffness
in some of his later poetry and prose. The late *Poems by the Way*
(1891) bring a flash of the old magic and include some of his
finest pieces.

The fullest imaginative expositions of his faith come in two
prose romances written late in his life. *A Dream of John Ball*
(1888) sends him back to the fourteenth century that he loved
to recount a vision of the peasant leader who refused to acknowledge any man as his master by accident of birth. It is an
extremely idealized picture, finding beauty in all aspects of the
medieval scene, but redeemed by its burning enthusiasm and
delight in his own fantasy and by his power to laugh in the
midst of seriousness.

News from Nowhere (1891) is a more considerable work. Here
he is transported in a dream into the twentieth century, where
socialism has been accomplished. People live in small communities, in beautiful houses with plenty of open space.
Money and commerce have been abolished. Everyone makes
the things for which he has aptitude and exchanges with others
for his needs. Government is by agreement in local 'motes';
there are no penal laws, no compulsion. These things have been
brought about by a series of civil disturbances culminating in
a great battle in Trafalgar Square in 1952; Morris was
remembering the events of 'Bloody Sunday' in 1887.[1]

It is a beautiful vision which, like most Utopias, leaves a lot of
questions unanswered. What is to be done with those who
refuse to conform to the new ideal? The problem of the nonconformist is a serious one for the Utopian revolutionary, who
spends his time encouraging people to revolt and turn against
society and is then faced with the need for agreement. Morris
takes the usual refuge of vaguely assuming that people will
become morally good when conditions are changed. Those who

[1] Morris wrote a poem for the funeral of Alfred Linnell who was killed in the
fighting.

do not accept the general ethos of the new society are sooner or later punished by their own remorse. *News from Nowhere* is full of loose ends and unjustified assumptions, political realities rubbing awkwardly against high-flown dreams. Yet it remains a magnificent statement of the belief in human brotherhood which was held by some of the best minds of the century, and of the peculiarly British desire to establish socialist principles while abolishing the industrial society for which they were designed. The ending is a fine statement of hope, of a vision not yet fulfilled but not quite extinguished in the grubbiness of party politics:

> Go back and be the happier for having seen us, for having added a little hope to your struggle. Go on living while you may, striving, with whatsoever pain and labour needs must be, to build up little by little the new day of fellowship, and rest, and happiness.

The concern of Morris about society is to be found in almost every activity of his life. As a craftsman and designer he did as much as any one man could do to change public taste. His love of simple medieval craft was sometimes idealized and led him to design furniture too massive for modern houses and too uncompromising to provide comfort. Yet he waged with some success the battle against elaborate ornamentation laid on without regard for function or basic design, against the mass-production which turned out identical articles without regard for their intended setting or user, against the shoddiness that hid poor work beneath fringes and beading. The joints on the furniture that he made were plain for all to see; their rough honesty showed what he meant by beauty. In furniture, wall-paper, printing and book-production he helped to start a reaction to greater simplicity and more intelligent use of the natural potential of materials. We may not care for all that he did, and he would be appalled by a great deal that we contrive to live with today, but we owe a debt to him that our urban civilization is not even uglier than it is.

Morris as a socialist, specifically understood, has to be sought in his books, essays and letters, in reprints of his lectures, in the record of his speeches in many parts of the country. In the earnest Victorian way, he read and reasoned himself into the principles of socialism, as Newman did into Roman Catholicism and George Eliot into agnosticism. He read Carlyle, Ruskin and John Stuart Mill; at the same time he surveyed the commercial squalor around him, contrasted it with his ideas of history and his love of beauty, and decided that the whole basis of society was rotten and had to be changed.

Although Morris was prepared to go farther than many of his contemporaries and press for 'the further development of democracy'[1] he yet suffered some tension between dream and reality. There is an escapist element in his work; his vision often soared ahead of the practical details. His description of himself in the 'Envoi' to *The Earthly Paradise* shows how far he was in some respects from the main channel of socialist development:

> Dreamer of dreams, born out of my due time,
> Why should I strive to set the crooked straight?
> Let it suffice me that my murmuring rhyme
> Beats with light wing against the ivory gate,
> Telling a tale not too importunate
> To those who in the sleepy region stay,
> Lulled by the singer of an empty day.

Yet he offers something that has remained within British socialism, never quite overlaid by the harder doctrinaire line. Life is right only if it can produce and enjoy beauty; art is a part of social morality and if it is not popular in the true sense it 'betokens that fatal division of men into the cultivated and the degraded classes which competitive commerce has bred and fosters'.[2] The dream of a medieval world where culture was serious and unified endured, to inspire Belloc and Chesterton in the next century. It is not a medievalism of Pre-Raphaelite languor but one which sees honest and satisfying work as man's greatest need.

Morris translated his vision into action more effectively than did Ruskin, who was hampered by personal insecurity. Sometimes idealistic to the point of naivety, Morris became an easy target for exploitation by the extreme and anarchist elements in the socialist organizations. The charm of his own nature emerges in all that he wrote, sometimes to his disadvantage when he writes of vitally important things in a gentle, dreamy tone and language, seeming to deny what he is really saying.

[1] *Four Letters on Socialism* (1894).
[2] Letter in the *Manchester Examiner*, 14 March 1883.

By the time of Morris's death, socialism had emerged as a definite political programme instead of a vague theory within existing institutions of state. The situation after mid-century became too complex for the emotional sympathy with the poor and the unformulated calls for a change of heart which had been characteristic of the forties. A new 'Condition of England question' was recognized and discussed, as the middle-class conscience was stirred by evidence of appalling conditions which previous legislation had not touched. The passion for enumeration and description shown by reformers at the start of the reign now assumed larger proportions: no previous age had been so well documented as the one which saw the establishment of the Statistical Department of the Board of Trade in 1832, the Royal Statistical Society in 1833, the Department of the Registrar-General in 1838. From about 1880, facts and figures were the tools of those who questioned anew the propositions of orthodox political economy – not with the wholesale denunciations of Carlyle and Dickens but with the determination to find a better system. The old theories of trade and wages were replaced by studies called social sciences. The Fabians researched, investigated and published; ideas of nationalization grew; Bernard Shaw was converted by hearing Henry George speak on the nationalization of land. Yet the real struggle was seen to be with capital rather than land ownership. It was not a question of dealing with individual masters but of beating the cartels and combines. To do this effectively, the State had to be invoked as the biggest combine of all.

The spirit of Christian Socialism was revived when Stewart Headlam founded the Guild of St Matthew in 1877. This fusion of Maurice's ideas with the developing social aims of the Tractarian successors attacked personal and social injustices, pressed for effective legislation on housing and conditions of work. It produced little of literary merit except some fine sermons by Stanton of St Alban's, Holborn. Headlam, who gave bail for Wilde after his committal, was the prototype of Morell in *Candida*. There was also the Christian Social Union, adding to similar ideas something of T. H. Green's political idealism.

By the last decade of the century, socialism was being debated often and frankly. 'An open letter to an Eton boy on the social question'[1] could present socialism as not only compatible with Christianity but as a necessary part of it and could describe the sufferings of the poor in graphic detail reminiscent of the novelists of the forties. In 1891 Oscar Wilde published in the *Fortnightly* his long essay *The Soul of Man under Socialism* after hearing Shaw make a political speech. The master must have been more amused than impressed by the disciple; for Wilde, socialism was a means to the end of individual fulfilment.

Wilde's essay shows that he could deal seriously with current issues and that he did not need imprisonment for mature thought. Under the flippancy of his aesthetic pose there was an astringency that could have led to greater things if he had not won fame too soon. He warns against the tendency of socialism to substitute economic tyranny for political tyranny. Like Morris, but with an idiosyncratic vision of Utopia, he sees art as a civilizing force. Extremes of poverty and riches alike degrade people; only equality can give play to individualism. Art is not urged as useful, nor manual work as elevating. Although it dodges many of the main issues, it is yet a lively piece of work which utters some profound truths. It stands for the young, gay aspect of socialism, the youthful protest against the moribund but still existing influence of Benthamism and *laissez-faire* economics. In a typical paradox, Wilde agrees that socialism is Utopian and impractical but suggests that this may be a good reason for trying it.

Most of the Victorian writers who look with favour on socialism mingle personal escapism with their sympathy, seeing it as a refuge from industrialism and class-conflict. That it was basically an economic doctrine requiring political power for its fulfilment, that it was linked with an industrialized society, were things that they could not or would not see. Morris hated the pressures of 'Podsnap's drawing-room'[2] but he came to hate the pressures of Marxism as well. Not until the next century did the real meaning of the new socialism find literary expression in the untidy but moving novel by 'Robert Tressel', *The Ragged-Trousered Philanthropists* (1914). Yet George Meredith, looking as he often did into the future, could see that

[1] James Adderley, *The New Floreat* (1894).
[2] *Justice* (the S. D. F. publication), 16 June 1894.

socialism was not destined to be a middle-class device for improving the lot of the poor:

The people are the Power to come. Oppressed, unprotected, abandoned; left to the ebb and flow of the tides of the market, now taken on to work, now cast off to starve, committed to the shifting laws of demand and supply, slaves of Capital – the whited name for old accursed Mammon; and of all the ranked and black-uniformed host no pastor to come out of the association of shepherds, and proclaim before heaven and man the primary claim of their cause: they are, I say, the power, worth the seduction of another Power not mighty in England now: and likely in time to set up yet another Power not existing in England now.[1]

[1] *Beauchamp's Career* (1876), Vol. 2, Ch. 1.

18

The Catholic Revival

To approach Victorian literature in complete ignorance of Christianity would be to start with a handicap amounting to disablement. The tenets of that religion were being challenged by many, and reconsidered by some who continued to hold them, but the majority still accepted them as part of the national background. It is impossible to read far at any level of writing without meeting the basic assumptions of faith. A private in the Crimea was reported seriously and without any imputation of religious mania when he exhorted a comrade before Alma:

'Eternity, Eternity, know and seek the Lord while He may be found. Call upon Him while He is near, for you cannot tell what tomorrow will bring forth, and it may be too late then.'[1]

It was not the missionary-explorer Livingstone but an ordinary manservant who said at a deathbed in the wilds of Africa:

'If it be the will of God to take you, Sir, you may confidently rely, as far as circumstances will permit me, on my faithfully performing all that you have desired; but I hope and believe that the Almighty will yet spare you to see your home and country again.'[2]

Is it surprising that so little of the greatest Victorian literature had the Christian religion as its principal theme? The common background of society may offer less inspiration than the areas of dispute, and those who did not pour their energy into some other commitment tended to acquiesce in faith rather than to be burningly impelled by it; religion was an underlying agreement within society more often than it was an all-informing force. The occasions when it burst into passion are all the more notable.

[1] Timothy Gowing, *A Voice from the Ranks*, edited by Kenneth Fenwick (London, 1954), p. 15.
[2] R. L. Lander, *Records of Captain Clapperton's Last Expedition*, in *African Discovery*, edited by M. Perham and J. Simmons (Harmondsworth, 1948), p. 128.

Homilectic and devotional literature poured out in a stream which has left few pools for our refreshment. The imaginative literature in which religion is a developed rather than an implicit assumption springs mainly from the two prongs of the Catholic revival: the Anglican successors to the Tractarians, and the growth of Roman Catholicism which began with Catholic emancipation in 1829 and became stronger after the restoration of the hierarchy in 1850. That revival indeed nurtured an aesthetic taste which had been starved for too long; it began a new extravagance in church architecture and ornament, vestments, music and incense. It turned into acceptable and even sanctified channels that upsurge of sensuous feeling which took a different course in the Pre-Raphaelites, the Aesthetes and the decadents. The Evangelical distrust of sensuous pleasure, coupled with a hearty condemnation of most literature as time-wasting and probably immoral, left the field open to writers with Catholic presuppositions.

The Anglo-Catholic revival owed almost as much to Romanticism as to theology. It came to many as a liberation from the artistic and emotional starvation which popular Evangelicalism had imposed, offering 'a religion which did not reject, but aspired to embody in itself, any form of art and literature ... which could be pressed into the service of Christianity'.[1] Even its theologians found much to attract them in the English expression of Romanticism, with its essential spirituality and its search for unity beneath the conflicts of the age. The early years of the Oxford Movement had the fabric of tragedy in its tensions, its seeming betrayals, its divided loyalties. The secession of Newman in 1845 wounded many whom he had inspired but appeared to others as a logical outcome of the search for true catholicity. The Tractarians made only too well the current appeal to history; their resort to continuity and tradition became fossilized, and the hopeful backward glance became a fixed stare. They were doomed, as the Chartists were doomed, by reactionary aims under the cloak of revolt. The reforms of the Whigs so hated by Newman saved the Church of England from the ruin prophesied gleefully by Bentham and gloomily by Thomas Arnold. Yet the best of the Tractarian

[1] Frederick Rogers (Lord Blachford), quoted in Wilfrid Ward, *The Oxford Movement* (London, N. D.), p. 31.

spirit had something still more precious to give to the future – 'the belief that the Church is a Divine Society and not a department of State'.[1]

With the exception of Newman, the Tractarians made little direct literary impact. The Tracts themselves, although by different hands, achieve a remarkably even style, which is serious without being portentous, dignified without excessive ornamentation. It was Newman who gave them much of their quality, but his contributions were only a tiny part of the production of his long life. He deserves a place in our literature as in our history, and his writings free him from the charge of narrowness as surely as does his life. He shared the frenetic energy of his time and committed himself to its needs, going devotedly among the cholera-victims and joining in the popular attacks on mismanagement in the Crimean campaign. His voice was as critical of the age as were those of Carlyle and Ruskin, Arnold and Morris; much of his writing sprang from challenges to be met and abuses to be remedied.

Newman handled most of the literary 'forms' of the time. His first novel, *Loss and Gain* (1848) was partly a counter to Froude's *Shadows of the Clouds* but also his first public defence after his conversion to Rome. It reaches no great heights but is readable as a story and invaluable as a picture of the movement in its early Oxford days. There is a good deal of auto-biography in the hero, Charles Reding – was there anything significant in the choice of name by a man who had read and studied his way towards Rome? *Callista* (1856) was a challenge to Kingsley's *Hypatia*: both are set in North Africa, Newman's being two generations the earlier, and the eponymous heroines of both are noble Greek pagans but Newman's is converted and martyred. Newman is too much of a propagandist to be a great novelist. The long expositions and speeches become wearisome, and the avoidance of sexual interest is remarkably thorough even for the time, but nevertheless his understanding of people is deep within the limits he gave himself.

Most of Newman's shorter poems appeared in *Lyra Apostolica* (1836), a collection of religious verse by various writers. His long work *The Dream of Gerontius* (1866) has, through Elgar's music, won approval from many who dislike or manage to

[1] T. M. Parker in *Ideas and Beliefs of the Victorians* (London, 1949), p. 122.

ignore its theological doctrine. It would be idle to pretend that Newman was a great poet, but his expository prose is a different matter. Much of the justification for his theology appears in *An Essay on the Doctrine of Development* (1845), which uses the current concern with evolutionary theory to tackle problems of absolute truth and relative understanding. His belief as it applied to his task as Rector of the new Catholic University in Dublin was expounded in *The Idea of a University Defined* (1873), an essay which once had influence in education but has fallen into neglect partly for insisting on theology as an essential of the university syllabus. The old appeal to history was made again in *The Grammar of Assent* (1870) which, influenced by Butler's *Analogy*, enshrines what 'assent' meant for him and for his followers – the quest for firm authority, for affirmation in an age of uncertainty.

It was, however, *Apologia pro Vita Sua* (1864) which chiefly won respect. This story and justification of his spiritual life was written quickly, to answer an imputation by Charles Kingsley that he had little regard for the strict truth. Its very manner refutes the charge; nothing could have more effectively convinced Englishmen that, for all his Roman robes, he was still one of them. It is the finest example of his style: in much of his work, but nowhere so strongly as here, we seem to hear him speaking. It is prose that is temperate in the best sense, sharing the warmth of emotion and the coolness of intellect without excess of either.

Newman stands high above the other Tractarians as a writer. In spite of their Romantic sympathies, none of them produced poetry of real value. John Keble's *The Christian Year* (1827) falls just outside our period but continued to be widely read all through the century. It was over-valued by those who, like Pendennis and his mother, 'whispered it to each other with awe',[1] but it is an interesting link between Romantic pantheism and the finer religious poetry of the next generation. Keble points towards Hopkins with his vision of the sacramental in all natural life and his inner loneliness which even religion cannot quite assuage. Where he is weak is where the Tractarians as a whole were weak: in being too well-read for his experience. There is more of the human warmth in Isaac Williams, whose

[1] Thackeray, *Pendennis* (1850), Bk. 1, Ch. 3.

Autobiography recalls the deep sincerity, the growing divisions, the essential tragedy of the Oxford Movement, with more of the true novelist's art than *Loss and Gain*. In spite of the palpable influence of Scott and Wordsworth, in spite of frequent technical faltering, there are fine things in *The Cathedral* (1838). Here he showed his devotion to the ancient Welsh Church with its warrant for non-Roman catholicity in Britain.

The popular sympathy won by men like Williams could be alienated by such as Richard Hurrell Froude whose *Literary Remains* (1838–9) caused offence by attacking the sixteenth-century reformers. The ebullient W. G. Ward angered many, and was deprived of his degree, for his praise of the Roman order in *The Ideal of a Christian Church* (1844). E. B. Pusey served the Church of England better than English literature with his appealingly devout sermons and tracts. Through him, and through its influence on men like R. W. Church, R. C. Trench and William Stubbs, the movement was important in factual and expository writing.

The revival of unfamiliar devotions had their effect far away from Oxford. There were many – too many – who tried to put their exciting rediscovery of the Catholic spirit into the form of fiction. Piety tends to outrun talent in the 'church novel', so full of introspection and self-analysis, of characters whose scruples stifle the plot. What makes them dull today was part of their appeal in an age when autobiographies and memoirs exposed the struggles of Christians and agnostics alike. Personal though the church-novelists may be, they are seldom indifferent to their age or resistant to the new realism of fiction. Their witness is restrained and very English, touching on social questions with piety rather than enthusiasm, avoiding the 'testifying' sprees of the Evangelicals.

Many of such novels are of little interest even to the specialist. There is not much reason to remember *Fabiola* (1854) except that it was written by Nicholas Wiseman, the first Cardinal in the restored hierarchy. A story of Constantinople, *Theodora Phranza* (1853–4), is part of the quest of J. M. Neale to find links with the Orthodox Church and thus by-pass Roman claims to sole Catholicity. Thomas Hughes, as a disciple of Thomas Arnold, depicted the spiritual upheaval of the forties in *Tom Brown at Oxford* (1861) without any hero-worship of Newman.

The most successful of them, who did well what many of her contemporaries were doing badly, was Charlotte M. Yonge (1823–1901). The comparison with Jane Austen is inevitable: the quiet life in a Hampshire village, the gentle observation of domestic life, the intense absorption in limited interests. The comparison is to Charlotte's disadvantage, but not so far as to make it ludicrous. She may lack her predecessor's irony and grasp of motivation, but she has the capacity to form moral judgements and the art of declaring them without seeming vapidly 'pious'. In her own century she was admired not only by Tennyson and Temple but also by William Morris and the soldiers in the Crimean trenches.

Her output, large even by Victorian standards, included such particular successes as *Heartsease* (1854), *The Daisy Chain* (1856) and historical novels like *The Dove in the Eagle's Nest*, but none passed in popularity *The Heir of Redclyffe* (1853). Here she gave most clearly that tone of new Anglican piety, coming in the wake of the Tractarians, which she had absorbed as a parishioner of Keble. It is an ordinary enough story of domestic life, with the rough course of love, heroic death and widow-hood, and with characters who today seem priggish – especially the hero Guy de Morville with his negative scruples about gambling and going to balls. Its success, and some lasting value, came from the introduction of a new moral sense into fiction; a morality which neither depends on stock axioms and quoted texts nor uses the melodramatic judgement of general platitudes drawn from artificial situations; a morality which recognizes the real tension between discipline and indulgence. She follows the idea of actions judged by consequences as resolutely as George Eliot, but from a religious instead of a humanist viewpoint, with less intellectual power but no less compassion. Philip Morville longs for the family inheritance; he receives it after a tragedy for which he is responsible, and it is loathsome to him. Above all, running through the book, is the theme of forgiveness.

Charlotte Yonge in fact does just what the Victorians have so often been blamed for not doing: she takes religion seriously and admits it to every aspect of life instead of keeping it in a separate Sunday compartment. Guy may be something of a Byronic hero, with his ancestral curse of a savage temper, but his struggle to conquer it reveals much about the Victorian fear of the beast in man and the black inheritance of the new society. She usually avoids the tear-jerking pathos, the bathetic sentimentality, which are the curse of the minor Victorian novel. If her characters are stiff in their views, they are also living personalities whom we can quickly accept. Their virtue is part of them, not a pious addition; whether we feel sympathy or impatience with their scruples, we recognize that the conflict is real for them. It is worth remembering that it was not only Christians who were sensitive about the minutiae of truth and loyalty; many agnostics would have felt just as strongly about the concealment from their parents practised by Philip and Laura.

Above all, Charlotte Yonge is a novelist of the family; the links of kinship often extend to characters over different novels. Here again the modern taste, nurtured on Samuel Butler and misreadings of Freud, may consider her picture idealized. It may be so, but it is done within realism, using a framework of details which can be verified from other sources. There was more than gloom and oppression in the Victorian family, where filial obedience was seen as a virtue but not always as an imposition. She idealizes as the age idealized itself, holding up a flattering but not a distorting glass.

One of the very few Evangelicals who wrote fiction was Dinah Maria Mulock, better known as Mrs Craik (1826–87). Her most famous book, *John Halifax, Gentleman* (1857), the story of a poor farm-boy who reaches success by honesty and hard work, was well calculated to appeal to the new reading-public with its watchwords of industry and self-help. She is more complacent than Charlotte Yonge, extolling virtues which lead to worldly success rather than to spiritual fulfilment. She had a point of view to express, however and she helped to make the novel more acceptable to Evangelical readers.

Another Anglican novel comes in a later period when doubt and questioning were more openly active: the period of Gissing and Rutherford, Hardy and Meredith. J. H. Shorthouse (1834–1903) came to the Church of England from Quakerism in 1861. The appeal to history for settling Anglican claims had been made from different viewpoints by the Froude brothers, and now Shorthouse made it with *John Inglesant* which he had

privately printed in 1880 and which was published by Macmillan in the following year. Set in the seventeenth century, it
relates the spiritual progress of a young man with old Catholic
loyalties and Jesuit training, through the mazes of intrigue in
England and Italy to the acceptance of something very like
Tractarian ideals. The earlier part perhaps owes a little to
Henry Esmond. Gladstone, the high Anglican admired by so
many nonconformist Liberals, praised the book and helped it
to success.

The modern reader becomes impatient with the large
amount that is practically transcribed from historical sources,
rather than with the inaccuracies which Lord Acton – a Roman
Catholic – found in the setting. More important than documentary truth is the author's desire to 'trace the conflict
between culture and fanaticism'.[1] Matthew Arnold would have
agreed, while disputing the interpretation of words. Shorthouse
wanted to show that Platonic ideals, which had played a
large part in early Christian culture, were compatible with high
Anglicanism. Further, he wanted to defend his Church against
those who denied her authority, and to strengthen the waverers
who were finding security in submission to Rome. Distinctively
Roman doctrines and practices are condemned as new bondage,
inessential to true Catholicism:

> The English Church, as established by the law of England, offers
> the supernatural to all who choose to come. It is like the Divine
> Being Himself, whose sun shines alike on the evil and on the good.
> Upon the altars of the Church the divine presence hovers as surely,
> to those who believe it, as it did upon the splendid altars of Rome.[2]

Not all, of course, would agree – then or now; but sentiments
like these, woven into narrative with a gentle, persuasive style,
could find supporters not deficient in either theological or
literary sense.

The Victorian religious poets retained some of the Romantic
spirit but tended to be less oracular and prophetic than their
predecessors, less passionate than those of their contemporaries
who were troubled by doubt. They used the quieter voice, the
personal rather than the public theme. Readers whose faith

[1] J. H. Shorthouse, *John Inglesant*, Preface to the 1881 edition.
[2] Ibid., Ch. 39.

was strengthened by the new revival but who found theology rather hard work, loved to anthologize religious 'messages' from them.

Christina Rossetti (1830–94) was two years younger than her brother Dante Gabriel. She began by publishing in *The Germ,* but her poetry soon developed far away from that of the Pre-Raphaelites and surpassed most of it. Her life was quiet: a spinsterhood in London punctuated by engagements which were broken because the suitors offended her Anglican devotion successively with Romanism and agnosticism. Many have preferred her early lyrics, with their clear imagery and light, lively metres, believing that her growing religious sense betrayed her talent, tamed her imagination and spoiled her first freshness.

Yet she never lost the sense of joy in natural beauty, domestic life and human love. She felt it right to renounce some of their manifestations and her religion did not fully compensate. The tension can be felt in the strange allegory of *Goblin Market* (1882), with its ambivalent attitude to the elder sister for whose restoration the heroine braves evil and nearly sacrifices herself. The idea of self-sacrifice is strong also in *The Prince's Progress* (1866). Although not all the tensions were admitted, the denunciation consciously exalted the claims of divine over human love, seen in the sonnets *Monna Innominata*. What does slip past the inward censor is expressed without self-pity, with a pathos that does not sentimentalize. It is personal and not condemnatory or proselytizing; its source is not the Calvinist fear of hell but a vision of greater happiness through present denial.

It was good for Evangelicals to be told that holiness was beautiful and for Anglo-Catholics to be reminded that it was difficult. Christina Rossetti did both, and if she is sometimes intense to a degree which the present day might consider morbid it must be remembered that such fervid devotion could find little socially acceptable outlet except in writing. She suffered as much as any overworked housemaid from the contemporary subjection of women.

The Victorian religious poets have been praised for being like the seventeenth-century Metaphysicals and condemned for not being like them. The fact is that the complexity of the age and the linguistic divergence between poetry and devotion made imitation impossible even if it had been desirable. Christina Rossetti comes near to Herbert in pieces like 'In the bleak mid-winter', and some of her allegories have a rich imagery which has been called Keatsian but is often more reminiscent of Crashaw. The contrast should be made not with them but with what her brother and his friends produced without religion to discipline their anxieties. Not that faith guaranteed good poetry: Christina Rossetti could express a mystical beauty in Anglo-Catholic devotion, but similar faith did less for Canon R. W. Dixon (1833–1900). His poetry is not contemptible, but it is seldom inspired and creaks heavily after Blake and Coleridge. Another poetic follower of the Oxford Movement was D. W. Dolben (1848–67), who died too young for his talent to be fairly assessed.

The palm for religious poetry must go to the Roman Catholics, mainly for the work of the two converts Patmore and Hopkins. Coventry Patmore (1823–96) began with the juvenile *Poems* (1844), followed after a long interval by *Tamerton Church Tower* (1853). Then came *The Angel in the House* (1854–6), an extended work on the simple Trollopian theme of the love-story of a Dean's daughter, into which accompanying 'preludes' weave the poet's philosophy. It was mauled by several reviewers, to whom its simple versifying seemed poor stuff, but has proved more to the taste of our own age. Its sequel, *The Victories of Love* (1860–2), continues the story into the married life of the first couple and the discontented marriage of the rejected suitor. The poet becomes less identified with the actions which he narrates, taking a more measured and objective view of the whole situation.

Both these long poems are celebrations of married love as a true and holy thing. The erotic and the mystic run into one another, without the hysterical neo-paganism of Swinburne or the autumnal morbidity of Rossetti. The religious element becomes stronger in *To the Unknown Eros* (1877), together with bolder experiments in prosody which continue in *Amelia* (1878). The abrupt, irregular metrical forms swing between splendid power and harsh disharmony but seldom fail to make their effect.

Like Christina Rossetti, Patmore develops much but changes little; a point dear to Newman in theology. Love is the major theme – love in physical human expression, love in spiritual manifestation, love as a mark of divine condescension. For Christina the tension between them was often strong. It was easier perhaps for the man, married and fulfilled in human love, to effect a harmony between the kinds. Patmore of all the Victorian poets comes nearest to the Metaphysicals in his ability to relate the concepts of faith to the details of contemporary life. The realism of his early work is often that of the novel, in which familiar domesticity is found to be an adequate frame for the imaginative world. Later the surface reference remains plain and simple, but the projection to things unseen is stronger. There is striking evocation of George Herbert in *The Toys*, with its challenging switch from trivial description to theological assertion, its human tenderness slanting into pathos, its self-criticism, its overwhelming realization of divine love, the quiet confidence of its closing lines:

> Ah, when at last we lie with trancèd breath,
> Not vexing thee in death,
> And thou rememberest of what toys
> We made our joys,
> How weakly understood
> Thy great commanded good,
> Then fatherly not less
> Than I whom thou hast modelled from the clay,
> Thou'lt leave thy wrath, and say,
> 'I will be sorry for their childishness'.

The praise of Patmore in the present century may be connected with the appearance in 1918 of the work of his co-religionist Gerard Manley Hopkins (1844–89). The fact that Hopkins had to wait so long before Robert Bridges gave his poetry to the world has made him seem a modern poet and he was adopted as a contemporary by those who approved of his linguistic experiments. His work in fact grew out of the religious situation of his own time; he was a poetic voice of that call to authority and 'assent' which Newman had made. His life touched Newman's more than once; whatever aesthetic promptings he may have had from Pater at Balliol, it was Newman who received him into the Roman Catholic Church and under whom he went to teach in Birmingham. He began Jesuit training in 1868, was ordained in 1877 and served in parishes in London,

Liverpool and Glasgow – cities where the Romanist section was among the most economically depressed. He later became Professor of Greek at Newman's new University in Dublin, and taught there until his death.

Hopkins burned his early poems in deliberate renunciation on beginning his ordination training. Those which survived in copies reveal a pleasant but not outstanding talent: a Keatsian influence filtered through Pre-Raphaelite channels. The years of silence were broken in 1875 when his superior encouraged him to write again. *The Wreck of the Deutschland* showed what he had learned while the suspension of poetic activity teased him with rhythms not yet to be tested. He had rediscovered the basic line of Old English poetry – or rather its looser medieval successor that appears in *Piers Plowman*. A number of fixed, alliterative stresses in each line can be linked by almost any number of unstressed syllables. It is a musical principle, in which the 'beats to a bar' can contain a variety of note-lengths; it is a full recognition that English poetic rhythm rests in stress and ought not to flirt with classical notions of length or quantity. Not all his poetry is written in what he called 'sprung rhythm', but common to it all is his ability to exploit certain features of English: the closeness to speech-rhythms of so much of its poetry, its gift for alliteration, the passing echo of assonance and internal rhyme, the facility for new word-formations by compounding.

More than technical brilliance goes to make a poet. Hopkins, like Christina Rossetti, fled from the prophetic roar of earlier and more confident poets into introspection. The particular interested him, the distinctive selfhood of things which he called 'inscape'; generalities were as repugnant to him as to Blake. He claimed theological warrant and appealed to the teaching of Duns Scotus that Nature reveals God. Wordsworth of course had said as much, and neither Nature nor religion was new subject-matter for poetry. What Hopkins could do is to sink himself in empathy with aspects of creation, while holding fast to orthodox teaching about the nature and place of Man as an individual. He praised beauty in all things created, praised them for their mere existence, without either the easy optimism of many of his contemporaries or the lacrymosity of the Romantics. The wonder of existence never deserted him, even when the weakness and failures of mortality afflicted him and he trembled at the transience of the farrier's strength and the bugler's innocence.

The Victorians too often discounted the presence of positive evil and held that everything could be solved by adequate knowledge and a right disposition of the will. Those who explored the darker shades of life often wrapped themselves in fantasy before shuddering back to the comfortable, familiar world. Hopkins recognized the markings of evil – his beloved word 'dappled' is a continual reminder of dark spots on our happiness. His later poems cry out in anguish at the monstrous tension of living with faith in an unfaithful world. It is no cry of arrogance or defiance, not the *non serviam* of the earlier and later literary rebel, but the protest from one who must submit because he has the secret to make sense of the darkness. The inner struggle is accepted as part of the cosmic struggle, but accepted only after radical questioning.

The tension of persistent evil which drove many Victorians to seek escape in some medieval or classical golden age never draws Hopkins from the moment of reality. He remains clear-sighted, taking experience by surprise with the immediacy of his observation. His work has the quality of a child's painting, looking freshly on the world, challenging sophistication. Perhaps he was over-praised for a time, but now he tends to get less than his due. Set in his own age he is a forward-looking poet, a conformist rebel who found freedom in the strictest of personal disciplines.

It is a decline to turn from Hopkins to Francis Thompson (1859–1907), who was once praised extravagantly. He was perhaps a necessary legend for the nineties, with his failures, his drug-taking, his sickness and destitution, his rescue and re-habilitation. His religious poetry is lushly ornate, too deeply touched by Swinburne; if it ever hints at the Metaphysicals it is towards Southwell or Crashaw at their most strained. No poem could show more clearly the gulf between the religious sensibility of the seventeenth century and that of the late nineteenth than the once-admired *Hound of Heaven,* where words spill over not with Donne's complexity but with Victorian profusion and the slick evocation of dead Romantic symbols. Yet there was something – a quest for mystical experience lost in a materialist age. Thompson had the eye of a visionary, but his fate was to be mastered by words. At his best he could see the world, if not in a grain of sand, at least in a convex mirror that concentrates a whole landscape in a Renaissance painting.

What is characteristic of the writers whose motivating force was a rediscovery of Catholicism? Their devotion was strong, directed towards a vision which had become clouded by concentration on immediate issues, formal worship and socially acceptable religion. There is distress and torment too. Patmore finds a unifying calm, but the happy confidence of Chesterton and the arrogantly hearty faith of Belloc were yet to be. To commit oneself, to venture on ecstasy, seemed to call for renunciation. The poets played their part towards a more sensuous apprehension of worship; yet the prevailing puritanism of the Evangelical spirit kept its hold even on those who had a different view of faith. The devotional manuals which appeared in large numbers towards the end of the century often combined ritualism with the stern perfectionism of Law and Wilberforce. Those who took religion really seriously did not know the meaning of compromise: that was their strength, sometimes their tragedy.

19

Religious Doubt and Revision

If any reading of Victorian literature soon arrives at some reference to religion, it may equally soon arrive at the subject of religious doubt. For centuries men had disputed, bitterly and sometimes bloodily, over matters of authority, interpretation and the details of worship, but the basis of faith was rarely questioned. By the end of the nineteenth century, frank and critical discussion of religion was no longer unsafe and scarcely even adventurous: churchgoing was still part of the general social pattern, but to stay away did not necessarily mean ostracism. The most striking change of all was that matters could now be considered without open reference to religion. The sphere of Christian influence had narrowed and was no longer assumed to include and measure every secular activity.

This change of outlook did not come about without anguish of mind. In spite of a warm enthusiasm for life which cushioned most of them from the dread of ultimate disaster, the great Victorians worried profoundly about their changing times. They worried about trade and politics, about class-divisions, about foreign expansion, about the viability of faith. Victorian unbelief covers many degrees, from outright atheism to a certain uneasiness in continuing to follow regular religious duties. Huxley coined the word 'agnostic' to cover the notion that spiritual things were not to be known by human minds and therefore could not be taken into their reckoning. Many writers expressed in various ways the idea that what had once seemed certain was certain no longer.

The reasons for the change are complex and not easy to disentangle. The growth of science may be named first, as it has tended to come first in the popular mind, but it is doubtful whether it was the most important. Scientific study had become more mechanistic; the determinist theory of evolution is discussed in another chapter. The cumulative effect was that Man was displaced from the centre. No longer the lord of creation, he found himself in a rapidly expanding universe with certainty retreating into stretches of time and distance never guessed at before. His pride in uniqueness of species was suddenly challenged by a family kinship with apes and lowlier forms of life. Science seemed to make relative what had been absolute, to make negative all the positive assertions about humanity.

The conflict between science and religion was unnecessary but was made inevitable by the increasingly exclusive attitudes of both sides and their insistence that their own mode of knowledge was the only valid one. Even so, the impact of science would have been lighter in an age less concerned with history. The ideas of evolution and relativism had touched historical as well as scientific method; the doctrines of thinkers like Comte were highly convenient for those inclined towards scepticism. If truth was no more static and uniform than creation, what was the use of claiming absolute certainty? 'It was not Science itself, but science interpreted as *History* which upset the orthodox cosmology'.[1]

There was also the social side of unbelief, the revolt against religion as identified with the ruling and comfortable classes. A tradition of working-class atheism extends from Paine through Robert Owen to Holyoake and the Secular Society. Christianity was indicted as a tool of repression, with the clergyman as a sinister enemy of the struggling masses – 'a black dragoon in every parish', John Sterling called him.[2] The Church of England was often identified with reaction and social inertia; the efforts of the Christian Socialists did not prevent the growth of rationalist and free-thinking groups, predominantly working-class in membership, which became stronger in the last thirty years of the century. The new popular press, with articles and snippets of Church news which were sometimes hostile and nearly always ill-informed, aided the decline of socially reverent attitudes.

The moral issue was often more influential than any of these. The search for standards after rejection of what had

[1] Noel Annan, 'The Strands of Unbelief', in *Ideas and Beliefs of the Victorians* (London, 1949), p. 151.
[2] Carlyle, *Life of John Sterling* (1851), Ch. 4.

claimed to be absolute truth troubled many minds. The sense of justice was offended by aspects of Christian doctrine, particularly in its prevailing Evangelical mode. Not only did the Atonement seem to be a dodging of personal responsibility, so dear to the earnest Victorian heart, but Calvinist pre-destination suggested that even the saved were only a small minority. To condemn vast numbers of mankind to eternal damnation seemed like the worst kind of laissez-faire indifferentism carried into spiritual spheres. Nothing could be more distasteful to many of those who considered it, and moral arguments helped to alienate George Eliot, Francis Newman, J. A. Froude and many more.

Sometimes the moral opposition to Christianity was inspired by hostile criticism of the previously sacrosanct Bible. But such criticism sometimes grew out of moral objections, producing the sacred texts of secularism which came in a steady stream from Paine's *Age of Reason* to Winwood Reade's *The Martyrdom of Man* (1872). Those who asked the moral question were forced to ask a number of others. If the teaching of Christianity is untrue, or at best a partial truth, is it possible to know truth at all? Can the real truth be presented more effectively than in the outworn modes of religion? Can human standards of behaviour survive the loss of supernatural sanctions or will the beast in man emerge and devour society? The earnest new agnostics asked, and were troubled.

Some of the troubled ones did not go so far as the rejection of faith, but tried rather to interpret and present it afresh with the stumbling-blocks cleared away. For most of the century religious orthodoxy pressed on and carried the majority with it, but it threw off the agnostics on one side and the liberal theologians on the other. The Oxford Movement started out to rescue the catholicity of the Anglican Church from 'liberalizing' tendencies, but it caused a spiritual and intellectual ferment which led to losses both ways.

Among its castaways to agnosticism was Francis Newman, brother of the Movement's leader. Stirred to take the Christian religion seriously, he followed the familiar path of finding its doctrine morally unsatisfactory and the worldliness of its official representatives offensive. Francis Newman is a classic case-study of the Victorian retreat from belief, and his spiritual history touches on many later attempts to find new freedom. From the Evangelical Anglicanism of his upbringing he became in turn Plymouth Brother, Baptist and Unitarian – all sects originally formed to protest against the constriction of orthodoxy. While his brother found peace in the monolithic authority of Rome, Francis ended in a vague spirituality attempting to synthesize various kinds of religious experience, clinging to Evangelical attitudes without dogma or authority. He recorded some of his spiritual struggles in *Phases of Faith* (1850).

J. A. Froude (1818–94) also dropped out of the Tractarian circle in which his brother Hurrell remained. He worked off the grudge against former friends, and justified himself to himself, by making the great appeal to history. His *History of England from the Fall of Wolsey* (1856–69) in fact got only as far as 1588, but that was far enough to chafe the Tractarians by making Henry VIII a hero and a reforming angel. Froude had already released some of his distress in the form of fiction and described his passage from ardent belief to doubt. *Shadows of the Clouds* published under the pseudonym of 'Zeta' in 1847, is a slight work that is interesting mainly for the thin disguise of its author as the hero 'Edward Fowler'. The school episodes, recalling Froude's own unhappy years at Westminster, are a good antidote to the jollier type of Victorian school story. *The Nemesis of Faith* (1849) is a more balanced work, with a sceptical hero 'Markham Sutherland' who is less hysterical than Fowler. The conflicts and weaknesses within the Oxford Movement are well brought out, with more sympathy for the personality of J. H. Newman. *The Nemesis of Faith* was publicly burned in Exeter College; the modern reader is more likely to be moved than shocked by the description of what loss of faith meant to a sensitive Victorian:

> You who look with cold eyes on such a one . . . could you see down below his heart's surface, could you count the tears streaming down his cheeks, as out through some church-door into the street come pealing the old familiar notes, and the old psalms which he cannot sing, the chanted creed which is no longer his creed, and yet to part with which was more agony than to lose his dearest friend; ah! you would deal him lighter measure.[1]

---

[1] *The Nemesis of Faith* (1849), pp. 117ff. Quoted in Basil Willey, *More Nineteenth-Century Studies* (London, 1956), p. 126.

Arthur Hugh Clough (1819–61) also knew some of the turmoil of the Movement. He was a close friend of Matthew Arnold, his contemporary at Rugby and Balliol, who commemorated him in *Thyrsis*. Arnold's doubts were more urbanely concealed and more fully sublimated; he was willing to let religion keep on for those who found it useful and to concede its value as a source of poetry and symbolism. His father Thomas Arnold, champion of the Broad Church and hammer of the Tractarians, had called the Old Testament story of Joseph a 'beautiful poem'.

Clough loved Matthew and revered Thomas, but he rejected such tolerance. He continued to worry about Christianity, convinced that it must be utterly rejected if it was not true. The honesty which made him resign his Oriel Fellowship underlies his rewarding but sometimes irritating poetry. His refusal to accept easy solutions and compromises is admirable but can lead to flabbiness in presentation. His work, surprisingly popular in his own century, is little enough in quantity; it consists mostly of four long poems: *The Bothie* (1848), *Amours de Voyage* (1858) and the posthumously printed *Dipsychus* and *Mari Magno*. There are also shorter pieces, mainly in the joint collection with Thomas Burbridge, *Ambarvalia* (1849).

It is poetry of a fine brain, making the search for moral and spiritual security through the doubts that were pressing down on the age. Clough regrets the turbulence of the present and longs wistfully for the religious certainties of the past, with a nostalgia less precisely grounded than that of Arnold. Tragic though the passing of faith may be, there is no retreat and no integrity except in honest acceptance. His *Epi-Strauss-ium* begins sadly:

> Matthew and Mark and Luke and holy John
> Evanished all and gone!

ends more confidently:

> The place of worship the meantime with light
> Is, if less richly, more sincerely bright,
> And in blue skies the Orb is manifest to sight.

Clough boldly faces the challenge of science to religion, for he respects scientific method and honours it for revealing new

aspects of truth. Its intellectual objectivity and honesty please
him, satisfying the aspirations which make the words *true* and
truth appear so often in his writings. The more mechanistic
tendency of science is less pleasing. A vague acceptance of
evolution in *Natura Naturans* (1849) contrasts with his sardonic
but troubled rendering of mechanistic physics:

> And as of old from Sinai's top
> God said that God is One,
> By Science strict so speaks He now
> To tell us, There is None!
> Earth goes by chemic forces; Heaven's
> A Mécanique Céleste!
> And heart and mind of human kind
> A watch-work as the rest![1]

He is typical of the Victorian agnostic in his honesty, his sadness
at the loss of the beauty in religion, and not least in the vague
spirituality with which he tries to keep open the door of faith.
He clutches at the idea of divinity resident in man's aspiration
to truth; he is neither peaceful in belief nor resigned in unbelief,
but tormented between the two with a masochistic persistence.
The oppression of public themes on his private problems is
also typical of the time. Like Ruskin, he became too burdened
with ideas and projects to see and synthesize clearly, defeating
himself by his own earnestness. His letters as well as his poems
reveal interest in current problems, in the status of women, the
problems of industry and state-control, the changes all through
society, the uncertainties imaged by:

> The whole great wicked artificial civilized fabric, –
> All its unfinished houses, lots for sale, and railway outworks.[2]

The use of narrative technique in his serious poetry is notable.
The Bothie is a mock-epic about a vacation reading-party,
brilliant with classical parodies which many of his readers
would have recognized. Here and elsewhere he uses the
hexameter, so difficult in English which depends on stress
instead of quantity. He uses the long classical line with skill,

---

[1] Clough here refers to the French scientist Pierre Simon Laplace (1749–1827),
who told Napoleon that he had no need for the hypothesis of a creating God.
Mécanique Céleste fills the first five of the seven volumes of his collected works.

[2] *The Bothie*, iv, lines 352ff.

and with a loose swing which points to the syncopated rhythm of later free verse. There is humour and satire in the character-sketches of *The Bothie* and in *Amours de Voyage*. The latter poem is in the form of verse-letters relating an English love-story in an Italian setting, with a hero remarkably like the poet in his inability to be quite wholehearted about the things which attract him most – about love or religion or Italian nationalism (Clough was present at the Siege of Rome in 1849). *Mari Magno* is a series of narratives told in the circumstances of an ocean voyage. *Dipsychus,* his most sustained achievement, tells of a Clough-like character sitting in a Venice café and conversing with a witty tempting Spirit.

A first reading of Clough gives the impression of vague and generalized poetic diction with little meaning. Deeper acquaintance reveals a remarkable if unorganized intellect, reaching beyond his own age to the perplexity of the next century. It is unfortunate that many know him only in the strained and archaic lines of 'Say not the struggle nought availeth', and ironical that this poem should have found a place in at least one collection of hymns.[1]

Newman, Froude and Clough shared an Oxford background, and the modes of their revolts were similar. A different world bred the revolt of Mark Rutherford, the pseudonym of William Hale White (1829–1913), who came to fiction in middle age with *The Autobiography of Mark Rutherford* (1881) and went on to write *Mark Rutherford's Deliverance* (1885), *The Revolution in Tanner's Lane* (1887) and *Catherine Furze* (1894). The first two are on the border between fiction and autobiography and are presented as 'edited by his friend Reuben Shapcott'. Rutherford grows up in a Midland dissenting family, undergoes the expected personal conversion, is trained and ordained before losing his conviction and drifting through Unitarianism into writing for rationalist papers. It is a pattern similar to that of Francis Newman in reality and Butler's Ernest Pontifex in fiction: to add to the likeness, Rutherford begins to lose his faith when he cannot answer the questions of an agnostic working man, just as Pontifex is confuted by an agnostic cobbler – working-class atheism meets the new intellectual doubts.

Yet it is a world far away from the middle-class Anglicanism

[1] *Songs of Praise,* No. 637.

of *The Nemesis of Faith* and *The Way of All Flesh*. White shows the material and intellectual poverty of the smaller dissenting groups, the narrowness of congregations who oppose the least innovation by their ministers. More especially, he castigates the rigidity into which they have fallen, these groups which started in protest against official conformity and claimed to offer men a new spiritual freedom. *The Revolution in Tanner's Lane* contrasts the visionary Zechariah Coleman in the early years of the century with the later indifference of the minister John Broad.

White writes of a type and class not new to English fiction, but seldom treated so seriously or in such depth. Earlier satirical portraits of dissenters abound, but the nature of their beliefs had made it virtually impossible for them to answer back through the medium of fiction. White came with dislike, with knowledge, above all with tremendous honesty. He never fails to show both sides of the case; if the lapse into unbelief was caused by the narrowness of the chapels, it is nevertheless seen as a human tragedy. He shows the struggle in which he himself had suffered, leading at last to agnosticism without pleasure or satisfaction. Different in so many ways from Newman and Clough, he could join them in the anguish which many others, less articulate, were feeling.

Butler took his personal grievances and made them appear to be universal. White took his inner conflict and gave it an external frame. He makes 'Shapcott' stress Rutherford's limitations, his morbidity, the gulf between his dreams and his capacity. White was in fact a reasonably successful Civil Servant, a good amateur astronomer, a frequent contributor to journals. Yet he shared with Rutherford something fundamental: the search for freedom from what seemed the malforming constriction of religion, which begins when Rutherford reads – not the 'higher critics' but – *Lyrical Ballads*, and feels a liberation that leads him on through Spinoza to worship the God of Nature. The same love of freedom moved White to write a pamphlet in favour of manhood suffrage. With the pathetic irony of the period, it was the honesty of his agnosticism which caused his small daughter to feel deprived when she watched other children setting off for Sunday School.[1]

[1] Irvin Stock, *William Hale White (Mark Rutherford): A Critical Study* (London, 1956), pp. 63ff.

White creates from experience, using that word to include the imaginative as well as the externally 'real' world. He could almost be called an existentialist, but he does not regard the individual as isolated within his own experience. He strives also to synthesize, to build a new freedom from the rejection of old beliefs. He does not fully succeed, but he states the case of the unsettled agnostic and creates a world where anguish is not despair. The clarity of his style emphasizes the modernity of his vision:

> What are the facts? Not those in Homer, Shakespeare, or even the Bible. The facts for most of us are a dark street, crowds, hurry, commonplaceness, loneliness, and, worse than all, a terrible doubt which can hardly be named as to the meaning and purpose of the world.[1]

Brought up to the doctrine of total depravity, he criticizes himself as well as others. The self-doubt that makes his rejection of faith negative and uncertain commends him to the twentieth century, in which he has won the admiration of Bennett, Lawrence and Gide.

The figure of Matthew Arnold appears on the agnostic scene again through his niece Mary Augusta Arnold, better known as Mrs Humphry Ward (1851–1920). Without his humour, urbanity or basic ease of mind, she put into the novel all the earnestness of his criticism of life. Like Clough, she seemed to gain from the Arnolds the power of criticism without the compensating willingness to compromise and accept the survival of institutions adaptable to present use. Hers are novels of serious purpose; none could apply to them the old charges of time-wasting fiction which were still being heard in her lifetime.

A comparison with the novelists of the forties who tried to use the novel as a serious factor in the 'condition of England question' is not to her advantage. Certainly her books are well constructed and logical where theirs are often loose. But they, even at their most polemical could create living characters whereas hers seem endlessly to project herself alone. Her pleas for change are assured where theirs are hesitant, intellectual where theirs are emotional. It is not the intellect of her friend

---

[1] *Last Pages from a Journal* (posthumously published, 1915), pp. 289ff. Quoted in Willey, op. cit., p. 218.

and fellow-doubter George Eliot, but it is powerful and disciplined enough to balance the lack of imagination and make her books a good deal better than recent judgements have allowed.

Fame, or rather notoriety, came to her in 1888 with *Robert Elsmere*. The story is slight enough: a young Anglican priest, seduced by a sceptical squire into reading new German critics of the Bible, loses his faith and resigns his living. He seeks to serve humanity by work among the poor of London, where he dies. It is a truly Victorian book in the melodramatic fall after temptation, the noble renunciation and death, but it is a Victorianism of its own decade and looks neither back nor forward. It caused a sensation because people were troubled by problems of belief, which only a few years later would not sustain the interest of a long novel. The scenes in the East End of London link with the new naturalism of Moore and Gissing. Elsmere's emotional distress at the mocking attitude to Christ of the secularists among whom he works is another indication of the poignancy and regret in sensitive Victorian agnostics.

Mrs Ward never equalled her first success. Another earnest hero, this time troubled by sensual rather than intellectual temptations, wins through to a serene but vague 'natural religion' in *The History of Daniel Grieve* (1892). Her own social work led to novels aiming at more direct political action on behalf of the poor: *Marcella* (1894) and *Sir George Tressady* (1895-6). Her demands are strong, her criticisms severe but limited; for instance, she says nothing directly on women's right to vote. The theological issue appears again in *Helbeck of Bannisdale* (1898), with the mixed marriage of a Roman Catholic and a Protestant; it is in some ways more mature, but less compelling, than *Robert Elsmere*. After the end of the century she went from ethical debate to novels of society similar to those of the old 'silver fork' school, and to fictional renderings of famous historical scandals. As late as 1911 she turned back to the old theme with *The Case of Robert Meynell*, in which Elsmere's son-in-law turns up as a clergyman clinging to the Church by virtue of its new modernism.

Meynell thus represents the other wing of the cleavage in orthodoxy, where churchmen tried to come to terms with new movements and ideas. Mark Pattison (1813-84), who influenced

Mrs Ward, was typical of them as he hovered on the frontier between belief and agnosticism. The conflict of new ideas in both intellect and emotion is shown, often movingly, in his *Memoirs* (1883).

To the Tractarians 'Liberalism' had been a dirty word, redolent of state encroachment and loss of orthodoxy. In spite of the diehards, it became theologically respectable before the end of the century. Its immediate origins may be found in the 'Noetics' whose rallying-point was Oriel College, Oxford, contemporarily with the rise of the Tractarians, and who included Thomas Arnold and Archbishop Whateley. The tendencies of the Noetics became general among the 'Broad Church' school – a title whose suggestion of latitudinarianism its members vigorously rejected. Frederick Denison Maurice was one of the best minds among them; although his fame was once as leader of the Christian Socialists, he has recently come to be valued as a theologian. His teachings about the Atonement and eternal punishment were indeed too broad for the authorities of King's College London and cost him his Chair there in 1853.

The trouble over Maurice's *Theological Essays* was a mere breeze compared with the storm that broke with the publication in 1860 of *Essays and Reviews*. The seven contributors, all clergymen save one, included Mark Pattison, Benjamin Jowett of Balliol (1817–93) and Thomas Arnold's pupil A. P. Stanley (1815–81). There was also a future Archbishop of Canterbury, Frederick Temple, who had befriended and advised Clough. The appellation *Septum contra Christum* was among the milder reactions to their work.

Today the appearance of the collection seems the inevitable result of various challenges to the Church. From 1832, legislation had reduced her privileged independence; judicial decisions had tended to go against the orthodox side in cases of theological dispute. Strauss with his *Leben Jesu*, soon followed by Renan's *Vie de Jésus* (1863), were among the Continental attacks on traditional acceptance of the Gospels as divine records. Within the Church, Bishop Colenso was excommunicated for his views on such matters as the literal authority of the Pentateuch. No wonder that it seemed a stab in the back when, on top of Lyell and Darwin, C. W. Goodwin's essay

'Mosaic Cosmogony' claimed that the first books of the Bible were not scientific history but only human utterances containing some divine truth.

Modern agnostics shrug off the issue as a boring irrelevance, and few modern Christians find anything startling in the whole book. Yet it was part of the vital concern of some churchmen to meet new challenges lest their Church perish by default. A year after its publication, Jowett wrote:

> In a few years there will be no religion in Oxford among intellectual young men, unless religion is shown to be consistent with criticism.[1]

Two of the contributors were suspended from their offices, but Lord Chancellor Westbury reversed the judgement on appeal, 'dismissed Hell with costs, and took away from orthodox members of the Church of England their last hope of everlasting damnation'.[2] The agnostics sourly accused the essayists of dishonesty.

Yet Liberalism had made its mark. In *Ecce Homo* (1865) J. R. Seeley tried to save the basic ethics of Christianity from being swallowed up in theological controversy. His presentation of a kind of natural, universal brotherhood, intensely aspiring to good, was generally well received. The climate of opinion changed, and the reception of *Lux Mundi* (1885) was much less hostile; yet the new collection, edited by Charles Gore (1853–1932), was in many ways more radical. Archbishop Davison attacked it but did not carry Convocation with him; and some old Tractarians like Dean Church approved of it.

Its authors claimed that much 'higher criticism' could be accepted without forsaking belief in divine inspiration of the Bible; they saw revelation and reason as related and complementary, not contrary to each other. They had a basic optimism, stemming from a general acceptance of evolution and the idea of progress and according with the late Victorian growth of immanentist philosophy. Such optimism was often a weakness in religious liberalism, but Gore and the rest showed that the Church was ready not merely to defend herself but to

[1] E. A. Abbott and Lewis Campbell, *Life and Letters of Benjamin Jowett* (London, 1897), Vol. 1, p. 345.
[2] Quoted in Alec Vidler, *The Church in an Age of Revolution* (Harmondsworth, 1961), p. 128.

take the offensive. The opposition again brought charges of insincerity: how could clergymen go on reciting things that they did not literally believe? By acting as authorized mouthpieces for the whole body of faith, was the reply of such apologias as E. A. Abbott's *The Kernel and the Husk* (1886).

Liberalism touched every party in religion, as in politics. Roman Catholics officially deprecated it but in practice accepted some of its attitudes. The Evangelicals, losing their earlier influence, stood apart on personal salvation and otherworldliness, with no outstanding thinkers in the later period except Henry Wace (1836–1924). The last few years of the century saw a new, anxious search for authority – in the Bible, the visible Church, mystical experience, personal conviction. Liberalism tended to be too optimistic and too intellectual. Nor, by its very nature, did it lend itself to the comfort of association, though it found some expression in the Churchmen's Union (1898).

As orthodoxy shook off its loose ends and began to regain strength, agnosticism had little cause for self-congratulation. The older agnostics found time passing them by, with their radicalism no longer daring and many churchmen prepared to say almost as much as they. Some of them fossilized sadly into the new century, like Shaw's Roebuck Ramsden.[1] Few found real satisfaction in the rejection of faith; a more positive humanist position was stated by Leslie Stephen (1832–1904) who, like Froude before him, found justification in the appeal to history with his *History of English Thought in the Eighteenth Century*.

The latter part of the century saw a proliferation of 'fancy religions' – sub-Christian heresies like the spiritualism which enraged Robert Browning, and vague attempts at synthesis like the theosophy acclaimed by Annie Besant. The Victorian period closed with less certainty but more tolerance in religious questions than it had opened. The optimism of agnostic humanism and of liberal religion was to be severely challenged in the next century, when the beast in man was unleashed with a savagery which few had suspected to exist.

[1] In *Man and Superman* (1903).

20

George Eliot

To say that the English novel comes of age with George Eliot is by no means to denigrate all that had gone before. Society needed a writer who could interpret through fiction some of its recent attempts to come to terms with its new conditions. Paradoxically, that masculine and overtly religious age was lectured by a woman who had rejected orthodox Christianity. George Eliot asserted the right which the Romantics had claimed in poetry: the right to reject social criteria if they conflicted with the call of the individual spirit. The earlier English novel had often displayed society on a canvas wide enough to allow for criticism, but it had largely been criticism from within an acceptance of involvement. George Eliot chose the new freedom of dissociation from behaviour and beliefs that were alien to her own point of view.

That point of view included disbelief in Christianity as it was currently taught. Consequently the student of the period approaches her work with excitement, eager for the answers to fundamental questions. What factors could, in the middle of the nineteenth century, make a young woman abandon the religion in which she had been brought up? What was the effect on the remainder of her life and work? How did she continue to deal with problems of conduct without religious sanctions? Questions like these were to be asked more often and more urgently as the century went on. George Eliot does not give us a master key to the Victorian loss of faith, but she opens a number of doors.

In the first place, she makes it entirely clear that agnosticism did not mean the abandonment of all ethical standards that many people feared. She brings to the novel a moral earnestness that had not been so expressed before (though perhaps, with less basic compassion, by Nathaniel Hawthorne), and which associates her with Lawrence and Forster and Woolf rather than with Fielding and Scott and Dickens. She did not write the novel of quiet, domestic activity, or of melodramatic sensation, or of social problems peculiar to the new age – though her books contain elements of all these. She was concerned above all with problems of individual conduct and its consequences, and in this she looked forward to the major preoccupations of the next age.

George Eliot is, however, beyond all doubt a Victorian – and not least in the extremes and contradictions which she presents. Born in 1819, in the same decade as Thackeray, Dickens, Reade, Trollope and Kingsley, she did not publish her first novel until the year of Meredith's *Ordeal of Richard Feverel*. She and Meredith were both influential in making literary critics look at the novel as a serious work of art. Her personal life defied convention, but she was no champion of women's rights. Her heroines accept marriage as the woman's career and do not agitate to be represented in Parliament, though Romola is said to derive something from the women's suffrage leader Mrs Bodichon.

Even her agnosticism is old-fashioned in its origins. The biography of George Eliot reads like a pious story in an Evangelical magazine, warning of the perils of keeping bad company and reading disturbing books. At the same time, it is like one of her own novels, full of challenges and moral decisions. She started life as Mary Ann Evans and spent most of her early years in Warwickshire where her father worked as steward of various large estates. The conditioning of her childhood is clear in her novels: most of them are set in the Midlands at the period when she was young, accepting the class-structure as she came to know it. Her father, strong, phlegmatic Robert Evans, gave birth to characters like Adam Bede and Caleb Garth; her mother, shrewd and shrewish, to Mrs Poyser; her brother Isaac, so much loved and admired in childhood, to Tom Tulliver. The rural stories that she heard reappeared in fiction.

She received a good education, considering the joint disabilities of the time, her social position and her sex. From the village school she went to boarding schools at Nuneaton and Coventry, until her mother's death in 1836 brought her back to take care of the family. She was twenty-two when her father retired and she accompanied him to Coventry. A more correctly conventional young woman could scarcely be imagined: devoted to her family and household, religious to a degree remarkable even for the period. Her immediate family's tepid loyalty to the Church of England did not satisfy the spiritual aspirations aroused by her pious Methodist aunt, Mrs Samuel Evans, and by the two dissenting ministers whose schools she had attended. The Evangelical spirit possessed her; she desired to be 'sanctified wholly'. But it was to be no fugitive and cloistered virtue; while she fed the contemplative appetite on Young and Wordsworth, she also conceived enthusiasm for the practical benevolence of Wilberforce and felt herself called to heroic goodness.

The Evangelicals were wont to warn the young that the devil had a knack of hiding under innocent disguises. Mary Ann began to occupy herself in making a huge chart of early Church history as a guide through the formative years of Christian orthodoxy. Before it was finished, she found that she had been anticipated by a similar compilation by A. P. Stanley. But the study which, about the same time, was leading Newman to accept the monolithic catholicity of the Roman Church, had started her mind doubting. The whole story seemed unedifying, so full of human pettiness and offence. However far back one went, the faults of later ages already seemed to exist. Could this be the absolute truth that its followers claimed?

We see Victorian agnosticism as the product of new discoveries about the natural world and the application of scientific reasoning to matters previously considered supernatural. Mary Ann Evans, and many others, were in an older tradition of scepticism running back to Hume through Paine, Priestley and Gibbon. She was already judging Christianity severely through the inadequacies of its recorded history and its human representatives when she met Charles Bray. An Owenite and a phrenologist, Bray had won some reputations as the author of *The Education of the Feelings* and *The Philosophy of Necessity* – titles which reveal their themes. He became a strong influence on the earnest girl, even to getting her to shave off her hair so that she could read the bumps on her head.

What Bray left unfinished was taken up by his brother-in-law Charles Hennell, a Unitarian who was interested in the historical approach to religion which had already affected Mary Ann. His *Inquiry Concerning the Origins of Christianity* (1838) came to conclusions similar to those of the German rationalist critics: Christianity had grown from myth, hallucination and pious desires on a slender base of human reality. He completed Mary Anne's rejection of Christianity, which she accomplished with a joyful sense of release. It seemed a moral triumph to cast out comfortable illusions in the name of truth.

Her gratitude to Hennell was tinged with growing personal affection, but possible hopes were squashed after the arrival in their little circle of a Miss Brabant who was to undertake the translation of Strauss's *Leben Jesu*. Instead she married Hennell and the work of translation fell to Mary Ann. By the time it was anonymously published in 1846, she felt herself to be 'Strauss-sick'. German thought was an addition to her previous scepticism, but Strauss seemed unsympathetic in his exclusion of the beauty and mystery which she could still feel; she hated his cold dissection of the Crucifixion story.

Her reviews were now attracting attention, and she went to London to become assistant editor of the *Westminster Review,* in a wider and more sophisticated society than that of the Coventry agnostics. She met Herbert Spencer, who introduced her to George Henry Lewes. This time her ever-ready hero-worship grew to something more. Lewes had been deserted by his wife and was unable to get a divorce from her; Mary Ann Evans moved into his home and lived faithfully with him until his death. Lewes added Comte's Positivism to her store of theories, but the 'religion of humanity' only conformed what she had already decided for herself. He also encouraged her to try creative writing, which she began in 1857 with some fictional sketches for *Blackwood's.*

Scenes of Clerical Life introduced to the world the pseudonym George Eliot, and a writer of fair but apparently not great talent. They did, however, arouse the interest of Dickens, who shrewdly guessed that the author was a woman; and they prepared for her first novel. Based on a story heard in her childhood, *Adam Bede* (1859) is a tale of seduction and repentance against a convincing background of rural life. Its success set her on a novelist's career. *The Mill on the Floss* (1860) has a more plainly biographical element and brings a sterner tone into the depiction of provincial society. *Silas Marner* (1861) is a study of avarice told through an unconvincing plot.

Like Dickens, George Eliot shows a leap in development from her first novels to those of her maturity. If her transition is earlier, it must be remembered that she came to fiction almost in middle age, already a respected writer on serious topics. Knowing and admiring her great predecessors in the novel, she was assured enough to look for a new use of it as a medium for ideas. They were ideas psychologically closed to most of her potential readers. They seemed unlikely to win over her imaginary butt Mrs Farthingale, 'who prefers the ideal in fiction; to whom tragedy means ermine tippets, adultery and murder; and comedy the adventures of some personage who is quite a "character".'[1]

The later novels, based less on early memories and more on acquired theories, fulfil her deeper purpose. The first departure from personal experience was not happy. She prepared by study and travel for *Romola* (1864) but this tale of the time of Savonarola is unconvincing and the heroine too much like Maggie Tulliver in Renaissance dress. *Felix Holt the Radical* (1866) makes the return to times and places which she understood, but with more directly polemical intent. Her excursion into dramatic verse, *The Spanish Gipsy* (1868), makes it clear that her talent was solely for prose. Greatness returns with *Middlemarch* (1872), an interweaving of provincial lives into her most profound and complex work. In *Daniel Deronda* (1876), although her didactic purpose sometimes overruns her function as a storyteller, she has a new vision of individual existence. Her faithful and happy association with Lewes ended when he died in 1878. She married John Cross, an admirer nearly twenty years her junior, in 1880 and died before the end of the same year.

In the last months of her life, George Eliot was married in a Christian church and buried, by her own wish, in unconsecrated ground with Lewes: an ironic conclusion to the irony of her adult years. Intellectually, she made up her mind against Christianity before she was thirty. Emotionally, she stayed involved with the faith of her youth, held in the categories and attitudes of Evangelical Christianity as firmly as was James Joyce in the Catholicism which he had overtly rejected. Her

[1] *Amos Barton*, Ch. 5.

imaginative world is a puritan one, weighted with the sense of duty, impatient of easy excuses, disapproving of self-indulgence, conscious of guilt. She mounted no violent attack on Christianity like Samuel Butler; her strictures on the Church are more obliquely implied. She adjudges organized religion guilty of stupidity and lack of perception rather than of positive badness. She praises the good clergy of any denomination, whether the Anglican Cleeves or the dissenting Lyons, but on the whole the Church of England seems to her sterile, the nonconformists narrow and repressive. Romanism had a slight exotic charm. She passed through the torment of rejection in pursuit of truth and felt little patience with the complacent masses who:

Were saved from the excesses of Protestantism by not knowing how to read, and by the absence of handlooms and mines to be the pioneers of Dissent: they were kept safely in the *via media* of indifference, and could have registered themselves in the census with a big black mark as members of the Church of England.[1]

This sort of thing would not do for George Eliot, but she was left in a dilemma about what would do. She found no full satisfaction in any of the offered substitutes; Comtism, science, Benthamism, all seemed too lacking in emotion and passion to fulfil her sense of wonder. In her last novel she flirts lightly with the new Zionist movement. Christianity might be dead, but it went on troubling her like the confession of Casaubon the sterile clergyman:

'I feed too much on the inward sources; I live too much with the dead. My mind is something like the ghost of an ancient, wandering about the world and trying mentally to construct it as it used to be, in spite of ruin and confusing changes.'[2]

Yet if the old belief had died in the progress of history, what was to take its place? She and those who thought like her had to face the implications of rejecting absolute certainty. Did the retreat from faith mean moral anarchy just when new ordering in society was demanding a decision on acceptable standards of conduct? The question was not so frightening if you believed implicitly in progress and thought that everything was certain to get better. George Eliot's attitude is ambivalent: personal

[1] *Felix Holt,* Introduction.
[2] *Middlemarch,* Bk. 1, Ch. 2.

improvement by a right disposition of the will is both possible and desirable, but there is no guarantee of either personal or social improvement through environmental change. She is no optimist about the moral effects of public health regulations and the spread of the franchise. It was already apparent, and not to her alone, that the reforms of earlier years had been to avoid disaster, not to inaugurate the golden age.

George Eliot shows no unqualified enthusiasm for the social and political forms of any age past, present or to come. The elections in her novels are full of bribery and deceit, organized mobs and meaningless violence. There is little faith in the political sense of ordinary people, though *Felix Holt* has glimpses of a socialist vision: 'The greatest question in the world is, how to give every man a man's share of what goes on in life'.[1] What she finds wrong with her own age is no new corruption but part of the long development through which mankind went astray. When she looks back to a generation earlier, it is with a mixture of detachment and involvement. She sees the influences on contemporary lives, including the disappointment of the great hopes pinned on the First Reform Act.

She follows the linear theory of history which was current, and which had inspired her early attempt at a chart of Church history. She tries to examine all the factors which have shaped people, to give a new sense of historical development underlying the individual form. In her view, there is no need either to preserve or to scorn past principles and institutions simply for being past. They were not absolutely right, but they had a significance in the human situation which can still be heeded.

Rejecting absolutes leads to certain dilemmas. Unless the agnostic is to become either antinomian or helplessly paralysed, he has to conceive right conduct as tending towards a certain ideal for societies and for individuals. George Eliot has her vision, and it is part of her greatness that, without using ready-made dogmatic patterns, she can show problems of choice as essential and not arising simply out of the immediate situation. She moved the serious novel from melodrama to tragedy; in the tension between the ideal and the actual, conscience is tormented and tragedy is born.

Yet if we may name tragedy in her work, it is not as we name

[1] *Felix Holt*, Ch. 30.

it in Hardy's. The force of unfolding destiny is not so stark and blind as Hardy's President of the Immortals. It has not sucked despair from the determinism of the new science (George Eliot was too late to get upset about Darwin, and her first novel was published in the year of *The Origin of Species*). Destiny for her means that moral choices bring consequences both logical and inescapable; with the old puritanism in her well to the fore, she shows the due rewards of vice and virtue and states the ethos of the Evangelicals with hell moved from the next world to this one. The 'good' clergyman Mr Irwine expresses it in words that could be an epigraph to her novels:

'Consequences are unpitying. Our deeds carry their terrible consequences, quite apart from any fluctuations that went before – consequences that are hardly ever confined to ourselves.'[1]

A single lapse brings its nemesis, perhaps after years of prosperity, to Godfrey Cass, Mrs Transome, Bulstrode, Gwendolen Harleth. The treatment of Bulstrode in *Middlemarch* is particularly interesting. He is a pious Evangelical, respected in the community but haunted by the memory of an old act of dishonesty. The revelation of his offence leads to utter disgrace and shatters his profession of religion. We can imagine how Dickens would have dealt with him, overflowing with delight in unmasking his hypocrisy before dismissing him like a broken clown. George Eliot treats him with compassion and movingly shows the loyalty in disaster given by his wife.

There is indeed a tension in her work between a stern sense of justice and an unwillingness to condemn the individual. There is the old Morality play element of the besetting fault that leads to ruin, but freedom and seriousness of choice are also urged and man is shown to be nothing if not responsible. George Eliot debates about free will and predestination, moved from the supernatural to the purely ethical plane. Her solution is the importance of self-knowledge: man must learn what he is and aspire to the best that his total situation offers. If he has flaws like Lydgate's 'spots of commonness' he must be aware of them and guard against their influence, for self-deception is the agnostic's Tempter, the power of darkness.

The duty to develop personality in the best way is no less for

[1] *Adam Bede*, Ch. 16.

the removal of religious sanctions. That is part of George Eliot's creed as she works it out in fiction. A character is formed by his moral choices. Some are blessed with a kind of natural goodness; others, who must aspire towards the good, are capable of greater nobility and greater evil. Yet what is the result of aspiration? The liberal agnostic, distrusting the assertion of absolutes, finds it hard to put his belief into external action; he may be in the dilemma of inertia from which Deronda escapes by assuming a hereditary duty. Is there a replacement for traditional morality except the sentimental 'change of heart?'

In true Evangelical fashion, George Eliot holds that actions are proved by their consequences. Good is what leads to fuller involvement with other people; bad is self-isolating and steadily increases its own failure to make contact. Casaubon, gaining only more isolation from marriage, is contrasted with Dorothea, whose fulfilment begins when she opens her bedroom window after a wretched night and sees people going about their lives:

> She felt the largeness of the world and the manifold wakings of men to labour and endurance. She was a part of that involuntary, palpitating life, and could neither look out on it from her luxurious shelter as a mere spectator, nor hide her eyes in selfish complacency.[1]

The idea of selfishness runs through George Eliot's work from start to finish, from the parasitical Countess Czerlaski in *Amos Barton* to Gwendolen in *Daniel Deronda*, reaching its fullest expression with the parade of types of egoism in *Middlemarch*. People express their moral choices through relationships, and there is power in contacts that may seem to come by chance. The unselfish person brings good, as Dinah to Hetty in *Adam Bede;* selfishness can cause ruin, as does the influence of Jermyn on Mrs Transome, of Rosamond on Lydgate.

When such clear moral conclusions can be drawn from fiction, we may wonder if the writer has sacrificed art to propaganda, and there is perhaps a continual conflict in George Eliot between intellect and imagination. Or is the conflict rather between her moral earnestness and her dislike of any appeal to absolute principles? Her commentary seldom appears as a laborious intrusion, but rather helps her characters to grow in our awareness: not visually, but through the presentation of

[1] *Middlemarch*, Bk. 8, Ch. 80.

how they behave and why they choose their behaviour. The complexity of their actions is clarified by a moral motivation which leaves the reader in no doubt.

This means that they do not live vividly in the visual imagination. Her art is far from the Dickensian gift of creating a new acquaintance out of a paragraph of description and a few idiosyncracies of speech; it is perhaps significant that she attracted no great illustrators. On the other hand, the inner conflicts of her characters are those which we can take into ourselves, to illuminate our own problems. We feel them not as part of our knowledge of the objective world but rather as part of that progress towards self-knowledge which was the ideal of their creator.

Yet they are by no means expressionist abstractions that could have been depicted against any background. Again like their creator, they are conditioned by their time without being fully committed to it. She had the full confidence and creativity of the Victorian writer within the known world; her skill shows up even more for the failure of *Romola*. In all her wide aspirations she knew the importance of the microcosm within which self-knowledge is found and personal relationships are expressed. Her microcosm is the Midland England of her childhood, and she never loses the sense of systematic, recurring routine in that rural community. Few novelists before her gave such attention to the problems of agriculture, and even fewer dealt so realistically with the details of daily work.

The microcosm, however, is no dimly-remembered lost paradise of innocence; it can be a bad influence, restricting the growth towards self-knowledge. Around the chief characters in the novels there seems to be a closed circle of the unimaginative, witnessing and containing the conflict, unwilling that any should pass in or out, sterile in their distrust of the stranger. Acceptance had to be striven for by Silas Marner, Felix Holt, Lydgate, Ladislaw; but goodness can come from the stranger accepted in infancy like Eppie and Esther.

The microcosm shares the corruption of the wider world. The rivalry in *Middlemarch* between Tyke and Farebrother for the hospital chaplaincy mirrors the chicanery of the Parliamentary election in the borough. George Eliot shared with many writers of the time a depressing realization of the power of money in society. Silas Marner's gold is a simple image of something given more complex expression in *Middlemarch*. Lydgate and Rosamond take money for granted until debts force them to face reality. Mr Brooke sees nothing hard to reconcile between his reforming principles and his bad land-lordism; Fred and the others wait impatiently to benefit from the death of Featherstone; and the tale is full of debts, loans and gifts offered or refused.

Middlemarch, a Study of Provincial Life – that is the full title and here George Eliot reached the height of her power to express basic realities through the microcosm. What seems to start as a *Bildungsroman* soon widens into the story of other lives that interweave and affect each other. With a reversal of Balzac's method, we go from the single character of Dorothea to the complexity of the provincial town where she lives. It is a work of maturity in every sense: the author's fullest achievement, the growth of self-knowledge in the principal characters, perhaps the same growth in the perceptive reader. We are in a society faced with changes that affect all classes – the aristocratic Chetham, the country gentleman Brooke, the *nouveau riche* Vincy, the old-fashioned yeoman Garth. Similar themes develop in different characters, as Casaubon and Lydgate show different kinds of incompatibility in marriage. They show also the comparative merits of dedicated work: Casaubon's 'Key to all the mythologies' is sterile, unscholarly, never to be completed (was she remembering her own frustrated work on Church history?) while Lydgate's search for the 'primitive tissue' has potential good for mankind until selfish living smothers it.

It is the handling of such themes that makes George Eliot a pioneer of new and serious possibilities in the novel. The minor pleasures of fiction are not absent – the comic characters strong but not allowed to overrun the serious plot, and the sharp-tongued countrywomen with their gnomic common sense. There is satisfaction in her handling of the novel-form, in the striking scene at a critical moment, in the rich vein of imagery with its Jamesian way of showing the disposition and experience of characters through symbols.

She looked forward to later developments in the novel, yet her age continued to hold her and the events of her life weave in and out of her books. The autobiographical element becomes ponderous with the clear wish-fulfilment of Maggie Tulliver who grows up beautiful and is reunited with her brother in death. Maggie's love for the slick Stephen Guest is a stumbling-block too, and so is Dorothea's for Ladislaw. Many critics have regarded these as impossible infatuations, but it is a fact of life that intelligent women may fall in love with the most unsuitable men. Ladislaw is more convincing when he appears simply as a virile young man than when his creator tries to make him a kind of sun-god, a symbol of liberation.

Her novels are Victorian in their touches of melodrama and sentimentality: the last-minute reprieve in *Adam Bede,* the flood in *The Mill on the Floss,* Lydia Glasher's curse on Gwendolen Harleth's marriage, the happy unions of Felix Holt and Esther, of Daniel Deronda and Mirah. Victorian too are the chances and coincidences such as the revealed relationship of Mordecai and Mirah, and Christian's pocket-book going to the one man who would understand its secret. So too are the forced reticences, so that Maggie does not really go astray during her escapade at sea, and Casaubon's impotence can be merely (but how brilliantly) hinted. Her own age deplored her personal life, admired her books, and tended to accept her gifts in the toned-down interpretation which in 1872 produced an anthology of *Wise, Witty and Tender Sayings* from her works.

To a generation reacting against the Victorians it was these occasional features that seemed obtrusive, unrelieved by the warm humour of Dickens. She seemed austere, unsympathetic, so that even an acute critic could say 'Her reputation has sustained a more catastrophic slump than that of any of her contemporaries'.[1] It is not so today, when a generation struggling with the question of ethics not linked to dogma recognizes the offer of help, while the Christian is forced to ask himself again what is distinctive and absolute in his faith. She anticipates the modern themes – the existential choice, the influence of people upon each other independently of desire or liking, the sense of alienation, the fear of meaninglessness. Her last novel, *Daniel Deronda* is not her best but in some ways her most forward-looking. Grandcourt is not such a convincing individual as Casaubon, but his marriage shows more terror of what one human being can do to another. Deronda himself,

[1] David Cecil, *Early Victorian Novelists* (London, 1934), p. 314.

despite an artificial sense of destiny at the end, is a figure of the twentieth century. He is alienated from society by his very virtues, impotent in his liberalism, a more compliant Stephen Daedalus. It is in a Joycean world too that Gwendolen suffers in coming to self-knowledge:

Solitude in any wide sense impressed her with an undefined feeling of immeasurable existence aloof from her, in the midst of which she was helplessly incapable of asserting herself. The little astronomy taught her at school used sometimes to set her imagination at work in a way that made her tremble: but always when someone joined her she recovered her indifference to the vastness in which she seemed an exile; she found again her usual world in which her will was of some avail.[1]

[1] *Daniel Deronda,* Bk. 1, Ch. 6.

21

Alienation and Despair

The novel as a literary form was inevitably affected by its increasing popularity. The new readers were willing to follow a serial in a magazine containing other miscellaneous fare, or to pick up a cheap edition to pass the time on a journey. They were less inclined to subscribe faithfully to a novel in monthly parts, or to expend time and money on a vast three-volume novel. The railway bookstall rather than the subscription library becomes the symbol of fiction-reading from about 1880. The three-volume novel, into which early-Victorian writers had poured both riches and dross, was doomed to extinction. The novelist was obliged to say what he had to say in one-third of the former length. Selection and compression replaced the old freedom to be discursive about life in general while the main plot waited in the wings for its next appearance.

The change was not only in length. For the early part of the period it is possible to speak with some assurance of the novel as a total conception. Names such as 'political', 'social', 'religious', 'scholastic', may be convenient for descriptive cataloguing, but there is still a high degree of coherence in the aims of the novelist and the expectations of the reader. As readership becomes wider and more diverse, so the novel begins to break into separate strata. The early-Victorian novelist was usually at one with his public; they admired him and he wooed them even when he was criticizing some of their attitudes. If he was successful, he shared the plaudits of the ordinary reader and the approval of the critics. There is no example of the novelist greatly admired by the few but ignored by the majority of readers: no Conrad, Joyce, Woolf or Compton-Burnett.

The reading public which was expanding in the years following the Education Act of 1871 found plenty of material to amuse and stimulate its new literacy. While Newnes and Harmsworth were catering for the many, some of the novelists began to look askance at the devouring, undiscriminating monster which the age had bred. They thought more deeply about the shape of the novel as a sophisticated work of art. At the same time, they began to feel alienated from the general public. The aesthetic principle affected the idea of the novel; fiction henceforth becomes more self-conscious, more limited in its scope and says less about society as a whole.

The new theory of fiction which was debated by writers and critics is often described as 'Naturalism'. Whether the word is as precise and as meaningful as it was for the French writers from whom it was borrowed may be doubted. It is true that French novelists were read and imitated in Britain as never before; but the likenesses between, for example, Zola and Maupassant, were more apparent to their English admirers than were their very marked differences. The name had been used from about 1850 by disciples and successors of Flaubert (who considered himself a classicist above all else); its most important expositions had been made by Maupassant in the preface to *Pierre et Jean* and by Zola in *Le Roman Expérimental*.

The Naturalists tried to study and describe Man objectively, as a part of the total natural world. All events were equally important for the purpose of record, equally evidential in the clinical study. Fiction was to present life as it was really lived, to be a slice out of the known world of observable phenomena. Men and women were to be seen in the environment which determined what they were and what they did. Against that background, the basic evolutionary drives for survival and propagation were continually being worked out. The great achievements of those who expounded these theories do not need to be stressed: the dangers of pseudo-scientism and the harm which it could and did do to art in lesser hands are perhaps no less obvious.

The impact of these ideas upon English writers was as an ally in the developing situation rather than as a complete revelation. Aspects of Naturalism were seized and sometimes only partly digested. Henry James, who properly belongs to American literature, greatly influenced the English novel through his theories of fiction as well as through his practice. He knew and

understood European writers better than did most of his
contemporaries in America or in Britain, and he helped to
make a bridge between English and French fiction. Nevertheless, a great deal of what passed for Naturalism in English
fiction was simply the old realism of previous decades taken a
step further. The 'new' idea of research and gathering factual
material as documentation for fiction had already been
assiduously followed by Reade, and indeed by Trollope and
Dickens.

The English approach to the novel continued to be more
pragmatic and less systematic than the French. The novelists
went on creating characters as outstanding and perhaps
eccentric individuals: if those characters happened to illustrate
general truths or personify abstractions, well and good, but
that was not the main purpose of their creation. Nor did
Naturalism become part of the wider artistic climate in this
country; it lacked the conscious link with painting which
French writers found in the work of the Impressionists.

What did happen was that some English novelists liked the
idea of describing all events dispassionately and with equal
candour. It gave them a new weapon in their running fight
with the moralists and the unofficial censors, and a fresh
argument in the controversy about what could and what could
not be permissibly described in fiction. Their distaste for the
new mass readership made them see themselves as 'advanced',
able to look beyond the prejudices and inhibitions which still
dominated the greater part of society. Naturalism became a
word to be bandied about by both sides when taboos were
broken. Of course, the revolt against the standards of the age
was not confined to those who openly claimed new freedom and
called themselves Naturalists; it is just as strong in writers like
Butler and Rutherford.

Although the Naturalist theory was vaguer here than in
France, the novelists were not slow in self-explanation and
apologia. The issue between realism and anti-realism was
fought in 1884 between Henry James's *The Art of Fiction* and
R. L. Stevenson's *A Humble Remonstrance*. George Moore
launched his attack on the restrictions imposed by the circulating libraries in his pamphlet *Literature at Nurse* in the following
year. The demand for freedom of expression was taken up in

Hardy's *Candour in English Fiction* (1890) and Gissing's *Realism in Fiction* (1895).

The practice of Naturalism in the English novel has to be seen against the background of considerable doubt and anxiety in the eighties. The comparative peace which had descended after 1848 was being shattered as class-bitterness grew again in a time of economic depression and widespread unemployment. The new trade unions were more militant and socialism was being proclaimed openly on street corners and in public meetings. There were riots and demonstrations, including the notorious 'Bloody Sunday' when shots were fired in Trafalgar Square. New investigations revealed the horrors of employment in trades untouched by reforming legislation. Bad housing conditions were making a mockery of the domestic ideal and the cult of family life.

Some brave spirits like William Morris looked forward to the coming Utopia when these horrors would be purged and forgotten. Others, more complacent, looked at the positive achievements of the age and decided that things were better than they had ever been. J. A. Froude considered that the present generation was more self-reliant and secure that its forerunners had been, and would never know 'what it was to find the lights all drifting, the compass all awry, and nothing left to steer by but the stars'.[1] Others again could find little comfort in a society that seemed to be getting more degenerate and more hopeless. There came a fascination with the evil forces in life, with the way in which human beings could be depraved and become utterly corrupt. The earnest questioning of the mid-Victorian agnostics began to give way to stark atheism and despair. Instead of the search for standards there came the assertions that no standards were possible.

The woes of urban life were portrayed in the novels of George Gissing, who tried honestly to express the basic sickness of his times. He succeeded in the presentation, but only within a limited range which prevented him from saying much that was constructive. His isolation was largely the result of his unhappy personal life: his career as a student was cut short when he started stealing in an attempt to reclaim a prostitute whom he afterwards married. He was, predictably, wretchedly unhappy

[1] *Carlyle's Life in London* (1884), Vol. 1, p. 291.

with her and little better with the woman he married after her death. Years of poverty in America and England preceded his reasonable success as a writer.

Like Butler, and others before and since, Gissing wrote a great deal of himself into his books, and his image of life tends to be shaped by personal grievances. He reappears in various guises, sometimes as the young man in revolt but without the zeal to reform or the hope to improve society. In this limitation, he gained the strength of refusing to comfort his readers with an easy solution. Some of his own story appears in *Workers in the Dawn* (1880), and his literary struggles inspired *New Grub Street* (1891), where he is the prototype of the cultured but exploited literary hack Reardon whose sad lot is contrasted with that of the confident and competent Milvain. There is something of Gissing also in the egoistic Godwin Peak of *Born in Exile* (1892), who cynically plays both sides in the controversy between science and religion until he is found out. The title of this book could stand for much of Gissing's work; his characters linger on an alien shore, discontented with their own sphere and belonging properly to none.

'Male and female, all the prominent persons of the story, dwell in a limbo external to society. They refuse the statistic badge.'[1]

Like Grail in *Thyrza* (1887), Peak presents the problem of the proletarian intellectual who has benefited by the new advances in popular education but finds no satisfaction, who is patronized by the privileged but hates his own class as well – 'All the grown-up creatures, who can't speak proper English and don't know how to behave themselves'.[2]

Gissing stands with the Naturalists in showing the effects of social environment on character and in his portrayal of corruption. His description of slum-life in *The Nether World* (1889) chimed in with the new concern about housing. It increased the fame which had begun with *Demos* (1886), a topical novel in a year of unrest and violent outbreaks, in which his purpose was to show that the poor have nothing to gain by agitation. Sordid and pessimistic though his books were, Gissing perhaps did something to reassure the consciences of

[1] Preface to *The Unclassed* (1884).
[2] *Born in Exile*, Part 1, Ch. 2.

middle-class readers by presenting the hopelessness of the situation and putting no faith in socialism.

He uses the methods of Naturalism also in *The Odd Women* (1893), yet another treatment of the perennial problem of the women who were slowly gaining emancipation but finding no acceptance in a predominantly masculine society. Yet he is in many ways nearest not to Zola or Maupassant but to Flaubert in his disgust with the general corruption of the age as judged by his own interpretation of classical standards. He loathed the cheapening of minds directed by the popular press under men like Whelpdale in *New Grub Street* whose 'Chit-Chat' prospers by having no article more than two inches in length.

Gissing has few rivals for showing the wretchedness of those who cling to the lowest middle-class stratum, striving for respectability but knowing no security, bullied by employers, lacking the protection of a strong trade union. Wells and Orwell were to tell their story again in the next century, and could not surpass his power of evoking urban squalor without either the fantastic horror or the alleviating jollity of Dickens. Gissing writes without much love, exposing the pretentious vulgarities of the new suburbs as well as the injustices; his most controlled and planned expression of this disgust is *In the Year of the Jubilee* (1894). His declared intention was to observe and record, not to take sides, to be, in Naturalist fashion, 'merely one who takes trouble to trace certain lines of human experience'.[1]

Gissing's novels are neither so dispassionate nor so advanced as he liked to suppose. He uses many of the stock Victorian devices of coincidence, commentary on the action, and exaggerated larger-than-life characters. He learned perhaps too much from Dickens, whom he greatly admired and about whom he wrote one of the best studies to appear in the nineteenth century.[2] He could write well about women, but his treatment of sexual matters is distinctly limited, through a combination of his personal problems and a lingering regard for the formal morality of the age. After achieving reasonable financial security, he produced a collection of semi-autobiographical musings under the title *The Private Papers of Henry Ryecroft* (1903), which has won more admirers than most of his

[1] Preface to *Isabel Clarendon* (1886).
[2] *Charles Dickens: A Critical Study* (1898).

other books. His assertion of old values and standards, freed now from contact with sordid reality, is presented in an artificial style reminiscent of the less successful pages of Lamb, and with a rather distasteful tendency to self-pity as well as self-satisfaction.

George Moore (1852–1933)[1] was in some ways more 'advanced' than Gissing and fits less easily into the story of the English novel. This is not surprising, since he was born in Ireland and spent some time in Paris before emerging into London as an art critic. From his studies in France he picked up the cults of Naturalism and Aestheticism, both of which he practised – the latter with less than happy results. He consciously and deliberately made himself into a creative writer, progressing from near-illiteracy to a fine but mannered prose. He saw himself as a man apart, a Romantic outsider who consorted oddly with the more urbane conventions of the late nineteenth century. 'Moore conducts his musical education in public', Oscar Wilde commented.[2] Yet for all his posing, Moore knew better than most of his contemporaries what Zola and Maupassant had done for fiction. The very fact that he remains odd and alien makes him a valuable commentator on his age.

Some of his best work went into his personal fantasies – one can hardly call them autobiographies since they are so committed to showing what a bad and daring lad he was – *Confessions of a Young Man* (1888) and the three volumes of *Hail and Farewell* (1911–14). His first novel, *A Modern Lover* (1883), deserved to be banned by the circulating libraries for its atrocious style and was in fact banned for its supposed immorality. It was in response to this censorship that Moore produced the pamphlet 'Literature at Nurse' mentioned above, which he put out with his next book *A Mummer's Wife* (1885). The study of an actor's wife who is ruined by drinking demands comparison with Zola's *L'Assommoir*. If Moore is the lesser artist, he is not far behind his master in his ability clinically to portray the degeneration of a human being, with details which arouse detached nausea more than compassion. That of course is what

---

[1] The date of his birth as given in various authorities ranges between 1852 and 1857; 1852 seems to be correct.
[2] Hesketh Pearson, *The Life of Oscar Wilde* (London, 1946), p. 183.

the Naturalists desired, and to achieve it Moore went with his notebook to Hanley where the story opens.

The same meticulous care about the background of the novel is shown in *Esther Waters* (1894). A much better book, this is the story of a woman who drifts from one kind of oppression and overwork to another, remaining faithful to her illegitimate child and its father in spite of chances of 'bettering herself'. The rare appearances of bastard children in Victorian fiction had been mostly furtive, apologetic and short-lived. That a fallen woman could be a good mother was not the sort of thing that people were supposed to say. Moore's saying of it was part of the recognition of the problems and rights of women; as women in fiction are given minds of their own, the remnants of the early-Victorian three-volume novel are gradually disappearing.

Moore treated frankly the situation of the unmarried woman in *A Drama in Muslin* (1886), with a recognition of the urges and frustrations that could be felt by girls looking out for husbands. He was not the first: in 1883 there appeared a novel by a young South African woman who, like Charlotte Brontë, had worked as a governess and resented the repression of her state. With a freedom for which the age was scarcely prepared, *The Story of an African Farm* gave a serious presentation of problems of religious doubt and sexual oppositions. A woman was not expected to have views on these matters, and certainly not unorthodox ones; Olive Schreiner achieved a brief notoriety but produced no other work of importance.

With one of the ironies in which the age abounds, Moore acquired some reputation as a social-problem novelist for his description of baby-farming in *Esther Waters*. More important, he showed himself a master of scenic and episodic description, with an awareness of the minutiae of English social life which only an outsider could reach so analytically. It is his best book, far superior to the Celtic mythicism which begins to appear with *Evelyn Innes* (1898) and to the more allegorical and poetic novels which he produced in the next century. At his best, he has no superior in recording the weary, half-resigned and half-bitter malaise of the late Victorians. His characters suffer the pressures of their environment and cannot break away by personal initiative; he has no heroes and no villains, but in a different way from Trollope. Yet he can show real sympathy when the warmth of his rebellious Irish nature breaks through the new convention of clinical observation.

Robert Louis Stevenson (1850–94) also studied in France, though in a gentler ambience than Moore's. He too perfected himself as a writer by conscious effort and imitation. There the resemblance would seem to end, and Stevenson is often regarded as a writer of boys' stories, as a romantic legend of untimely death in the South Seas, as a leader of anti-realism. He was all these, but he shared with Gissing and Moore a sense of evil, of a doomed society, of individual degradation. *Kidnapped* (1886) and *Treasure Island* (1883) have all the ingredients of popular adventure tales – the mysteries, the pursuit and evasion, the bursts of action. They have more: the authenticity of historical setting, and a recognition of the real evil which is distinct from the conventional opposition of 'good' and 'bad' characters. It is felt, for instance, in the first and subsequent appearances of Pew.

These features are stronger in *The Master of Ballantrae* (1889). The collapse of the second Jacobite rising is convincingly described, with the mixture of involvement and detachment as the old steward tells the story. The Master himself is a study in evil, moving in a sinister, gloomy atmosphere, who totally corrupts his inoffensive brother. Stevenson's Scots ancestry and upbringing added the doctrine of predestination to the current preoccupation with human wickedness. He could believe in a soul doomed to evil, spreading poison through society.

Stevenson left his finest work unfinished at his death. In *Weir of Hermiston* (1897) his ability to evoke the life of Edinburgh early in the century makes it reasonable to compare him with Scott. Apart from his adventure stories he is best known for *Doctor Jekyll and Mr Hyde* (1886), a specimen of the *novella* length of which there are so few successful ones in English. It has passed into popular folklore in a similar way to *Frankenstein*; as a psychological study of evil, it needs to be rescued from the realms of sensationalism.

In spite of his declaration, Stevenson cannot be firmly ranked with the anti-realists. He helped to bring something new into the novel of romantic adventure, something which writers like Haggard, Doyle and Weyman also reveal: a willingness to show the hero as less than a superman, as subject to normal human weaknesses. His understanding of Scots settings and characters might have given him an outstanding place among novelists if he had lived longer.

The sense of evil and corruption, the despair, the deliberate dwelling on sordid aspects of life – all these are to be found in poetry as well as in the novel. There is also a more determined and militant atheism, replacing the melancholy agnostic musings of poets like Clough. One aspect of it is seen in the *Rubaiyat of Omar Khayyam,* the first English version of which appeared in 1859 – the year of *The Origin of Species.* The work done on it by Edward Fitzgerald (1809–93) was that of adapter and interpreter rather than pure translator. He gave the rather banal aphorisms of the Persian poet a flavour of Romantic melancholy as well as a sense of continuous meditation upon life in general.

Eastern fatalism offered a refuge for many who were troubled by the loss of traditional faith. The blend of scepticism and hedonism which the *Rubaiyat* offered was welcomed by those who felt guilty but impotent about the materialism and corruption of the age. It was a complacent alternative to the nagging of Ruskin and Morris: nothing could be done, so why try to do anything?

More stark was the poetry of James Thomson (1834–82) who is often known as BV to distinguish him from the eighteenth-century poet of the same name (he wrote under the name 'Bysshe Vanolis'). Thomson's world is an image in verse of what Gissing described in prose. His own life was not happy and he became a mouthpiece for the bleak pessimism which was affecting many of his contemporaries. He could write more lightly, as in some of his shorter pieces, but his outstanding work is the long *City of Dreadful Night* (1880). Refusing what glimmers of hope the various voices of the time might offer, he here attempts a statement of utter negation. The attempt of course does not succeed, being cancelled by the positive action of writing a poem. Yet one aspect of the age finds its voice here.

A. E. Housman (1859–1936) wrote most of his best poetry as the result of a personal crisis early in his life. Within his range he is an important poet: not for his statements, which are commonplaces of the gloomy outlook. Life is a rotten job, best got over quickly and with whatever moments of pleasure may be possible – this finds its parallel in the novelists and in other poets. Housman's quality lies in his poetic expression of deep feeling with classical restraint. In spite of his glum atheism, there is a frequent declaration of courage against impossible odds, of refusal to give in to evil, which is essentially religious. His reflections on human life are set against evocations of nature, whose changing moods themselves go along with what people are feeling.

The word 'classical' was used in the previous paragraph, and it is just; but there is also a strong medievalism, coming much closer to the traditional anonymous ballad than anything that Morris wrote. The words are deceptively simple, the rhythms seem familiar yet rouse unexpected emotions. To compare 'Is my team ploughing'[1] with something like 'Two red roses across the moon' is to realise how profoundly medievalism was misunderstood by those who most deliberately made it their Utopia.

By the end of the century a definite atheism and pessimism about life was not confined to a few notorious outsiders. Was the protest a liberating one, an honest confrontation of man's coming of age such as Shelley had dreamed of? There is an emptiness in novelists and poets alike which prevents the modern reader from seeing them as pioneers of a new understanding. The restrictions and failures of official Christianity have been described often enough. The churches often resisted social reform, but their members were just as often leading it. The atheists claimed to assert the dignity of human beings without God, but Charles Bradlaugh could oppose a Bill to reduce the hours worked by shop assistants and describe it as 'opening the door to legislation which might be of the most terrible character'.[2]

It is no easy refuge to put people into labelled categories; they remain individuals, capable of blessed inconsistency. What is certain is that atheism in its principal literary manifestations offered no joy or hope, and no release from mounting guilt.

[1] *A Shropshire Lad* (1896), No. 27.
[2] E. S. Turner, *Roads to Ruin* (London, 1950), Penguin edition, 1966, p. 87.

22

The Impact of Evolution

By the mid-Victorian period science was more highly respected than it had ever been. It had taken a long time to become free from the suspicions of magic and forbidden knowledge which had dogged its practitioners since medieval beginnings. Despite marks of favour like the foundation of the Royal Society in 1662, the ghost of Faust continued to haunt the western world until such spirits were virtually canonized by the Romantics. Mary Shelley's *Frankenstein* had moved the 'novel of terror' from the supernatural realm to the pseudo-scientific and hailed the eponymous hero as 'The Modern Prometheus'.

The impact of scientific discoveries on religious and social thinking was therefore strengthened by the new prestige of science and the feeling that the spirit of inquiry was on the whole beneficent. Applied science had revolutionized economic and social life; the principles of empiricism were spreading. Darwin's work came not as a sudden revelation but rather as the culmination of ideas which were already arousing hopes and fears. The broad concept of evolution is as old as the Greeks, who had arrived at the idea that higher types of life had developed from lower ones, and the notion as a philosophical theme became common enough in such post-Renaissance thinkers as Bacon and Descartes. Its first truly scientific expression was made by the French naturalist Lamarck (1744–1839), who postulated the production of new species through the inheritance of modifications caused by the new needs (*besoins*) of changing environment. Similar ideas were expressed by Erasmus Darwin (1731–1802), grandfather of the more famous Charles Darwin.

In spite of such speculations, most European biologists held to the creationist theory that species were made, complete and immutable, in their present forms. The discovery of fossils of extinct species caused scarcely a ripple of doubt, and was regarded as evidence of catastrophic annihilation rather than supersession. Evolution was in the air, but as a subject for light conversation rather than spiritual anguish. 'I do not believe I was ever a fish' says the hero of *Tancred*. 'Oh! but it is all proved,' counters Lady Constance, who has been reading a book on the subject.[1] Without a scientifically acceptable statement of *how* species had evolved, the subject seemed unlikely to reach much higher levels than this.

Charles Darwin (1809–82) was one of those who have greatness thrust upon them. After proving himself an unsatisfactory student of medicine at Edinburgh and of theology at Cambridge, he set off in 1831 on a government-sponsored scientific expedition around South America. His observations on that voyage were the foundations of his life's work, but fulfilment came only after years of semi-retirement when he was hardly known outside a limited circle.

Darwin was still working on his theory when he received from abroad a paper written by A. W. Wallace, who had arrived at virtually the same conclusions. With characteristic generosity, Darwin placed both Wallace's work and his own before the Linnaean Society, and then hastily made his findings into a book. The first edition of 1,250 copies was sold on the day of publication, and the shy scientist found himself suddenly at the centre of a national controversy. Though he tried to avoid the fray, militant disciples were always ready to attack realms which he had never intended to threaten.

Why did *The Origin of Species by Natural Selection* (1859) arouse such passions? The answer is in the second half of the title: Darwin had provided a basis of experimental science for the old speculative theory of evolution. His interpretation was that species evolved by the survival and more prolific breeding of individuals best physically fitted for life within their environment. In over-simple terms, the giraffe's long neck results from generations of leaf-eating creatures whose longer-necked members had access to more fodder. He applied to nature the principle of selection which had long been consciously exercised in the breeding of domestic animals. Less dogmatic than many

[1] *Tancred* (1847), Bk. 2, Ch. 9.

of his followers, he was careful to describe Natural Selection as 'the main but not exclusive means of modification'.[1]

Darwin's book gave evolutionists the proofs which they needed, and stimulated new research. Behind it stood other works, influential in themselves and contributory to the evolutionary battle. Thomas Malthus reappears at this point, as he did do at unexpected times during the century. Darwin read him in 1838 and deduced that variations favourable to survival would tend to be preserved and perpetuated in the struggle for existence. Wallace came more quickly to his own theory after the same reading. The new ideas which alarmed the later Victorians were no more pessimistic than the teaching of Malthus that population tended to grow beyond the means of subsistence unless checked by natural catastrophes; but they had the new prestige of science behind them.

A satisfactory theory of evolution needed a long time-scale, and this was supplied by another branch of science. Sir Charles Lyell's *Principles of Geology* (1830–33) had an influence comparable to that of Darwin. Lyell, to whom Darwin confided some of his theory before publication,[2] utterly rejected the more orthodox current theory of catastrophic changes and asserted the minority uniformitarian view of 'one uninterrupted succession of physical events, governed by the laws now in operation'. The discovery of fossils of extinct species at low subterranean levels had made it possible to state the age of the earth with some certainty. In the year when Lyell finished his book, a human skull was unearthed in the Meuse valley along with remains of extinct mammals; the first remains of Neanderthal Man were discovered in 1857. Not only was the earth found to be older than tradition had taught, but man himself had become more difficult to identify as a unique species.

Thus Darwin's book was a catalyst in many arguments that had already begun. Some hailed him in Shelleyan terms as a new liberator; to give scientific proof to evolution was a triumph for those who would enlist evolution itself under the banner of progress. The new theory accorded well with the current faith in progress: if man had emerged from primitive life by his fitness to survive, was there any limit to what the human race

[1] Introduction to *The Origin of Species*.
[2] Basil Willey, *Darwin and Butler* (London, 1960), p. 11.

might yet accomplish? The Godwinian belief in human perfectibility found a new course, with new and stronger reasons for optimism. Had natural creation been set to evolve in minute stages, with a design of progress for the species and a gambler's chance for the individual? Such a proposition fitted in very well with ideas of general progress and free competition.

Optimism was felt by some who saw God behind creation, as well as by those who were content with a vague First Cause. Charles Kingsley welcomed Darwin's theory, in words which few of his fellow-clergy would have echoed:

Men find that now they have got rid of an interfering God – a master-magician as I call it – they have to choose between the absolute empire of accident, and a living, immanent, ever-working God.[1]

Such enthusiasms were in part a tribute to the benefits of applied science. After the worst results of industrialization had begun to turn to greater prosperity, it seemed that science could bring nothing but good. At the height of the railway mania in 1846, Charles Mackay was eloquent if not notably poetic:

Blessings on Science, and her handmaid Steam!
They make Utopia only half a dream;
And show the fervent, of capacious souls,
Who watch the ball of Progress as it rolls,
That all as yet completed, or begun,
Is but the dawning that precedes the sun.[2]

The belief of those lines grew stronger as science seemed more and more to suggest that movement in time was a supersession of the past and not a decline from it. This is the thesis of Henry Thomas Buckle's *History of Civilization in England* (1857), where the historian approaches his subject in the spirit of Darwin's then unpublished theory. European man is seen as the finest work of creation, the bearer of human destiny because of his degree of control over his environment, bringing the benefits of his civilization influence to the whole world. War would disappear with the advance of science and economics, as better means of communication and the panacea of a free market

[1] Quoted by C. E. Raven in 'Man and Nature', in *Ideas and Beliefs of the Victorians* (London, 1949).

[2] 'Railways', printed in *A Book of Science Verse*, edited by W. Eastwood (London, 1961).

overcame the dangers of national hatred, prejudice and jealousy.

While some rejoiced, others retreated with alarm into the protective fold of conservative orthodoxy. Where was the place of human striving and aspiration in this mechanical weeding-out of individuals for their physical survival-value? Not only the theologians but many of the scientists preferred still to believe that nature produced higher forms of life in succession, rather than to accept the organic evolution which Darwin had postulated. There were also many scientists who continued to reject all evolutionary theory in favour of the creationist view. With or without Darwin, evolution seemed to many people a process of running down towards maximum entropy. If man was in the middle of a long biological development, what abiding faith could be put into current ideas and institutions? This last was a gloomy thought for many, but a happy one for Samuel Butler and later for Bernard Shaw.

As a facet of organic nature, subject to mechanistic laws, man no longer seemed such a splendid figure. Was a Newton the helpless object of those laws which his own genius had seemed to formulate? The increasing tendency to give objective reality to 'laws of nature' could engender despair like that of Tennyson's *Locksley Hall Sixty Years After* (1886). The narrator has eschewed his youthful optimism and sees science failing to touch the evils of the age:

Let us hush this cry of 'Forward' till ten thousand years have gone. If science seemed to be doing little or nothing to improve the present, where would it all end? The fear of the machine evolving into control of mankind is heard – a theme from Butler to Capek's *RUR* and beyond:

> Humanity shall faint and fail,
> And on her ruins will prevail
> The Conquering Machine![1]

Besides all these fears, evolution seemed to be challenging orthodox religious belief. To accept the chronology of Lyell was to reject that which had been painstakingly worked out from the Bible – the kind of dating which George Rawlinson seriously discussed

[1] 'The Conquering Machine', in *Dreams to Sell* (1887), by May Kendall (Mrs Andrew Lang).

in his Bampton Lectures in 1859. The awkward fossils could perhaps be explained by the extinction of whole species in the Flood; or, as Philip Gosse suggested, the world and all its species had been created entire by God, with the appearance of having slowly evolved.[1] The new challenge to the supreme place of man in nature was more serious. Darwin, who had no great interest in theological questions, came in for a great deal of abuse which was increased by his *Descent of Man* (1871).[2]

Evolution as a stick to beat the theologians was heartily wielded by Thomas Henry Huxley (1825–95) who, unlike Darwin, was an enthusiastic public speaker and a lover of controversy. He was the archetype of the new scientist, the visionary who saw hope in a world where knowledge could increase and make men free. Huxley had largely educated himself and was able to speak for the intelligent workmen, the frequenters of Mechanics' Institutes who were caught up in Holyoake's Secularism and Bradlaugh's defiance of religion. He set out to make popular the Darwinian theory of evolution.

In doing so he also made it sensational, drawing out with almost pathological intensity the elements of cruelty and violence which natural selection seemed to involve. He worked on the ambivalent Victorian attitude to struggle and competition, more deliberately than Malthus had done. The tension grew: the individual must develop in freedom, but was there or was there not a relationship of duty between him and society? Some, like Grant Allen in *A Ballade of Evolution* (1894), saw only bitter strife and the loss of compassion following from Darwinism. Huxley was important in achieving the dominance of scientific thinking and the cult of scientific method at the end of the century. Yet he himself was no utter materialist; he could see a kind of poetry in science and could write, as in *Man's Place in Nature* (1863), a good style of prose which carried on the tradition of expository writing developed since the Restoration.

The philosophical implications of evolution were engaging

---

[1] *Omphalos: An Attempt to Untie the Geological Knot* (1857) – an interesting though extreme example of the efforts to 'reconcile' geology and religion.

[2] Butler once said that *The Origin of Species* had destroyed his faith in a personal God, but his quarrel with Christianity had in fact begun before Darwin's theory was published; see John Butler Yeats, 'Recollections of Samuel Butler', in *Essays Irish and American*.

the attention of Herbert Spencer (1820–1903) even before Darwin's work was published. Over his long lifetime he wrote a great deal, attempting to make a synthesis of knowledge, a bridge across the various disciplines. It was a noble venture, but in that expanding and fragmenting age no one could hope to rival Bacon's claim to take all knowledge to be his province.

Spencer's application of scientific method to the study of human behaviour, seeking to fit social phenomena into a mechanical framework, was the beginning of sociology as a serious study in Britain. His approach is essentially optimistic, though shadowed in true Victorian fashion by the possibility of disaster. Mankind is seen to be moving towards a society emancipated by science, where the individual will be all-important. Yet the happy end can be delayed; men may even take the wrong turning and regress. The principle of progress is the basic law of the universe, but there are human tendencies to break it. State interference is anathema to Spencer, who takes up the old cry of complete individualism and gives it the scientific backing which Darwin gave to biological evolution.

In effect, he was trying to reconcile evolution and the Utilitarian philosophy. His influence was perhaps greater than his achievement, his statement of the Victorian dilemma more meaningful today than his attempts to solve it. Like George Eliot, who greatly admired him, he was searching for an ethical system that could survive the loss of religious faith. Like her too, he held a strong sense of the responsibility of the individual and the continuing consequences of action. He might well have been a novelist: he explored new aspects of man in society and man as an individual which were to become dominant in fiction within a generation. His enthusiasm for science was influential on the course of education, giving theoretical backing to the practical need to become technically equipped to face foreign competition.

The essential materialism with which Buckle and Spencer applied evolutionary theory to human society is seen also in *Physics and Politics* (1869) by Walter Bagehot (1826–77). The sub-title is a fair comment: *Thoughts on the Application of the Principles of Natural Selection and Inheritance to a Political Society.* Bagehot considers the forces which enable society to survive and suggests that the 'cake of custom' tends towards sterility as well as cohesion until it is broken by inquiring intelligence growing to replace instinct. He shows Victorian amplitude in full measure: he became the editor of *The Economist* and made a notable contribution to the theory of public finance with *Lombard Street* (1873). He also produced a large amount of literary criticism, and *The English Constitution* (1867) for long remained a standard work in its field. He has the tincture of greatness without the essence. Always shrewd in perception and often brilliant in expression, he proves at last to be more stimulating than satisfying.

The new interest in science did not lead universally to loss of faith. There were some unedifying attempts to reconcile *Genesis* with Lyell's *Principles* – after all, how long was a 'day' of creation? Controversy raged to the end of the century and into the next, but there were plenty of Christians who welcomed the spirit of inquiry, acknowledging that truth was indivisible and that faith rested on essentials not on accidents. The Meta-physical Society, founded in 1869 for the encouragement of scientific discussion and research, included among its members agnostics like John Morley, Leslie Stephen, John Tyndall and Huxley (who coined the very word *agnostic*), but also Tennyson, Gladstone and Cardinal Manning.

Although science was not seen as purely destructive, a new feeling of revolt was following its advance. The early part of the period had produced outpourings from many social critics, but their attacks had usually been on particular abuses for which remedies were suggested, or appeals for a general change of heart within the existing framework. Now came a more icono-clastic assault on the whole basis of society, a questioning of traditions in politics, in religion, in education, in social structure.

Samuel Butler (1835–1902) did not limit himself to a single target, but kept up a series of skirmishes. As the son of a clergy-man and the grandson of a bishop – who had been Darwin's headmaster at Shrewsbury – he might have seemed likely to become the epitome of Victorian conformity and orthodoxy. Instead, he succeeded in posthumously shocking the Edwardians. He went down from Cambridge with the plan of ordination, but growing doubts led to acrimonious corres-pondence with his father and a hasty departure for New Zealand. There he became a sheep-farmer, did well financially, and returned home to a dilettante life as a bachelor who could write, paint and compose. Out of his family quarrels he built an opposition to established conventions. He attacked vigorously but often with something of the child seeking for attention and basically wanting the security of orthodoxy. He is often perverse, sometimes absurd, in the prejudices which he opposes to the prejudices of society – and he often shows that he knew it. He was an evolutionist who dared to dispute the new master Darwin and look back to Lamarck.[1]

Butler wrote on many subjects, but the modern reader finds little of interest in such pieces of misplaced ingenuity as *The Authoress of the Odyssey* (1897) and *Shakespeare's Sonnets Reconsidered* (1899). His fame rests on a few books, starting with *Erewhon* which appeared anonymously in 1872 and was attributed by some to Lytton until Butler revealed his authorship. It takes its setting from New Zealand and its theme from reflections on English society. The hero, Higgs,[2] stumbles on an unknown community in the interior of the country and spends some time there before making his escape in a balloon. The society of *Erewhon* is Utopia with a difference. (The word is 'Nowhere' reversed and slightly changed: both the association and the inversion tell us what to expect.) It is the England of Victoria as clearly as Lilliput was the England of George 1; some of the characters even have English names reversed, like 'Nosnibor'.

In *Erewhon* Butler worked out some of his venom against the things which he hated because his parents revered them. The Church is parodied in the 'Musical Banks' where people can build up accounts which are payable only in the next world but whose servants insist on being paid in real, immediately usable currency. He mocks at religion for its social respectability and the insurance-policy calculations of certain types of Evangelical piety. It continued to haunt him all his life, and he kept sniping at it without ever shooting it down. More unusual for the time is his recognition of the connection between crime and poverty

---

[1] Bernard Shaw later called him 'a prophet who tried to head us back when we were gaily dancing to our damnation across the rainbow bridge which Darwinism had thrown over the gulf which separates life and hope from death and despair'. Preface to *Back to Methusaleh*.

[2] He is not so called in *Erewhon* but it is convenient to use here the name given to him in *Erewhon Revisited*.

and his attack on the injustice of punishing actions for which an unequal society was responsible. In Erewhon people are imprisoned for being ill but sent to hospital and visited with sympathy when they break the law. Higgs sees the trial of a poor man for 'labouring under pulmonary consumption', and the irony came too near to truth for the comfort of his readers. He returned to the style and theme many years later with *Erewhon Revisited* (1901), a slighter work out of a weary mind. The new parody of Christianity is dreary: Higgs has been deified by the people because of his previous disappearance into the sky.

The comparison with Swift is not to Butler's advantage. There is nothing in *Erewhon* so savagely ironical as Swift's *Modest Proposal* that the surplus Irish children should be killed and eaten. Nor does the framework of the story contain such a convincingly organic whole as the even more fantastic realms of *Gulliver's Travels*. At his best, Butler can be as stimulating as Swift, but the irony is seldom sustained to be carried to its logical conclusion and beyond. The fact is perhaps that Butler, like many late Victorians who railed against their age, was a man with a zest for life in all its vigour and shared the prevailing optimism that a better society was attainable and indeed probable. The lack of depth in much that he wrote is often hidden under the easy style which invites the reader's confidence and glossed by the quality of his best descriptive passages. The opening scenes of *Erewhon* were written by a man whose paintings were later hung in the Royal Academy.

That Butler did not abandon convention, decent feeling or whatever we may choose to call it, is shown by the fact that he did not allow *The Way of All Flesh*, written over a long period from 1872, to be published until 1903 when the prototypes of most of the characters were dead. It tells the story of Butler's life, with imaginative changes, until his Cambridge years, and goes on to suggest what his later life might have been if he had resolved his doubts and been ordained. The hero, Ernest Pontifex, falls into disgrace in his first curacy by making a pass at a respectable girl, is sent to prison, comes out and marries a drunken slut, eventually escaping from degradation by the discovery that she was already married and that he has a rich inheritance.

What made the book notorious even to its first Edwardian readers is Butler's attack on the institution of the family and the duty to parents. Ernest's troubles are blamed on his narrowly Evangelical upbringing (Butler also has some bitter fun with 'Simeonites' in the Cambridge section), with its morbid sense of guilt and complete suppression of sexual knowledge. Continually the point is made that parents are a poisonous, stunting influence on children, the family home is a place of horror where the mistakes and tensions of one generation are passed on to the next. We are not so startled by these things since Freud taught us to understand in a new sense what it means to visit the sins of the fathers upon the children. Once again, Butler's skill should not lead us into excessive admiration. He said much that needed saying, but he said it mainly out of his own experience. He was one of those whose technical brilliance can make the particular seem universal. There was more to the Victorian family than hypocrisy and repression; the very conventionality which he attacked might build greater security in the child than the permissiveness without moral certainty of some later homes. Butler has the perception, and also the limitation, of the 'wretched little heavy-eyed mite sitting on the edge of a chair' who, like Ernest in Dr Skinner's study, observes the scene and one day writes about it.[1]

Not objective enough to be pure fiction, too fictional to be documentary, *The Way of All Flesh* still has a great deal to say about Victorian society. Butler attacks his age where it felt most confident – or perhaps was most stoutly defending its anxiety. He strikes at the middle-class values, the axioms of respectability. At a period when satire was a rare literary form, though self-criticism was increasing, he combines the two and batters away at the walls which are bastions for the majority but prisons for him. Writing before Gissing and Moore had brought a new naturalism to fiction, he uses the accepted realism of the contemporary novel to criticise things hitherto beyond criticism. It was one thing to attack the factories and workhouses because they interfered with family life, quite another to suggest that the family ought to be abolished.

There is destruction in plenty, but little attempt to rebuild. The rehabilitated Ernest Pontifex is a dull prig, cultivating his

[1] *The Way of All Flesh*, Ch. 28.

private garden and seeming untroubled by the continuance of things from which he has suffered. He has freedom from responsibility, but freedom for what? In his end there is an image of Butler himself, as a figure who becomes increasingly common: the 'advanced' thinker who has settled his model of the world and sits complacently congratulating himself on being so much more enlightened than the others.

As a comic novel, *The Way of All Flesh* has higher quality. The portraits of Ernest's parents and Dr Skinner are excellent, though they fall off into farce before the end as the comic monsters of Dickens often do. Few writers caught so well the weakness of aspects of Evangelicalism and the comedy of the parsonical manner. The detached, satirical tone is maintained by Butler's dual role in the story, as the immature Ernest and as the sceptical narrator Overton.

Yet no book would have had such an impact if it were purely negative. Through the advocacy of Shaw and others, and with benefit of the new psychology, its influence may be traced in Bennett, Joyce, Maugham and other chroniclers of the young man who is rejecting as well as seeking. Butler's interest in evolution gave him a deeper insight into human development within society. He studies and dissects the current manners and conventions almost like an anthropologist with a strange tribe, starting well back in Ernest's ancestry and tracing the dominant pattern of behaviour emerging as each generation grows up. Ernest comes to believe that evolution works in the mind as well as in physical nature: the human will prevails to break taboos and social superstitions.

Now this is clearly not the pure Darwinian gospel. Butler read *The Origin of Species* and embarked on a number of books on evolution which challenged the mechanistic determinism of Darwin's theory.[1] He carried on a running fight with Darwin as well as with the Church, appealing back to Lamarck and the idea of mind and will working on the evolutionary pattern. It is not those fitted by the chance of body who survive, but those who best use their skill and cunning. Useful habits are unconsciously stored and transmitted to the next generation – so

---

[1] They are too numerous, and of too limited interest today, to deal with here. The most important are: *Evolution Old and New* (1875), *Life and Habit* (1877), *Unconscious Memory* (1880), *Luck or Cunning?* (1886–7).

the hidden strength of an ancestor saves Ernest from the final disaster to which parental influence would have led him.

This is a more cheerful doctrine than Darwin's, putting the stakes not on physical chance but on individual virtue and the will to succeed. Butler was a good Victorian after all, not least in his fear of a new tyranny in place of the old. He saw danger in the assumption that mankind was being carried on the tide of progressive nature, with more complex forms always evolving. If men were subject to evolution, why not machines? He deals with this new fear of the time in *Erewhon*, where the people banish the machines that threaten to evolve and destroy them.[1]

The Victorians drew some optimism but more pessimism from the doctrine of evolution. If man had evolved and superseded other species, who was to say that he was evolution's last word? The dominance of Darwinism made people fear that there could be little hope for the race if the laws of selection pronounced it doomed. In the next century, a lively Irish playwright, stimulated by Lamarck and Butler, tried to shake his contemporaries into action to will their own development. Darwin was long dead by then, having in his lifetime recorded his loss of literary and artistic appreciation in the process of 'grinding general laws out of large collections of facts'.[2] All in all, it is unlikely that he would have made much of *Man and Superman* or *Back to Methusaleh*.

[1] *Erewhon*, Chs. 23 and 24. The substance of this section had already appeared in an essay 'Darwin among the Machines' published in New Zealand in 1863.

[2] *The Autobiography of Charles Darwin*, ed. Nora Barlow (London, 1958), p. 139.

23

Meredith and Hardy

The last quarter of the nineteenth century seemed, to those who lived through it, to be producing doubts and difficulties at every turn. Many of the problems which had confronted the early Victorians had found solutions; but areas of life which had seemed safe and stable were becoming insecure. The physical and biological sciences had changed the idea of man's position within time and space; social studies of the individual and of the community were reducing him to an object for clinical description; spiritual certainties were being shaken by sceptical reappraisal both outside and within the Christian churches. Man no longer stood aloft, the special favourite of the Creator in a specially favoured corner of the universe.

There was thus a severe shock to the stability and complacency which had endured through decades of particular and local insecurities. The intelligent man was forced to take himself both less and more seriously: his cosmic significance might be less, but the need to make up his own mind seemed greater. Prose fiction, well established as the dominant literary form, took on a new seriousness of purpose. It began to incorporate new interpretations of experience, to be concerned with the inner motivation of characters and the implications of behaviour. The two important British novelists who embarked on the deeper exploration of life (Henry James makes an English-speaking third) were cast by birth and upbringing firmly in the Victorian mould. In 1875 Meredith was forty-seven and Hardy thirty-five.

George Eliot had said, and was still saying, a great deal about motives and consequences. The moral problems in her novels are those of particularized individuals: her genius gives them universal application. She is touched with the prevailing Victorian melodrama, which passes moral judgements more on particular cases than on general principles, and she rises above it only as the quality of her mind prevails over literary fashion. The maturity of thinking in concepts, which proclaimed that the novel had reached new intellectual growth, comes with Hardy and Meredith. They achieve that universalizing of abstractions in a single creation which is found in the French novelists – achieve it more effectively than do the direct admirers of Naturalism.

Unlike other major Victorian novelists, they were both important poets as well. Great though their work in fiction was, they both sometimes were irked by the restrictions of plot and narrative. Poetry seemed to give them a greater freedom for the expression of ideas, and they felt it as their first love. In the years of success as a novelist, Hardy could write:

> It sometimes occurs to me that it is better to fail in poetry than to succeed in prose. At any rate, more mental satisfaction is to be got out of verse, if you have not to cover so many pages a year, like some of us.[1]

The novels of George Meredith (1828–1909) are important partly because his personal affairs and the pressures of his age so frequently complemented one another. His grandfather had been a tailor in Portsmouth who had prospered during the Napoleonic wars and lived in some style. His father – like the fathers of several other novelists – had failed in business, gone bankrupt and moved to London. The young George had received some private schooling in England and Germany through money left by his mother. He had thus experienced the contemporary upheaval of classes and the transcience of riches in the new economy. His sense of being somehow un-classed was emphasized by pride in his Welsh ancestry and his grandfather's boasts of descent from princes.

He married a daughter of Thomas Love Peacock, a widow several years his senior, who eventually ran off with a young painter and left him with a son to care for. Meredith, who had already begun writing poetry without much financial success, was virtually driven to the practice of prose. It is perhaps not

[1] Quoted in 'Hardy's Letters to Sir George Douglas' by W. M. Parker in *English*, Vol. 14, No. 84, p. 218.

surprising that the themes of his mature work were the causes and effects of tension in human relationships, the evil of selfishness and the search for individual integrity and self-knowledge.

His start was uncertain with *The Shaving of Shagpat* (1855), an imitation of the *Arabian Nights* genre with an uneasy blend of burlesque and Gothic horror, in which the study of egoism is already being made. In *Farina* (1857) he takes a setting of medieval folklore; a light-hearted telling of the legendary origin of *eau de Cologne* comprehends more serious reflections. With *The Ordeal of Richard Feverel* (1859) the true Meredith emerges and his private problems become the basis of fiction. Sir Austin Feverel is deserted by his wife and devotes himself to the strict education of his son; young Richard grows up selfish and arrogant, and communication between father and son breaks down although affection is not lost. There are elements of the common Victorian melodrama in such episodes as the secret marriage and the duel. What makes the book outstanding is its examination of problems almost new to English fiction, its ruthless analysis of the dishonesty in intimate relationships, its hatred of egoism and sentimentalism as the main faults of the age. What was said earlier about the ability to think in concepts Is pertinent here; previous novelists had attacked these vices as manifested in particular aspects of life, but Meredith was able to give his exposure a wider validity.

Evan Harrington (1860–1) drew much from his own family history – too much for some of his surviving relatives. A comic approach again conceals serious purpose, particularly the theme of class-divisions and the maturing of the hero to realise (like Pip in *Great Expectations*) the futility of social climbing. *Emilia in England* (1864) examines the artistic temperament in the person of the daughter of an Italian street-musician: once more sentimentalism and the current attitude to social class come under attack. The insecurity of the middle class, leading to artificiality and pretentiousness is exposed mordantly:

If with attentive minds we mark the origin of classes, we shall discern that the Nice Feelings and the Fine Shades play a principal part in our human development and social history. I dare not say that civilized man is to be studied with the eye of a naturalist; but my vulgar meaning might almost be twisted to convey that our sentimentalists are a variety owing their existence to a certain prolonged term of comfortable feeding.[1]

This novel was reissued as *Sandra Belloni* in 1887. Its sequel *Vittoria* (1866–7) shows the heroine, now a famous prima donna, devoted to the Italian nationalist movement of 1848; it is a less satisfactory book, suffering from Meredith's tendency to hover uncertainly between realism and romanticism.

Rhoda Fleming (1865) is a more straightforward narrative, in a rustic setting with which Meredith was not entirely happy. *The Adventures of Harry Richmond* (1870–1), which appeared anonymously in the *Cornhill*, returns to the father-and-son theme. The wild adventurer Richmond Roy, claiming royal lineage, is seen through the eyes of his son Harry who is dragged in the wake of his exploits. Despite a strong romantic element, the tensions and experiences of Meredith's own early life are clear, not least some happier memories of schooldays in Germany. The hero of *Beauchamp's Career* (1874–5) was based on Meredith's friend, the Radical F. A. Maxse, in support of whose campaign he had received some insight into politics. Beauchamp is a dedicated idealist who cannot sort out his own emotions; he dies nobly in rescuing a child, after a life of muddle and failure.

Meredith's next book, *The Egoist* (1879), is his most intellectual and the one which makes fewest concessions to the casual reader. Its sub-title is 'A Comedy in Narrative' and it comes soon after the lecture on *The Idea of Comedy and the Uses of the Comic Spirit*[2] a condensation of which appears at the opening of the novel. His ability to cast dramatic poetry into the form of prose fiction is exemplified here: a great deal of the book is in the form of dialogue, with the formal construction of classical comedy. The anti-hero Sir Willoughby Patterne[3] is an egoist whose vice is ruthlessly dissected; his arrogance in love affairs leads to a humiliation from which he does not emerge cleansed as other Meredithian heroes do. He is contemptible, yet we feel

---

[1] *Sandra Belloni*, Ch. 1.

[2] This lecture was given on 1 February 1877, in the austere setting of the London Institution for the Advancement of Literature and the Diffusion of Useful Knowledge. It appeared in the *New Quarterly Magazine* in April of the same year, and was published separately in 1897.

[3] The very name, with its conjuration of 'Willow Pattern', emphasizes the formal, stylized nature of the action.

for him the stab of pity that we feel for creations of comedy when the real world overtakes them: for Malvolio, for Sir Peter Teazle, supremely for Falstaff in his rejection. The critics were kinder about *The Egoist*, despite its metaphorical, allusive style and its frequent quotations from the imaginary *Book of Egoism;* the art of the novel was coming to receive more serious intellectual consideration.

Meredith's return to a subject of recent history in *The Tragic Comedians* (1881) was not very successful, but he did better with *Diana of the Crossways* (1884). Based on the scandal of Mrs Norton early in the reign, and bringing in under thin disguises such characters as Lord Melbourne and Sidney Herbert, it has a feeling of the old 'silver fork' school. Meredith's serious intent was to show how even a clever woman could go wrong through the failure of society to discipline creatively her emotions. Young 'emancipated' women of the time mistook the point and made something of a cult-symbol out of the heroine who was prepared to leave her husband. *One of Our Conquerors* (1891) has the theme of money which had preoccupied so many Victorian novelists. The magnate Victor Radnor degenerates from influence and power to insanity, through his unhappy marriage and the pressure of his financial speculations. Meredith's last two books, *Lord Ormont and his Aminta* (1894) and *The Amazing Marriage* (1895), both include the themes of incompatibility in marriage and the alliance of an elderly man with a young woman.

Time and again, Meredith deals with the problem of the individual finding his true self through some kind of ordeal which brings release from inhibiting self-centredness. For him, true self-knowledge was the real purpose of experience. The significance of this in the intellectual conditions outlined at the beginning of this chapter cannot be overlooked. Meredith affirmed the basic freedom of the individual when many factors seemed to deny it. Darwin's evolutionary theory seemed to challenge and inspire him: man might be an animal, but he was one that could use the developed powers of intellect and will to rule sense and emotion. 'For him evolution was a series of steps from earth to mind, and thence to spirit.'[1]

Yet he recognizes in full the animal element, recognizes not

[1] Bonamy Dobrée, *The Broken Cistern* (London, 1954), p. 94.

with a dread of the latent beast which troubled many of his contemporaries but with acceptance of man's interaction with the natural world. The shared sexuality, in the widest sense, of man and nature had been understood by Blake and also, hysterically, by Swinburne. For Meredith it was an exhilarating fact, driving the individual to ally himself with total creative purpose towards the progress of the race – an anticipation of a basic Shavian message. The working out of such ideas inevitably brought sharp reactions from the critics; *The Ordeal of Richard Feverel* was severely handled by the *Spectator* and the *Athenaeum*, and Mudie's refused to circulate the three hundred copies which had been ordered. His early poems too were unfavourably compared with Tennyson's, more for their moral tone than their skill of execution:

No word-painting or clever analysis can atone for a choice of subject which we cannot help regarding as a grave moral mistake.[1]

If Meredith's view of society is incomplete, it is because it is in the deepest way a comic view. The clash between reality and illusion is ever before him, and he deals with serious themes in that artificial mood which supposes that much of life is deception. His lecture on comedy discussed laughter as a clarification and a cleansing: the laughter of dispassionate and clear-sighted perception of folly and conceit. That is how he presents society, and the consequent feeling of aloofness makes him neither easy nor particularly attractive on first reading. Other factors increase the alienation, notably his style, which seems hopelessly ornate and discursive until one comes to enter his dramatic concept of the novel and read it more like speech with its ellipses and rapid transitions. The beauty and the difficulty of the novels both derive largely from the fact that Meredith was a poet. He makes use of symbolism and he rises to passages of great lyrical emotion – the first meeting of Richard Feverel with Lucy is a good example.

Meredith's poetry in the technical sense is large in bulk and varied in prosodic form. It contains some of the themes which he worked out in his novels, notably that of unfortunate marriage in the series of sixteen-line sonnets called *Modern Love* (1862). He knew too the happiness and ecstasy of love, shown

[1] *Saturday Review*, 24 October 1863.

in such poems as 'Love in the Valley'. The interaction of man and nature is a frequent subject, treated with lively excitement in a manner sometimes reminiscent of Coleridge.

As a publisher's reader, Meredith rejected the first manuscript of Thomas Hardy (1840–1928). The two writers shared a pride in their ancestry, but Hardy came of Dorset yeoman stock. He grew up in a region as yet little touched by change, a region where contemporary events often seemed less real than the memory of Napoleon's threatened invasion. He was apprenticed to an architect, made drawings of old churches scheduled for restoration, and did so well that he found a position in London; but he disliked the metropolis and returned home to devote himself to writing.

His first published novel, *Desperate Remedies* (1871) displeased the reviewers, mainly because of its treatment of illegitimacy. He makes the modern reader impatient by following the fashion for sensational fiction and by an over-complex plot. *Under the Greenwood Tree* (1872), which he described as 'a rural painting of the Dutch school', has kept more favour. It is a light, derivative and rather sketchy piece of work with delightful glimpses of the country way of life that was already moribund. The more typical Hardy emerges with *A Pair of Blue Eyes* (1873) in which two rivals for the same woman return to England and find they are travelling on the train that carries her coffin.

Hardy's reputation was established when *Far from the Madding Crowd* (1874) appeared in volume-form under his name after anonymous publication in the *Cornhill*. His dramatic power, his gift of characterization, were now reaching maturity. *The Hand of Ethelberta* (1876), a story of female struggle similar to that of Becky Sharp, also appeared first in the *Cornhill*. His first really great work was *The Return of the Native* (1878). From the opening description of Egdon Heath, his ability to use natural settings as more than mere background becomes apparent. The Heath becomes a part of the conflict, potent and variable as a human character; no one but Emily Brontë had done as much, and she had not lived long enough to develop her genius. His characters too assume the mighty proportions that we associate with him: Eustacia may be too much a romantic conception and Clym may be too weak in human terms for the significance he is supposed to have, but there is grandeur in their portrayal which makes them bear existence beyond the simple plot.

With *The Trumpet-Major* (1880) Hardy took the Napoleonic setting of which he had heard so much in his youth. The main characters are simpler and more conventional, but the final dismissal of John Loveday 'to blow his trumpet till silenced for ever upon one of the bloody battlefields of Spain' has all of Hardy's irony and compassion. *A Laodicean* (1881) draws on his early years as an architect. Not an outstanding novel (it was written during a period of illness) it is interesting for its treatment of the effect of the new technical age on rural life. The railway magnate John Power, a strong Dissenter, who buys up an old castle which causes a diversion of a new line, is a type familiar in Victorian fiction and reality. *Two on a Tower* (1882) sets human affairs against the vast stellar universe through the character of a young astronomer.

Hardy's treatment of the clash between the old and the new ways of life is typified in *The Mayor of Casterbridge* (1886). The earthy, powerful but ignorant Mayor Henchard declines into ruin while the alert, modernist Farfrae prospers. The transition in English agriculture around the time of Corn Law Repeal is the background of the personal conflicts which begin with the primitive, brutal act of Henchard in selling his wife and child at a fair. The working-out of natural scenes within human affairs is used again in *The Woodlanders* (1887), where the question of the rights of women is raised in condemnation of the system which compels Grace to remain with her unfaithful and dissolute husband. *Tess of the d'Urbervilles* (1891) deals with a situation similar to that of *Adam Bede,* but with a different attitude and very different consequences. Hardy's sympathy for the 'fallen' woman is defiantly expressed in the sub-title 'A Pure Woman Faithfully Presented'.

The handling of *Jude the Obscure* (1896) brought to an end Hardy's long warfare with the critics. The outrage which it caused may seem strange to a later generation which is not so easily shocked by reading of a character who finds relief through drink and sex. The hero, Jude Fawley, is a latecomer in a long line of Victorian fictional characters: the talented and ambitious young working man who is trying to better his position against the odds of society. Perhaps what upset the first readers was not only the frankness of the book but also its pessimism. The gloom which Hardy had cast over his previous novels now seemed to break out and envelop the reader's world. *Jude* has a markedly late-Victorian setting in time and its attitudes were the more threatening to security. An age already troubled by new ideas was not delighted to read the verdict on the macabre episode in which Jude's eldest boy kills the small children and then himself 'because we are too menny':

> The doctor says there are such boys springing up amongst us – boys of a sort unknown in the last generation – the outcome of new views of life. They seem to see all its terrors before they are old enough to have staying power to resist them. He says it is the beginning of the coming universal wish not to live.[1]

Hardy wrote no more novels; most of his poetry belongs to the twentieth century. His shorter pieces are often less bold in prosody and less polished in execution than those of Meredith, but they have few rivals in English for the capturing of a mood as it passes away into regretful memory. The Greek classicism which contributed to the sense of inexorable fate in his novels gave him also this skill in lyrical epigram. It helped also to form *The Dynasts* (1903–8), an epic drama of Napoleon's last ten years of power against which the common peasant-soldier moves on his helpless way, while the immortals look on in impotent pity at the workings of the blind First Cause. Much that Hardy had said in his novels comes out with wild power of poetry which gave him new freedom. The recurring myth of Napoleon which had moved nineteenth-century writers from Byron through Carlyle and onwards now found its post-Victorian and most splendid expression.

While Meredith writes almost entirely about the urbane world where a baronet is found on every corner, Hardy depicts the rustic life that was yielding to industrialism as the norm of English society. He is one of the few Victorian writers to give extended treatment to the agricultural worker and to enter fully into his mind and outlook. He has the old tradition of the oral ballad and legend which his talent weaves into prose fiction, a tradition which contains much that is horrific, tragic and

[1] *Jude the Obscure*, Part 6, Ch. 2.

morbid.[1] He has the gift of the exciting incident, the memorable anecdote.

Yet he was learned too, at home in the world of Mill, Spencer and Darwin. The traditions of his Dorset home combined with his intellectual understanding of what time and space had come to mean in the new age. Personal experience had taught him to recognize the continuity of British life – 'Casterbridge announced old Rome in every street, alley and precinct'[2] but science was opening longer vistas of time. Hardy was eight years old when Layard's *Nineveh* was published; he produced his second novel in the year when George Smith deciphered a Chaldean description of the Deluge and threw another cat among the fundamentalist pigeons. Hardy's novels move against a background of infinite time even when the events in them seem to be precisely located.

His faith in Christianity went early, and it went mainly through the apparent challenge of science; in that way he was in the new rather than the old tradition of scepticism. He came to the idea of a universe moved by blind chance, not by conscious power either good or bad. Man is tossed hither and thither in the ruthless struggle for survival, in which the talented and the strong-spirited suffer more as they impotently try to resist the sweep of destiny. It is a complete contrast to the exhortations of Meredith and Shaw for individual co-operation with the Life Force. Man is only the more wretched for his long evolution since he alone of creatures is conscious of his state and has aspirations never to be fulfilled.

Yet man is not a cosmic mistake. His consciousness is the necessary crown of all natural things:

Above the plain rose the hill, above the hill rose the barrow, and above the barrow rose the figure. Above the figure was nothing that could be mapped elsewhere than on a celestial globe.

Such a perfect, delicate and necessary finish did the figure give to the dark pile of hills that it seemed to be the only justification for their outline.[3]

Hardy's characters often seem, as does Eustacia in this passage, to embody the very elemental forces which are their masters

[1] Douglas Brown, *Thomas Hardy* (London, 1954), pp. 108ff.
[2] *The Mayor of Casterbridge*, Ch. 11.
[3] *The Return of the Native*, Bk. 1, Ch. 2.

and against which they struggle in vain. Although he asserts that destiny is neither good nor evil in intent, most readers have felt that he overloads the odds against his characters. A chain of coincidences thwarts reasonable human plans; his people seem like victims driven to sacrifice, an impression made explicit in the long vigil of Tess at Stonehenge. 'In Hardy the *deus ex machina* has become a *diabolus ex machina*.'[1]

The truth may be that the pessimism accentuated by the pressure of his age and by some of his reading was continually in conflict with his personal compassion. In spite of the cosmic sweep and the protestations that there is no sense in the universe, his novels leave one with the certainty that individuals matter. He was as unhappy with the bland prophecies of the new scientism as with the apparently discredited optimism of the Church. Both of them seemed to deny the importance of people and of what they do to each other. Man's inhumanity to man becomes a stronger force in the later novels, and combines with a surge of social protest in *Jude*. He pities those who suffer not only from the common human lot but from the miseries of a transitional time when the old certainties are departing and the natural rhythms of life are broken.

Both Hardy and Meredith were affected by Darwinism, in the different ways that their different temperaments encouraged. Meredith fed his sense of comic irony upon it and offered to his readers the struggle for survival in nature as a reason for overcoming self-seeking and attaining the full stature of humanity. Hardy saw more grimly the ruthlessness and the waste from which mankind did not seem to be exempt: was there any logical reason why the young of the human race should not be hunted down for sport like any other animal?[2] It all seemed to fit in with his tragic sense that human endeavour was doomed to frustration. Meredith and Hardy between them gave imaginative voice to the extremes of optimism and pessimism which Darwinism engendered in its time. In doing so, they formed a bridge towards problems unknown in their time but whose nineteenth-century origins are now too plainly visible.

---

[1] Lionel Stevenson, *The English Novel* (London, 1960), p. 388. Hardy himself would not have accepted this. See, for instance, F. E. Hardy, *The Life of Thomas Hardy* (London, 1933), Vol. 2, pp. 4 and 217.

[2] F. E. Hardy, op. cit., Vol. 2, p. 106.

24

The Theatre

By the beginning of the Victorian period, drama had long ceased to be a dominant mode of literary expression. It was to rise during the reign from its nadir to, if not a summit, at least to a plateau from which higher peaks would once again be reached. The Romantic poets had essayed dramatic form without producing anything that was a serious theatrical possibility; Shelley's *Cenci* was out of consideration because of its incest theme, though it has in recent years proved that it can hold the stage. Those who were writing for the theatre in the first half of the nineteenth century were often over-anxious to assert the claim to be 'literary' and were fearful of being thought 'low'.

The theatre had lost its power to interpret imaginatively the society from which its audience was drawn. It had become mere entertainment, and the reader is asked to note that stress should fall on the word *mere*; while the popular theatre was often trivial in content, the better writers who attempted drama did not always realize that the one unforgivable fault in a play is boredom. The early Victorian drama was more often an escape from society than a reflection of society. The changing conditions of life had been accompanied by no comparable change in the conception of drama and the chief traditional genres had been debased.

In place of tragedy, the 'serious' form of play was melodrama; in place of comedy, audiences expected farce. The two types are not always dramatically despicable but their predominance does not indicate a healthy theatrical situation. They concentrate on situation and incident instead of character: what people are becomes less important than what happens to them. Melodrama is full of moral judgements, but it makes them in relation to particular situations, drawing on general criteria only for supporting aphorisms. We have seen how strong this element was in the contemporary novel. Both types over-simplify life for the sake of rapid and startling action. By the 1830's they had lost touch with normal communication and taken on a debased form of the old 'high style' of speech.

A monopoly granted by Charles II meant that Drury Lane and Covent Garden were the only theatres in London where plays could be publicly performed (the Theatre Royal, Haymarket, had a limited patent for the summer months). These two privileged giants, destroyed and rebuilt in earlier years, had developed into vast arenas too large for any subtlety of presentation. The actors had to bellow to reach the top galleries when they were allowed to speak at all; for much of the time the stage might be filled with an elaborate spectacle. The auditoria were dirty and uncomfortable in the legal houses, worse in the many unlicensed theatres which just managed to keep on the right side of the law – or got on its wrong side and were suppressed. A straight play was the monopoly of the licensed theatres but there was no prohibition of other kinds of public show. A little dramatic action could be introduced between the turns of a circus or an equestrian show; or, if enough musical pieces were strewn through its course, the play could pass off as a 'burletta'.

When the facts are considered, the wonder is not that the drama sank so low but that it survived at all. Not only were new and trivial pieces doctored to get them within the law, but there was no mercy for any of the old masters from Shakespeare onwards. Despite their monopoly, the licensed theatres were obliged to make similar concessions to compete for the fickle London audience. The straight theatre was also challenged by 'hippodromes', pleasure gardens with tight-rope walkers and balloonists, pastimes such as dog-fighting and rat-catching, as well as the even less demanding attraction of cheap liquor.

There seemed little hope of attracting an audience that would raise the demand for better drama. In some periods the theatre has flourished under aristocratic patronage which has eventually crippled it. The early-Victorian theatre was suffering from the other extreme: it was not part of the fashionable round for those most influential in society. The middle class that was beginning to feel and show its strength stayed away from the grim physical conditions and the usual behaviour of the audiences. The 'mob' continued to dominate the theatre, still almost as unruly as when they had rioted against the new prices at Covent Garden for sixty-one successive nights in 1809. Their drab surroundings made them demand colour and spectacle; their monotonous daily insecurity called for escape into fantasy; their weary bodies and untrained minds wanted no more than the familiar mixture where sides were clearly marked and attitudes predetermined. A visit to the theatre in 1850 was not for the timid:

> The place was crammed to excess in all parts. Among the audience were a large number of boys and youths, and a great many very young girls grown into bold women before they had well ceased to be children. These last were the worst features of the whole crowd, and were more prominent there than in any other sort of public assembly that we know of, except at a public execution.[1]

Conditions gradually improved, but there was still room for progress at the end of the century, if we can believe Bernard Shaw's experience:

> I regret to say that the patrons of the gallery at the Princess's, being admitted at half the usual west-end prices, devote the saving to the purchase of sausages to throw at the critics. I appeal to the lady or gentleman who successfully aimed one at me to throw a cabbage next time, as I am a vegetarian and sausages are wasted on me.[2]

The middle-class cult of home and family did not encourage much wandering abroad at night, and the dominant Evangelical spirit had a special bias against the theatre. The old puritanical arguments were heard, as they had been heard in Elizabethan days. The theatre was said to be an excuse for unruly assemblies (there was some truth in this!); it was full of worldliness; it showed things that might corrupt the young and inflame the passions of the mature; above all, it was a manifest and self-declared falsehood, full of pretence. The actors were suspected to be little more than criminals, lacking a proper place in a society which was still troubled by the sixteenth-century spectre of the 'masterless man'. As for actresses – pious

---

[1] 'The Amusement of the People', in *Household Words*, 30 April 1850.
[2] G. B. Shaw in *The Saturday Review*, 1 February 1896; the play being performed was Dion Boucicault's *The Colleen Bawn*.

mothers hastily changed the subject. The clergy were not so easily silenced; Charles Spurgeon would excommunicate those of his flock who went to the theatre, and Bishop Wilberforce declared that the 'resolution to attend theatres or operas was an absolute disqualification for Holy Orders'.[1]

During the first years of the period, the theatre was kept alive largely by hack-writers and adventurers. Following a tradition that they imperfectly understood, throwing together hackneyed situations with stock characters to fit the company for which they wrote, the melodramatists prevented the art of drama from being entirely submerged. Deriving from the eighteenth-century examples of Pixérécourt in France and Kotzebue in Germany, melodrama had come to be well established in its own English kind. As well as the musical interludes which gave its name, its characteristics were the sufferings of innocence, the final discomfiture of villainy at the hands of heroism, and the vindication of true love. It is easy to dismiss it as a formless and heterogeneous mass, but in fact it shows development from remote, exotic themes towards a reflection of more familiar society. As that society becomes more urbanized, melodrama tends to leave the rustic scene and migrate to the city: the wicked squire often becomes the wicked financier; the simple hero may appear in a policeman's uniform. Melodrama was not lacking in social awareness or in the capacity for adaptation. It was still drawing audiences up to the end of the century, taking advantage of new stage techniques which could involve the heroine in a gigantic train smash instead of merely an overturned carriage.

As well as the hacks, there were men who loved the theatre in spite of its faults and were willing to write for it. Most of their work now reads for what it is: the attempts of talented amateurs who had neither the time nor the inclination to master full theatrical technique. James Sheridan Knowles (1784–1862) was an actor and might have done something worthwhile if he had not slavishly followed the prevailing fashion for melo-drama. The Hunchback (1832) has a good part for a stock heroine; his better work, on historical subjects, falls outside the period. Thomas Noon Talfourd (1795–1854) was a successful lawyer, a friend of Dickens and a leading figure in the small

[1] S. D. Collingwood, The Life and Letters of Lewis Carroll (London, 1899), p. 74.

group of writers who were hopeful of bringing back poetic drama to the English stage. He was fortunate in having Macready to play the lead in his first play *Ion* at Covent Garden in 1836, and its success then and in later revivals may be attributable as much to the actor as to the dramatist. The blank verse of *Ion* is not really bad, but it is lacking in dramatic power and the easy fluency that stage speech needs. Yet there is a deeply human quality here and in Talfourd's later plays *The Athenian Captive* (1838) and *Glencoe* (1840). All three depict the misfortunes of innocent youth – a theme common in Dickens and other novelists as well as in melodrama – and all three show the hero compelled to kill for the sake of law or custom. We are given surprising insight into the liberal mind of a judicial officer in an age of frequent capital punishment. The assertion of liberalism against oppression appears also in Sir Henry Taylor's (1800–86) two-part play *Philip van Artevalde* (1834). The blank verse here is a little stronger but still far from theatrically adequate. Yet neither its artificiality nor the fourteenth-century setting can obscure its interest in a period of continuing struggle for the vote and the growth of working-class movements. Talfourd and Taylor show how drama was striving to say something valid about contemporary society.

Lytton applied himself to the theatre as well as to the novel and public life. His first two plays, *The Lady of Lyons* (1838) and *Richelieu* (1839), had the benefit of Macready's acting and were revived many times. They read as flatly as other verse plays of the time, and Lytton was wise to write his next play in the prose that he had already learned to handle in fiction. *Money* (1840) cannot be said to make a great breakthrough in the English theatre, but it did foreshadow better things to come. Its theme is a familiar one in drama: the hero becomes rich, tests his new-found friends by pretending to lose everything, and sinks into cynical misanthropy at the result. It is the Timon story, but with a particular relevance in this age of rapid fortunes, industrial expansion and wild speculation. Prose, a contemporary setting and a growing mastery of theatrical craft – these were good auguries for the future.

The old monopoly was broken in 1843 when the Act for Regulating the Theatres lifted restriction on the production of straight plays. The freeing of the theatre was necessary before dramatists could begin to experiment, to build again a vital relationship with emerging society and new ideas of the nature and destiny of man. Now at last the theatre and the drama started to draw together again into harmony. It was the age of realism; although this country produced no Ostrovsky, she did produce those who could break with convention and close the gap between the theatre and society. The English playhouse in the first half of the nineteenth century was the lineal descendant of the Elizabethan, with an apron stage projecting well beyond the proscenium. The new theatres that started to open from about the middle of the century were different, designed neither for spectacle nor for rapid action, but for scenes that were smaller and more intimate yet also more detached. The disappearance of the apron stage framed the whole action within the proscenium arch, which was itself deprived of its front doors so that all entrances and exits were made 'on the set'. Instead of the old backcloth with rows of sliding wings before it, the stage was now more often enclosed in a box-set, with the spectator looking through the missing fourth wall. The scene would be crowded with furniture and ornaments, a reproduction of the rooms which most of the audience had just left.

All this was not without precedent, for Madame Vestris had treated the stage thus as early as 1831. The real establishment of the new theatre can, however, be conveniently dated from 1865 when Marie Wilton and Squire Bancroft renovated the battered old Queen's Theatre near Tottenham Court Road and opened it as the Prince of Wales's. The second-generation change of name was indeed suitable for the new venture, with its smart, comfortable auditorium to attract a new type of audience.

The new theatre was not a pure gain to the drama. The detached effect of the retracted proscenium, aided at first by gas and later by electricity, reduced that participation of the audience which some modern dramatists are trying to recover. The theatre entered the era of the 'eavesdropping convention'.[1] The mania for realism gave a new twist to the old demand for spectacle: leaves would drift across the woodland scene and gallons of wet salt descend when the text referred to snow. The

[1] The phrase of Henry Arthur Jones, quoted in Lynton Hudson, *The English Stage 1850–1950* (London, 1951), p. 53.

expensive sets and new scenic effects tended to bring the designer into competition with the actor.

Yet the gains outweighed the losses. Plays which needed long runs if they were to make a profit had to be carefully rehearsed, and the producer became an important member of the theatrical team. The old stock companies began to disappear and the wanderings of Vincent Crummles were replaced by the smart touring company, guided by a respected actor-manager and travelling by the ever-increasing railway network. The theatre itself came to be regarded as a profitable speculation, and there began the modern practice of leasing a theatre for profit and hiring the company for a particular run; the effect has not been wholly good. There was good, however, in the return of a more intelligent audience. When the Bancrofts took over the Haymarket Theatre in 1880 they did away with the old Pit; the precedent was followed by other managers, and henceforth the seats nearest to the stage were occupied by the wealthier, and presumably less unruly, members of the audience. By the last decade of the century, the ultra-respectable Mr Pooter was willing to take his family to the 'Tank Theatre, Islington'.[1]

For twenty years or more after the Theatre Act, there was no great step forward in the writing of plays. Tom Taylor (1817–80) borrowed unblushingly from existing sources, especially from the French, and had the gift of turning out efficient work for the resources then available. His name was singularly appropriate; one can see him snipping and stitching away at old pieces to fit the new season's fashions. He retained the melodramatic element in plays with contemporary semi-realistic settings, and he constantly respected the solid domestic virtues. He wrote over seventy plays, some of which are not negligible. There is still a lively appeal in *Masks and Faces* (1852), a comedy in a seventeenth-century setting written with Charles Reade. *Still Waters Run Deep* (1855) was unusually outspoken for its time – its derivation from a French novel would have confirmed the darkest suspicions about Gallic literature. *The Ticket-of-Leave Man* (1863) shows the vogue for crime and police detection within melodrama; 'Hawkshaw the detective' held the stage for many years.

[1] George and Weedon Grossmith, *The Diary of a Nobody* (1892), Ch. 3.

Dion Boucicault (1822–90) was an actor and therefore more intimately acquainted with the theatre, but shared Taylor's talent for plagiarism and adaptation. He had more, a liveliness of wit and dialogue together with the ability to look clearly at his own age. He might have done greater things if he had lived at a time more congenial to satire. The coming reaction against the Victorian ethos is hinted at in *The School for Scheming* (1847). He continued the romantic tradition of melodrama in his rendering from the French, *The Corsican Brothers* (1852). That he was not living only in the past was proved by *The Octoroon* (1859), in which he looked seriously at the problems of the American South before the Civil War, and also used scientific detection by having a murder committed before an exposed camera. His most distinctive and original plays were set in his native Ireland: *Arrah-na-Pogue* (1864), *The Colleen Bawn* (1860) and *The Shaughraun* (1875). Melodramatic in the extreme, they yet catch something of the spirit of the country which was passing through such sad times. He could bring a touch of romance and mystery into the domestic setting, and he knew what could be done effectively on a stage.

Taylor and Boucicault were not the arch-plagiarists of the time, only the most able; in the absence of international copyright, anyone could adapt or translate from foreign sources. France was the favourite source of plunder and yielded, if not literary riches, at least theatrical profits in the 'well-made' plays of Scribe, Sardou, d'Ennery and others.[1] There were competent enough English writers who, at a more propitious time, might have produced original work of merit but who now occupied themselves mainly in putting together themes from other men's plays. Such was W. G. Wills (1828–91), who drew a regular salary to turn out plays for the Lyceum. Sidney Grundy (1848–1914) did some original work, though some of his biggest successes were taken from the French. He is of interest in showing aspirations towards the new realism being strangled by the endurance of melodramatic conventions.

At this time of change it took considerable talent to produce something both original and theatrically viable. Talent,

[1] The reader will recall Nicholas Nickleby's interview with Vincent Crummles: 'Do you understand French? ... Just turn that into English and put your name on the title page.' *Nicholas Nickleby*, Ch. 23.

though not genius, was exercised by Thomas William Robertson (1829–71) who came from a theatrical family and himself acted until he attained success as a dramatist. His name is inextricably linked with the Bancrofts and the Prince of Wales's, where most of his work was produced. As the hugely overgrown theatres and open stages had been cut down and enclosed, so Robertson cut down the extravagance of dramatic dialogue and plot. In his work, the still-limpid stream of melodrama begins to flow into a backwater while the new realism occupies the main channel. The very titles of his plays show the change, with their monosyllables instead of the old verbosity: *Society* (1865); *Ours* (1866); *Caste* (1867); *Play* (1868); *School* (1869); *The MP* (1870); *War* (1871). The last title indicates one of Robertson's preoccupations – the effect of war upon society. It is the Crimea in *Ours*, the Indian Mutiny in *Caste*, the Franco-Prussian War in *War*.

Robertson's thinking is seldom in advance of his time; his ideas, like his dialogue, carried no hazards for the respectable audiences which the Bancrofts were beginning to attract. The new 'teacup-and-saucer' comedy was realistic without any of the 'nastiness' which was rumoured to exist in Continental realism. The result was a return of elegance, refinement and true theatrical professionalism which had been absent from the English playhouse for many years. These plays of ordinary people, with human but not satanic failings and noble but not angelic virtues, were just what a large section of society needed to restore its confidence in the theatre.

James Albery (1838–89) seemed a possible successor to Robertson; there is humour superior to the usually flippant type of the period in *Red Roses* (1870). Albery never repeated this success, though his other plays show signs of strong psychological penetration. *Red Roses* gave Irving an early appearance, but he went on to greater fame while Albery declined through play after play, including *Apple Blossoms* (1871), *Forgiven* (1872), *The Crisis* (1878) and *Duty* (1879). Albery could write a good scene, even a good act, but not quite a good play; his talent flames brightly but never settles to a steady blaze.

It was Henry Arthur Jones (1851–1929) who took the next big step on the road of realism. He helped to establish the new autocracy of the author over the actor-manager that was to increase with Shaw and Wilde. Where others had been content to adapt the French dramatists, Jones learned from them, gaining in technique but keeping his own imagination free to write dialogue less stilted than Robertson's. After escaping from the servitude of a draper's shop, he came to establish himself as a playwright; his years in business gave him an eye for commercial success, while deeper talents made him understand what the theatre was capable of offering to society. The play that made his name, *The Silver King* (1882), is in the tradition of melodrama with much of the action transferred to the United States. It pleased Matthew Arnold, who accorded it the title of 'literature' and contrasted it with the feeble 'transpontine' melodramas that were being presented south of the Thames.[1]

The Silver King was indeed melodrama with a new look, drawing its power more from the inner conflict of the wronged hero than from external sensations. Jones continued to look both forwards and backwards throughout his dramatic career, moulding the form which had held the popular stage so long into a medium for social criticism. Mild as the criticism seems today, it was too strong for his contemporaries who gave a hostile reception to *Saints and Sinners* (1884) and were scandalized by the suggestion that adultery was neither more nor less blameworthy in a woman than in a man made in *The Case of Rebellious Susan* (1894). *Michael and his Lost Angel* (1896) lived up to its title by losing its leading actress in protest before it opened and being withdrawn after ten nights. The clergy had been coming in for attack from socialists and agnostics, but the time was not yet ready for the public stage to show that a priest might be guilty of adultery. By these, and perhaps by *The Liars* (1897) and *Mrs Dane's Defence* (1900), Jones deserves to be remembered. He came near to writing the Ibsenite type of problem play, yet he disliked Ibsen and the extent to which he fell short of realism that was dramatically significant is a measure of how low the English drama had previously sunk.

The influence of Ibsen is more marked in the work of Arthur Wing Pinero (1855–1934). Less apt than Jones to fall into melodrama, he may be regarded as the first of the modern

[1] He calls the 'outer drama' of sensational incidents 'transpontine', but says that in the 'inner drama of thought and passion there is nothing transpontine'. *Pall Mall Gazette*, 6 December 1882.

British dramatists. Yet though his technique is in advance of what has gone before, he is a clear manifestation of his age with its faults and its virtues. He fed the appetites of the late-Victorian playgoer: with farce in *Dandy Dick* (1887), with sentimentality in *Sweet Lavender* (1888), with social problems in *The Profligate* (1889), *The Second Mrs Tanqueray* (1893) and *The Notorious Mrs Ebbsmith* (1895). He surpassed his predecessors in being able to take a plausible situation with credible characters and develop it in theatrical terms. Yet the people of his plays are usually well-to-do and thoroughly committed to the conventions of social morality. With Jones, morality wins in the end after some sharp protests against its power. With Pinero, morality never has to fight very hard for its victory and is opposed for a time with little more than well-bred regret. The tragic element in Pinero is less in the plays themselves than in the world which inspired and accepted them. Outwardly comfortable and secure but always in danger of losing everything by a moral lapse, Pinero's characters are fixed within the framework of their own time and do not reach universal validity. Yet to manage serious themes without asides, long soliloquies, the continual bustling of entrances and exits – that is something which deserves praise.

A different tradition was developing concurrently with the growth of realism. The melodrama, starting with settings and situations remote from familiar life, had shown increasing tendencies towards social criticism. For the submerged classes there was both emotional satisfaction and a spur to intellectual questioning in seeing the sufferings of the poor at the hands of the rich. At the same time, the purely escapist element was an even stronger attraction, and the pressures of the advancing century did not fall on the poor alone. The flight from reality was manifested in various theatrical forms, in pantomime and burlesque and extravaganza, which turned to their own advantage the early need to evade by music and spectacle the restriction on straight plays. These entertainments were vehicles for the virtuosity of the actor rather than the craft of the playwright; only James Robinson Planché (1796–1880) has gained an important place in theatrical history for work of this kind. Planché had some respect for the theatre, but most of the contemporary hacks were anxious only to produce more startling effects and more outrageous puns. The trials of life could be forgotten in fantastic worlds of the imagination, in stories drawn from fairy-tales or unashamedly parodied from Shakespeare. The visual attraction generally included a good deal of semi-nudity, and the growth of stricter morality had its effect on the gradual decline of this aspect of the theatre.

Fantastic stories, musical interludes and puns burst out in new splendour in the work of W. S. Gilbert (1836–1911). In his own comedies and in the libretti which he wrote for Arthur Sullivan he brought to the theatre a keener intelligence and a readier wit than it had seen for some time. His acquaintance with Robertson and Bancroft gave him insight into the possibilities of the new stage; he is far more than a comic versifier. He expresses the growing insecurity and discontent of the Victorian age, but the criticism is always masked with a smile. The Savoy operettas gave psychological satisfaction by expressing general insecurity through specific satire. *H.M.S. Pinafore* (1878) casts doubt on national strength under its light burlesque of the Navy; the follies of Japan in *The Mikado* (1885) hit nearer home; questions of constitution, representation and democracy in *The Gondoliers* (1889) are more English than Venetian.

The combination of shrewd satire with welcome escapism is perhaps a specially British trait, one which requires fidelity to a particular kind of logic and an intellectualism that appears to mock the intellect. Gilbert's work is the essence of comedy, demanding acceptance of outrageous postulates within which the rest of the action is orderly and blandly logical. If the world seems dangerously irrational, the stage counters it by persuading us that reason will not fail in the most trying circumstances. If life is cruel, the stage sublimates our fears by showing that no one is really hurt in the end by the rack in the Tower, the torture chamber with illustrated papers in the waiting room, the threat of punishment 'humorous but lingering'. If society feels guilty about the position of women and challenged by the call for emancipation, it is comforting to laugh at Katisha. Gilbert showed his contemporaries the flaws in their structure by exaggerating them in other settings, and they loved him for it. To the stage he gave better plot construction, a disciplined sense of comedy, and a new liveliness of comic dialogue.

These were also the gifts of Oscar Wilde (1854–1900), who

made the world of comedy his own escape from the tension of reality. Few today are interested in the early *Vera* (1880) and *The Duchess of Padua* (1883); not until *Lady Windermere's Fan* (1892) did he reveal himself as a dramatist not to be ignored. Here and in *A Woman of No Importance* (1893) a slight and conventional plot is rescued by brilliant dialogue. There is more ingenuity in *An Ideal Husband* (1895), but his full genius was shown in *The Importance of Being Earnest* (1895). Now the Victorian capacity for dramatic extravagance and escapism were joined with the elegant sophistication of Congreve, made more decorous but not stifled by contemporary morality. Its first night drew all fashionable London, despite the worst snowstorm for many years, and the storm that soon devastated Wilde's own life has not dimmed its brilliance. Not even Gilbert had so fully mastered the theatre's need for speech that is economical, formal, a little exaggerated, yet never losing touch with everyday social communication.

The comedies of Wilde have little hint of the darker appetites which were already making him notorious and had caused the Lord Chamberlain to suppress *Salome* (1892) where they seemed to verge on sacrilege. In this last decade of the century, the theatre seemed to be celebrating its new freedom from repression and mediocrity. The actor's profession was respectable at last, crowned by Irving's knighthood in 1895. With the coming of more serious themes in drama, aided by the gradual extension of copyright protection, plays were being increasingly published and read as well as acted, and criticism was giving attention to the text as well as the presentation. It was the period of new dramatic criticism, of Clement Scott, A. B. Walkley and William Archer. Dramatic criticism gave employment to Archer's Irish protégé George Bernard Shaw, himself beginning to get a name for writing plays on subjects distasteful to the censor. By 1901 there were thirteen theatres and forty-two music halls licensed by the LCC, and forty-four theatres in the whole metropolitan area.[1] Serious actors and music-hall artists alike were happy to play at outlying theatres: the drama had won the approval of the suburbs at last.

The paradoxes of late Victorianism appear nowhere more strongly than in the theatre. Side by side with the new realism

[1] A. E. Wilson, *Edwardian Theatre* (London, 1951), p. 22.

and the witty comedies of manners, the old melodramatic tradition lingered in plays like *The Prisoner of Zenda* (1896), and the old demand for sensation and spectacle was met with *The Sign of the Cross* (1895). *Salome* might be banned, but there was approval for the macabre elements in Irving's famous role in *The Bells* and the sinister para-psychology in the stage adaptation of *Trilby*. Shakespeare was no longer raided as material for extravaganza, but elaborate staging and realistic effects often meant mutilated texts and distorted interpretations. The old and once necessary tradition of musical interludes meant that 'a polka or a quadrille is inflicted on you between each act of *Hamlet* or *Othello*'.[1] However, William Poel was working hard with his Elizabethan Stage Society to re-establish fast-moving productions on an open stage in Elizabethan dress and with sixteenth-century music. Victorian prejudices sometimes conflicted with his archæological ideals, and he made cuts where his moral sense was offended. Yet a new understanding of the Elizabethan stage was to influence the writing as well as the production of plays in the next generation; 'directors like Poel, and Granville-Barker himself, climbed out of the drawing-room on Shakespeare's back'.[2]

The drama was once again versatile and vital enough to be a significant reflection of society, and the harvest of Victorian progress was reaped in the following century. It is tempting to overrate the achievement of the best Victorian dramatists by contrast with what had gone before. To see the drama in perspective, it is necessary to remember what the period produced in the novel, and also that by the end of the century other countries had the work of Ibsen, Strindberg, Chekhov and Turgenev. In the theatre, as in many other ways, the greatness of the Victorians was shown in overcoming problems which they had partly inherited and partly created.

[1] 'Max O'Rell' (Paul Blouet), *John Bull and his Island* (London, N. D. c. 1885), p. 174.
[2] Laurence Kitchin, *Drama in the Sixties* (London, 1966), p. 80.

25

Writers and Opinions

There is a twofold danger in seeking the expression of social history in literature. The first is that we may assume 'society' to be intellectually and emotionally homogeneous, even though it is manifestly varied in its conditions. The second is the failure to realize that writers do not necessarily come from the section of society which is most strongly influencing the course of events. Yet the search is not in vain; we can know very little of a past age beyond those things which were made articulate and recorded in writing. A writer is not a god, but an individual bounded by particularities of time and space, subject to the same pressures as his contemporaries. It is reasonable to suppose that themes which frequently recur in the literature of a period will reflect the general presuppositions of that period. The reverse may not be true: the argument from silence is seldom satisfactory.

Literary criticism based on social revelation may turn out to be bad criticism from other points of view. Carried to extremes, it would value the official document more than the personal fantasy. It is important to maintain one's criteria of literary art, even while praising or deploring the extent to which a writer reveals his period. The main purpose of this book has meant that some writers have been given more scanty treatment than their qualities might deserve and that some who have minor delights of their own have been omitted. However, the injustice may not be too great, since the major writers of the Victorian age mostly have their significance in the history of social life and ideas. The greater number of them show and express a strong awareness of their times and a desire that the connection between literature and life should be close.

The status of the writer rose to new heights during the period, and his confidence rose with it. Troubled as they might be by the world around them, most of the writers felt moved to utter their ideas with authority, yet with respect for the public. The relationship between writer and reader was closer in the early and middle part of the century than it has been before or since. The economic conditions were propitious, the circulation of books and periodicals steadily increased, most of the writers came from the class which was providing most of the readers. Ironically, the new detachment of the writer which becomes apparent towards the end of the century was due partly to the great spread of the reading public and the trivial matter which was produced to satisfy it. With certain exceptions, the later Victorian writers reached more limited sections of society. This was true in the twentieth century until the pressures of war brought new cohesion, and it is sadly true again today.

Throughout the period, the novel is dominant among the literary forms. The existence of a comparatively few outstanding books has tended to give the 'Victorian novel' an image which it does not altogether deserve. Even the best novelists wrote some inferior stuff and the number of second-rate or worse practitioners is staggering. Who now finds any attraction in F. H. Burnett, Augusta Noel, George Fleming, E. M. Archer, Amy Dunsmuir, Ellice Hopkins, Katherine Cooper?[1] The novel became the melting-pot of idleness and slight talent as well as genius, of fanatical theories as well as human insight. Scarcely any social reform did not throw up a novel or two in the preceding agitation.

We have seen how and why the drama failed to take a high place in the literature of the time. Poetry, though highly respected and even bought in the bookshops, did not keep the supreme place which the Romantics had given it. The Victorian image of the writer is not that of the poet. Carlyle could see the poet as one archetype of the Hero, but society as a whole saw him as only one among many types of artist. The change is reflected in linguistic usage: the general sense of creativity and imagination which Shelley could give to the word *poet* was linked before the end of the century with the word *artist*.[2]

---

[1] These names are taken at random from the advertisements appended to Macmillan's 1883 edition of *John Inglesant*. Every major publisher of novels yields lists of forgotten names.

[2] L. L. Schucking, *The Sociology of Literary Taste* (London, 1944), p. 30.

The Victorian poet was often most respected when his manner was most public and vatic: when he was giving out a 'message' and was comprehensible by minds accustomed to extensive novel-reading. The growing retreat into aggressive aestheticism perhaps owed something to this popular appetite. On the other hand, there was a co-existent feeling that poetry was essentially light in manner and trivial in content, a passing fancy not to be taken seriously. Both the portentous tone and the deliberate evasion of seriousness are traceable to aspects of Romanticism; the great Romantics produced no true disciples, though most of the important Victorian poets started writing under the clear influence of Keats and Shelley.

The novelists were more adventurous, more willing to break new ground in manner as well as subject. From early distrust and even hostility in some quarters, the novel came to command serious respect. There was a new concern about what the novel could and should be like, a preoccupation with fiction as a craft. The concern does not start with Henry James, important though his influence undoubtedly was, but is already clear in the statements of novelists and reviewers in the first decade of our period. No poet fully expressed even one aspect of the age, though many made brave efforts to do so. The novelists sometimes expressed ideas only too well and became turgid in the process; the minor Victorian novel is often a bloodsucker, gorged to bursting with other men's ideas.

Nevertheless, the major novelists have left us a valuable record even when they were not specifically conveying propaganda or theories. Well before the end of the eighteenth century, the novelists were already countering adverse criticism of their art by claiming to reflect the manners of society and to inculcate true morality. Their apologias presuppose a fairly stable and depictable society, but the Victorians were often concerned to discover society before describing it. The sense of transition and insecurity gave them greater awareness. They too wanted to know what it was all about, and they sometimes used the novel to work out their own understanding. The result gave them immediacy and sympathy with their readers but often produced untidy and ill-planned books.

The writers did not cheerfully give themselves up to an orgy of speculation. There is detectable in most Victorian writers a determination not to give in and be submerged under the weight of theories. It was an age full of ideas and counter-ideas; the writers recognized the danger to their artistic integrity. Indeed, the modern reader's occasional irritation with the Victorians is not so often caused by their crusading zeal. Rather is there a sense of negativism, of being against things more than for them, of rejecting ideas which are being accepted by the nation in general. The most fervent writers rise to their greatest rhetorical heights when they are refuting some current belief but fall into pious generalities when they come to offer their own alternative. This is true of Carlyle and Dickens and those who wrote at the same time; less true in the following generation.

For many the pressures of the age led not to defiance but to retreat. Various ways in which great minds found the life around them unsatisfactory can be seen in the Oxford Movement, the Pre-Raphaelite Brotherhood and the extremes of aestheticism. Some put their faith in art, others in science; some shut out the world by a closed-circle religion, others by an equally closed humanism. Some, like Lewis Carroll and Edward Lear, created a world of fantasy where fears could be projected into impossible creatures, made safe because they had been formed from imagination. Yet it was not an age of obvious neurotic manifestation nor was it so strongly shadowed by the dread of madness as the eighteenth century had been. Those whose several retreats show their inward lack of adjustment were often the most calm and conformist in their outward lives. Eccentricity of behaviour found less tolerance in the late-Victorian period than it had in the Regency, but eccentricity of thought and opinion found more.

Whether battling or retreating, the major writers were in some way critical of their age. Some uttered open denunciations; others, like Trollope, expressed apparent satisfaction but let traces of distress slip through. A great myth of the Victorian spirit was built up in the first quarter of the twentieth century by such as Lytton Strachey. It is a myth of complacency, outward piety, indifference to suffering that is not seen, complete satisfaction that all is for the best in the best of all possible worlds. It is a myth based to some extent on recorded reality, but the interesting thing is that it was seen, stated and attacked by most of those Victorian writers whose names we now remember.

What, more specifically, did they attack? In the first years of the period they set out to denounce, especially through the novel, callous attitudes to the sufferings of the poor. In that age of economic upheaval, the victims who won most literary sympathy were the industrial workers; the grim lot of the agricultural labourer was not treated nearly so often. The work of the 'Condition of England' writers shows a new compassion and a new sense of social responsibility: the more significant since it was aroused by evils which had existed for some time and were in fact beginning to retreat. The sufferers were made known and immortalized, though the even more pathetic victims of the previous generation had found few voices to speak up for them. By the time yet another generation had grown up, the concern of literature was more for their mental than their physical deprivation. The appalling conditions of work and housing which endured in the sixties and seventies were more effectively exposed by the non-literary writer, the researcher with his notebook and tables of statistics, while the novelists were lamenting the stifled ambitions and starving intellects of the poor.

Even the most reforming writers were troubled by fears of revolt and class-warfare. In the imaginative writers the sense of class-distinction is generally implicit and unquestioned. While they were moved by extreme poverty, they were distrustful of 'levelling' tendencies. Few indeed said as much in so many words, but they were not far from Herbert Spencer in his views on the proposal to restrict absolute copyright to one year. The consequent flow of early cheap editions would, he thought, mean that:

> People with smaller amounts of money shall have no disadvantages from their smaller amounts of money. It is communistic practically: it is simply equalizing the advantages of wealth and poverty.[1]

The great mass of the poor still held something of the menace which the 'mob' had held in the eighteenth century, a menace increased by the shadow of Malthus. There was the fear that established society and its decencies would be overwhelmed in

[1] Quoted in R. D. Altick, *The English Common Reader* (Chicago, 1957), p. 311.

a flood of faceless, uncontrollable people. As late as 1890, T. H. Huxley was warning that:

> The population question is the real riddle of the sphinx, to which no political Oedipus has as yet found the answer. In view of the ravages of the terrible monster over-multiplication, all other riddles sink into insignificance.

The only hope still seemed to lie in the responsible and informed individual. The hatred of Benthamite Utilitarianism shown by most of the important writers in the early part of the period was based largely on its apparent denial of the individual. The theories of political economy seemed bent towards disaster because they made people grey, shadowy statistical units. Both compassion and anxiety combined in the outbursts against the *laissez-faire* attitude in all aspects of industry, business and trade. Ironically, those attitudes are so strongly associated today with the period largely because the writers denounced them.

We have seen how the power of money became a symbol in the work of writers very different in other ways: in Dickens and Trollope, in Lytton and Eliot. The financier was as sinister to many serious novelists as to the later writers of melodrama. The real economic issue of capital and labour was less often understood and seldom fully examined, though Ruskin and Morris among others worked past the symbol to the reality. Here again the negative tone seems very strong, as the call for a general change of heart takes precedence over specific plans for the changing of society.

From the sixties, the rights and duties of the individual tend to become detached in literature from his membership of the total society. There is a revival of the Romantic spirit, a new emotionalism that calls almost hysterically for attention to the wonder of human life. As real frontiers were opened by exploration, so the possibilities of mental pioneering came to be the concern of literature. There was a sense that the great social problems had been solved and that the new age was bringing new individual challenges. Some, indeed, continued to grapple with the problems of society as a whole: others found only alienation and despair as mankind was subjected to new pressures.

---

[1] 'On the Natural Inequality of Man', in *The Nineteenth Century*, January 1890.

As religion became less the social norm, as it became clearer that British people were not automatically churchgoing Christians, so the problems of faith became more overtly literary themes. Both Charlotte M. Yonge and George Eliot stress the importance of individual conduct, personal responsibility for actions and their consequences. The agnostics shared and even sometimes outdid the moral earnestness of thinking Christians. As religion was seen to be losing its power as a national institution, Malthusian and related fears became stronger. Was the Beast in Man about to be unleashed?

The Beast lurked particularly under fears about sex. The inhibitions which society laid on the frank portrayal of sexual problems have been noted as they affected literature. There is an imbalance in the great Victorian novels as a result, but the writers did not submit entirely. Their repressions sometimes broke through in unconscious symbolism, but they also managed to live within the situation and to say what they wanted to say without offending too many readers. How masterly is the tact with which Thackeray deals with the question of Becky Sharp's adultery, and George Eliot with Casaubon's impotence. Yet even restraint did not always meet approval: 'every important novelist of the period [1850–70] ... was attacked, most novelists more than once, for lowering the standard of "purity" of the English novel.'[1] In the later part of the century, controversy raged around the new freedom to discuss sexual matters, whether it was the legality of publicizing birth-control or the novels of those who claimed to follow French Naturalism.

The anxiety about sex did not, of course, appear only in direct treatment or obvious evasion. The threat to innocence in a hostile and evil world is a common theme and has sexual origins. It is frequent in Dickens, with Oliver Twist, Pip, Nell, Little Dorrit and others, it appears in *The Water Babies* and, less frighteningly but clearly, in the *Alice* books. Growing to maturity seems to be dangerous, liable to involve a sullying of purity. The happiest are those who come through to new knowledge but remain essentially children. Like Alice, they cross the battlefield of the chess-board and join the grown-up

[1] Richard Stang, *The Theory of the Novel in England 1850–1870* (London, 1959), p. 217.

Queens, but waking proves that 'it really *was* a kitten after all'.

Although their heroines might be monuments of purity, the writers did not generally succumb to the prevailing view of the woman as a strange idol with no acknowledged existence above the ears or below the waist. They worried about the problem of the unemployed spinster and the challenge of increasing emancipation. Many of them, especially the male writers, suffered a tension between the ideal of untutored innocence and a realistic concern for the situation. The power of women in social relationships is more strongly expressed in the latter part of the century: Wells was not revolutionary in his creation of Ann Veronica.

In one way, however, literature generally acquiesces in the popular outlook. The writers are seldom internationally-minded; they share the mingled pity, scorn and amusement with which Englishmen as a whole regarded other nations. There are of course outstanding exceptions, such as Carlyle's admiration for Germany and Arnold's for France. Dickens makes fun of Podsnap's insularity but does not portray convincing foreigners. Even the rebels and reformers usually concentrated on the national situation, remained loyal to the idea of constitutional monarchy and spent most of their lives at home. From Carlyle to Kipling, there are appeals to the British spirit, appeals for a national revival and a rediscovery of past greatness. The belief that Britain had a special role to play, in example and leadership, which had grown strong during the Napoleonic years, did not often falter. There was general agreement with Thomas Arnold:

> I do not wish to lose . . . all those thousand ties, so noble and so sacred and so dear, which bind us to our country, as she was and as she is, with all her imperfections and difficulties.[1]

Patriotism was often backed by the appeal to history and tradition, which we have seen to be common and important throughout the period. The idea of history played its part in the revival of Romantic attitudes mentioned above. The ancient world, as interpreted by the younger Romantics, was explored

[1] Letter to Carlyle on Arnold's proposal to form a society to 'collect information as to every point in the condition of the poor throughout the kingdom' (1840). Printed in *English Letters of the Nineteenth Century*, ed. James Aitken (Harmondsworth, 1946), p. 165.

again by Tennyson and Browning and, in different vein, by Swinburne. The Middle Ages, variously understood or misunderstood, became the exemplar of all that was good. Carlyle held up the medieval situation to shame the present; so did Ruskin and Morris. The followers of the Tractarians, whose first theological appeal had been to primitive Christianity, looked to the medieval Church for interpretation and practice. In architecture the 'battle of the styles' was joined: Gothicist and classicist disputed with almost theological fervour, and indeed there were some devotees of the medieval style who regarded classical churches like those of Hawksmoor and Inwood as almost pagan.

It would be as true as generalizations can be to say that the great Victorian writers looked back rather than forwards. Though they were often deeply perceptive about current events and had flashes of prophetic insight, they tended to take the old-fashioned position in intellectual matters. Their view of history was Elizabethan in drawing lessons from the past for the edification of the present: whether to emulate or to shun, the purpose of learning about history seemed to be the pointing of morals. This was far from the new scientism in historiography which percolated from Germany to later Victorian historians like Stubbs, Freeman and J. R. Green. Perhaps the new method seemed to stultify the imagination and lead to the cold determinism of science itself.

Certainly the scientific outlook found little imaginative expression, though there were a number of writers interested in scientific speculation and laudatory of the results of applied science. The whole scientific method, however, seemed to be touched by the same disregard of the individual as Benthamism was. It sought to put people into categories like other observable phenomena, to classify and label them, to express the particular in terms of the general. Hence the distrust of many of the systematic means of reform which were being canvassed during the century, the refusal to believe that men and women could be improved by outside pressures even in the shape of higher education and the development of reason. There was a spirit in the land which most of the writers feared and disliked. It was a spirit of planning, systematizing and directing; in various ways it seemed incarnate in Bentham and Ricardo, in

Marx and Darwin, in the Poor Law Commission and the Board of Education. It seemed inimical to the free and responsible choice of the individual and to the exercise of the imagination which F. D. Maurice described as 'A terrible object of the dread, the hatred and hostility of the mistresses of establishments and the governesses of young ladies'.[1]

In a sense, then, the outlook of Victorian literature tends towards reaction, in the way that some outstanding movements of the period like Chartism and the Oxford Movement were reactionary. Like them in another way, there was an understanding of deeper aspects of the contemporary scene and the ability to correct values that had fallen out of balance. Nor is it reaction in the way commonly associated with oppression and autocracy in the political sense, but a burning desire to reassert the worth of the individual which seemed to be in danger of extinction. The writers were prepared to tackle great issues while scorning the specialization of knowledge which was in fact making the modern state emerge without too much bruising.

Yet though they deplored much in their time, they shared something of the prevailing optimism that wrongs could be righted. The moments of deep existential terror are rare, and come perhaps in brief revelations disguised as fantasy.[2] Deep concern need not be paralysing anxiety, and moral earnestness need not be plunged in gloom. That, perhaps, is one of the things that modern society can still learn from the Victorians.

[1] Quoted in R. L. Archer, *Secondary Education in the Nineteenth Century* (Cambridge, 1921), p. 232.

[2] For example, 'the wood where things have no names' in *Through the Looking Glass*. See also the fates of various characters in Edward Lear's verse, such as that exemplar of *angst* the Old Man of Cape Horn,

> Who wished he had never been born;
> So he sat on a chair
> Till he died of despair,
> That dolorous man of Cape Horn.

Bibliography

In order to provide a more serviceable reading-list, attention has been given mainly to fairly recent works.

The reader who wishes to study any aspects of the subject in more detail will find all that he needs in the bibliographies cited below.

Bibliographies

BATESON, F. W., ed., *Cambridge Bibliography of English Literature* (Cambridge, 1940), Vol. 3.

EHRSAM, T. G., and DEILY, R. H., *Bibliographies of Twelve Victorian Authors* (New York, 1936).

FAVERTY, F. E., *et al.*, *The Victorian Poets: a Guide to Research* (Cambridge, Mass., 1956).

SADLEIR, M., *Nineteenth Century Fiction: a Bibliographical Record* (London, 1951).

STEVENSON, L., *Victorian Fiction: a Guide to Research* (Cambridge, Mass., 1964).

TEMPLEMAN, W. D., *Bibliographies of Studies in Victorian Literature 1932–44* (Urbana, 1945).

WATSON, G., ed., *Cambridge Bibliography of English Literature: Supplement* (Cambridge, 1957).

The Year's Work in English Studies (London, annually since 1919).

General Studies of Victorian Literature

(*Books marked with an asterisk contain extensive bibliographies*)

BAKER, J. E., ed., *The Re-interpretation of Victorian Literature* (Princeton, 1950).

*BATHO, E., and DOBREE, B., *The Victorians and After* (London, 1938).

BUCKLEY, J. H., *The Victorian Temper* (London, 1952).

CECIL, D., *Early Victorian Novelists* (London, 1934).

CHURCHILL, R. C., *English Literature of the Nineteenth Century* (London, 1951).

COOKE, J. D., and STEVENSON, L., *English Literature of the Victorian Period* (New York, 1949).

DAVIS, H., ed., *Nineteenth Century Studies* (Ithaca, New York, 1940).

EVANS, B. I., *English Poetry in the Later Nineteenth Century* (London, 1933).

*FORD, B., ed., *From Dickens to Hardy* (Harmondsworth, 1958).

GOODE, H. L., *Tradition and Tolerance in Nineteenth-Century Fiction* (London, 1966).

GRIERSON, H. J. C., *Lyrical Poetry from Blake to Hardy* (London, 1928).

HUDSON, W. H., *A Short History of English Literature in the Nineteenth Century* (London, 1918).

JOHNSON, E. D. H., *The Alien Vision of Victorian Poetry* (Princeton, 1952).

KNOEPFLMACHER, U. C., *Religious Humanism and the Victorian Novel* (Princeton, 1965).

LEAVIS, F. R., *New Bearings in English Poetry* (London, 1932).
The Great Tradition (London, 1948).

MILLER, G. M., *English Literature: Victorian Period* (New York, rev. ed. 1933).

PINTO, V. de S., *Crisis in English Poetry* (London, 1951).

PRAZ, M., *The Hero in Eclipse in Victorian Fiction* (Oxford, 1956).

ROUTH, H. V., *Towards the Twentieth Century* (London, 1937).

STANG, R., *The Theory of the Novel in England* (London, 1959).

THOMSON, P., *The Victorian Heroine* (Oxford, 1956).

TILLOTSON, G. and K., *Mid-Victorian Studies* (London, 1965).

TILLOTSON, K., *Novels of the Eighteen Forties* (Oxford, 1954).

VINES, S., *A Hundred Years of English Literature* (London, 1950).

WARD, A. W., and WALLER, A. R., eds., *Cambridge History of English Literature* (Cambridge, 1915), Vols. 13 and 14.

WARREN, S. H., *English Poetic Theory 1835–1865* (Oxford, 1950).

WILLEY, B., *Nineteenth Century Studies* (London, 1949).

The Victorian Age

ASHWORTH, W., *English Economic History 1800–1870* (London, 1960).

BERNAL, J. D., *Science and Industry in the Nineteenth Century* (London, 1953).

BRIGGS, A., ed., *Chartist Studies* (London, 1959).
Victorian Cities (London, 1963).
Victorian People (London, 1954).

BROOKE, I., and LAVER, J., *English Costume in the Nineteenth Century* (London, 1947).

BUTLER, J. R. M., *A History of England 1815–1918* (London, 1928).

The Victorian Debate

COURT, W. H. B., *A Concise Economic History of Britain from 1750* (Cambridge, 1954). *British Economic History 1870–1914* (Cambridge, 1965).

ENSOR, R. C. K., *England 1870–1914* (Oxford, 1935).

FINER, S. E., *The Life and Times of Sir Edwin Chadwick* (London, 1952).

FRAZER, W. M., *A History of English Public Health 1834–1939* (London, 1950).

GREGG, P., *A Social and Economic History of Britain 1760–1950* (London, 1950).

HALÉVY, E., *A History of the English People 1815–1914* (London, rev. ed. 1951).

HOBSBAWN, E. J., *The Age of Revolution* (London, 1962).

KITSON CLARK, G., *The Making of Victorian England* (London, 1962).

LICHTEN, F., *Decorative Arts of Victoria's Era* (New York, 1950).

MACOBY, S., *English Radicalism 1832–1914* (London, 1935–53), 3 vols.

MATHER, F. C., *Chartism* (London, 1965).

PEVSNER, N., *High Victorian Design* (London, 1951).

SINGER, C., *A Short History of Science in the Nineteenth Century* (London, 1941).

SMELLIE, K. B., *A Hundred Years of British Government* (London, rev. ed. 1951).

THOMSON, D., *England in the Nineteenth Century* (Harmondsworth, 1950).

TREVELYAN, G. M., *English Social History* (London, 1944).

WOOD, A., *Nineteenth-Century Britain* (London, 1960).

WOODWARD, E. L., *The Age of Reform 1815–1870* (Oxford, 1934).

YOUNG, G. M., ed., *Early Victorian England* (Oxford, 1934).

Victorian Ideas

BRINTON, C., *English Political Thought in the Nineteenth Century* (London, 1933).

BUCKLEY, J. H., *The Victorian Temper* (London, 1952).

COCKSHUT, A. O. J., ed., *Religious Controversies of the Nineteenth Century* (London, 1966).

ELLIOTT-BINNS, L. E., *English Thought 1860–1900; the Theological Aspect* (London, 1956).

HALÉVY, E., *The Growth of Philosophic Radicalism* (London, rev. ed. 1949).

HOLLOWAY, J., *The Victorian Sage* (London, 1966).

HOUGHTON, W. E., *The Victorian Frame of Mind* (Yale, 1957).

Ideas and Beliefs of the Victorians, BBC talks, (London, 1949).

KELLETT, E. E., *Religion and Life in the Early Victorian Age* (London, 1938).
KROOK, D., *Three Traditions of Moral Thought* (Cambridge, 1959).
MEAD, G. H., *Movements of Thought in the Nineteenth Century* (Chicago, 1936).
METZ, R., *A Hundred Years of British Philosophy* (London, 1938).
PETRIE, C., *The Victorians* (London, 1960).
ROSENBAUM, R. A., *Earnest Victorians* (London, 1961).
SMITH, K., *The Malthusian Controversy* (London, 1951).
SOMERVELL, D. C., *English Thought in the Nineteenth Century* (London, 1950).

Books and Readers

ALTICK, R. D., *The English Common Reader 1800–1900* (Chicago, 1957).
BIRCHENOUGH, C., *History of Elementary Education in England and Wales from 1800* (London, 1938).
BOAS, L. S., *Women's Education Begins* (London, 1938).
CRUSE, A., *The Victorians and their Books* (London, 1935).
GETTMAN, R. A., *A Victorian Publisher* (Cambridge, 1960).
HARRISON, J. F. C., *Learning and Living, 1790–1960* (London, 1961).
JAMES, L., *Fiction for the Working Man 1830–1860* (London, 1963).
LEAVIS, Q. D., *Fiction and the Reading Public* (London, 1932).
SMITH, J. W. A., *The Birth of Modern Education* (London, 1954).

Magazines and Periodicals

ADRIAN, A. A., *Mark Lemon, first editor of Punch* (London, 1966).
BEVINGTON, M. M., *The Saturday Review 1855–68* (New York, 1941).
CASFORD, E. L., *The Magazines of the 1890's* (Eugene, Oregon, 1929).
EVERETT, E. M., *The Party of Humanity: the Fortnightly Review* (Chapel Hill, 1939).
GRAHAM, W., *English Literary Periodicals* (New York, 1930).
Tory Criticism in the Quarterly Review (New York, 1921).
The History of The Times (London, 1935–52).
MARCHAND, L. A., *The Athenaeum: a Mirror of Victorian Culture* (Chapel Hill, 1940).
MORISON, S., *The English Newspaper* (Cambridge, 1932).
NESBIT, G. L., *Benthamite Reviewing* (New York, 1934).
ROBERTSON SCOTT, J. W., *The Story of the Pall Mall Gazette* (London, 1950).
THOMAS, W. B., *The Story of the Spectator* (London, 1928).
THRALL, M., *Rebellious Fraser's* (New York, 1934).

The Victorian Debate

TILLOTSON, G., *Criticism in the Nineteenth Century* (London, 1951).
WELLEK, R., *A History of Modern Criticism* (London, 1955).

Thomas Carlyle

BRYANT, A., *Macaulay* (London, 1932).
GOOCH, G. P., *History and Historians in the Nineteenth Century* (London, rev. ed. 1952).
HOLME, T., *The Carlyles at Home* (Oxford, 1965).
LEHMANN, B. L., *Carlyle's Theory of the Hero* (Durham, N. Carolina, 1928).
MARRIOTT, J., *English History in English Fiction* (London, 1940).
NEFF, E., *Carlyle* (New York, 1932).
ROE, F. W., *Social Philosophy of Carlyle and Ruskin* (New York, 1921).
SYMONS, J., *Thomas Carlyle* (London, 1952).
TENNYSON, G. B., *Sartor called Resartus* (Princeton, 1965).
WOODWARD, E. L., *British Historians* (London, 1943).
YOUNG, L. M., *Carlyle and the Art of History* (Philadelphia, 1939).

The Progress of the Novel

COOPER, L., *R. S. Surtees* (London, 1952).
DALZIEL, M., *Popular Fiction a Hundred Years Ago* (London, 1957).
DAVIES, R., *A Voice from the Attic* (New York, 1960).
ELLIS, S. M., *The Solitary Horseman* [G. P. R. James] (London, 1927).
William Harrison Ainsworth and his Friends (London, 1911).
HOLLINGSWORTH, K., *The Newgate Novel 1830–1847* (Detroit, 1963).
LYTTON, Earl of, *Bulwer-Lytton* (London, 1948).
ROSA, M. W., *The Silver Fork School* (New York, 1936).
WARNER, O., *Captain Marryat: A Rediscovery* (London, 1953).

Dickens

BUTT, J., and TILLOTSON, K., *Dickens at Work* (London, 1957).
COCKSHUT, A. O. J., *The Imagination of Charles Dickens* (London, 1961).
COLLINS, P., *Dickens and Crime* (London, 1962).
Dickens and Education (London, 1963).
CRUIKSHANK, R. J., *Dickens and Early Victorian England* (London, 1949).
ENGEL, M., *The Maturity of Dickens* (Oxford, 1959).
FIELDING, K. J., *Charles Dickens: A Critical Introduction* (London, new ed. 1964).
GARIS, R., *The Dickens Theatre* (Oxford, 1965).

GROSS, J. and PEARSON, G., eds., *Dickens and the Twentieth Century* (London, 1962).

HOUSE, H., *The Dickens World* (London, 1941).

JACKSON, T. A., *Charles Dickens: The Progress of a Radical* (London, 1937).

MARCUS, S., *Dickens from Pickwick to Dombey* (New York, 1965).

MILLER, J. H., *Dickens: The World of his Novels* (New York, 1958).

POPE-HENNESSY, U., *Charles Dickens* (London, 1945).

STOEHR, T., *Dickens: The Dreamer's Stance* (Oxford, 1966).

The Social and Political Novel

ALLOTT, M., *Elizabeth Gaskell* (London, 1960).

BLAKE, R., *Disraeli* (London, 1966).

CAZAMIAN, L., *Le Roman Social en Angleterre 1830–1850* (Paris, new ed. 1935).

HALDANE, E., *Mrs Gaskell and her Friends* (London, 1930).

HOPKINS, A. B., *Elizabeth Gaskell: Her Life and Work* (London, 1952).

KENDALL, G., *Charles Kingsley and his Ideas* (London, 1947).

MARMO, M., *The Social Novel of Kingsley* (Salerno, 1937).

MARTIN, R. B., *The Dust of Combat* (London, 1960).

MASEFIELD, M., *Peacocks and Primroses: A Study of Disraeli's Novels* (London, 1953).

POLLARD, A., *Mrs Gaskell: Novelist and Biographer* (Manchester, 1966).

POPE-HENNESSY, U., *Canon Charles Kingsley* (London, 1948).

WRIGHT, E., *Mrs Gaskell: The Basis for Reassessment* (London, 1965).

Thackeray

DODDS, J. W., *Thackeray: A Critical Portrait* (New York, 1941).

ENNIS, L., *Thackeray, the Sentimental Cynic* (Evanston, 1951).

GREIG, J. Y. T., *Thackeray: A Reconsideration* (Oxford, 1950).

LOOFBOUROW, J., *Thackeray and the Form of Fiction* (Princeton, 1964).

RAY, G. N., *Thackeray* (New York, 1955–8).

STEVENSON, L., *The Showman of Vanity Fair* (New York, 1947).

TILLOTSON, G., *Thackeray the Novelist* (Cambridge, 1954).

The Brontës

DRY, F. S., *The Sources of Wuthering Heights* (Cambridge, 1937).

EWBANK, I-S., *Their Proper Sphere* (London, 1966).

GERIN, W., *Anne Brontë* (London, 1959).

The Victorian Debate

HANSON, L. and E. M., *The Four Brontës* (Oxford, 1949).
HINKLEY, L. L., *The Brontës* (London, 1947).
MARTIN, R. B., *The Accents of Persuasion* (London, 1966).
RATCHFORD, F., *The Brontës' Web of Childhood* (New York, 1941).
WISE, T. J., and SYMINGTON, J. A., *The Brontës* (Oxford, 1932).

Realism and Sensation

BIGLAND, E., *Ouida, the Passionate Victorian* (London, 1950).
BURNS, W., *Charles Reade* (New York, 1961).
DAVIS, N. P., *Wilkie Collins* (Urbana, 1956).
ELWIN, M., *Charles Reade* (London, 1931).
PHILLIPS, W. C., *Dickens, Reade and Collins: Sensation Novelists* (New York, 1919).
ROBINSON, K., *Wilkie Collins* (London, 1951).

Trollope

BOOTH, B. A., *Anthony Trollope* (Bloomington, 1958).
BOWEN, E., *Trollope: A New Judgement* (Oxford, 1946).
BROWN, B. C., *Anthony Trollope* (London, 1950).
COCKSHUT, A. O. J., *Anthony Trollope* (London, 1955).
SADLEIR, M., *Trollope: A Commentary* (London, rev. ed. 1945).
STEBBINS, L. P. and R. P., *The Trollopes: The Chronicle of a Writing Family* (New York, 1945).

Tennyson and Browning

BAUM, P. F., *Tennyson Sixty Years After* (London, 1949).
COHEN, J. M., *Robert Browning* (London, 1952).
DAVIES, H. S., *Browning and the Modern Novel* (Hull, 1962).
DREW, P., ed., *Robert Browning* (London, 1966).
DUCKWORTH, F. G. R., *Browning: Background and Conflict* (London, 1931).
DUFFIN, H. C., *Amphibian: A Reconsideration of Browning* (London, 1956).
KILLHAM, J., ed., *Critical Essays on the Poetry of Tennyson* (London, 1960).
Tennyson and 'The Princess': Reflections of an Age (London, 1958).
MARTIN, H., *The Faith of Robert Browning* (London, 1963).
SHANNON, E. F., *Tennyson and the Reviewers* (Oxford, 1952).
SMITH, E. E., *The Two Voices: a Tennyson Study* (Lincoln, Nebraska, 1964).

Ruskin

CLARK, K., ed., *Ruskin Today* (London, 1964).

EVANS, J., *John Ruskin* (London, 1954).

HAGSTOTZ, H. B., *The Educational Theories of Ruskin* (Lincoln, Nebraska, 1942).

LADD, H., *The Victorian Morality of Art* (New York, 1932).

LEON, D., *Ruskin: The Great Victorian* (London, 1949).

LUTYENS, M., *Millais and the Ruskins* (London, 1967).

QUENNELL, P., *Ruskin* (London, 1949).

ROSENBERG, J. D., *The Darkening Glass* (London, 1963).

WHITEHOUSE, J. H., *Vindication of Ruskin* (London, 1950).

Society and Personal Responsibility

ALEXANDER, E., *Matthew Arnold and John Stuart Mill* (London, 1965).

ANSCHUTZ, R. P., *The Philosophy of J. S. Mill* (Oxford, 1953).

BAUM, P. F., *Ten Studies in the Poetry of Matthew Arnold* (Cambridge, 1958).

BRITTON, K. W., *Mill* (Harmondsworth, 1953).

CHAMBERS, E. K., *Matthew Arnold* (Oxford, 1947).

CONNELL, W. F., *The Educational Thought and Influence of Matthew Arnold* (London, 1950).

DUFFIN, H. C., *Arnold the Poet* (London, 1962).

GOTTFRIED, L., *Matthew Arnold and the Victorians* (London, 1963).

JAMES, D. G., *Matthew Arnold and the Decline of English Romanticism* (Oxford, 1961).

JUMP, J. D., *Matthew Arnold* (London, 1955).

MCCARTHY, P. J., *Matthew Arnold and the Three Classes* (New York, 1964).

ROBBINS, W., *The Ethical Idealism of Matthew Arnold* (London, 1959).

Escape through Art

ASHCROFT, T., *English Art and English Society* (London, 1936).

BOASE, T. S. R., *English Art 1800–1870* (Oxford, 1959).

CECIL, D., *Walter Pater* (Cambridge, 1955).

CHEW, S. C., *Swinburne* (Boston, 1929).

CHILD, R. C., *The Aesthetic of Pater* (New York, 1940).

DOUGHTY, O., *Dante Gabriel Rossetti* (London, 1957).

ECKHOFF, L., *The Aesthetic Movement* (Oslo, 1959).

FLEMING, G. H., *Rossetti and the Pre-Raphaelite Brotherhood* (London, 1967).

GAUNT, W., *The Aesthetic Adventure* (London, 1945).

GAUNT, W., *The Pre-Raphaelite Dream* (London, 1943).
HUBBARD, H., *A Hundred Years of British Painting 1851–1951* (London, 1951).
IRONSIDE, R., *Pre-Raphaelite Painters* (London, 1948).
JOHNSON, R. V., *Walter Pater* (Cambridge, 1962).
MASON, S., *Oscar Wilde: Art and Morality* (London, 1915).
NICOLSON, H., *Swinburne* (London, 1926).
PEARSON, H., *The Life of Oscar Wilde* (London, 1946).
The Man Whistler (London, 1952).
TINKER, C. B., *Painter and Poet* (Cambridge, Mass., 1938).
WELLAND, D. S. R., *The Pre-Raphaelites in Literature and Art* (London, 1953).
WINWAR, F., *The Rossettis and their Circle* (London, 1934).
Wilde and the Yellow Nineties (New York, 1940).

Socialism

ARNOT, R. P., *William Morris: The Man and the Myth* (London, 1964).
BEER, M., *A History of British Socialism* (London, 1920).
CLUTTON-BROCK, A., *William Morris: his Work and Influence* (London, 1914).
EVANS, B. I., *Morris and his Poetry* (London, 1925).
GLASIER, J. B., *William Morris and the Early Days of the Socialist Movement* (London, 1921).
MACKAIL, J. W., *The Life of William Morris* (Oxford, 1950).
RECKITT, M. B., *Maurice to Temple* (London, 1947).
THOMPSON, E. P., *Morris: Romantic to Revolutionary* (London, 1955).
WOOD, H. G., *Frederick Denison Maurice* (Cambridge, 1950).

The Catholic Revival

BAKER, J. E., *The Novel and the Oxford Movement* (Princeton, 1932).
BATTISCOMBE, G., *Charlotte Mary Yonge* (London, 1943).
BIRKHEAD, E., *Christina Rossetti and her Poetry* (London, 1930).
CAMERON, J. M., *John Henry Newman* (London, 1956).
CULLER, A. D., *The Imperial Intellect: a Study of Newman's Educational Ideal* (New Haven, 1955).
DAWSON, C., *The Spirit of the Oxford Movement* (London, 1933).
DOWNES, D. A., *Gerard Manley Hopkins: a Study of his Ignatian Spirit* (London, 1960).
FABER, G., *Oxford Apostles* (London, 1933).
GORCE, A. de la, *Francis Thompson* (London, 1933).
GARDNER, W. H., *Gerard Manley Hopkins* (London, rev. ed. 1958).
MAISON, M., *Search Your Soul, Eustace* (London, 1961).

NEWSOME, D. H., *The Parting of Friends* (London, 1966).
OLIVER, E. J., *Coventry Patmore* (London, 1956).
PETERS, W. A. M., *Gerard Manley Hopkins* (London, 1948).
REID, J. C., *The Mind and Art of Coventry Patmore* (London, 1957).
SAMBROOK, J., *A Poet Hidden* [R. W. Dixon] (London, 1962).
SAWTELL, M., *Christina Rossetti* (London, 1955).
TREVOR, M., *Newman* (London, 1962), 2 vols.
WRIGHT, T. H., *Francis Thompson and his Poetry* (London, 1927).

Religious Doubt and Revision

ANNAN, N., *Leslie Stephen* (London, 1961).
CHORLEY, K., *Arthur Hugh Clough* (Oxford, 1962).
MACCARTHY, D., *Leslie Stephen* (Cambridge, 1937).
MACLEAN, M., *Mark Rutherford* (London, 1955).
ROBBINS, W., *The Newman Brothers* (London, 1966).
STEWART, H. L., *Modernism, Past and Present* (London, 1932).
STOCK, I., *William Hale White* (London, 1956).
STONE, W., *Religion and Art of William Hale White* (Oxford, 1954).
WILLEY, B., *More Nineteenth-Century Studies: a Group of Honest Doubters* (London, 1956).

George Eliot

ALLEN, W., *George Eliot* (London, 1965).
BENNETT, J., *George Eliot: her Mind and her Art* (Cambridge, 1948).
HALDANE, E. S., *George Eliot and her Times* (London, 1927).
HANSON, L. and E., *Mary Ann Evans and George Eliot* (London, 1952).
HARDY, B., *The Novels of George Eliot* (London, 1959).
HARVEY, W. J., *The Art of George Eliot* (London, 1961).
KITCHELL, A. T., *George Lewes and George Eliot* (New York, 1934).
LERNER, L., and HOLMSTROM, J., *George Eliot and her Readers* (London, 1966).
PARIS, B. J., *Experiments in Life* (Detroit, 1965).
STANG, R., ed., *Discussions of George Eliot* (Boston, 1960).
THALE, J., *The Novels of George Eliot* (London, 1959).

Alienation and Despair

BROWN, M. J., *Moore: a Reconsideration* (Seattle, 1955).
BYRON, K. H., *The Pessimism of James Thomson (BV) in relation to his times* (The Hague, 1965).
COLLINS, M., *George Gissing* (Oxford, 1954).

DAICHES, D., *Stevenson and the Art of Fiction* (New York, 1951).
ELWIN, M., *The Strange Case of Stevenson* (London, 1950).
GETTMANN, R. A., *George Gissing and H. G. Wells* (London, 1961).
MEINTJES, J., *Olive Schreiner* (Johannesburg, 1965).
NOEL, J. C., *George Moore: l'homme et l'oeuvre* (Paris, 1966).
ROBINSON, O., *Angry Dust: the Poetry of Housman* (Boston, 1950).
SCHAEFFER, W. O., *James Thomson (BV): beyond 'The City'* (Cambridge, 1967).
STARKIE, E., *From Gautier to Eliot* (London, 1960).
WALKER, L. B., *Thomson: a Critical Study* (Ithaca, 1950).
WARD, A. C., *Gissing* (London, 1959).
WATSON, G. L., *Housman: a Divided Life* (London, 1957).

The Impact of Evolution

BURROW, J. W., *Evolution and Society* (Cambridge, 1966).
CLODD, E., *Thomas Huxley* (London, 1902).
COLE, G. D. H., *Butler and the Way of All Flesh* (London, 1947).
FURBANK, P. N., *Samuel Butler* (Cambridge, 1948).
HENKIN, L. J., *Darwinism in the English Novel* (New York, 1940).
HOLT, L. E., *Samuel Butler* (New York, 1964).
HUXLEY, L., *Charles Darwin* (London, 1921).
IRVINE, W., *Apes, Angels and Victorians* (London, 1955).
MUGGERIDGE, M., *Earnest Atheist* (London, 1956).
STEVAS, N. ST J., *Walter Bagehot: a Study of his Life and Thought* (London, 1960).
STEVENSON, L., *Darwin among the Poets* (London, 1932).
WILLEY, B., *Darwin and Butler* (London, 1960).
WILLIAMS-ELLIS, A., *Darwin's Moon* [A. R. Wallace] (London, 1966).

Meredith and Hardy

ABERCROMBIE, L., *Thomas Hardy: a Critical Study* (London, 1912).
BAILEY, E. J., *The Novels of George Meredith* (New York, 1910).
BOWRA, M., *The Lyrical Poetry of Hardy* (Nottingham, 1937).
BRAYBROOKE, P., *Thomas Hardy and his Philosophy* (London, 1928).
BROWN, D., *Thomas Hardy* (London, 1954).
CECIL, D., *Hardy the Novelist* (London, 1943).
DUFFIN, H. C., *Hardy* (London, rev. ed. 1937).
ELLIOTT, A. P., *Fatalism in the Works of Thomas Hardy* (Philadelphia, 1935).
PEEL, R., *The Creed of a Victorian Pagan* (Cambridge, Mass., 1931).

SASSOON, S., *Meredith* (London, 1948).

TREVELYAN, G. M., *The Poetry and Philosophy of George Meredith* (London, 1906).

WEBER, C. J., *Hardy of Wessex* (London, 1965).

WRIGHT, W. F., *Art and Substance in George Meredith* (Lincoln, Nebraska, 1953).

The Theatre

BOOTH, M. P., *English Melodrama* (London, 1965).

CORDELL, R. A., *Henry Arthur Jones and the Modern Drama* (London, 1932).

CUNLIFFE, J. W., *Modern English Playwrights* (New York, 1927).

DISHER, M. W., *Blood and Thunder: Mid-Victorian Melodrama and its Origins* (London, 1949).

FRANK, M. A., *Ibsen in England* (London, 1919).

HUDSON, L., *The English Stage 1850–1950* (London, 1951).

NICOLL, A., *A History of Early Nineteenth Century Drama* (Cambridge, 1930). *A History of Late Nineteenth Century Drama* (Cambridge, 1946).

PEARSON, H., *Gilbert and Sullivan* (London, 1947).

REYNOLDS, E., *Early Victorian Drama* (Cambridge, 1936).

ROWELL, G., *The Victorian Theatre* (London, 1956).

SAVIN, M., *Robertson: his Plays and Stage Craft* (Providence, R. I., 1950).

TOLLES, W., *Taylor and the Victorian Drama* (New York, 1940).

Index

Index

Index

Index

Index

Index